BCBA Reference Manual

TrainABA Supervision Curriculum: Volume 1

Edited by:
Benjamin Theisen
Zachary Bird

erence Manual
Supervision Curriculum: Volume 1

njamin Theisen & Zachary Bird
15

356329-3-9
17 16

Hollywood, CA 91601

BCBA Reference Manual
TrainABA Supervision Curriculum: Volume 1

Edited by Benjamin Theisen and Zachary Bird

Table of Contents

About the Authors

Executive Editors

Ben Theisen founded TrainABA in January 2014 as an excuse to deliver supervision seminars. He is a BCBA and has worked in applied behavior analysis since 2006.

 Email: ben@trainaba.com

 Cell: 1+310-801-5450

My name is Zachary Bird. I'm a BCBA and a managing partner at TrainABA. You won't find my phone number here but I still share the same vision you hear when Ben speaks passionately about TrainABA.

I'm currently working on my PhD in Behavior Analysis at Simmons College. I used to live near Los Angeles, but Boston was as far away as my wife and I could get from Ben without leaving the country.

I work hard each day to learn ways to advance the field of behavior analysis. ABA is my greatest passion. Everyone who knows me, knows this about me. I've spent time in center-based programs, non-public schools, in-home programs, and worked as a consultant internationally. TrainABA is a company designed to provide tools for the behavior analytic community in general, whether it be in a university setting, an ABA center, or in-home ABA program.

I hope the work Ben and I have done over the last two years will result in a supervision system you appreciate and can use every day. If you don't like it, or you don't use a Train-ABA product in your work or school every day, please bombard Ben's cell phone with discouraging text messages.

Additional Editors

Casey Clay is a BCBA-D. He earned his Ph.D. in the Disability Disciplines program at Utah State University and his Master of Science in Applied Behavior Analysis from Northeastern University. He has several years of clinical experience at the New England Center for Children and the Utah Behavior Support Clinic. His research interests include assessment and treatment of challenging behavior, social interaction and preference assessment methodologies, and training procedures in these areas. His work has been published in multiple peer-reviewed journals. He has also served as a guest reviewer for the Journal of Applied Behavior Analysis (JABA) and the Journal of Positive Behavior Interventions (JPBI).

Caleb Davis is a BCBA. Currently, he is a PhD student in the Behavior Analysis program at Simmons College. He received his Master of Science in Applied Behavior Analysis from Western New England University. During graduate school he received his BCBA supervision requirements while working at the New England Center for Children. His research interests include the assessment and treatment of severe problem behavior and errorless learning procedures. Caleb has presented his research at both national and regional conferences.

This book would not have been made possible without contributions from a set of behavior analysts. Their roles were crucial in developing this book. The editors offer a special thank you to Jason Zeigler for his extraordinary contributions to this project, which would not have been completed without him.

Jason Zeigler is a BCBA currently working for the Walpole Public School District in Walpole, Massachusetts. He received his Master's of Education with a concentration in autism spectrum disorder and applied behavior analysis from Cambridge College in 2011. He has worked in a variety of settings serving students of various age ranges and cognitive abilities. Previously, Jason had worked as a head teacher at the Evergreen Center, an assistant clinical director at the May Institute, and as a BCBA in the Marlborough Public School district. This wide range of experiences has given him a well-rounded professional outlook with experience serving students with various disabilities as well as typically developed students with behavioral issues. His research interests include functional behavior assessment, behavioral skills training, sensory processing disorder, interventions for students with ADHD, sensory deficits, and anxiety, and effective training methodologies. Jason's current position has him consulting, assessing, and providing programming and behavioral support for a number of students ranging from preschool to high school. He enjoys research,

training others in applied behavior analytic principles, assessment, and problem solving various maladaptive behavior concerns to create effective interventions for students on his case load.

Additional Authors

Dalena Anzivino is a BCBA. She completed her undergraduate degree from York University, a post-graduate certificate program from George Brown College, and a Master's of Applied Disabilities Studies with a Specialization in ABA from Brock University, Canada. Her studies at Brock University led to a publication as a contributing author of a chapter in a handbook for ABA practitioners on genetic syndromes and ABA. Over the past ten years, she has worked with children and adolescents diagnosed with autism, providing direct service, clinical supervision for both home based and centre based Intensive Behavioural Intervention (IBI) programs, as well as facilitating training workshops for direct support staff and parents.

Candice Colón-Kwedor is a BCBA. She was first introduced to behavior analysis as an undergraduate at Virginia Tech. She then received her Master of Science in Applied Behavior Analysis from Northeastern University and fulfilled her graduate assistantship requirements and BCBA supervision requirements at the New England Center for Children. Her research interests include the treatment of automatically maintained behavior, verbal behavior and the assessment and treatment of severe challenging behavior. Her research has been published in the Journal of Applied Behavior Analysis (JABA) and has been presented at national and regional conferences. She has also served as a guest reviewer for The Analysis of Verbal behavior (TAVB) and Behavioral Interventions (BI). She is currently a doctoral candidate in the Behavior Analysis Ph.D. program at Western

New England University and is a Senior Clinical Director at the May Institute's May Center for Autism and Developmental Disabilities in Randolph, Massachusetts.

Emma Martin graduated in 2007 from the University of Bath with a Bachelor's degree in Psychology. Her Bachelors included a placement year and as such she spent a year working at the Institute of Child Health in London with two research teams conducting research on autism. She worked as a Lead Teacher at the Jigsaw School in the UK, which is an Independent Day School for children with autism and severe learning difficulties. At that time, she also completed a Master's Degree in Education with a concentration in high-incidence disabilities with Nicholls State University. In 2011, she moved to Bermuda and began work as a Senior Verbal Behavior Therapist for Tomorrow's Voices, an Autism Early Intervention Centre. She became a Board Certified Behavior Analyst in 2012.

Angela Pao-Johnson is a BCBA and has been in the field since 2004. She was first introduced to applied behavioral analysis while interning at UC San Diego's Autism Center for Excellence. Since then, she has worked with a wide range of individuals ages 1 to 70 across a multitude of settings, which include home, schools, clinics and adult group homes. She has created protocols for several agencies, designed and implemented social skills classes, overseen the training of over 100 behavioral interventionists and led a series of behaviorally based trainings for teachers across Los Angeles School District. She currently resides in Los Angeles with her loving husband, Mike and their daughter Imogen.

Pamela Shea is currently the clinical supervisor of Behaviour Services at Ottawa Children's Treatment Centre. She completed her Masters in Applied Disabilities (Brock University), a Graduate Certificate in Behavior

Analysis (University of North Texas), Behavioural Science Technology (St. Lawrence College), an Honours Degree in Psychology (Queen's University), and is a BCBA. She has over 25 years of experience in the field of ABA, has worked as a clinical supervisor, a behaviour consultant, senior therapist, a BCBA supervisor and has taught at two colleges. She has worked in community based behaviour services and the provincial IBI within multidisciplinary teams, in residential, vocational, home, day care and school environments. She is a member of OCTC's Ethics Advisory Committee and has spearheaded the development of a Functional Analysis Ethical Review Committee for medium and high severity functional analyses and is a member of the Christian Horizons Ethical Review Committee.

Carolyn E. Stephens has worked in the field of autism and applied behavior analysis for over 30 years. Her academic training includes intervention in early childhood, learning disabilities, and moderate and severe intellectual disabilities. She has completed single subject research related to joint attention in children with autism. As an assistant professor in special education she taught and supervised undergraduate and graduate students in special education at the university level. She is currently working as a behavior analyst to design and implement individual behavior support plans for children and adults. To address the gap between needs and behavior training within public agency systems, she has designed and presented a year-long workshop to introduce applied behavior analysis concepts and skills to supervisors in an eight-county area serving adults with developmental disabilities.

Sarah Teske grew up in a small, historic town in New Hampshire. She studied Psychology and English at the University of New Hampshire. She spent three years teaching at the

New England Center for Children while she acquired a master's degree in applied behavior analysis through Northeastern University. Sarah went on to receive her certification as a BCBA and also obtained her special ed. teaching certification in the state of N.H. She has been working in the field of autism for 15 years and currently works for William J. White Educational and Behavioral Consulting Services Inc., consulting for schools in both Maine and New Hampshire. In her spare time Sarah likes to write children's books and garden. She has been collaborating with other professionals to enhance the field of ABA. She currently lives on the seacoast of Maine with her husband and two sons.

Kelly Workman, M.A., M.S., is a BCBA who started her career in ABA in 2007. Her work in ABA has focused on assessment and intervention programs for individuals with autism and other developmental disabilities across the lifespan in the home, school, workplace, and group home settings. Kelly has also provided supervision, training, and consultation for several years. Kelly has an avid interest in clinical behavior analysis and is currently completing a doctoral program in clinical psychology at the University of La Verne, with the goal of applying behavior analysis to chronic and severe mental health issues. She received extensive training in behavioral and cognitive-behavioral therapies including ACT, DBT, CBT, and CBASP, and incorporates principles of operant conditioning to facilitate behavior change when treating individuals with mental health concerns. Kelly is passionate about her clinical work and is receiving specialized training in working with populations who present with pervasive emotional dysregulation, life-threatening suicidal and non-suicidal self-harming behavior, and trauma-related concerns.

Acknowledgments

We would like to thank certain individuals whose professional activities influenced the development of this book in some way.

Brooke Mackenzie was contracted for administrative edits and worked expeditiously.

Natasha Harris helped organize legal and administrative paperwork.

Rabeha Motiwala helped with early research in summer 2014.

Angie Bird provided feedback and great ideas throughout the editing process.

Stephanie Ortega evaluated the logic of the supervision system to help Ben and Zach develop a conceptually-systematic approach. Her razor-sharp analysis and creativity was a tremendous help.

Christie Caccioppo, Vivienne Nelson, and Sharon Noble provided insightful feedback in an early stage collaboration group in summer 2014.

Ellie Kazemi's own work in supervision curriculum is important to the ethical practice of evidence-based supervision and we encourage readers to explore her resources. Ben had the privilege to work with Dr. Kazemi at the Southern California Consortium for Behavior Analysis, which she founded. It helped Ben understand the role project management played in helping service providers collaborate.

Gary Geer provided much-needed coaching support for project management. When the editors were fully immersed in the messy writing process, Mr. Geer helped us step back, prioritize, and focus.

Eduard S. Alterson generously provided his economic genius and industry knowledge in summer 2014, helping Ben analyze the ABA supervision industry mathematically. Mr. Alterson's calculations helped create a financial forecast for completing the book.

John Youngbauer coined the name of "Associated Aardvarks for Autism," a fictitious behavioral service provider. Ben borrowed the name for the case study in the Supervisor book. Dr. Youngbauer's lifelong contributions to behavior analysis could fill volumes of books this size.

OBMNetwork is an excellent resource with annual subscriptions available for the price of one dinner. At the time of publishing the first edition of this book, there were 21,233 BACB certificants and only 236 members of the OBMNetwork – a mere 1.11%.

Paula Braga-Kenyon provided support throughout entire book writing/editing process whether she was aware of it or not.

Olga Shapovalova provided insight and support with initial stages and various parts of editing. She inspires us with her work in multiple languages while we struggle to work in just one.

Carl Cheney contributed to our solid resource list on a few of the more difficult to find topics.

Gregory Hanley provided and continues to provide his vision for our field and a simple call-to-action to behavior analysts everywhere: "Read JABA."

Michael Ballard contributed ideas, inspiration and support.

Bill Ahearn advocated and continues to advocate for taking a big-picture perspective on our field and promoting systems to increase the quality of training in our field.

Foreward

Imagine my surprise when I returned to applied behavior analysis from a 3-year sabbatical in 2013. How different could things be? It was night and day. In less than a presidential term, the BACB® had doubled its membership, supervision had guidelines, and universities had ABA master's degrees online. My MBA no longer met the degree requirements. ABA students were talking about SAFMEDs. What the heck were SAFMEDs?

That was around the time I leaned back in an old squeaky chair at a school startup outside Los Angeles, manding to Zach Bird, my new colleague, from across the hall. "Zach," I said, waiting for him to unpeel his eyes from the computer screen. Zach's desk contained a red pen, no papers, and a week's worth of vegetarian meal replacement bars, some of which were opened. "Yeah?" he responded. He blinked a few times to let me know he was ready. I put my hands behind my head and stretched my heels onto the Craigslist desk. "What's a SAFMED?"

Zach looked at me like I had two heads. Then, he gave me a full explanation. Zach was different than any BCBA® I had met. He had just left New England Center for Children, where new BCBAs provided direct care, and arrived in Southern California, where every BCBA® was made an automatic manager. Here, exam pass rates were around 40% at popular schools and negative reinforcement was occasionally defined as taking away a preferred item to decrease behavior. Our differences were what brought us together.

Zach was hands-down the biggest behavior analysis geek I had ever met. Yet there was something lovable about the way he answered my questions that made me keep asking. As I write these words, I can hear his voice in my mind saying, "Reinforcement, Ben."

What was so reinforcing about talking ABA with Zach? We talked philosophy, private events, things Skinner said, and, of course, anything by Patrick Friman. I introduced Zach to some of my non-ABA friends and they thought he was the most interesting person they had ever met. He was bright, enthusiastic, and incredibly humble.

Zach and I cared deeply about the same thing – the future of ABA. My approach was through business and marketing, hoping to see a world where ABA organizations ran like clockwork and other industries would want to know our secrets. Zach was into technology and research.

We agreed that behavior analysts would benefit globally if supervisors had resources at a molecular level. This book may not look like much but it took us a very long time to make, not to mention our countless webchats, whiteboard sessions, Elon Musk blogs, and epic plans to change the world. We envisioned a world where behavior analysts could focus on supervision instead of spending time figuring out how to supervise. This book was a step in the right direction.

Yet we walked those steps slowly. Months passed. We made slow progress. And then there was Jason. Mr. Jason Zeigler was a Boston-area BCBA and absolute powerhouse. We worked with Jason 10 months before meeting him face-to-face, filming Registered Behavior Technician training videos at our "studio" (my tiny 1-bedroom apartment in the North Hollywood Arts District of Los Angeles). Jason was charismatic, fun, and cool.

Gary Geer, my longtime mentor and partner in TrainABA, had a good joke about Jason. He said, "Did you see his Cooper book, Ben?" I said, "Yeah. Lots of underlining and margin notes, right?" Gary laughed. "He could use a black highlighter, if you know what I mean," Gary said, playfully. "Yeah, xii

because he has the whole thing memorized so he doesn't need to see the words," I replied. "Exactly," Gary said. From that day forward, whenever I thought of Jason I imagined him blacking out the Cooper text after memorizing each section. I was grateful that Jason lended his talents to finishing this book. He is an outstanding resource and gifted presenter, full of passion and creativity.

At the time this book was finished, we had plans to launch a mobile app version that would forever change the field of ABA. Buying this book was like voting with your dollars. With this purchase, you voted for Train-ABA's vision – *to save time*. It was a vote for Zach and me to keep being ambitious, humble social entrepreneurs trying to bring the

world more ABA. We thank you for buying this book – even if you have no idea who we are – and we look forward to seeing you someday soon. Launching this book is the biggest thing we have ever done. Thank you for sharing the moment with us. We appreciate you so much.

Here's to a better field. We will keep working hard to save you time. I hope this book helps you find a few hours to do something you love.

Ben Theisen, *Editor*

SECTION ONE
Getting Started

Chapter 1
Introduction

Thank you for purchasing this book as part of the *TrainABA Supervision Curriculum* system. It will save you dozens of hours – enough to plan a nice vacation for yourself or find extra time throughout the week to jump on Facebook, search Google, add Ben on Twitter, or catch up on Netflix.

The system was built in response to two things happening at the same time – like weather when warm air mixes with a cold front and creates a storm. The warm air was the developing industry of applied behavior analysis (ABA) professional services, marked by variability in university training and fieldwork that resulted in low Behavior Analyst Certification Board® (BACB®) exam pass rates. The cold front was the shock of Ben's 15-month old niece dying from Sudden Unexplained Death of a Child in 2012. At the wake, her father urged parents to, "read one more story" or "give one more piggy back ride." Time was precious.

Ben was deeply affected. In the months that followed, he ran supervision webinars and was struck by how many unpaid hours BCBAs completed at home. "We have to," some would say, "There's no time to do it at work." Supervisors described reading emails during family dinners and writing reports with a laptop from the bleachers at soccer practice. It made Ben sad to think of what his brother-in-law said at the wake. Time was precious. If his sister had worked through dinner the night before his niece died, they may have regretted it forever. Ben knew the industry would eventually correct itself but it could take decades before supervision was structured.

Ben pondered the warm and cold weather conditions, metaphorically, and used his economics training to calculate when and who would create standardized supervision curriculum. Private agency supervisors created makeshift solutions but stopped developing them once the systems met their minimum needs. Universities focused on their own practicum programs.

The *TrainABA Supervision Curriculum* system took two years of full time effort to develop. There were only 3,000 BACB®-exam candidates in 2013. Even if Ben sold books to 25% of them, he would have made less than minimum wage. It was a pet project that Ben took way too seriously. Zach joined in to help, probably because he felt sorry for Ben and also realized Ben would finish the project but did not know enough ABA literature to do it justice. They made slow progress until Jason Zeigler joined the party. That guy was a powerhouse. (Other contributors are mentioned in the About the Authors section.) The result was the overly sophisticated TrainABA system that you hold today. We hope it keeps you organized and saves you time while the ABA profession develops.

In the coming years, we will see a more perfect ABA world. It will be beautiful. We are privileged to have a front row seat to the development of our field. We are honored to take this journey with you.

Okay, enough storytelling. Thank you for purchasing the system. Here is what you bought:

TrainABA Supervision Curriculum includes the items below.

1. **TrainABA Supervision Curriculum: BCBA Reference Manual**
2. **TrainABA Supervision Curriculum: Independent Fieldwork** (this book)
3. **TrainABA Supervision Curriculum: RBT Credential**

The *TrainABA Supervision Curriculum* system helps you:

a. Grow your company's management team with less stress on the system
b. Get from start to finish with a page-by-page, week-by-week program (supervision contract → fieldwork → BACB® application)
c. Find systems to help you track supervision hours and signature forms to email to the BACB®
d. Use Individual and Group meeting agendas
e. Save dozens of hours by not reinventing the wheel
f. Check pre-assigned homework

g.   Track ongoing progress on the 4th Edition Task List™ assessment

h.   Prepare for BACB®-exam with test topics built into fieldwork

i.   Organize essential supervision materials and meetings in one place, accessible by phone or computer

TrainABA is a BACB®-Approved Continuing Education (ACE) provider. We specialize in responding to supervision-related problems that are global in scope and too complex or time-consuming for other organizations and universities to solve.

The 4th Edition Task List™ face sheets are organized by "segments" (more about those later) to make it easier to complete and check homework assignments.

TrainABA Supervision Curriculum: Independent Fieldwork contains exercises for the supervisee to complete in a week-by-week progression that cover all 168 items on the 4th Edition Task List with the following:

1.   Individual meeting agendas
2.   Group meeting agendas
3.   Ongoing homework assignments
4.   4th Edition Task List™ assessment

The hours are not tracked in the book as a safeguard in case the book was lost. Keep your signature forms on a storage cloud online and in a paper file for seven years.

ABA Internship Process

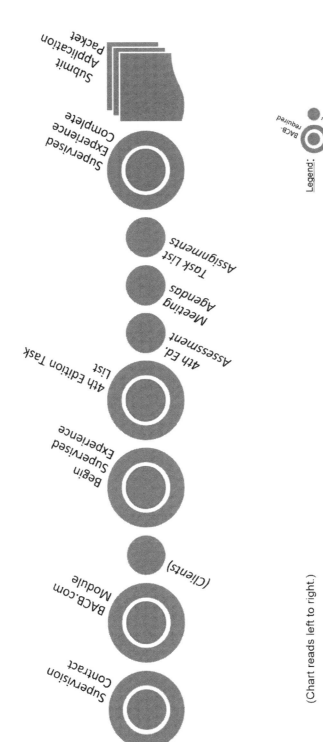

Supervision Contract

BACB.com Module

(Clients)

Begin Supervised Experience

4th Edition Task List

4th Ed. Assessment

Meeting Agendas

Task List Assignments

Supervised Experience Complete

Submit Application Packet

Legend:

BACB-required

Supplemental

(Chart reads left to right.)

Chapter 2
Supervision Taxonomy

1. What is ABA supervision?
2. A Taxonomy of ABA supervision
3. BACB® Influence in the Development of Formal Behavior Analysis Supervision

What is ABA Supervision?

What is "supervision"? Most definitions indicate that it is the act of providing supervision or oversight, involving directing in relation to execution and performance.

Supervision in Management

"Supervision" is most used in relation to business administration, in the realm of management. Human supervisors are employed to supervise humans and systems.

Supervision of Humans and Systems

It would be unusual to use the term "supervisor" to describe a machine that monitors information (including that generated by a human), or to describe a human that oversees information generated solely by a machine. The typical use of the word, "supervisor" implies a human to human interaction related to execution or performance.

Supervision in ABA Settings

The words, "execution" and "performance" are commonly used in business settings and could be used within the context of behavior analysis. However, more precise language further locates "supervision" in the field of applied behavior analysis. A manager at a typical business corporation "supervises" an employee to monitor performance and execution of tasks. In ABA settings, managers would more likely say they, "supervise staff to measure how effectively they implement a behavioral plan."

Direct vs. Indirect ABA Supervision

One might also describe ABA supervision as, "Overseeing direct implementation" or "following the procedures. An ABA subordinate may be evaluated on procedural integrity, procedural drift, and other direct measures of staff performance. The client's progress may be a direct measure of the subordinate's performance. However, client progress is an indirect measure of supervision efficacy.

Increase of Management Problems in ABA Organizations

The proliferation of autism behavior services has accompanied the rise in management problems at private practice ABA agencies, centers, and special education school settings. Management at such organizations have not widely adopted management practices to solve the repetitive problems occurring at the workplace in daily operations.

The primary reasons include:
1. Decision makers are unaware of how to identify the problem
2. Unaware of how to solve it
3. Have made unsuccessful attempts to solve it in the past and believe they either exhausted possible solutions or that the problem cannot be solved
4. Lack resources in behavior analytic literature and have come to view the problem as a non-issue because it does not seem to be covered in ABA

The above reasons are potential barriers if all resources are equal. However, more important barriers include time constraints, lack of money to pay consultants, and a tendency to focus on work that is expressly billable as opposed to management strategies, which require time, creativity, and a willingness to gather and analyze data over time to find "what works" at a particular organization using an experimental approach.

What Is Being Done

It is perhaps surprising that behavior analysis professionals are not leading the managerial movement to solve such problems, given the curious nature of behavior analysis professionals and their propensity for solving problems in the world around them.

A Taxonomy of ABA Supervision

In the 8 Hour Supervisor Training workshops, TrainABA moderators generally introduce the supervision taxonomy by addressing the "big picture" of policy-level issues governing the professional practice of applied behavior analysis. The presenter posits that such policy both necessitated and helped define how ABA supervision would be practiced. Policy varies across countries, states, and provinces, and various funding sources share properties with specific differences.

As such, we acknowledge that no single "source", whether an academic, private, or government model created ABA supervision. It has evolved with the proliferation of professional behavior analytic services for individuals with developmental disabilities, namely autism. ABA supervision existed prior to the formation of the Behavior Analyst Certification Board® (BACB®) in 1999. However, the BACB® has grown. It has served as the primary centralized regulatory organization for professional ABA services.

After introductions, the workshop presenter often asks the following set of questions:

How Does Policy Influence How Funding Sources Choose Providers?

And

How do funding source requirements influence the professional practice of applied behavior analysis services?

In the USA, the answer is generally that policy is written and a licensing body enforces compliance. However, the professional practice of behavior analysis is currently experiencing an early stage developmental period. More states are passing legislation. Some states are still in the process of licensure for ABA professionals.

Generally, the process involves policy language for licensure that acknowledges the BACB® certification credential and identifies an established licensing board to regulate practitioners. Other practices, such as psychology, have their own licensing boards and may opt to include behavior analysts within their board.

Other service delivery professions, such as psychology, have similar requirements as the BACB®, such as required education, supervised experience (1500 hours), ethical compliance code, continuing education requirements, etc.

As states adapt to the growing demand for professional behavior analytic services, many have acknowledged the BACB® certification as a requirement for billing. The BACB® is not a licensing body but serves as the central regulatory body for certified professional behavior analysts. It is the authoritative body for certification and credentialing in professional ABA services around the world. The BACB® is an influential global organization. Its international impact has been possible, in part, because it is not bound by a specific state or federal government. Such would not be the case if the BACB® was created as a licensing organization in Florida, its state of origin. The BACB® is currently headquartered in Littleton, Colorado, USA. Its strong influence in shaping the practice of professional behavior analysis services merits a prominent role in a taxonomy for ABA supervision today.

- Licensing body standardizes practitioner KSAs, ethics, practice (medicine, psychology, counseling, etc.).
- If no licensing body available, some authoritative body for certification

or credentialing assumes that role (BACB in 1998).

BACB® Influence in the Development of Formal Behavior Analysis Supervision

In recent years, the BACB® has established a model for the professional delivery of behavior analytic services for insurance providers. It involved a hierarchy upon which a BCBA or BCBA-D oversees a BCaBA, who supervises a behavior technician. It is common practice for companies to omit the BCaBA. In such cases, the BCBA or BCBA-D may oversee the behavior technicians directly.

Individuals with BACB® certification are not required to supervise. Some certified practitioners work directly with clients, particularly in group home settings and other consulting situations where monthly hours are low and hiring a direct implementation professional would not be appropriate. However, the global rise in autism diagnoses has warranted a high demand for appropriate structure of professional behavior analytic services that serve children with autism. Such services are delivered in homes, schools, and centers. Applied behavior analysis practitioners typically train and supervise professionals who implement behavior analytic programming directly with staff.

Generally, the certificant acts as a supervisor who analyzes data, conducts most or all elements of the assessment, designs and develops behavioral programming, and reports on progress. It is typical for ABA certificants to function in a supervisory role under such a service delivery model. However, not every certificant supervises staff.

Most, but not all certificants, supervise clinical staff. Some work directly with clients or in research roles.

The BACB® established the BCBA, BCBA-D and BCaBA credentials in its early years. However, the organization has grown from roughly 200 members in 2000 to over 19,200 active participants at the time this book was published.

In the summer 2014, the BACB® introduced the Registered Behavior Technician (RBT) Credential. This was a standardized credential for individuals who provided direct implementation of behavior analysis programs.

It should be noted that some confusion over terminology has arisen among practitioners as the RBT credential is becoming more common.

A rule-of-thumb:

"Certification" is for Supervisors and "credentialing" is for Direct Implementation staff.

The ABA Supervision taxonomy, therefore, applies to individuals who either hold or are candidates for BACB® certification. RBT Credentialees are supervised by individuals who hold a BACB® certification. However, credentialees do not supervise.

We draw this distinction to help define and locate the meaning of an ABA supervisor. The following chart identifies the basic difference in requirements for supervisors – ABA certification – versus those they supervise – RBT credentialees.

(This book is for developing supervisors.)

(This book is NOT for developing behavior technicians.)

Directors and Supervisors

Behavior Technicians

ABA Certification

- BCBA-D
- BCBA
- BCaBA*

ABA Credential

- RBT

Training

- University diploma
- University hours (270)
- Supervised Experience
- Certification exam

Training

- High school diploma
- RBT 40 hour Training
- RBT Assessment
- Fingerprints/RBT application

Ongoing Quality Assurance

- Ethical/Disciplinary Standards
- *Ongoing Supervision for BCaBAs
- Continuing Education Units
- 8 Hour Supervisor Training Workshop

Ongoing Quality Assurance

- Ethical/Disciplinary Standards
- Ongoing supervision

*BCaBAs require ongoing supervision from a BCBA or BCBA-D

Supervised Experience Hours

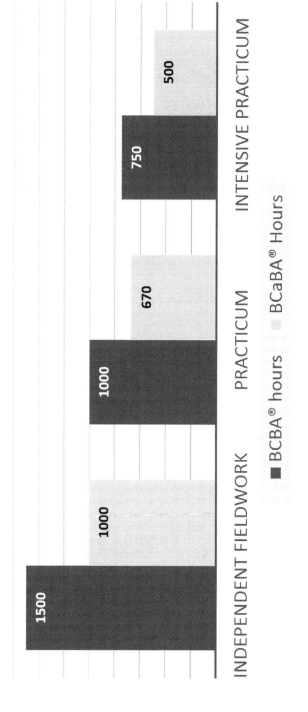

INDEPENDENT FIELDWORK   PRACTICUM   INTENSIVE PRACTICUM

■ BCBA® hours   ■ BCaBA® Hours

The following chart depicts the typical arrangement for ABA service delivery for an organization whose staff hold BACB® credentials.

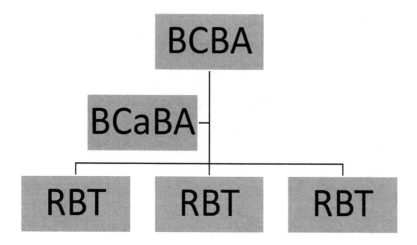

In the above chart, where is the *candidate* – the intern who is accruing hours toward satisfaction of her or his credential application criteria?

Suppose the position is called the *supervisor intern*. Is the *supervisor intern* billable? Herein lies the problem – or solution – for many ABA professionals around the world.

Consider the *supervisor intern*. Such a position is occasionally covered by policy or funding source, especially when a unique negotiation has been reached. The problem is simple: how can you bill for supervision hours if your supervisor does not hold a credential? The answer is often complicated by economic conditions of supply and demand for autism intervention services. Autism is a public health crisis that is difficult to solve because there are far more people with autism than credentialed behavior analysts to serve them. The challenge at the policy-level is to provide enough legislation to safeguard clients with qualified service providers. Legislation that is too rigid makes it difficult for companies to "keep the lights on," or meet minimum expenses to turn a profit. Often, practitioners assume that a company is making a lot of money because they see clients, employees, laptops, trainings, catered lunches, and office space. Yet organizations in the ABA industry must exercise restraint and deliberation for their business practices. For example, what happens when a company can only be paid for services provided by a BCBA, yet all the BCBAs in the area are gainfully employed?

Let's say a local university observes the growing *demand* for professional behavior analysts has increased. That university creates a certification program as a hybrid or standalone master's degree that satisfies the university hours required by the BACB. A few years pass. The university has graduated its first class. Yet the university does not have a practicum and it is the responsibility of the graduates to complete their supervised experience hours. What would the students do? They would reach out to local companies for employment – after all, it will soon be time to repay student loans – in hopes that a company can provide a training system for the individual.

The recent graduate may face a mixed landscape, shaped by the contingencies the company faces for promoting and/or billing for that *supervisor intern*. There are a few common scenarios:

- Two local funding sources reimburses companies ONLY for supervision hours performed by a BCBA.
  - One source formally allows the agency to have the supervision hours performed at the rate of a Behavior Technician (lower rate).
  - The other source does not reimburse work performed by a non-credentialed supervisor. They will discontinue services unless all supervisor hours are performed by a credential holder.

Billing Process for ABA Internship

Funding Source

- Required BCBA credential for billing as supervisor
- Intern was billable only as behavior technician (*not as a supervisor*)
- Company only reimbursed for <u>direct implementation hours</u> performed by intern

Company Employs Intern

- Intern hired as paid employee. (Title: *"Behavior Technician"*)
- AAA paid wages out-of-pocket for indirect activities (e.g., *program development; shadowing supervisor*)
- Intern counted ≤50% <u>direct implementation</u> toward BCBA supervised exerience

Internship Complete

- Company could not bill for *supervision* hours until intern passed required credential/licensing exams
- Company began to recoup internship expenses after employee met funding source's requirements for *supervisor*

Case Study: *Associated Aardvarks for Autism (AAA)*

Associated Aardvarks for Autism (AAA) was a fictitious ABA agency. Their directory was tasked with deciding whether to offer an internship program for university graduates of a local ABA master's program. AAA would select one intern to pilot the program. The internship was meant to fulfill the 1,500 hours of supervised experience toward the BCBA® credential. AAA hoped the program would result in developing a new supervisor who could be on the AAA team, rising from the ranks of the company. This supervisor would, AAA presumed, be more loyal to AAA in appreciation for the internship. Also, the intern would have learned how to get things done at AAA. These were attractive characteristics that were almost impossible to find from outside BCBA®s, which were in scarce supply anyway.

AAA's Accountant

AAA's director asked the accounting department to create Table 2.1, which summarized cashflow for the internship. The accountant assumed they would hire the intern at $45,000. That included a 50-week year at 30 hour/week, for which half of the hours were to be provided as direct implementation of behavioral programming. The engagement culminated in a complete 1,500-hour internship, satisfying the requirements toward the BACB®'s credentialing application.

The 30 hours per week led to the quickest possible completion of the supervised experience hours for the ABA credential internship. The accountant interviewed the clinical director and was informed that the BACB® permitted up to 50% of intern hours for direct implementation. What were the other hours? The accountant asked about scheduling meetings, billing, drive-time, and planning meetings that were not clinical. Unfortunately, those things were considered "non-clinical"

of "administrative" hours. They could not be counted toward the intern's credentialing hours.

The accountant knew that at least half of the intern's hours needed to be clinical but could not be direct implementation of behavioral programming. For that reason, the accountant only calculated 15 hours per week of billable work for the intern to serve as a behavior technician. He knew the other half included program development, report writing, parent education, and staff training. The company had one funding source that allowed interns to bill for these services. However, two other funding sources required the full credential for reimbursement. For that reason, the accountant described the "other 50%", as he called it, as a gray area category that may or may not be billable. But how could he help offset more of the cost of internship, so the company would not have to pay so much money out of pocket?

Funding Sources

The accountant considered the types of reimbursement contingencies the company faced. The most lenient funding sources allowed the company to bill for the intern's program development and report writing, generally under the supervision of a credentialed individual. Other funding sources will not pay for any supervisor hours performed by a noncredentialed ABA professional. The most conservative funding sources only reimburse for supervision performed in the presence of the client by a credentialed ABA professional.

In the AAA Company for Table 2.1, the funding source allowed only direct implementation hours to be billed by the intern. These hours are performed by a behavior technician and take the form of direct service.

The accountant recommended AAA to minimize the out-of-pocket expense of the internship by assigning a salaried individual as the supervisor for the 75 hours a supervisor would need to spend supervising that intern.

The director asked how much money that would save.

Estimating Supervision Costs

The accountant created *Table 2.2* to estimate costs if the intern's supervisor would have been paid hourly. The table reflected $45 per hour for the supervisor wage. It was a safe estimate considering the BACB® and Association of Professional Behavior Analysts (APBA) 2012 study which showed that most supervisor hours were reimbursed $40-$50 per hour. The accountant found those data in a BACB® newsletter from 2012. The director forwarded those emails to him regularly. He was glad to have the opportunity to show he had read them.

Billing for Parent Education Groups

AAA also recognized that the intern could run Parent Education Groups as part of their 50% of non-direct implementation hours. Fortunately, AAA could be reimbursed for these hours. It was not a huge savings, but it neutralized some of the costs of the intern's hourly rate. The Parent Education Groups only added 4 hours per week to the Intern's workload.

Consulting the Clinical Director

The accountant approached the clinical director for ideas on the rest of the internship hours. It looked like AAA needed to meet the 30 hours per week in the agreement but they were short. Adding 1.5 hours per week of supervision, 4 hours for parent education, and 15 hours of direct implementation left a deficit pf 9.5 hours to fill. The company met those hours by scheduling the intern for staff training, along with program development and report writing for clients on the intern's direct implementation caseload.

Putting It Together

As a result, the intern was able to satisfy a requirement toward the BACB® credential application and was paid $45,000 for the year. Admittedly, it was not a huge amount of money for someone with a master's degree. The intern felt it was fair because she was only asked to work 30 hours per week. There were some travel time hours and expenses, which were handled separately in compliance with law. The company ultimately lost $12,750 for the year.

AAA knew they would lose the money this year but hoped the intern would pass the credentialing exam soon and stay with AAA, billing at a full supervisor rate. That would allow AAA to earn a higher reimbursement rate for the hours the supervisor worked. More importantly, it meant AAA could add some clients from their waiting list, placing these clients on the new supervisor's caseload.

A Risk for the Company

AAA recognized that the main incentive for a company to sponsor an intern was the possibility of serving more clients once the intern earned the credential. It was a gamble for AAA. Not every intern passed the credentialing exam. In this case, they requested transcripts from the possible interns they were considering. They wanted an intern with the highest possible grades because they believed previous academic performance suggested a history of work habits and a higher likelihood of having acquired the skills needed to pass the credential exam.

Final Decision

AAA knew that other ABA agencies in the area were using contracts to keep interns at their companies for long enough to recoup the cost of the internship. They weighed the pros and cons of contracts but chose to revisit that issue at a later date.

Ultimately, they were ambivalent about the internship. The director said, "If someone told you to pay $12,750 today and there was only a 58% you could get that money back in 2 years, would you invest?" She was referring to passing rates on the exam. The clinical director looked up the university pass rates for graduates of that local program and found that 60% of graduates passed the exam on the first try.

These data did not impress the director. The decision was made to offer the internship as a trial. The clinical director selected a salaried supervisor and put pressure on her to make sure the intern learned the BACB® 4th Edition Task List fully. "If she doesn't pass the exam, I'm holding you responsible," said the clinical director. The supervisor accepted the challenge and implemented the procedures in Section 2 of the TrainABA supervised experience book. Years later, the intern had passed the exam on her first attempt and was successfully managing a caseload of 12 clients. She was a success story. AAA realized that not all internship stories have happy endings.

See the following pages for Table 2.1 and 2.2 to see what the accountant gave the director at AAA.

Table 2.1 - AAA Expense Sheet for Hiring a 50-week Supervisor Internship, Salaried Supervisor

Expense	Hours	Hourly Rate	Total
Intern works 30 hours/week (out of pocket)	1,500	($30)	($45,000)
Intern bills 50% hours as direct implementation (company reimbursed by funding source)	750	$35	$26,250
Company assigns salaried supervisor to intern (1.5 hours/week)	75	--	--
Supervisor conducts 50% of supervision meetings individually (reimbursed for supervision)	37.5	$65	--
Intern conducts Parent Education Groups 4 hours/week (billable)	200	$30	$6,000
Intern conducts staff training and program development 9.5 hours/week (non-billable)	9.5	--	--
		Total Loss:	($12,750)

Table 2.2 - AAA Expense Sheet for Hiring a 50-week Supervisor Internship, Hourly Supervisor

Expense	Hours	Hourly Rate	Total
Intern works 30 hours/week (out of pocket)	1,500	($30)	($45,000)
Intern bills 50% hours as direct implementation (company reimbursed by funding source)	750	$35	$26,250
Company assigns salaried supervisor to intern (1.5 hours/week)	75	($45)	($3,375)
Supervisor conducts 50% of supervision meetings individually (reimbursed for supervision)	37.5	$65	--
Intern conducts Parent Education Groups 4 hours/week (billable)	200	$30	$6,000
Intern conducts staff training and program development 9.5 hours/week (non-billable)	9.5	--	--
		Total Loss:	($16,125)

Resources for the Supervised Experience Process

Items in Bold are required by the BACB® for credentialing. Non-bold items are supplemental materials.

Supervisee

1. **Contract**
2. **BACB.com module**
   a. **"Registration" (See page 23)**
3. Clients (generally)
4. **4th Ed. Task List**

5. **Experience Verification Forms**
6. Supplementary Materials
7. Homework

Supervisor

1. **Contract**
2. **BACB.com module**

3. Clients
4. **4th Ed. Task List**
   a. Assessment
   b. Meeting agendas
5. **Experience Verification Forms**
6. Supplementary Materials
7. Homework
8. Create Performance Management Plan
   a. Personal Development
   b. Modeled after IEP, BSP, PBIP
9. Ongoing Payment
   a. Company
   b. University
   c. Private pay
10. Time Retainer
11. Technology
    a. Journals, online videos, etc.
12. Communication
    a. Synchronous: Phone, streaming webcam, video chat
    b. Asynchronous: Email, recorded audio/video

Beyond the Taxonomy

Have you located yourself as an ABA supervisor in the taxonomy? Can you write the steps of the Supervised Experience Process? If not, please review the charts above. The goal of this chapter was to identify the type of supervision you offer, or plan to offer, as a supervisor in the field of applied behavior analysis.

The next chapter identifies pre-requisites needed for supervising certification candidates. It includes checklists to identify the requirements.

Rules and Guidelines for Supervision of BACB® Experience Hours

This document reflects the BACB®'s recent supervision standards, effective January 1, 2015.

BACB® Rules for Supervision

1. **Each supervisee must have a valid supervision contract.** Multiple exemplars and comprehensive guidelines are available at bacb.com®
2. Each supervi**sor** must have completed both of the following by December 31, 2014.
a. Complete 8 Hour Supervisor Training from a BACB® ACE provider (Available from TrainABA as a live webinar)
b. Complete an online, competency-based supervision module on BACB.com
c. Complete 3 CEUs for supervision for every recertification cycle
3. Each supervision period is 2 *consecutive weeks*
4. Ratio of Independent Fieldwork to Direct Supervision must be *no less than 5%* by the end of the 2 week period (You MUST provide Direct Supervision 5% or more of their Independent Fieldwork by the end of each 2-week period.)
5. Per 2 week supervision period, no more than 50% of supervision can be direct care. The other 50%+ must be behavior analytic in nature
6. Start/end dates may not be more than 5 years apart.
7. Supervision must be face to face. Real-time video is okay. Think of Google Hangouts, FaceTime, Skype, etc.
8. 5% of 1500 hours = 75 hours of independent fieldwork experience
9. Supervision hours may be counted toward total experience hours
10. No more than 50% of supervision (per 2-week period) can be in a group format
11. Group maximum = 10 supervisees
12. You do not need to provide Direct Supervision every week
13. Must meet at least once for every 2 week period
14. Content must be behavior analytic (Do not discuss billing, travel time, non-clinical scheduling, etc.)

Mathematical Assumptions

- Supervisors must provide 5% of 1,500 Independent Fieldwork hours = 75 hours
- Supervision period is two weeks in duration
- (75 hours total) DIVIDED BY (maximum of 3 hours per 2-week period) = 25 meetings, one per 2 weeks
- Up to 50% of supervised experience hours can be delivered in group format
- Therefore, deliver group supervision meetings that are 1.5 hours in duration, once per 2 week period
- Also provide individual supervision for 1.5 hours in duration for each 2 week period
- Given the math above, Train ABA recommends you make group supervision meetings 1.5 hours long (90 minutes) for full time staff. We built the agendas around the 90 minute model

- If your supervisees do not work 30 hours per week during both weeks of the 2-week supervision period, you will need to adjust the math to provide exactly 5% of the hours they provided. See rules below.

Rules for Calculating How Many Hours Your Supervisee Has Completed

1. Your supervisee must work at least 10 and up to 30 hours during both weeks of each 2-week supervision period
2. You must provide supervision for 5% of these hours
3. You do not need to provide exactly 50% of group supervision every 2-week period, but we use that model for this protocol because it makes the math easier
4. When your supervisee works less than the expected amount of hours for a week or 2-week period, adjust your supervision hours to equal 5% of their hours worked
5. If they work more than 30 hours in one week, the company can pay wages but the BACB® will not recognize extra hours

Registration Process

There is a new BACB® requirement for supervisees to "register" before beginning Experience Hours. It was first mentioned in the BACB®'s September 2012 Newsletter. The Supervisor must complete the module immediately if she has not already done so. All supervisees must complete the process at the outset of the supervised fieldwork.

The registration process has two steps:
1. Create a login at bacb.com®
2. In that login, complete the same Supervision Policies Module required by individuals who wish to supervise those accruing Experience Hours. In plain English, your supervisees must complete the same supervision module as you. Additionally, they are expected to do it at the outset of supervision. Some supervises may not know of this requirement. Please advise your supervisees to complete this module immediately. It takes approximately 1.5 hours and is available free of charge.

NOTE: Supervisees need only complete the module once, regardless of how many approved supervisors with whom they have completed Supervised Experience.

Chapter 3

Refresher: Key Takeaways from the 8-Hour Supervisor Training Workshop

The BACB® 8-Hour Supervisor Training Workshop curriculum has 6 sections:
- Part 1 – Purpose of Supervision
- Part 2 – Features of Supervision
- Part 3 – Behavioral Skills Training
- Part 4 – Delivering Performance Feedback
- Part 5 – Evaluating the Effects of Supervision
- Part 6 – Ongoing Professional Feedback

These sections are summarized briefly in visuals and charts below. This chapter is meant to serve as a refresher for the concepts presented in the 8-Hour Supervisor Training workshop. It is not a substitute for the workshop. These materials are taken from the TrainABA 8-Hour Supervisor Training Workshop. For more information, or to sign up a colleague for the workshop, visit:

http://trainaba.com

Purpose of Supervision

"The purpose of supervision is to improve and maintain the behavior-analytic, professional and ethical repertoires of the supervisee and facilitate the delivery of high-quality services to his/her clients."

--*BACB® 8-Hour Curriculum Training Outline, 2012*

Features of Supervision

Appropriate Supervision Activities

- Focus on developing new ABA skills
- Use BACB® Fourth Edition Task List
- Follow 7 Dimensions of Behavior Analysis (BATCAGE) (Baer, Wolf, & Risley, 1968)
- Give supervisees multiple sites, varied experiences, different supervisors
- Conducting assessments to determine the need for behavioral intervention
- Designing, implementing, & systematically monitoring skill-acquisition and behavior-reduction programs
- Oversee implementation of behavior-analytic programs by others
- Training, designing behavioral systems, and performance management
- Using behavioral skills training to Model and rehearse various behavior analytic skills and procedures.
- Engaging in role-play scenarios in natural and contrived situations for various skills
- Other items directly related to ABA

Inappropriate Supervision Activities
(Non-examples of content for group supervision meetings)

- Attending meetings with little or no behavior-analytic content
- Scheduling, travel time, billing
- Using unproven or non-behavior analytic interventions
- Non-behavioral administrative activities, non-behavioral assessments (diagnostic or intellectual assessments)

Features of Supervision

Effective January 1st, 2015, the BACB® will only permit individuals who completed a training experience to supervise individuals pursuing BCBA® or BCaBA® credentials.
- 8-hour workshop
- Modules on BACB.com
- 3-hours Supervision CEs
--BACB®, 2012 newsletter

Recertification Requirements Before January 1, 2015

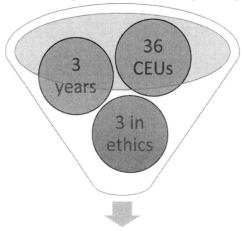

Recertification

Recertification Requirements After January 1, 2015

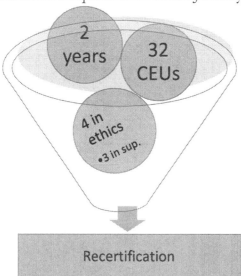

Recertification

Using Behavioral Skills Training

Why is Behavioral Skills Training (BST) popular in ABA supervision now?

In 2012, the Behavior Analyst Certification Board® created a document called the "Supervision Training Curriculum Outline". It contained the required topics for Approved-Continuing Education (ACE) providers who would provide the 8-Hour Supervisor Training curriculum. Section (3) of this (6) section document was titled, "Behavioral Skills Training (BST)".

BST is found in various JABA articles and books by behavior analysts. Perhaps the best example of BST is found in Raymond Miltenberger's 2011 textbook, "Behavior Modification Principles and Procedures."

An 8-step BST procedure is outlined on the following page.

Behavioral Skills Training

1. Provide a rationale for why the target skills are to be trained
2. Provide a succinct, written description (instructions) of the target skills
    a. Scripts are included in this document. Be sure to provide a script to employees.
3. Provide a detailed, vocal description (instructions) of the target skills
    a. Trainer reads script aloud to trainee
4. Demonstrate (model) each of the target skills
    a. Trainer is first to role play, demonstrating correct behavior for trainee
    b. Include examples and non-examples
    c. If training scenario is a non-example, trainer deviates from script and scenario is terminated with positive feedback.
5. Require trainee to practice (rehearse) each target skill
    a. Trainee role plays scenarios from the list
    b. Include examples and non-examples
    c. If training scenario is a non-example, trainee deviates from script and scenario is terminated with positive feedback
6. Provide positive and corrective feedback to supervisee
    a. Provide it vocally, immediately following trainee role play
    b. Deliver positive feedback to trainee throughout training, aiming for 4:1 ratio
    c. Deliver corrective feedback directly.
7. Repeat the previous step until supervisee performs each target skill correctly
8. Assess application and generalization of skills to new targets, clients, and settings, when appropriate

Delivering Performance Feedback
Corrective Feedback

1. Provide an empathy statement
2. Describe ineffective performance
3. Provide a rationale for desired change in performance
4. Provide instructions and demonstration for how to improve designated performance
5. Provide opportunities to practice the desired performance
6. Provide immediate feedback

Evaluating the Effects of Supervision

Evaluate supervision with evidence-based, intervention specific criteria for:

- Client performance
- Staff performance
- Supervisory behavior

Ongoing Professional Development

> 1.03 Professional Development (+RBT)
> Behavior analysts who engage in assessment, therapy, teaching, research, organizational consulting, or other professional activities maintain a reasonable level of awareness of current scientific and professional information in their fields of activity, and undertake ongoing efforts to maintain competence in the skills they use by reading the appropriate literature, attending conferences and conventions, participating in workshops, and/or obtaining Behavior Analyst Certification Board certification.
>
> --BACB Professional and Ethical Compliance Code, Ver. 9/23/2014

The supervisor should be able to describe the following methods for his/her ongoing professional development as a supervisor
• Creating a continuous learning community to enhance supervisory and training behavior
• Regular review of resources and research for best practices in supervision

The supervisor should be able to describe the following methods for his/her ongoing professional development as a supervisor *and to the supervisee*:

- Supervisory study groups
- Attending conferences
- Seeking peer review
- Seeking mentorship
- Regular review of resources and research relevant to supervisee's area of practice
- Seeking consultation when necessary

SECTION TWO
Supervised Fieldwork Curriculum

Chapter 4
Annotated 4th Edition Task List™

A-01 Measure Frequency

Definition:
Frequency - "A ratio of count per observation time; often expressed as count per standard unit of time and calculated by dividing the number of responses recorded by the number of standard units of time in which observations were conducted (Cooper, Heron, & Heward, 2007, p. 85)"*

Example:
- Hand Raising - A student is sitting in an hour long class. The student raises his hand 3 times to ask and answer questions during the class. The bell rings once and the student goes to his next class. Frequency of hand raising is 3 per hour.

Assessment:
- Ask your supervisee to identify the frequency of hand raising above.
- Ask your supervisee to create another example and non-example of his/her own.
- Have supervisee measure a frequency of a behavior on the job or in a role play.
- Have supervisee graph the frequency measured on the job or in a role play.

Relevant Literature:
Catania, A. C. (2013). *Learning* (5th ed.). Cornwall-on-Hudson, NY: Sloan.
Cooper, J. O., Heron, T. E., & Heward, W.L. (2007). Applied behavior analysis.

Related Lessons:
I-01 Define behavior in observable and measurable terms
H-01 Select a measurement system to obtain representative data given the dimensions of the behavior and the logistics of observing and recording
FK-47 Identify the measurable dimensions of behavior (e.g. rate, duration, latency, interresponse time)

Footnotes:
* Alternatively, frequency is not always defined synonymously with rate throughout the discipline of behavior analysis. Catania (2013, p. 443) defines frequency as "total responses over a fixed time, over a session of variable duration or, in trial procedure, over a fixed number of trials." Cooper, Heron, & Heward (2007) functionally defines "count" as Catania defines "frequency".

A-02 Measure Rate

Definition:

Rate - "A ratio of count per observation time; often expressed as count per standard unit of time and calculated by dividing the number of responses recorded by the number of number of standard units of time in which observations were conducted (Cooper, Heron, & Heward, 2007, p. 85)."*

Examples:

- Eating Chips
    - Example: A young child is sitting at a table where there is a bag of potato chips. They eat 8 chips, stand up, and walk to the living room to watch TV for the rest of the hour. Rate of chip eating is 8 per hour.
- Basketball Dribbles
    - Example: Child is playing basketball for 30 minutes. Dribbles 7 times and then practices foul shots. He shoots 15 times and between each shot he dribbles 3 times. Frequency of dribbling is 52 dribbles per 30 minutes.

Assessment:

- Ask your supervisee to identify the frequency of chip eating or basketball dribbles in examples.

- Have supervisee measure a frequency of a behavior on the job or in a role play.

Relevant Literature:

Catania, A. C. (2013). *Learning* (5th ed.). Cornwall-on-Hudson, NY: Sloan.

Cooper, J. O., Heron, T. E., & Heward, W. L. (2007). Applied behavior analysis.

Related Lessons:

I-01 Define behavior in observable and measurable terms

H-01 Select a measurement system to obtain representative data given the dimensions of the behavior and the logistics of observing and recording

FK-47 Identify the measurable dimensions of behavior (e.g. rate, duration, latency, interresponse time)

Footnotes:

* Alternatively, rate is not always defined synonymously with frequency throughout the discipline of behavior analysis. Catania (2013) defines rate as "responses per unit time" (p. 458) but frequency as "total responses over a fixed time, over a session of variable duration or, in trial procedure, over a fixed number of trials" (p. 443) Cooper, Heron, & Heward (2007) functionally defines "count" whereas Catania defines "frequency".

A-03 Measure Duration

Definition:
Duration – "A measure of the total extent of time in which a behavior occurs" (Cooper, Heron, & Heward, 2007, p. 79).

Examples:
- Sarah gets a fancy new piece of furniture from one of those Swedish companies. When it arrives, Sarah realizes that it is not assembled. She reads the complicated set of directions and begins putting it together at 2:12pm. Armed with a screwdriver and an Allen wrench, she consistently works to put it together until 3:43pm. Phew! Maybe next time she will order the one that comes fully assembled! The duration of the project was 1 hour and 31 minutes.
- Benny gets a new yo-yo for his birthday and plays with it for 20 minutes after eating his cake and ice cream. He puts it down to play tag with his sister. The duration of yo-yo playing is 20 minutes.

Assessment:
- Ask your supervisee to identify the duration of furniture assembly from the example above

- Ask your supervisee to create another example and non-example of his/her own
- Have your supervisee measure the duration of another behavior on the job or in role-play.
- Have the supervisee graph the duration of another behavior measured on the job or in a role-play.

Relevant Literature:
Cooper, J. O., Heron, T. E., & Heward, W. L. (2007). Applied behavior analysis.
DeLeon, I. G., Iwata, B. A., Conners, J., & Wallace, M. D. (1999). Examination of ambiguous stimulus preferences with duration-based measures. *Journal of Applied Behavior Analysis*, *32*(1), 111-114.

Related Lessons:
H-01 Select a measurement system to obtain representative data given the dimensions of the behavior and the logistics of observing and recording.
I-01 Define the behavior in observable and measurable terms
FK-47 Identify the measurable dimensions of behavior (e.g., rate, duration, latency, interresponse time).

A-04 Measure Latency

Definition:

Latency - "A measure of temporal locus; the elapsed time from the onset of a stimulus (e.g., task direction, cue) to the initiation of a response" (Cooper, Heron, & Heward, 2007, p. 80).

Example: Hitting the snooze button or hitting the break

- Example: Gertrude is not a morning person. Her alarm goes off at precisely 5:30AM. She hears the annoying wail but doesn't respond immediately. After 32 seconds of beeping, she whacks the snooze button, rolls over and goes back to sleep. Latency to turning off the alarm is 32 seconds.

- Example: Marty is driving down a country road. Out of nowhere a herd of deer dart out in front of his car. It takes Marty 5 seconds from the time he first sees the deer to hit the break. Latency from the time the deer are spotted to applying pressure to the break is 5 seconds.

- Non-example: Gertrude is not a morning person. Her alarm goes off at precisely 5:30 AM. She does not respond to its annoying wailing and continues to sleep despite the noise. The alarm stops on its own 1 hour later.

Assessment:

- Ask your supervisee to identify the latency of a few responses of your choosing.
- Ask your supervisee to create another example and non-example of his/her own.
- Have your supervisee measure the latency to another behavior on the job or in role-play.

Relevant Literature:

Cooper, J. O., Heron, T. E., & Heward,W. L. (2007). Applied behavior analsis. Upper Saddle River, NJ: Pearson Education.

Thomason-Sassi, J. L., Iwata, B. A., Neidert, P. L., & Roscoe, E. M. (2011). Response latency as an index of response strength during functional analyses of problem behavior. Journal of Applied Behavior Analysis, 44(1), 51-67.

Related Lessons:

H-01 Select a measurement system to obtain representative data given the dimensions of the behavior and the logistics of observing and recording.

I-01 Define the behavior in observable and measurable terms

FK-47 Identify the measurable dimensions of behavior (e.g., rate, duration, latency, interresponse time).

A-05 Measure Interresponse Time (IRT)

Definition:

Interresponse time (IRT) - "…the elapsed time between two successive responses" (Cooper, Heron, & Heward, 2007, p. 80).

Example: Frisky pets

- Example: Sparky loves to bark at passing cars. He hears a car drive by the house and barks. Thirty-seven seconds later another car passes by and Sparky barks again. Interresponse time between barking at the vehicles is thirty-seven seconds.

- Example: Doodles the cat likes to scratch the furniture. She walks over the chair and sinks her claws in. Eleven seconds later Doodles walks over to the couch and begins to scratch again. Interresponse time between scratches is eleven seconds.

- Example: Roger the rooster doesn't know that he's only supposed to crow at dawn. He lets out crows all day long. He is observed to crow at 3:43 in the afternoon. He crows again at 3: 59. Interresponse time between crows is sixteen minutes.

- Non-example: Sparky's owner accidentally steps on his tail. Sparky yelps from the pain.

Assessment:

- Ask your supervisee to identify the interresponse time in the examples above.

- Ask your supervisee to create another example and non-example of his/her own.

- Have your supervisee measure the interresponse time of a behavior on the job or in a role-play.

- Have your supervisee graph the interresponse time measured on the job or in a role-play.

Relevant Literature:

Blough, D. S. (1963), Interresponse Time as a Function of Continuous Variables: A New Method and Some Data. *Journal of Experimental Analysis Behavior*, 6: 237–246.

Cooper J.O, Heron T.E, Heward W.L. (2007). *Applied behavior analysis* (2nd ed.) Upper Saddle River, NJ: Pearson

Favell, J.E., McGimsey, J.F., & Jones, M.L. (1980). Rapid Eating in the Retarded: Reduction by Nonaversive Procedures. *Behavior Modifications*, 4, 235-239.

Related Lessons:

A-05 Measure Interresponse time (IRT)

I-01 Define behavior in observable and measurable terms

H-01 Select a measurement system to obtain representative data given the dimensions of the behavior and the logistics of observing and recording

FK-47 Identify the measurable dimensions of behavior (e.g. rate, duration, latency, interresponse time)

A-06 Measure Percent of Occurrence

Definition:
Percent of occurrence - "A ratio formed by combining the same dimensional quantities such as count or time; expressed as a number of parts per 100; typically expressed as a ratio of the number of responses of a certain type per total number of responses. A percentage represents a proportional quantity per 100" (Cooper, Heron & Heward, 2007, p. 701)

Example: Greeting
- Example: Twelve strangers walk by an elderly man. He greets three of them and ignores the rest. The percent of occurrence of greeting strangers is 25%.
  o To compute: Divide number of greetings emitted by the man (3) by the total number of opportunities to greet (12) and multiply that product by 100 to yield a percentage (3/12= 0.25 x 100= 25%).
- Non-example: Twelve strangers walk by an elderly man. He greets three of them and ignores the rest. The percent of occurrence of greeting strangers is 0.25.

Pros:
- Demonstrates proportional relations well (e.g. can indicate how many times an individual engaged in a target response given a set number of opportunities available).

Cons:
- Has no dimensional quantities (e.g. does not indicate how many target responses were emitted nor how many opportunities were given)
- When there are few response opportunities (e.g. fewer than 20), percent occurrence measures may skew performance (e.g. An individual answering 1 out of 2 problems correct on a math test will receive the same

score of 50% as an individual answering 25 out of 50 problems correct).
- Imposes an artificial ceiling of measurement (e.g. 100% may be subjective; suggests that a learner performing at 100% cannot improve) (Cooper et al., 2007).

Assessment:
- Provide hypothetical situations and ask your supervisee if using percent of occurrence measures are appropriate
- Provide various hypothetical situations and ask your supervisee to calculate percent of occurrence
- Have supervisee graph percent of occurrence measured on the job or in a role play

Relevant Literature:
Cooper, J. O., Heron, T. E., & Heward, W. L. (2007). *Applied behavior analysis* (2nd ed.). Upper Saddle River, NJ: Prentice Hall.

Related Lessons:
I-01 Define behavior in observable and measurable terms
H-01 Select a measurement system to obtain representative data given the dimensions of the behavior and the logistics of observing and recording
FK-47 Identify the measurable dimensions of behavior

A-07 Measure Trials to Criterion

Definition:

Trials to criterion - "A special form of event recording; a measure of the number of responses or practice opportunities needed for a person to achieve a pre-established level of accuracy or proficiency" (Cooper, Heron & Heward, 2007, p. 87).

To use, one must first determine what constitutes a response opportunity, and what the criteria for mastery will be. Response opportunities can vary depending on the target behavior. For example, an opportunity for spelling accuracy could be a 10-question spelling test. An opportunity for responding to one's name within five seconds might be every time someone called the individual's name. Other measures such as latency, percent occurrence, rate and duration can be used to compute trials to criterion data. For instance in the latter example to compute whether the individual is responding to his name within 5 seconds, data would have to be taken on latency to respond per opportunity (Cooper et al., 2007).

Example:

- A behavioral interventionist is teaching a child how to brush her teeth. She teaches this using a task analysis that involves backwards chaining. She provides two opportunities per session for the child to complete this skill. Data reflect that it takes the child on average four opportunities before she is able to complete the step being taught independently and to move to the next step in the task analysis.

Assessment:

- Have your supervisee list uses for trials to criterion data.
- In a clinical setting or during role-play, have your supervisee determine which intervention is more efficient using trials to criterion data.
- Have your supervisee complete trials to criterion data in various scenarios.

Relevant Literature:

Cooper, J. O., Heron, T. E., & Heward, W. L. (2007). *Applied behavior analysis* (2nd ed.). Upper Saddle River, NJ: Prentice Hall.

Lahey, B. B., & Drabman, R. S. (1974). Facilitation of the acquisition and retention of the sight-word vocabulary through token reinforcement1. *Journal of applied behavior analysis*, 7(2), 307-312.

Related Lessons:

H-01 Select a measurement system to obtain representative data given the dimensions of the behavior and the logistics of observing and recording.

H-03 Select a data display that effectively communicates relevant quantitative relations.

A-08 Assess and Interpret Interobserver Agreement

Definition:

Interobserver agreement (IOA) – "…refers to the degree to which two or more independent observers report the same observed values after measuring the same event" (Cooper, Heron, & Heward, 2007, p. 113).

There are four basic types of IOA as described by Johnston and Pennypacker (2009):

Total agreement - Smaller total ÷ Larger total X 100 = % Agreement

Exact agreement – Total agreements ÷ Total number of intervals X 100 = % Agreement

Interval agreement –Total agreements ÷ Total number of intervals X 100 = % Agreement

Occurrence/nonoccurrence agreement – Total agreements ÷ Total number of intervals X 100 = % Agreement

"By reporting the results of IOA assessments, researchers enable consumers to judge the relative believability of the data as trustworthy and deserving interpretation" (Cooper et al., 2007, p. 114). It, however, should be noted that the "…fact that two observers reported the same measure of the target behavior for a session says nothing about the accuracy or reliability of either" (Johnston & Pennypacker, 2009, p. 149).

Example:

John is conducting a functional analysis (FA) on aggression in one of his students. He has asked Mary to observe the behavior and record data simultaneously with him to calculate Interobserver agreement. He plans on conducting a 5-minute session with 30, 10-second intervals. He plans to use interval agreement IOA. He records 4 instances of aggression during the FA in the 21st, 22nd, 23rd and 24th interval. Mary records 4 instances in the 21st, 22nd, 23rd, and 25th interval. He calculates IOA to be 97% or 29/30 intervals.

Non-example:

John is conducting a functional analysis on aggression in one of his students. He asks Mary to come in and observe but does not provide her with a data recording sheet to take data on the behavior. At the end of the session he asks Mary if she saw any aggression during the session.

Assessment:

- Have supervisee watch a video of client exhibiting target behavior. Ask him/her to record frequency data on the behavior. Record data on the same video and compare data after completion.

- Provide supervisee with 2 sets of data sheets based on the observance of the same behavior. Have him/her calculate Interobserver agreement based on the data provided.

- Assign supervisee recommended article on Interobserver agreement. Have him/her summarize the article and share this with peers

Relevant Literature:

Boyce, T.E., Carter, N., & Neboschick, H. (2000). An Evaluation of Intraobserver Reliability versus Interobserver Agreement. *European Journal of Behavior Analysis*, 1, (2), 107-114.

Cooper, J.O., Heron, T.E. & Heward W.L. (2007). *Applied Behavior Analysis* (2nd Ed.), Upper Saddle River, NJ. Pearson Prentice Hall. 113-122.

Johnston, J. M., & Pennypacker, H. S. (2009). Strategies and tactics of behavioral research.

Watkins, M.W. & Pacheco, M. (2000). Interobserver Agreement in Behavioral Research: Importance and Calculation. Journal of Behavioral Education, 10, 4, 205-212.

Related Lessons:

A-01: Measure Frequency (i.e., count)

A-09: Evaluate the accuracy and reliability of measurement procedures.

B 02: Review and interpret articles from the behavior-analytic literature.

G-06: Provide behavior-analytic services in collaboration with others who support and/or provide services to one's clients.

H-02: Select a schedule of observation and recording periods.

I-01: Define behavior in observable and measurable terms.

I-05: Organize, analyze, and interpret observed data.

J-09: Identify and address practical and ethical considerations when using experimental designs to demonstrate treatment effectiveness.

K-05: Design and use systems for monitoring procedural integrity.

A-09 Evaluate the accuracy and reliability of measurement procedures

Evaluating the accuracy and reliability of measurement procedures involves "measuring the measurement system" (Cooper, Heron, & Heward, 2007, p. 110). As human error is the biggest threat to the accuracy and reliability of data, measurements must be evaluated to determine trustworthiness. Accuracy of measurement is determined when the observed values equal the true values. Establishing a true value requires the use of a different measurement procedure than the one used to record the observed value. This often makes it difficult to determine a true value for many of the behaviors of interest. Measures of reliability should be used when a true value cannot be established. Reliability of measurement is determined when the same value is given across repeated measures of the same event, thus reliability reflects consistency.

Examples:

- Accuracy: You and a friend decide to go on a 5-mile run. Your friend tells you that she can monitor the distance because her legs always start to hurt once she runs 5 miles. You, being a data-driven behavior analyst, decide that your friend's measurement procedure might not be the most accurate so you use your smart phone app to track the distance. Your measurement system will likely reveal a better estimate of the true value of the distance you ran.
- Reliability: Using the example for accuracy, both measures can be reliable if at the end of the run your friend tells you that you must have run 5 miles because her legs hurt and your app indicates you ran 5 miles.

Assessment:

- Ask supervisee to evaluate the accuracy and reliability of a measurement procedure that is being used with a client.
- Ask supervisee to provide definitions and examples of accuracy and reliability.

Relevant Literature:

Cooper, J. O., Heron, T. E., & Heward, W. L. (2007). Improving and assessing the quality of behavioral measurement. *Applied Behavior Analysis* (pp. 102-124). Upper Saddle River, NJ: Pearson Prentice Hall.

Johnston, J. M., & Pennypacker, H. S. (1993a). *Strategies and tactics for human behavioral research* (2nd ed.). Hillsdale, NJ Erlbaum.

Related Lessons:

A-01 Measure frequency (i.e., count).

A-02 Measure rate (i.e., count per unit time).

A-03 Measure duration.

A-04 Measure latency.

A-05 Measure interresponse time (IRT).

A-06 Measure percent of occurrence.

A-07 Measure trials to criterion.

A-08 Assess and interpret interobserver agreement.

H-01 Select a measurement system to obtain representative data given the dimensions of the behavior and the logistics of observing and recording.

H-02 Select a schedule of observation and recording periods.

A-10 Design, plot and interpret data using equal-interval graphs

Definition:

Line graph - "In applied behavior analysis, each point on a line graph shows the level of some quantifiable dimension of the target behavior (i.e. the dependent variable) in relation to a specified point in time and/or environmental condition" (Cooper, Heron, & Heward, p. 129).*

The behavior analyst defines behavior in quantifiable, observable terms to measure consistently and accurately. The behavior is measured in terms of a pertinent aspect of behavior that can be counted or assessed across observers. When data are plotted, the patterns they make provide for a visual analysis of levels of the behavior (shown on the vertical, y-axis) as the behavior occurs at a specific point in time or environmental condition (shown on a horizontal, x-axis). Graphs are drawn with the y-axis in a two-thirds ratio to the x-axis in order to enable accurate comparison of intervention results across graphs. The analysis interprets levels of data points, directions (trend), and stability or variability of data paths within a single condition or viewed across different conditions. These factors help an analyst assess if an individual is responding to intervention efforts in a therapeutic or non-therapeutic direction. As a result of this systematic interpretation of results, the analyst continues treatment strategies or alters them until the line graph shows consistent behavior change in a therapeutic direction.

Designing an equal interval line graph:
- Approximate ratio of y to x-axis is 2:3
- The target behavior to measure was the percent (dimension) of math homework (varied number of problems assigned) a student completed each morning when math homework was assigned (session).
- Lowest possible percent of homework completed was zero and highest possible percent (100%) is shown at equal intervals of outside tic marks.

Example:

- Before intervention began, John showed a baseline pattern of completing between zero and 10% of his assigned math homework.
- Zero value is raised above the x-axis to see data points clearly.
- Baseline lasted 4 sessions in a non-therapeutic pattern.
- Conditions changed from baseline to intervention between Session 4 and 5.
- The intervention included John's teacher praising him each day that he returned any part of his math homework assigned.
- In the first session of intervention, John turned in 10% of his homework. The second day after receiving teacher praise, John increased his completed amount of homework to 40% of the assignment.
- John did not always increase the percent of homework completed each day that math homework was given.
- The intervention data path shows an increasing trend overall throughout the intervention condition of teacher praise for math homework completion.
- Although data showed some variability, John reached criteria of at least 90% of math homework completed for 3 consecutive days on the 12th day of teacher praise for his efforts to return homework.

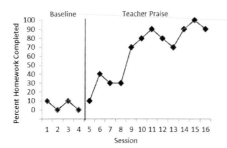

Figure 2   Percent of daily math homework
        John completed in September

*AB designs can show relations between base-
line and intervention responding but
cannot be used to show cause and effect.

Assessment:

- Ask the supervisee to explain why
  the percent of homework completed
  was the correct dimension to measure for this intervention.

- Ask supervisee to explain the reason
  the AB graph design cannot be used
  to demonstrate experimental control
  but can be used in applied settings to
  indicate consistent and therapeutic
  change.

- Ask supervisee to find missing elements in a line graph you design.

- Ask the supervisee to operationally
  define a repetitive behavior of a
  friend or family member, identify a
  dimension of that behavior that
  would accurately represent occurrences of the behavior, and then design a line graph to show results.

- Give the supervisee a line graph you
  design and ask supervisee to interpret level, trend, variability, and data
  path characteristics within and
  across conditions.

Relevant Literature:

Alberto, P., & Troutman, A. C. (2013). *Applied
    behavior analysis for teachers* (9th ed). Bos-
    ton: Pearson.

Cooper, J. O., Heron, T. E., & Heward, W. L.
    (2007). Applied behavior analysis.

Gast, D. L., & Ledford, J. R. (Eds.).
    (2010). *Single subject research methodology in
    behavioral sciences*. Routledge.

Vanselow, N. R., & Bourret, J. C. (2012).
    Online Interactive Tutorials for Creat-
    ing Graphs with Excel 2007 or 2010. *Be-
    havior analysis in practice*, *5*(1), 40.

Related Lessons:

H-01 Select a measurement system to obtain
representative data given the dimensions of
the behavior and the logistics of observing
and recording.

H-02 Select a schedule of observation and recording periods.

H-03 Select a data display that effectively
communicates relevant quantitative relations.

H-04 Evaluate changes in level, trend, and
variability.

I-05 Organize, analyze, and interpret observed
data.

FK-47 Identify the measurable dimensions of
behavior (e.g. rate, duration, latency, interresponse time)

J-15 Base decision-making on data displayed
in various formats.

A-11 Design, plot, and interpret data using a cumulative record to display data

<u>Definition:</u>

Cumulative record – recording method that involves "the number of responses recorded during each observation period is added to the total number of responses recorded during previous observation periods" (Cooper, Heron & Heward, 2007, p. 138). The value on the y-axis represents the cumulative number of responses recorded and the value on the x-axis represents time (i.e., observation periods). Once the response rate exceeds the maximum value on the y-axis, the curve resets to zero and begins again. Cumulative records display the overall response rate and visually depict the learner's rate of acquisition for a series of behavior targets (e.g., total number of skills mastered throughout services, number of sight words learned). Data are interpreted on a cumulative record by analyzing the slope in which the steeper the slope, the higher the response rate.

<u>Examples:</u>

- The cumulative record below indicates the number of attributes learned by a first grade student. The overall response rate is 13 attributes across 181 sessions. In general, data in this graph suggests that there was a fairly slow rate of acquisition. However, the slope is much steeper between sessions 1 and 61, indicating that the rate of acquisition was quicker during the first part of the intervention.

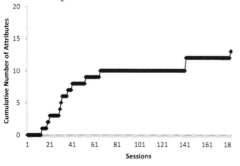

<u>Assessment:</u>

- Ask supervisee to identify behavioral targets that would be appropriate to graph in a cumulative record
- Ask supervisee to create a cumulative record graph.
- Show supervisee various examples of cumulative records and ask supervisee to interpret the data.

<u>Relevant Literature:</u>

Cooper, J. O., Heron, T. E., & Heward, W. L. (2007). Constructing and interpreting graphic displays of behavioral data. *Applied Behavior Analysis* (pp. 126-157). Upper Saddle River, NJ: Pearson Prentice Hall.

Ferster, C. B., & Skinner, B. F. (1957). Schedules of reinforcement. New York, NY: Appleton-Century-Crofts.

<u>Related Lessons:</u>

A-10 Design, plot, and interpret data using equal-interval graphs.

H-01 Select a measurement system to obtain representative data given the dimensions of the behavior and the logistics of observing and recording.

H-02 Select a schedule of observation and recording periods.

H-03 Select a data display that effectively communicates relevant quantitative relations.

H-04 Evaluate changes in level, trend, and variability.

H-05 Evaluate temporal relations between observed variables (within &between sessions, time series).

A-12 Design and implement continuous measurement procedures (e.g., event recording)

Definition:

Event recording – "measurement procedure for obtaining a tally or count of the number of times a behavior occurs" (Cooper, Heron, & Heward, 2007, p. 695).

Examples:
Examples of contexts that are likely to be appropriate for an event recording procedure:
- Property destruction that typically occurs two to five times a week.
- Correct responses to the question, "What do you want?" when asked in at least six distributed trials each day.

Examples of contexts that may be inappropriate for an event recording procedure:
- Vocal Stereotypy that occurs on and off so rapidly that an observer would not be able to accurately determine the start and end of the stereotypy.
- Aggressive behavior in a classroom setting with one teacher, who must conduct instruction, interact with other students, and count hitting behavior that often includes multiple students.

An observer may increase counting accuracy by using a counting device with low-technology (i.e., masking tape around the wrist for tally marks or a golf-stroke counter or with high technology (i.e., iPad or laptop direct observation programs).

Assessment:
- Ask the supervisee to describe situations that would be appropriate to use event recording procedures.
- Ask the supervisee to describe situations that may not be appropriate to use an event recording procedure.
- Ask the supervisee to use an event recording procedure to measure 3 responses at one time. Ask the student to design a datasheet and method for counting that will help the observer record the responses accurately.

Relevant Literature:
Cooper, J. O., Heron, T. E., & Heward, W. L. (2007). Applied behavior analysis. Upper Saddle River, NJ: Pearson Education.

Kelly, M. B. (1977). A review of the observational data-collection and reliability procedures reported in the Journal of Applied Behavior Analysis. *Journal of Applied Behavior Analysis*, 10 (1), 97-101.

Sasso, G. M., Reimers, T. M., Cooper, L. J., Wacker, D., Berg, W., Steege, M., & Allaire, A. (1992). Use of descriptive and experimental analyses to identify the functional properties of aberrant behavior in school settings. *Journal of Applied Behavior Analysis*, 25 (4), 809-821.

Related Lessons:
A-09 Evaluate the accuracy and reliability of measurement procedures.

H-01 Select a measurement system to obtain representative data given the dimensions of the behavior and the logistics of observing and recording.

I-01 Define behavior in observable and measurable terms.

FK-47 Identify the measurable dimensions of behavior (e.g. rate, duration, latency, interresponse time).

FK-48 State the advantages and disadvantages of using continuous measurement procedures and discontinuous measurement procedures (e.g. partial- and whole-interval recording, momentary time sampling.)

A-13 Design and implement discontinuous measurement procedures (e.g., partial & whole interval, momentary time sampling)

Definition:

Time sampling – "…refers to a variety of methods for observing and recording behavior during intervals or at specific moments in time. The basic procedure involves dividing the observation period into time intervals and then recording the presence or absence of behavior within or at the end of interval… Three forms of time sampling used often by applied behavior analysts are whole-interval recording, partial-interval recording and momentary time sampling" (Cooper, Heron, & Heward, 2007, p. 90).

Whole-Interval Recording

Once the interval has ended, the observer records whether the behavior has occurred throughout the *entire* interval. Whole-interval recording tends to underestimate how much a behavior is occurring because the behavior has to be emitted for the entire interval in order to get recorded (Cooper, Heron, & Heward, 2007).

Example:

- *Hand-flapping: student moves one or both hands repeatedly and rapidly by bending at the wrist, such that fingers move more than 2 inches.*
- *Non-example: waving hand to say "hello" or "goodbye."*
- An observer divides a 5-minute observation period into intervals of 5 seconds. A student flaps his hands for the *entire* 5-second interval. At the end of the 5-second interval, the observer records the behavior as having occurred.

Example:

- *Palilalia: student repeats a word, phrase, or sentence with no direct, observable relationship with the immediate environment.*

- An observer divides a 5-minute observation period up into intervals of 10 seconds. A student emits palilalia for the *entire* 10-second interval. At the end of the 10-second interval, the observer records the behavior as having occurred.

Partial-Interval Recording

With the partial-interval recording method, the time of observation is again divided into intervals and a behavior is recorded as having occurred if it has occurred *at some point* during the interval. Data are usually reported as percentage of intervals (Cooper, Heron, & Heward, 2007).

Example:

- *Calling-out behavior in a pupil: student raises voice above conversation level when not called on by teacher.*
- A 30-minute observation period is divided into one-minute intervals. At the end of the one minute interval, the behavior is recorded as having occurred because the pupil called-out after the first 30 seconds of the interval.

Example:

- *Toy play: child touches or manipulates toys.*
- A 5-minute observation period is divided up into 10-second intervals. The observer records the behavior as having occurred in the last 10-second interval because the child had engaged with the toy at some point during the interval.

Momentary Time Sampling

With this type of measurement, a period of time is divided up into intervals and the observer records whether the behavior is occurring at the precise moment the interval ends. (Cooper, Heron and Heward, 2007)

Example:

- *Movie watching: client is seated, and head and eyes are oriented toward screen.*

- An observer is measuring a client's engagement with a movie across a 2-minute period. The 2-minute period is divided up into 5-second intervals. The observer records the behavior as being present at the end of the first 5-second interval as the client was watching the movie appropriately at that specific point in time.

Assessment:

- Ask your Supervisee to describe each of the 3 types of time sampling methods listed above.

- Have your Supervisee practice each type of data collection method in his/her job role or through role-playing.

- Ask them to tell you which time sampling method is being employed in each of the following examples:

  o An observer is interested in a client's interactions with his/her peers. They observe him/her across a 10-minute period; at the end of each 10-second interval, they record the behavior as being present if the client has had any interaction with his/her peers at all during the interval. **(Answer = Partial-interval recording).**

  o An observer is examining a client's on-task behavior in class. They observe him/her for a 60-minute period and divide the hour up into 5-minute intervals. If the client is on-task at the end of the 5-minute interval, on-task behavior is scored as having been

observed. **(Answer = Momentary time sampling).**

  o A client's humming behavior is being observed; the observer divides a 15-minute observation time up into 30-second intervals. If humming was observed throughout the entire 30-second interval, the behavior is scored as having occurred in that interval. **(Answer = Whole-interval recording).**

Relevant Literature:

Daboul-Meany, M. G., Roscoe, E. M., Bourret, J. C., Ahearn, W. H. (2007). A comparison of momentary time sampling and partial-interval recording for evaluating functional relations. *Journal of Applied Behavior Analysis, 40* (3), 501-514.

Powell, J., Martindale, A., & Kulp, S. (1975). An evaluation of time-sample measures of behavior. *Journal of Applied Behavior Analysis, 8*, 463-469.

Suen, H. K., Ary, D., & Covalt, W. (1991). Reappraisal of momentary time sampling and partial-interval recording. *Journal of Applied Behavior Analysis, 24*, 803-804.

Related Lessons:

A-12: Design and implement continuous measurement procedures (e.g., event recording)

H-01: Select a measurement system to obtain representative data given the dimensions of the behavior and the logistics of observing and recording

I-01: Define the behavior in observable and measurable terms

FK-47: Identify the measurable dimensions of behavior (e.g., rate, duration, latency, interresponse time)

FK-48: State the advantages and disadvantages of using continuous measurement procedures and discontinuous measurement procedures (e.g., partial- and whole-interval recording, momentary time sampling)

A-14 Design and implement choice measures

Types of Choice Measures

- Stimulus preference assessment – "a variety of procedures used to determine the stimuli that a person prefers, the relative preference values (high versus low) of those stimuli, the conditions under which those preference values remain in effect, and their presumed value as reinforcers" (Cooper, Heron, & Heward, 2007, p. 705).
- Single-stimulus preference assessment – also called a "successive choice" method. A stimulus is presented one at a time. Approaches to the items are recorded. Preference is based on whether or not individual approached item. (Pace, Ivancic, Edwards, Iwata, & Page, 1985)
- Paired choice preference assessment –also called a "forced choice" method. Consists of the simultaneous presentation of two stimuli. The observer records which of the two stimuli the learner chooses. Presentations continue until all stimuli are paired with each other stimulus. A hierarchy can then be formed using the choices. (Fisher, Piazza, Bowman, Hagopian, Owens, & Slevin, 1992).
- Multiple stimulus assessment – an extension of the paired-stimulus procedure developed by Fisher and colleagues (1992). The person chooses a preferred stimulus from an array of three or more stimuli. (Cooper, Heron, & Heward, 2007)
- Multiple stimulus without replacement assessment – an extension of the procedures described by Windsor and colleagues (1994). Once an item was selected, DeLeon and Iwata (1996) did not replace previously chosen stimuli. Each choice was among the remaining stimuli.

- Free-operant assessment – Developed by Roane and colleagues (1998), participants had free and continuous access to the entire array of stimuli for 5 minutes. Duration of item manipulation is recorded.
- Response restriction assessment– Developed by Hanley and colleagues (2003), a free operant arrangement was used to measure preference. Stimuli with high interaction relative to the other stimuli during a session were restricted for the remaining sessions.
- Duration assessment – Developed by Hagopian and colleagues (2001), items were presented one at a time. Duration of engagement was measured for each item.
- Concurrent-chain assessment (Concurrent-chain schedules) – "concurrent schedules in which the reinforcers are themselves schedules that operate separately and in the presence of different stimuli" (Catania, 2013, p. 433). Completion of the initial link schedule of reinforcement gives access to the terminal link schedule of reinforcement. Preference for particular schedules of reinforcement, or other environmental arrangements can be measured by responding in the initial links (Hanley, Iwata, & Lindberg, 1999).

Assessment:

- Ask your Supervisee to identify the pros and cons of each type of preference assessment.
- Have Supervisee memorize the authors and years for the publications of each type of preference assessment. Use flashcards to learn to fluency.
- Have Supervisee demonstrate the use of at least 5 types of preference

assessments on the job (or in a role play).

Relevant Literature:

Catania, A. C. (2013). *Learning* (5th ed.). Cornwall-on-Hudson, NY: Sloan.

Cooper, J. O., Heron, T. E., & Heward, W. L. (2007). Applied behavior analysis. Upper Saddle River, NJ: Pearson Education.

Fisher, W., Piazza, C. C., Bowman, L. G., Hagopian, L. P., Owens, J. C., & Slevin, I. (1992). A comparison of two approaches for identifying reinforcers for persons with severe and profound disabilities. *Journal of applied Behavior analysis, 25*(2), 491-498.

Hagopian, L. P., Rush, K. S., Lewin, A. B., & Long, E. S. (2001). Evaluating the predictive validity of a single stimulus engagement preference assessment. *Journal of Applied Behavior Analysis, 34*(4), 475-485.

Hanley, G. P., Iwata, B. A., Lindberg, J. S., & Conners, J. (2003). Response-restriction analysis: I. Assessment of activity preferences. *Journal of Applied Behavior Analysis, 36*(1), 47-58.

Hanley, G. P., Iwata, B. A., & Lindberg, J. S. (1999). Analysis of activity preferences as a function of differential consequences. *Journal of Applied Behavior Analysis, 32*(4), 419-435.

DeLeon, I. G., & Iwata, B. A. (1996). Evaluation of a multiple-stimulus presentation format for assessing reinforcer preferences. *Journal of Applied Behavior Analysis, 29*(4), 519-533.

Pace, G. M., Ivancic, M. T., Edwards, G. L., Iwata, B. A., & Page, T. J. (1985). Assessment of stimulus preference and reinforcer value with profoundly retarded individuals. *Journal of Applied Behavior Analysis, 18*(3), 249-255.

Roane, H. S., Vollmer, T. R., Ringdahl, J. E., & Marcus, B. A. (1998). Evaluation of a brief stimulus preference assessment. *Journal of Applied Behavior Analysis, 31*(4), 605-620.

Smith, R. G., Iwata, B. A., & Shore, B. A. (1995). Effects of subject-versus experimenter-selected reinforcers on the behavior of individuals with profound developmental disabilities. *Journal of Applied Behavior Analysis, 28*(1), 61-71.

Windsor, J., Piché, L. M., & Locke, P. A. (1994). Preference testing: A comparison of two presentation methods. *Research in Developmental Disabilities, 15*(6), 439-455.

Related Lessons:

I-07: Design and conduct preference assessments to identify putative reinforcers.

J-04: Select intervention strategies based on client preferences.

B-01 Use the dimensions of Applied Behavior Analysis (Baer, Wolf, & Risley, 1968) to evaluate whether interventions are behavior analytic in nature

"Baer, Wolf, and Risley (1968) recommended that applied behavior analysis should be *applied, behavioral, analytic, technological, conceptually systematic, effective,* and capable of appropriately *generalized outcomes….*" In 1987 Baer and colleagues reported that the "seven self-conscious guides to behavior analytic conduct" they had offered 20 years earlier "remain functional; they still connote the current dimensions of the work usually called applied behavior analysis" (Baer, et al., cited in Cooper et al., 2007, p. 16).

1. **Applied** - The applied dimension relates to choosing target behaviors to change that are socially significant.
2. **Behavioral** - The behavioral dimension refers to the target behavior being systematically chosen for intervention based on its significance and this behavior must be measurable. Baer et al. (1968, p. 93) summarized this point by stating, "Since the behavior of an individual is composed of physical events, its scientific study requires their precise measure."
3. **Analytic** - The analytic dimension refers to "… a functional relation between the manipulated events and a reliable change in some measurable dimension of the targeted behavior" (Cooper et al. 2007, p. 17). Baer et al. (1968, p. 94) stated that, "An experimenter has achieved an analysis of behavior when he can exercise control over it."
4. **Technological** - "A study in applied behavior analysis is technological when all of its operative procedures are identified and described with sufficient detail and clarity" (Cooper et al., 2007, p. 17).
5. **Conceptually systematic** - Conceptual systems refer to the application of behavior analytic principles to create behavior change. "The field of applied behavior analysis will probably advance best if the published descriptions of its procedures are not only precisely technological, but also strive for relevance to principle" (Baer et. al. 1968, p. 96).
6. **Effective** - "An effective application of behavioral techniques must improve the behavior under investigation to a practical degree" (Cooper et al., 2007, p. 17).
7. **Generality** - The final dimension of applied behavior analysis outlined by Baer et al. (1968) was generality. "A behavior change has generality if it lasts over time, appears in environments other than the one in which the intervention that initially produced it was implemented, and/or spreads to other behaviors not directly treated by the intervention." (Cooper et al., 2007, p. 18).

Example:

- Tim was evaluating the effectiveness of an intervention to decrease inappropriate comments for a first grade student on his case load. The data indicated that the behavior had decreased across all settings including when the child was home, displaying generalization of the intervention. He also noticed that the intervention was analytic because the data indicated that on days there was a substitute who was not thoroughly trained on the intervention there was a significant increase in rates of inappropriate commenting. Finally, Tim deemed the behavior of inappropriately commenting to be socially significant because it impeded the student from effectively accessing the classroom curriculum.

- Students learning the 7 dimensions of ABA often use the acronyms GET-A-CAB or BAT-CAGE to remember them.

Assessment:
- Have supervisee create SAFMEDs cards for each of the dimensions of ABA.
- Have supervisee identify, define, and give examples of each of the 7 dimensions of Applied Behavior Analysis mentioned in the Baer, Wolf, & Risley (1968) article.
- In reference to the "applied" dimension of ABA, have supervisee list 5 types of behavior that they feel are social significant in their life. Have him/her describe why these are socially significant types of behavior.
- Have supervisee identify types of socially significant behavior they target with clients.

Relevant Literature:
Baer, D.M., Wolf, M.M., & Risley, T.R. (1968). Some Current Dimensions of Applied Behavior Analysis. *Journal of Applied Behavior Analysis, 1*, 1, 91-97.
Baer, D.M., Wolf, M.M., & Risley, T.R. (1987). Some Still Current Dimensions of Applied Behavior Analysis. *Journal of Applied Behavior Analysis, 20*, 4, 313-327.

Cooper, J.O., Heron, T.E. & Heward W.L. (2007). *Applied Behavior Analysis* (2nd Ed.), Upper Saddle River, NJ. Pearson Prentice Hall. 16-18, 235, 247-252.
Stokes, T.F. & Baer, D.M. (1977). An Implicit Technology of Generalization. *Journal of Applied Behavior Analysis*, 10, 2, 349-367.
Wolf, M.M. (1978). Social Validity: The Case for Subjective Measurement or How Applied Behavior Analysis Is Finding its Heart. *Journal of Applied Behavior Analysis*, 11, 2, 203-214.

Related Lessons:
B-04: Use withdrawal/reversal designs
B-05: Use alternating treatments (i.e., multi-element) designs
B-06: Use changing criterion designs
B-07: Use multiple baseline designs
B-09: Conduct a component analysis to determine the effective components of an intervention package
B-11: Conduct a parametric analysis to determine the effective values of an independent variable.
H-04: Evaluate changes in level, trend, and variability.
I-01: Define behavior in observable and measurable terms.

B-02 Review and interpret articles from the behavior-analytic literature

Applied behavior analysis is an applied science that develops its technology via the discovery of environmental variables that produce socially significant behavior change. The process of putting the science into practice begins with basic researchers discovering the principles of behavior that are then tested on socially significant behavior by applied researchers and then ultimately implemented by practitioners (Cooper, Heron, & Heward, 2007). Whether a behavior analyst is solely a practitioner or a practitioner and a researcher, it is important that they maintain close contact with the scientific literature and its possible applications by regularly reviewing and critically interpreting articles from the behavior analytic literature.

When engaging in a review of the literature it is useful to consider the criteria that define applied behavior analysis which are outlined by Baer, Wolf, & Risley (1987). These criteria referred to as the seven dimensions (applied, behavioral, analytic, technological, conceptually systematic, effective and generality) can not only assist in determining if an intervention meets the standards of applied behavior analysis but it can also conclude whether a research intervention is prepared to translate into practice or if further investigation is necessary prior to effective clinical implementation.

Cooper, Heron and Heward (2007, p. 5), assert that "scientific knowledge is built on above all, empiricism - the practice of objective observations of the phenomena of interest." Therefore, a behavior analyst should also remain objective when reviewing and interpreting articles. For example, when reviewing an article it is important to make an unbiased interpretation regarding whether or not experimental control (internal validity) was established by acknowledging possible subject, setting, measurement and/or independent variable confounds (Cooper, Heron, & Heward, 2007). Furthermore, it is important to remain objective when conducting visual analyses of

the data to determine the extent that a functional relation is demonstrated. To assist in this process, Johnston and Pennypacker (2009) suggest that a behavior analyst have extensive experience with graphical analyses both as a designer and a reader. They also note that the first step to analyzing behavioral data is to ask whether the data presentation is straightforward and productive toward the research question by orienting to the graph's scale, axes and legend. Next, one should conduct a visual analysis by acknowledging the number of data points, variability, level and trend for each experimental condition followed by a visual analysis across conditions and then across participants to draw comparisons and begin to establish conclusions (Cooper, Heron, & Heward, 2007).

In summary, a behavior analyst's ability to critically and empirically analyze the literature requires a thorough understanding of the science and acknowledgment of the bidirectional relationship between research and practice.

Assessment:
- Provide the supervisee with an article and ask them to outline and possible threats to internal validity in the article.
- Provide the supervisee with an article that has the results and discussion removed. Ask Supervisee to give a precise summary of the results based upon the figures and tables. Afterward, provide the results and the discussion to compare and facilitate further supervisory discussion.
- Ask supervisee to determine if there is a function relation based on the data presented in an article and provide a rationale to their assertion.
- Ask the supervisee to evaluate an article to determine if it includes the seven dimensions of applied behavior analysis

- Throughout the course of supervision, ask the supervisee to determine whether a literature review or research article (considering past research cited) is applied, basic or both and whether there is adequate support to use the intervention in clinical practice.

Relevant Literature:

Baer, D. M., Wolf, M. M., & Risley, T. R. (1968). Some current dimensions of applied behavior
  analysis. *Journal of applied behavior analysis, 1*(1), 91-97.
Cooper, J. O., Heron, T. E., & Heward, W. L. (2007). *Applied behavior analysis (2nd ed.). Upper Saddle River, NJ: Pearson.*

Johnston, J. M. (2009). Pennypacker Jr. Strategies and tactics of behavioral research.

Related Lessons:

B-01 Use the dimensions of applied behavior analysis (Baer, Wolf, & Risley, 1968) to evaluate whether interventions are behavior analytic in nature.

H-04 Evaluate changes in level, trend, and variability.

I-05 Organize, analyze and interpret observed data

FK-04 Empiricism

FK-09 Distinguish between the conceptual analysis of behavior, experimental analysis of behavior, applied behavior analysis, and behavioral service delivery.

FK-33 functional relations

B-03 Systematically arrange independent variables to demonstrate their effects on dependent variables

Definitions:

Independent Variable - "The variable that is systematically manipulated by the researcher in an experiment to see whether changes in the independent variable produce reliable changes in the dependent variable. In applied behavior analysis, it is usually an environmental event or condition antecedent or consequent to the dependent variable. Sometimes called the intervention or treatment variable" (Cooper, Heron, & Heward, 2007, p. 697).

Dependent Variable - "The variable in an experiment measured to determine if it changes as a result of the manipulations of the independent variable; in applied behavior analysis, it represents some measure of a socially significant behavior" (Cooper et al. 2007, p. 693).

Dependent variables must be operationally defined to allow for consistent assessment and replication of the assessment process, measured repeatedly within and across controlled conditions, recording is assessed for consistency across the experiment using inter-observer agreement, and dependent variables must be socially significant to the individual or those around them. (Horner, Carr, Halle, McGee, Odom, & Wolery, 2005) Experimental control is achieved when predicted change in the dependent variable (i.e., the behavior) covaries with manipulations of the independent variable (i.e., the intervention) showing the effectiveness of the independent variable on the dependent variable of a participant. (Horner et al., 2005)

Example:

- *A student consistently disrupts group activities. When given visuals for appropriate behavior (i.e., quiet voice, calm body) paired with gestural redirection, disruptive behavior in group lessons decreases. The teacher then takes the visuals away for a week to see if fading these supports would be an option. The gestural redirection for inappropriate behavior is still in place. The student's disruptive behavior remains low. When the redirection is removed the following week. The student engages in increased disruptive behavior during this week, so the teacher decides to continue the gestural prompts and the disruptive behavior decreases again.*

Non-example:
A student with attention deficits consistently disrupts group activities. His teacher occasionally uses the visuals for appropriate behavior outlined in the BSP and the disruptive behavior does not decrease.

Assessment:
- Give supervisees article abstracts on single subject research. Have them identify the dependent variable and independent variable for the study.
- Have supervisees identify the independent and dependent variables in the example listed above.
- Have supervisees read Horner et al., (2005) The Use of Single-Subject Research to Identify Evidence-Based Practice in Special Education and complete a brief summary of the article and ask them to identify what compromises the integrity of a functional relationship and define the quality indicators outlined for effective single-subject research.

Relevant Literature:
Cooper, J.O., Heron, T.E. & Heward W.L. (2007). *Applied Behavior Analysis* (2nd Ed.), Upper Saddle River, NJ. Pearson Prentice Hall.

Horner, R.H., Carr, E.G., Halle, J., McGee, G., Odom, S., Wolery, M. (2005). The Use of Single-Subject Research to Identify Evidence-Based Practice in Special

Education. *Exceptional Children*, 71, 2, 165-179.

<u>Related Lessons:</u>
B-04: Use withdrawal/reversal designs
B-05: Use alternating treatments (i.e., multi-element) designs
B-06: Use changing criterion designs
B-07: Use multiple baseline designs

B-09: Conduct a component analysis to determine the effective components of an intervention package
B-11: Conduct a parametric analysis to determine the effective values of an independent variable.
H-04: Evaluate changes in level, trend, and variability.
I-01: Define behavior in observable and measurable terms.

B-04 Use withdrawal/reversal designs

Definition:

Reversal design - "Any experimental design in which the researcher attempts to verify the effect of the independent variable by "reversing" responding to a level obtained in a previous condition; encompasses experimental designs in which the independent variable is withdrawn (A-B-A-B) or reversed in its focus (e.g., DRI/DRA)" (Cooper, Heron, & Heward, 2007, p. 703).

Withdrawal design - "A term used by some researchers as a synonym for an A-B-A-B design; also used to describe experiments in which an effective treatment is sequentially or partially withdrawn to promote the maintenance of behavior changes" (Cooper, Heron, & Heward, 2007, p. 708).

Examples:

- An experiment that entails exposing a participant to a condition of no programmed reinforcement for a work task (baseline) until steady state is achieved, then exposes a participate to a condition in which they earn stickers contingent on a work task (intervention) and then repeats these two conditions respectively.

- An experiment in which baseline consists of the reinforcement of challenging behavior and the treatment consists of differential reinforcement of an alternative/replacement behavior and both conditions are replicated at least twice.

Assessment:

- Ask the supervisee to either describe a time that they used of a withdrawal or reversal design or have them describe a hypothetical experiment using a withdrawal or reversal design.

- Have supervisee look at the figures in the articles (such as those listed below) as well as other articles and determine which ones are reversal/withdrawal designs.

- Have the supervisee look at figures in the articles below and describe what characteristics make it a reversal or withdrawal design

- Have the supervisee describe the pros of using a reversal design and the condition in which

the use of a reversal design would not be desirable

Relevant Literature:

Anderson, C. M., & Long, E. S. (2002). Use of a structured descriptive assessment methodology to identify variables affecting problem behavior. *Journal of Applied Behavior Analysis*, *35*(2), 137-154.

Baer, D. M., & Wolf, M. M. (1970). Recent examples of behavior modification in preschool settings. *Behavior modification in clinical psychology*, 5-12

Cooper, J. O., Heron, T. E., & Heward, W. L. (2007). *Applied behavior analysis (2nd ed.). Upper Saddle River, NJ: Pearson.*

Falcomata, T. S., Roane, H. S., Hovanetz, A. N., Kettering, T. L., & Keeney, K. M. (2004). An evaluation of response cost in the treatment of inappropriate vocalizations maintained by automatic reinforcement. *Journal of Applied Behavior Analysis*, *37*(1), 83-87.

Lerman, D. C., Kelley, M. E., Vorndran, C. M., Kuhn, S. A., & LaRue, R. H. (2002). Reinforcement magnitude and responding during treatment with differential reinforcement. *Journal of Applied Behavior Analysis*, *35*(1), 29-48.

Related Lessons:

B-03 Systematically arrange independent variables to demonstrate their effects on dependent variables
J-09 Identify and address practical and ethical considerations when using experimental designs to demonstrate treatment effectiveness

Footnotes

Some authors exclusively use the term reversal design for studies in which the contingency is reversed (or switched to another behavior) as in DRO and DRA/DRI reversal techniques and the term withdrawal design for studies that employ an A-B-A-B approach where the A signifies baseline condition and B the treatment condition (Cooper, Heron, & Heward, 2007).

A multiple treatment reversal design can also be used to compare the effects of two or more treatment conditions to baseline and/or to the other treatments (e.g., ABABACAC, ABABCBCB) (Cooper, Heron, & Heward, 2007).

B-05 Use alternating treatments designs

<u>Definition:</u>

Alternating treatments design - "An experimental design in which two or more conditions (one of which may be a no treatment control condition) are presented in rapidly alternating succession (e.g., on alternating sessions or days) independent of the level of responding; differences in responding between or among conditions are attributed to the effects of the conditions (also called concurrent schedule design, multielement design, multiple schedule design)" (Cooper, Heron, & Heward, 2007, p. 689).

<u>Examples:</u>

- An experiment that entails conducting DRA and no programmed treatment during alternating sessions to compare treatment to the no treatment.

- An experiment that entails conducting DRI, DRO and DRA on alternating days to compare all treatments to each other.

<u>Assessment:</u>

- Ask the supervisee to either describe an alternating treatment design they have used in the past or have them describe an alternating treatments design.

- Have supervisee look at various figures from the articles (such as some of those below) as well as articles that did not use an alternating treatment design and have them determine which figures depict the use of an alternating treatment design.

- Have the supervisee look at figures in the articles below and describe what characteristics make it an alternating treatment design

- Have the supervisee describe the pros of using an alternating treatment design and the condition in which the use of an alternating treatment design would not be desirable

<u>Relevant Literature:</u>

Barbetta, P. M., Heron, T. E., & Heward, W. L. (1992). Effects of active student response during error correction on the acquisition, maintenance, and generalization of sight words by students with developmental disabilities. *Journal of applied behavior analysis*, *26* (1), 111-119.

Barlow, D. H., & Hayes, S. C. (1979). Alternating treatments design: One strategy for comparing the effects of two treatments in a single subject. *Journal of Applied Behavior Analysis*, *12*(2), 199-210.

Cooper, J. O., Heron, T. E., & Heward, W. L. (2007). *Applied behavior analysis (2nd ed.)*. Upper Saddle River, NJ: Pearson.

Iwata, B.A., Dorsey, M. F., Slifer, K .J. Bauman, K. E., & Richman, G. S. (1994). Toward a functional analysis of self-injury. *Journal of Applied Behavior Analysis, 27*, 197-209. (Reprinted from *Analysis and Intervention in Developmental Disabilities, 2*, 3-20, 1982).

Martens, B. K., Lochner, D. G., & Kelly, S. Q. (1992). The effects of variable-interval reinforcement on academic engagement: A demonstration of matching theory. *Journal of Applied Behavior Analysis*, *25*(1), 143-151.

Singh, J., & Singh, N. N. (1985). Comparison of word-supply and word-analysis error-correction procedures on oral reading by mentally retarded children. *American Journal of Mental Deficiency*.

Ulman, J. D., & Sulzer-Azaroff, B. (1975). Multielement baseline design in educational research. *Behavior analysis: Areas of research and application*, 377-391.

<u>Related Lessons:</u>

B-03 Systematically arrange independent variables to demonstrate their effects on dependent variables

J-09 Identify and address practical and ethical considerations when using experimental designs to demonstrate treatment effectiveness

B-06 Use changing criterion designs

Definitions:

Changing criterion design - "An experimental design in which an initial baseline phase is followed by a series of treatment phases consisting of successive and gradually changing criteria for reinforcement or punishment. Experimental control is evidenced by the extent the level of responding changes to conform to each new criterion" (Cooper, Heron & Heward, 2007, pp. 691-692).

"The design requires initial baseline observations on a single target behavior. This baseline phase is followed by implementation of a treatment program in each of a series of treatment phases. Each treatment phase is associated with a stepwise change in criterion rate for the target behavior. Thus, each phase of the design provides a baseline for the following phase. When the rate of the target behavior changes with each stepwise change in the criterion, therapeutic change is replicated and experimental control is demonstrated" (Hartmann & Hall, 1976, p. 527).

Guidelines for using the changing criterion design include:

1. Manipulation of the length of phases. Each phase serves as a baseline to compare responding to the next phase. Each phase must be long enough to display stable responding before moving to the next phase.
2. "Varying the size of the criterion change enables a more convincing demonstration of experimental control." (Cooper et al., 2007, p. 222). Criterion change magnitude must be carefully considered so that the criterion is not too large and unattainable but also not too small in magnitude which would not demonstrate sufficient experimental control.
3. Experimental control is demonstrated through replication of treatment effects. Therefore, as the number of phases increases, so does the

opportunity to replicate treatment effects and enhance experimental control.

Example:

- Jim created a class wide reinforcement program to increase the vocabulary test scores of a 1st grade class. He wanted to make sure that the reinforcement program was effective so he set specific score criterion for the class, to monitor their progress. Average baseline test scores were 55 % correct for the entire class. Jim set the first criterion phase at 70% of the test questions answered correctly for the entire class. After 4 weeks, the class met these criteria for 3 consecutive tests, so Jim set the classroom performance criterion to 80% of the test questions answered correctly. This time the class met the criterion in 3 weeks and Jim increased the criterion to 90%. Once again, the class met these criteria for 3 consecutive tests. Jim concluded that his intervention was likely responsible for the change in test scores, since the test score reliably increased when the criteria were altered and required a greater score.

Non-example:

John created a reinforcement program to increase Larry's rate of answering questions during class. After 3 weeks, the data indicated that Larry was answering more questions appropriately in class. However, there was a new teacher in the classroom and other variables that may have accounted for this change. John wanted to see if the program was increasing this behavior, so he decided to remove the reinforcement program for a week to see if Larry's rate of answering questions decreased.

Assessment:

- Have supervisee describe the changing criterion design and state when it may be most appropriate, strengths of this design, as well as limitations of the changing criterion design.

- Have supervisee create a hypothetical analysis using the changing criterion design. Have him/her state why the changing criterion design was the most effective design to display experimental control.

- Have supervisee label the parts of a completed changing criterion design graph and describe how the graph displays experimental control.

Relevant Literature:

Cooper, J.O., Heron, T.E. & Heward W.L. (2007). *Applied Behavior Analysis* (2nd Ed.), Upper Saddle River, NJ. Pearson Prentice Hall.

Hartmann, D.P. & Hall, R.V. (1976). The changing criterion design. *Journal of Applied Behavior Analysis*, 9, 4, 527-532.

McDougall, D. (2005). The range-bound changing criterion design. *Behavioral Interventions*, 20, 2, 129-137.

McLaughlin, T.F. (1983). An examination and evaluation of single subject designs used in behavior analysis research in school settings. *Educational Research Quarterly*, 7, 4, 35-42.

Hall, R.V., & Fox, R.G. (1977). Changing criterion designs: An alternative applied behavior analysis procedure. In B.C. Etzel, J.M. LeBlanc, & D.M. Baer (Eds.). *New developments in behavioral research: Theory, method, and application* (pp. 151-166). Hillsdale, NJ: Erlbaum.

Allen, K.D., & Evans, J.H. (2001). Exposure-based treatment to control excessive blood glucose monitoring. *Journal of Applied Behavior Analysis*, 34, 497-500.

Related Lessons:

B-04: Use withdrawal/reversal designs

B-05: Use alternating treatments (i.e., multi-element) designs

B-07: Use multiple baseline designs

B-09: Conduct a component analysis to determine the effective components of an intervention package

B-11: Conduct a parametric analysis to determine the effective values of an independent variable.

H-04: Evaluate changes in level, trend, and variability.

I-01: Define behavior in observable and measurable terms.

B-07 Use multiple baseline designs

Definition:

Multiple baseline design – "An experimental design that begins with the concurrent measurement of two or more behaviors in a baseline condition, followed by the application of the treatment variable to one of the behaviors while baseline conditions remain in effect for the other behavior(s) After maximum change has been noted in the first behavior, the treatment variable is applied in sequential fashion to each of the other behaviors in the design" (Cooper, Heron & Heward, 2007, p. 699).

Multiple baselines are useful when the target behavior is likely to be irreversible, for example, in skill acquisition. And are also useful when it may be impractical or undesirable to implement a reversal design. For example, in decreasing aggression toward peers. One drawback of the multiple baseline design is potentially the length of time that treatment or intervention is withheld for the last behavior or setting being targeted.

In the delayed baseline design, collection of baseline data for other target behaviors is taken after baseline measurements for the previous behaviors. This design may be effective when a reversal design is not possible, when resources are limited, or when a new behavior or subject becomes available. Behaviors must be measured at the same time and the independent variable cannot be applied to the next behavior until the previous behavior change has been established. There should be a significant difference in the length of baseline conditions between the different behaviors and the independent variable should first be applied to the behavior demonstrating the greatest level of stable responding in baseline.

Other variations in multiple baselines designs are concurrent and nonconcurrent uses of the design. In concurrent multiple baseline designs the data are collected in the same time period. In nonconcurrent multiple baseline designs data can be collected at different times, and different lengths of baselines are

collected, following which implementation of the treatment or intervention is conducted—creating multiple A-B experiments. The experiments are then arranged by length of baseline to create a multiple baseline design. "According to single-case design logic, the nonconcurrent MB design demonstrates only prediction and replication, and not the critical verification of the intervention's effects" (Carr, 2005, p. 220).

Example:
- Rod conducted an FBA on Billy's aggression and property destruction. Both behaviors were determined to be maintained by escape from demands. Rod decided to implement the same intervention for each behavior using a multiple baseline design because they both served the same function and a reversal would possibly reestablish the dangerous behavior after therapeutic effects were observed.

Non-example:
Bob wanted to determine the effects of response blocking and redirection on hand flapping with one of his students. He implemented this procedure and once it proved effective, decided to eliminate the intervention to determine if this procedure was the likely cause of the behavior decrease.

Assessment:
- Have supervisee describe the multiple baseline design and state when it may be most appropriate, strengths of this design, as well as limitations of the multiple baseline design.
- Have supervisee create a hypothetical analysis using the multiple baseline design. Have him/her state why the multiple baseline design was the most effective design to display experimental control.

- Have supervisee label the parts of a completed multiple baseline design graph and describe how the graph displays experimental control.

Relevant Literature:

Barger-Anderson, R., Domaracki, J.W., Kearney-Vakulick, N., & Kubina, R.M. (2004). Multiple baseline designs: The use of a single-case experimental design in literacy research. *Reading Improvement*, 41, 4, 217.

Carr, J.E. (2005). Recommendations for reporting multiple-baseline designs across participants. Behavioral Interventions, 20, 3, 219-224.

Cooper, J.O., Heron, T.E. & Heward W.L. (2007). *Applied Behavior Analysis* (2nd Ed.), Upper Saddle River, NJ. Pearson Prentice Hall.

Harris, F.N., & Jenson, W.R. (1985). Comparisons of multiple-baseline across persons designs and AB designs with replication: Issues and confusions. *Behavioral Assessment*, 7, 2, 121,127.

Harvey, M.T., May, M.E., & Kennedy, C.H. (2004) Nonconcurrent multiple baseline designs and the evaluation of educational systems. *Journal of Behavioral Education*, 13, 4, 267-276.

Watson, P.J., & Workman, E.A. (1981), The non-concurrent multiple baseline across-individuals design: An extension of the traditional multiple baseline design. *Journal of Behavior Therapy and Experimental Psychology*, 12, 3, 257-259.

Zhan, S. & Ottenbacher, K.J. (2001). Single subject research designs for disability research. Journal of Disability and Rehabilitation, 23, 1, 1-8.

Related Lessons:

B-03: Systematically arrange independent variables to demonstrate their effects on dependent variables.

B-04: Use withdrawal/reversal designs.

B-08: Use multiple probe designs.

B-09: Use combinations of design elements.

B-10: Conduct a component analysis to determine the effective components of an intervention package.

B-11: Conduct a parametric analysis to determine the effective values of an independent variable.

E-01: Use interventions based on manipulation of antecedents, such as motivating operants and discriminative stimuli

H-03: Select a data display that effectively communicates relevant quantitative relations.

I-05: Organize, analyze, and interpret observed data.

FK-33: Functional relations.

B-08 Use multiple-probe designs

Like multiple baseline designs (MBD), multiple probe designs (MPD) are "rigorous in their evaluation of threats to interval validity; and are practical for teachers and clinicians who want their research efforts to be wholly compatible with their instructional or therapy activities" (Gast, 2009, p. 277). Multiple probe designs have an additional advantage in applied settings in that intermittent measures of baseline conditions streamline data collection and still maintain the requirement that responding does not change until intervention is applied (baseline logic). Either one probe is taken periodically in baseline conditions and at least three days immediately before applying intervention, MPD (days), or probes occur in brief sessions of a few baseline measurements taken at least three consecutive days before intervention, MPD (conditions). Experimental control is demonstrated if probe evidence across each tier of similar, but functionally different behaviors, participants, or conditions remains relatively stable until intervention is implemented.

Examples:

- Multiple probe designs are particularly useful for researchers and teachers in educational settings to efficiently demonstrate results of instructional interventions when teaching across functionally different new skills (behaviors), across multiple students (participants), or across different sets of skills (conditions).

- Multiple probe designs might not be appropriate if assessing the effects of intervention on severe behaviors that result in injury or property destruction because of the requirement that intervention be delayed across each tier while a person continues to engage in severe behaviors with lasting consequences.

Assessment:

- Ask the supervisee to explain the meaning of "baseline logic" and the reason it enables measurement of experimental control.

- Ask the supervisee why MPD across behaviors requires similar, but functionally different behaviors in each tier of a MPD.

- Give the supervisee three articles in which researchers based their conclusions on MPD line graph data. Ask the supervisee to interpret results of the study based on the graphic data. Compare to the conclusions written by study authors.

Relevant Literature:

Gast, D. L., & Ledford, J. R. (2009). Single subject research methodology in behavioral sciences. Routledge.

Horner, R. D., & Baer, D. M. (1978). Multiple-probe technique: A variation of the multiple baseline. *Journal of Applied Behavior Analysis*, *11*(1), 189-196.

Thompson, T. J., Braam, S. J., & Fuqua, R. W. (1982). Training and generalization of laundry skills: A multiple probe evaluation with handicapped persons. *Journal of applied behavior analysis*, *15*(1), 177-182.

Related Lessons:

B-03 Systematically arrange independent variables to demonstrate their effects on dependent variables.

B-07 Use multiple baselines designs.

H-01 Select a measurement system to obtain representative data given thedimensions of the behavior and the logistics of observing and recording.

H-02 Select a schedule of observation and recording periods.

H-04 Evaluate changes in level, trend, and variability.

I-05 Organize, analyze, and interpret observed data.

FK-36 response generalization

B-09 Use combinations of design elements

When designing an experiment it is sometimes useful to combine experimental design elements to strengthen the demonstration of experimental control. For instance it may be valuable to combine a multiple baseline design with a reversal design.

For example, Colón et al. (2012) used a non-concurrent multiple baseline design across participants to analyze the effects of verbal operant training on appropriate vocalizations and vocal stereotypy. RIRD was implemented and examined using a reversal design for each participant exposed to their procedure.

In 1985, Alexander used a multiple baseline across students with reversal design to evaluate the effects of a study skill training procedure.

Johnston and Pennypacker (2009) point out that experimenters often combine and intermingle many different types of designs as necessary. Categorizing types of designs is really a more valuable thing for the student than it is for the researcher.

Murray Sidman in *Tactics of Scientific Research* says that it is not valuable to say that there are rules to follow when designing an experiment. He says "this would be disastrous" (Sidman, 1960/1988, p. 214). Simply put, he says, "The fact is that *there are no rules of experimental design*" (Sidman, 1960/1988, p. 214).

The most important thing is that the experiment is designed to answer some question we have about the natural world. Sidman says, "We conduct experiments to find out something we do not know" (Sidman, 1960/1988, p.214).

Assessment:

- Have your supervisee design an experiment that would be best suited to use a combination of design elements.
- Ask your supervisee to point to the sections of the graphs in Colon et al. (2012) and Alexander (1985) that reflect the types of experimental designs used.
- Ask your supervisee to describe what Sidman meant when he said that having rules for designing an experiment would be "disastrous."

Relevant Literature:

Alexander, D. F. (1985). The effect of study skill training on learning disabled students' retelling of expository material. *Journal of applied behavior analysis, 18*(3), 263-267.

Colón, C. L., Ahearn, W. H., Clark, K. M., & Masalsky, J. (2012). The effects of verbal operant training and response interruption and redirection on appropriate and inappropriate vocalizations. *Journal of applied behavior analysis, 45*(1), 107-120.

Iwata, B. A., Wallace, M. D., Kahng, S., Lindberg, J. S., Roscoe, E. M., Conners, J., ... & Worsdell, A. S. (2000). Skill acquisition in the implementation of functional analysis methodology. *Journal of Applied Behavior Analysis,33*(2), 181-194.

Johnston, J. M., & Pennypacker, H. S. (2009). *Strategies and tactics of behavioral research*. Routledge.

Related Lessons:

B-03 Systematically arrange independent variables to demonstrate their effects on dependent variables.
B-07 Use multiple baselines designs.
H-01 Select a measurement system to obtain representative data given the dimensions of the behavior and the logistics of observing and recording.
II-05 Organize, analyze, and interpret observed data.

B-10 Conduct a component analysis to determine the effective components of an intervention package

Definition:

Component analysis - "An experiment designed to identify the active elements of a treatment condition, the relative contributions of different variables in a treatment package, and/or the necessary and sufficient components of an intervention. Component analyses take many forms, but the basic strategy is to compare levels of responding across successive phases in which the intervention is implemented with one or more of the components left out" (Cooper, Heron, & Heward, 2007, p. 692).

Examples:
- An experiment that compares response blocking with and without redirection.
- An experiment that compares differential reinforcement of alternative behavior with and without extinction
- An experiment that removes one procedure at a time from a treatment package consisting of three procedures (e.g., Token system, response cost and extinction) and compares responding under each condition to responding during implementation of the full treatment package.

Assessment:
- Ask Supervisee to explain why component analysis research is important to clinical practice (e.g. efficiency)
- Ask the supervisee to either describe a treatment package they use in their fieldwork or practicum that could

be tested via a component analysis or have them describe a hypothetical treatment package that could be tested via a component analysis
- Have supervisee look at the figures in the articles listed below and explain the findings of the analysis by determining the effective components of the intervention package.

Relevant Literature:

Cooper, J. O., Heron, T. E., & Heward, W. L. (2007). *Applied behavior analysis (2nd ed.). Upper Saddle River, NJ: Pearson.*

Hardesty, S. L., Hagopian, L. P., McIvor, M. M., Wagner, L. L., Sigurdsson, S. O., & Bowman, L. G. (2014). Effects of specified performance criterion and performance feedback on staff behavior: A component analysis. *Behavior Modification, 38*(5), 760-773. doi:10.1177/0145445514538280

Ward-Horner, J., & Sturmey, P. (2010). Component analyses using single-subject experimental designs: A review. *Journal of Applied Behavior Analysis, 43*(4), 685-704. doi:10.1901/jaba.2010.43-685

Ward-Horner, J., & Sturmey, P. (2012). Component analysis of behavior skills training in functional analysis. *Behavioral Interventions, 27*(2), 75-92. doi:10.1002/bin.1339

Related Lessons:

B-03 Systematically arrange independent variables to demonstrate their effects on dependent variables

B-11 Conduct a parametric analysis to determine the effective values of an independent variable

Definition:

Parametric analysis - "An experiment designed to compare the differential effects of a range of values of the independent variable" (Cooper, Heron, & Heward, 2007, p. 701).

Examples:

- An experiment designed to analyze different magnitudes of a punishment procedure to determine the least intrusive magnitude of a stimulus to decrease behavior.
- An experiment designed to analyze the optimal quality of attention necessary to reinforce appropriate behavior

Assessment:

- Ask Supervisee to list some parameters (schedule, immediacy, quality, quantity) of an independent variable that can be manipulated experimentally
- Have supervisee describe a hypothetical parametric analysis inclusive of the independent variable parameter to be manipulated and the functional relation to be tested
- Ask the supervisee how they could use a parametric analysis to test for the optimal level of treatment integrity. Then discuss what parameter they would measure (i.e., schedule, immediacy) and which values they would select to answer this experimental question.

Relevant Literature:

Cooper, J. O., Heron, T. E., & Heward, W. L. (2007). *Applied behavior analysis (2nd ed.). Upper Saddle River, NJ: Pearson*

Lerman, D. C., & Iwata, B. A. (1996). A methodology for distinguishing between extinction and punishment effects associated with response blocking. *Journal of Applied Behavior Analysis, 29*, 231-233. doi:10.1901/jaba.1996.29-231

Lerman, D. C., Kelley, M. E., Vorndran, C. M., Kuhn, S. C., & LaRue, R. J. (2002). Reinforcement magnitude and responding during treatment with differential reinforcement. *Journal Of Applied Behavior Analysis, 35*(1), 29-48. doi:10.1901/jaba.2002.35-29

Related Lessons:

B-03 Systematically arrange independent variables to demonstrate their effects on dependent variables

FK-33 functional relations

C-01 State and plan for the possible unwanted effects of reinforcement

Reinforcement has been long been defined as a crucial element to behavioral change. However, there are considerations that behavioral analysts should explore before implementing reinforcement strategies. Here are some considerations for the use of positive reinforcement:

- May suppress the desired response
  - e.g. The availability of the reinforcer elicits behavior that may compete with the target response (Balsam & Bondy, 1983).
- May not be feasible for an individual that has little or no learning history with that reinforcement contingency.
  - e.g. An individual that is being taught to swallow solid food may not progress with a program solely using positive reinforcement due to low baseline levels of swallowing solid foods (Riordan, Iwata, Wohl & Finney, 1984).
- Increases the frequency of the target behavior, thereby reducing the frequency in other responses that may also be desirable
  - e.g. While teaching a student to raise their hand and wait until they are called on in class, the student no longer garners others' attention by calling their name (Balsam & Bondy, 1983).
- May evoke aggression in others, especially in conditions which there are limited quantities of the reinforcer.
  - Aggression may be directed at individuals that are also competing for the same reinforce (Balsam & Bondy, 1983).
- May also evoke aggression when group contingencies are used.
  - Individual may become aggressive towards lower-performing teammates (Balsam & Bondy, 1983).
- Removal of positive reinforcer has been correlated with lower than baseline levels of responding (Balsam & Bondy, 1983).

There are also considerations for the use of negative reinforcement. Here are some:

- Can result in more challenging behavior due to the continuation of aversive stimulation if target behavior is not displayed
- Research shows that even for escape-maintained behavior, positive reinforcement contingencies may compete with negative reinforcement contingencies, therefore, decreasing escape-maintained behavior (Lerman, Volkert & Trosclair, 2007).
  - A child that engages in aggression to escape tasks may be more likely complete tasks without aggression if access to an iPad was given contingent on work completion. This may be more effective than reducing aggression by providing breaks contingent on appropriate asking.
- Negative reinforcement contingencies may reinforce minimal requirements needed to avoid/escape aversive stimulus; does not focus on quality of target response (Balsam & Bondy, 1983).
- Requires continuous aversive stimulation and aversive stimulation often elicits aggressive responses.

These unwanted effects of reinforcement can be curbed taking baseline levels of the target behavior before setting criteria for reinforcement, implementing preference assessments routinely, ensuring reinforcement schedule and reinforcers chosen are as natural to the individual's environment as possible to promote generalization, systematic thinning of the reinforcement schedule, and having concurrent schedules of reinforcement for positive and negative reinforcement when negative reinforcement is utilized.

Assessment:

- Ask supervisee to list considerations for the use of positive reinforcement.
- Ask supervisee to list considerations for the use of negative reinforcement.
- Have supervisee outline which considerations may affect a particular client and what behavioral strategies can be used to curb these unwanted effects.

Relevant Literature:

Balsam, P.D., & Bondy, A.S. (1983). The negative side effects of reward. *Journal of Applied Behavioral Analysis, 16(3)*, 283-296.

Flora, S.R. (2004). *The power of reinforcement.* Albany: State University of New York Press.

Lerman, D.C., Volkert, V.M., & Trosclair, N. (2007). Further examination of factors that influence preference for positive versus negative reinforcement. *Journal of Applied Behavioral Analysis, 40(1)*, 25-44.

Riordan M.M., Iwata B.A., Wohl M.K., Finney J.W. (1984). Behavioral treatment of food refusal and selectivity in developmentaly disabled children. *Journal of Applied Behavioral Analysis. 17(3)*, 327-341.

Related Lessons:

D-01 Use positive and negative reinforcement.

D-02 Use appropriate parameters and schedules of reinforcement.

D-21 Use differential reinforcement (e.g. DRO, DRA, DRI, DRL, DRH).

E-11 Use pairing procedures to establish new conditioned reinforcers and punishers.

I-07 Design and conduct preference assessments to identify putative reinforcers.

J-04 Select intervention strategies based on client preferences.

J-05 Select intervention strategies based on client's current repertoires.

J-06 Select intervention strategies based on supporting environments.

J-07 Select intervention strategies based on environmental and resource constraints.

J-11 Program for stimulus and response generalization.

C-02 State and plan for unwanted effects of punishment

Punishment is sometimes used to change or shape behavior and may cause unwanted side effects.

- For instance, those individuals who are being treated using punishment procedures may become aggressive (Azrin & Holz, 1966) or may have strong emotional reactions to such measures.
- An adult or child may become subject to negative modeling (such as imitating scolding or hitting behavior).
- Those treated through the use of punishment may seek out escape/avoidance of the punisher or the contingencies surrounding punishment.
- In extreme cases, the use of punishment can result in harm or injury to the child or adult.

Punishment may also have unwanted effects with regards to an individual's future learning. It may not appropriately generalize to new situations requiring further intervention. When used as the sole intervention in a treatment package, it fails to teach an individual an alternative behavior to engage in and consequently individuals may revert back to old behaviors without a replacement strategy. These behaviors may diminish temporarily only to be subject to a recovery of responding (Catania, 1998) at a later period of time.

As a result, the majority of those in the field agree that "punishment be limited to those situations in which other interventions have failed" (May, Risley, Twardosz, Friedman, Bijou, Wexler et al., 1975 as cited in Iwata et al., 1994, p. 198). Iwata et al., (1994) described that reinforcement approaches to behavior reduction were just as effective as punishment approaches and that if a functional analysis of the problem behavior was done, the need for the use of punishment procedures was greatly reduced.

During the supervision process, be diligent in choosing interventions, which are based on reinforcement and not solely on punishment. The function of a problem behavior should always be assessed before making decisions regarding an individuals program to ensure effective treatment. If a team has deemed that punishment is necessary as a part of a treatment package, it is important to state any potential unwanted effects of any procedure being utilized and to attempt to plan for these.

Consider the following when planning for punishment effects:

1. A team should always adhere to the "Fair Pair Rule" when using punishment. This states that a "practitioner should choose one or more alternatives to increase for every behavior targeted for reduction" (White & Haring, 1980, p. 423).
2. Be sure to plan for continuation of the procedure to different environments, staff and stimuli (any and all that apply).
3. Avoid modeling any behavior which you do not want the adult or child to imitate
4. The team should develop a contingency plan for managing aggression or extreme emotional responses (should they occur) and have safety measures in place to avoid accidental injury to the individual.
5. The team should develop a plan to manage any escape/avoidant behaviors that may occur
6. Be aware the effects of punishment can be difficult to predict. Staff may need to adjust the plan over time if the affects are not therapeutic or effective.

Assessment:
- Ask the supervisee to state the unwanted effects of punishment.

- Ask the supervisee to plan for unwanted effects of punishment. The supervisor should provide examples of commonly used punishment procedures within agency (such as restraint, time outs, or other punitive measures) and ask the supervisee to propose solutions to these problems.
- Ask the supervisee to select one behavior to target for increase for each behavior targeted for decrease.

Relevant Literature:

Azrin, N.H., & Holz, W.C. (1966). Punishment. In W.K. Honig (Ed), *Operant Behavior: Areas of Research and Application.* New York: Appleton-Century-Crofts.

Catania, C.A. (1998). *Learning (4th ed.)* Upper Saddle River, NJ: Prentice-Hall, Inc.

Cooper J.O, Heron T.E, Heward W.L. (2007). *Applied behavior analysis* (2nd ed.) Upper Saddle River, NJ: Pearson

Iwata, B. A., Dorsey, M. F., Slifer, K. J., Bauman, K. E. and Richman, G. S. (1994). Toward a Functional Analysis of Self-injury. *Journal of Applied Behavior Analysis*, 27: 197–209.

May, J. G., Risley, T. R., Twardosz, S., Friedman, P., Bijou, S., Wexler, D., et al. (1975). Guidelines for the use of behavioral procedures in state programs for the retarded. *NARC Monograph*, M. R. Research, 1.

White, O.R. & Haring, N.G. (1980). *Exceptional Teaching* (2nd e.d.). Columbus, O.H.: Charles E. Merrill.

Related Lessons:

C-02 State and plan for the possible unwanted effects of punishment.

D-16 Use positive and negative punishment.

D-17 Use appropriate parameters andschedules of punishment.

D-19 Use combinations of reinforcement with punishment and extinction.

E-07 Plan for behavioral contrast effects.

FK-31 Behavioral contingencies.

C-03 Use Extinction

Extinction "occurs when reinforcement of a previously reinforced behavior is discontinued; as a result the frequency of that behavior decreases in the future" (Cooper, Heron & Howard, 2007, p. 457). Extinction renders target behavior useless and is often a significant component contributing to the effectiveness of a behavioral program. However, extinction should be used with caution. Two common side effects may occur when extinction is utilized: an extinction burst, defined as "an immediate increase in the frequency of the response after the removal of the positive, negative, or automatic reinforcement" (Cooper, Heron & Howard, 2007, p. 462), and extinction-induced aggression.

Studies have compared withdrawal of reinforcement as an aversive event and responses to extinction are similar to attack responses in laboratory subjects exposed to aversive stimulation, such as heat, shocks and physical blows (Lerman et al., 1999). Extinction should not be used as a singular intervention when self-injury or aggression is severe and cannot be prevented and appropriate safe-guards cannot be put in place. Other considerations include extinction being inappropriate in settings where maladaptive behaviors are likely to be imitated by others (e.g., classroom setting) and when extinction is not feasible (e.g. if an individual engages in physical aggression for attention, response-blocking may be enough to reinforce the individual's behavior).

Research has shown that there are other behavioral strategies that can be utilized to mitigate the unwanted effects of extinction. These include using differential reinforcement of alternative behavior in conjunction with extinction procedures. In situations in which using extinction is not possible, research has shown that by manipulating reinforcement schedules and reinforcement parameters (e.g. quality, duration, immediacy of reinforcement) to favoring appropriate behavior rather than problem behavior, problem behavior has also been shown to decrease (Athens & Vollmer, 2010).

Assessment:

- Ask your supervisee to list the possible unwanted effects of extinction.
- Ask your supervisee in which situations should extinction not be utilized.
- Ask your supervisee what behavioral strategies can mitigate the unwanted effects of extinction.
- Have your supervisee determine which of his/her clients could benefit from extinction and which clients should avoid the use of extinction.

Relevant Literature:

Athen, E.S., & Vollmer, T.R., (2010). An investigation of differential reinforcement of alternative behavior without extinction. *Journal of Applied Behavioral Analysis, 43(4),* 569-589.

Cooper, J. O., Heron, T. E., & Heward, W. L. (2007). *Applied behavior analysis* (2nd ed.). Upper Saddle River, NJ: Prentice Hall.

Lerman, D.C., & Iwata, B.A.,(1995). Prevalence of the extinction burst and its attenuation during treatment. *Journal of Applied Behavioral Analysis, 28(1),* 93-94.

Lerman, D.C., Iwata, B.A., & Wallace, M.D., (1999). Side effects of extinction: Prevalence of bursting and aggression during the treatment of self-injurious behavior. *Journal of Applied Behavioral Analysis, 32 (1),* 1-8.

Related Lessons:

D-02 Use appropriate parameters and schedules of reinforcement.

D-18. Use Extinction.

D.-19 Use combinations of reinforcement with punishment and extinction.

E-01 Use interventions based on manipulation of antecedents, such as motivating operations and discriminative stimuli.

E-08 Use the matching law and recognize factors influencing choice.

D-01 Use positive and negative reinforcement

The principle of reinforcement is in operation when immediately following a behavior, a stimulus event occurs and this serves to increase the future frequency of that behavior (Cooper, Heron & Heward, 2007).

Positive Reinforcement
Positive reinforcement has occurred when a stimulus is *added* to the environment, or is increased in intensity, immediately following a behavior, and this serves to *increase* the frequency of that behavior occurring in the future (Cooper, Heron & Heward, 2007).

Example:
Mommy Singing
A mommy sings a verse from "The Wheels on the Bus" nursery rhyme to her baby. The baby giggles immediately following the nursery rhyme being sung. The mommy is more likely to sing this nursery rhyme to her baby in the future, because the baby's giggling serves as a reinforcer.

Example:
Accessing food
A rat is in a cage, which has a food dispenser lever. To access food, the rat pushes the lever and food pellets are dispensed. In the future, after a few hours of food deprivation, the rat is more likely to push the lever to access food.

Negative Reinforcement
Negative reinforcement has occurred when a stimulus is *removed*, or decreased in intensity, immediately following a behavior, and this *increases* the frequency of that behavior in the future (Cooper, Heron & Heward, 2007).

Example:
Removal of loud music
A child asks her friend to turn down the music, as it is too loud for her. The music is immediately turned down. The child is more likely to ask for music to be turned down in the future when it is too loud.

Example:
Raining
It is raining so you put up your umbrella and immediately reduce the amount that you are getting wet. You are more likely to put up your umbrella in the future when it is raining to avoid getting wet.

Assessment:
- Ask your Supervisees to define both positive and negative reinforcement and give an example of each type.
- Ask your Supervisee to demonstrate an example of positive and negative reinforcement through role-playing.
- Ask your Supervisee to identify which type of reinforcement is operating in these examples:
  - A Supervisee sees her BCBA Supervisor coming in to the classroom to run teaching evaluations. The Supervisee takes her client for a reinforcer break in another room and thereby avoids having a teaching evaluation completed on her. The next day, when her Supervisor comes back in to do more evaluations, she takes her client outside to play. (Answer = the Supervisee's behavior of leaving the classroom is negatively reinforced by avoiding having teaching evaluations completed on her).
  - A client regularly has challenging behavior when working with his teacher at the table, as he does not enjoy the work. However, on this occasion he has worked really well so has immediately been given a 3-minute break to run around in the playground. He continues to work well at the table after his break. (Answer = the client's hard work at the table

may be being negatively reinforced. This is because his work behavior is being reinforced with removal from the table environment).

o A Father calls his son down to the dishes. His son comes down and does the dishes. His Father says "Thanks, Son" and gives him a dollar to get some candy. The next day when the son is asked to do the dishes again, he quickly comes down to do them. (Answer = the son's compliant behavior was probably positively reinforced with praise and/or money).

Relevant Literature:

Hall, R. V., Lund, D. & Jackson, D. (1968). Effects of teacher attention on study behavior. *Journal of Applied Behavior Analysis, 1*, 1-12.

Hart, B. M., Reynolds, N. J., Baer, D. M., Brawley, E. R. & Harris, F. R. (1968). Effect of contingent and non-contingent social reinforcement on the cooperative play of a preschool child. *Journal of Applied Behavior Analysis, 1*, 73-76.

Michael, J. (1975). Positive and negative reinforcement, a distinction that is no longer necessary; or a better way to talk about bad things. *Behaviorism, 3* (1), 33-44.

Osborne, J. G. (1969). Free-time as a reinforcer in the management of classroom behavior. *Journal of Applied Behavior Analysis, 2*, 113-118.

Skinner, B. F. *The behavior of organisms.* New York: D. Appleton-Century, 1938.

Thomas, D. R., Becker, W. C., & Armstrong, M. (1968). Production and elimination of disruptive classroom behavior by systematically varying teacher's behavior. *Journal of Applied Behavior Analysis, 1*, 35-45.

Related Lessons:

C-01: State and plan for the possible unwanted side effects of reinforcement

D-02: Use appropriate parameters and schedules of reinforcement

D-16: Use positive and negative punishment

D-17: Use appropriate parameters and schedules of reinforcement

D-19: Use combinations of reinforcement with punishment and extinction

D-20: Use response-independent (time-based) schedules of reinforcement (i.e., non-contingent reinforcement)

D-21: Use differential reinforcement (e.g., DRO, DRA, DRI, DRL, DRH)

E-10: Use the Premack principle

E-11: Use pairing procedures to establish new conditioned reinforcers and punishers

F-02: Use token economies and other conditioned reinforcement systems

FK-14: Respondent conditioning (CS-CR)

FK-15: Operant conditioning

FK-17: Unconditioned reinforcement

FK-18: Conditioned reinforcement

FK-19: Unconditioned punishment

FK-20: Conditioned punishment

FK-21: Schedules of reinforcement and punishment

FK-23: Automatic reinforcement and punishment

D-02 Use appropriate parameters and schedules of reinforcement

<u>Definition:</u>
Schedule of reinforcement - "A rule specifying the environmental arrangements and response requirements for reinforcement; a description of a contingency of reinforcement" (Cooper, Heron & Heward, 2007, p. 703).

There are two basic schedules of reinforcement: continuous (CRF) and intermittent (INT). CRF is useful when teaching a new response. With CRF, reinforcement is provided each time the target behavior occurs. As a result, the desired behavior is strengthened. INT is used for thinning schedules of reinforcement and transitioning to naturally occurring reinforcement contingencies.

INT may be defined as having a fixed ratio schedule, variable ratio schedule, fixed interval schedule, or variable interval schedule.

When learning basic schedules of reinforcement, it is not only important to understand how the schedules are defined, but also understand the effects of each type of INT. Ferster and Skinner (1957) and Cooper et al. (2007) thoroughly discuss these concepts and it is strongly encouraged that supervisors and supervisees read this material. The table below serves as a reference and briefly illustrates the key points of basic INT.

<u>Assessment:</u>
* Ask supervisee to define basic schedules of reinforcement.
* Ask supervisee to provide examples of basic schedules of reinforcement.
* Supervisor can graph response rates of INT schedules and ask supervisee to analyze graphs and identify which INT schedule is in place.

	Fixed Ratio (FR)	Variable Ratio (VR)	Fixed Interval (FI)	Variable Interval (VI)
Definition	A fixed number of target responses must be completed to produce a reinforcer.	A variable number of target responses must be completed to produce a reinforcer.	Reinforcement is provided for the first target response following a fixed duration of time.	Reinforcement is provided for the first target response following the end of variable durations of time.
Example	FR 7 means that every seventh target response produces a reinforcer.	VR 15 means that on average, every fifteenth target response produces a reinforcer.	FI 5 means that first target response following the end of a five minute period produces a reinforcer.	VI 12 means that the first target response following the end of an average duration of 12 minutes produces a reinforcer.
Schedule Effects	Produces a typical pattern of responding and high rates of responses. Post reinforcement pause occurs.	Produces a consistent, steady response rate, usually without a post reinforcement pause.	Produces a post reinforcement pause during the initial part of the interval. Rate of responding accelerates toward the end. Slow to moderate response rates observed.	Produces a constant, stable, yet low to moderate response rate.

Relevant Literature:

Cooper, J. O., Heron, T. E., & Heward, W. L. (2007). Schedules of reinforcement. *Applied Behavior Analysis* (pp. 304-323). Upper Saddle River, NJ: Pearson Prentice Hall.

Ferster, C. B., & Skinner, B. F. (1957). *Schedules of reinforcement*. New York, NY: Appleton-Century-Crofts

Related Lessons:

D-19 Use combinations of reinforcement with punishment and extinction

D-20 Use response-independent (time-based) schedules of reinforcement (i.e., non-contingent reinforcement)

D-21 Use differential reinforcement (e.g., DRO, DRA, DRI, DRL, DRH)

FK-21 Schedules of reinforcement and punishment

FK-40 Matching law

FK-41 Contingency maintained behavior

D-03 Use prompts and prompt fading

Definitions:

Prompts – "…antecedent stimuli that increase the probability of a desired response" (Piazza, & Roane, 2014, p. 256)

Prompt fading – "…transfer stimulus control from therapist delivered prompts to stimuli in the natural environment that should evoke appropriate responses" (Walker, 2008 as cited in Fisher, Piazza, & Roane, 2014, p. 412).

Prompts are used when teaching skills. Prompts can be used when teaching in task analysis, discrete trial, incidental teaching, etc. Prompt fading is important as the learner begins to show competence with the skill being taught. Fading allows the learner to become independent and meet naturalistic reinforcers for his/her behavior.

Prompts are generally divided into two categories: stimulus prompts and response prompts.

Stimulus prompts – "…those in which some property of the criterion stimulus is altered, or other stimuli are added to or removed from the criterion stimulus" (Etzel & LeBlanc, 1979 cited in Fisher, Piazza, & Roane, 2014, p. 256)

Examples:
Stimulus shaping
Stimulus fading

Response prompts – "…addition of some behavior on the part of an instructor to evoke the desired learner behavior" (Fisher, Piazza, & Roane, 2014, p. 256).

Examples:
Most-to-least prompting
Least-to-most prompting
Time delay prompts

Assessment:
- Ask your supervisee to role-play several types of prompt strategies.
- Ask your supervisee to role-play several types of prompt fading procedures.
- Ask your supervisee to describe the transfer of stimulus control when a prompt is faded out e.g., what stimulus is controlling behavior while prompting vs what stimulus is controlling behavior after the prompt has been faded out.

Relevant Literature:
Etzel, B. C., & LeBlanc, J. M. (1979). The simplest treatment alternative: The law of parsimony applied to choosing appropriate instructional control and errorless-learning procedures for the difficult-to-teach child. *Journal of Autism and Developmental Disorders, 9*(4), 361-382.

Fisher, W. W., Piazza, C. C., & Roane, H. S. (2014). *Handbook of applied behavior analysis.* New York: Guilford Press.

Walker, G. (2008). Constant and progressive time delay procedures for teaching children with autism: A literature review. *Journal of Autism and Developmental Disorders, 38*(2), 261-275.

Related Lessons:
D-04 Use modeling and imitation training.
D-05 Use shaping.
D-06 Use chaining.
D-07 Conduct task analyses.
D-08 Use discrete-trial and free-operant arrangements.
E-01 Use interventions based on manipulation of antecedents, such as motivating operations and discriminative stimuli.
E-02 Use discrimination training procedures.
E-13 Use matching-to-sample procedures.
FK-24 stimulus control

D-04 Modeling and Imitation training

Definitions:

Imitation - "A behavior controlled by any physical movement that serves as a novel model excluding vocal-verbal behavior, has formal similarity with the model, and immediately follows the occurrence of the model (e.g. within seconds of the model presentation). An imitative behavior is a new behavior emitted following a novel antecedent event (i.e., the model)" (Cooper, Heron, & Heward, 2007, p. 697).

Model - "An antecedent stimulus that evokes the imitative behavior" (Cooper, Heron, & Heward, 2007, p. 413)

- Imitation training is a method often used to teach learners new imitation skills. During imitation training the learner learns to imitate the behavior of the person providing the model (Cooper, Heron, & Heward, 2007). Reinforcement is typically delivered for imitation of the model. Prompt fading is often used.

Example: Modeling a new behavior

- Example: A therapist sits across from his student Zeke in the pre-school classroom. The therapist prompts the student to "do this," and claps her hands. Zeke responds within two seconds of the therapist's prompt and claps. The therapist responds by adding a token to Zeke's token board.
- Example: During job training, the job coach, Flora, demonstrates to her new employee, Fauna, how to turn the copy machine off at the end of the workday. Fauna then imme-

diately flicks the switch, demonstrating that she understands the expectation. Flora praises Fauna for paying attention.

- Non-example: A therapist sits across from his student Zeke in the pre-school classroom. The therapist prompts the student to "do this," and claps her hands. Zeke does not imitate the model and reinforcement is not delivered. Later during the day Zeke excitedly claps his hands when his favorite song is playing on the t.v.

Assessment:

- Ask your Supervisee to define both "imitation" and "model."
- Ask your Supervisee to state the purpose of imitation training.
- Ask your supervisee to give several examples of some new skills that one might want to select for imitation training (other than the ones listed above).

Relevant Literature:

Baer, D. M., Peterson, R. F. and Sherman, J. A. (1967), The development of imitation by reinforcing behavioral similarity to a model. *Journal of the Experimental Analysis Behavior*, 10: 405–416.

Cooper J.O, Heron T.E, Heward W.L. (2007). *Applied behavior analysis* (2nd ed.) Upper Saddle River, NJ: Pearson.

Striefel, S., Bryan, K. S. and Aikins, D. A. (1974), Transfer of stimulus control from motor to verbal stimuli. *Journal of Applied Behavior Analysis*, 7: 123–135.

Related Lessons:
D-04 Use modeling and imitation training.

D-05 Use Shaping

Definition:
Shaping – "Using differential reinforcement to produce a series of gradually changing response classes; each response class is a successive approximation toward a terminal behavior. Members of an existent response class are selected for differential reinforcement because they more closely resemble the terminal behavior" (Cooper, Heron, & Heward, 2007, p. 704).

•

Examples:
• Bernice's infant is babbling. She has been trying to get him to say, "mama." While playing with him she happens to catch him making the "mmm" sound. She smiles and praises him for making the vocalization. Over the next several days she continues to applaud when he makes this sound. After a few weeks she observes the baby making a "ma" noise. She praises him more enthusiastically giving him tickles. Although she still continues to commend him for making the "mmm" sound, the social reinforcement delivered for saying "ma" is differentially delivered. Some time later she catches him babbling "ma ma ma." She praises him, saying, "You said 'mama'," giving him big hugs and kisses. Verbal praise and affection is almost exclusively delivered for saying "ma ma ma" now. Eventually the baby who continually hears him mother say "mama" (and not "ma ma ma") echoes his mother when she gives the verbal model. She demonstrates the highest level of excitement for this vocalization and the baby continues to emit this response.

• Petunia is pet sitting for a friend. On her way out the door the cat, Mr. Boots, escapes outside. Petunia tries to call the feline back indoors, but every time she gets near him, Mr. Boots runs away. Petunia has an idea. She places a bowl of cat food outside. Mr. Boots goes to the bowl but only when he thinks the coast is clear. Over the next few days, she successively moves the bowl of food closer to the front door. On the fourth day, Petunia puts the bowl just inside of the doorway. Mr. Boots takes the bait. While he gobbles down the food, Petunia, who had been hiding nearby shuts the door and captures the beloved cat.

Non-example:
Bernice's baby has gotten bigger. While looking at a picture book she points out a picture of a farm animal. She tells him that this is a cow and that the cow says, "moo." The baby immediately echoes the word "moo" and Bernice praises him. He continues to say "moo" when seeing pictures of cows in other books as well.

Assessment:
• Ask your Supervisee to identify the steps taken to shape the desired behavior of saying "mama" above.
• Ask the supervisee to identify how differential reinforcement is used to shape desired behavior.
• Ask your supervisee to create another example and non-example of his/her own.

Relevant Literature:
Cooper J.O, Heron T.E, Heward W.L. (2007). *Applied behavior analysis* (2nd ed.) Upper Saddle River, NJ: Pearson.
Lovaas O.I. The autistic child: Language development through behavior modification. New York: Irvington; 1977.
Newman, B., Reinecke, D., & Ramos, M. (2009). Is a Reasonable Attempt Reasonable? Shaping Versus Reinforcing Verbal Attempts of Preschoolers with Autism. *The Analysis of Verbal Behavior*, 25(1), 67–72.
Pryor, K. (1999). Don't Shoot The Dog [rev. ed.]. New York: Bantam.
Ricciardi, J. N., Luiselli, J. K., & Camare, M. (2006). Shaping approach responses as intervention for specific phobia in a child with autism. Journal of Applied Behavior Analysis, 39(4), 445-448.
Skinner, B. F. (1979). *The shaping of a behaviorist: Part two of an autobiography.* New York: New York University Press.

Related Lessons:
D-01 Use positive and negative reinforcement
D-05 Use Shaping
D-21 Use differential reinforcement (e.g., DRO, DRA, DRI, DRL, DRH)
FK -41 Contingency-shaped behavior

D-06 Use Chaining

Definition:

Behavior chain - "A sequence of responses in which each response produces a stimulus change that functions as conditioned reinforcement for that response and as a discriminative stimulus for the next response in the chain; reinforcement for the last response in a chain maintains the reinforcing effectiveness of the stimulus changes produced by all previous responses in the chain" (Cooper, Heron, & Heward, 2007, p. 691).

Often behavior chains are taught using a task analysis. This involves breaking down steps of a sequence or routine and sequentially teaching them one at a time. Reinforcement is delivered following the first step, then following each succeeding step if the previous steps were completed in correct order.

According to Cooper, et al., "a behavior chain has the following three important characteristics: (a) A behavior chain involves the performance of a specific series of discrete responses; (b) the performance of each behavior in the sequence changes the environment in such a way that it produces conditioned reinforcement for the preceding responses and serves as an S^D for the next response; and (c) the responses within the chain must be performed in a specific sequence, usually in close temporal succession" (2007, p. 436).

"In forward chaining, behaviors are linked together beginning with the first behavior in the sequence. In backward chaining, behaviors are linked together beginning with the last behavior in the sequence" (Cooper ct al., 2007, p. 436).

Example:
- Brad is going to teach shoe tying to one of his students. He decides to use a forward chain and writes down all the smaller steps involved in tying ones shoes. He teaches the steps at the beginning, like crossing the laces.

After the student has completed this step Brad delivers reinforcement. Then moves down the steps in sequential order delivering reinforcement at the completion of the last step that was taught.

Non-example:

Joe decides to use video modeling to help his student learn to tie their shoes. He has them watch the video daily and then model what they learned from that video in an attempt to have them learn how to tie their shoes.

Assessment:
- Have supervisee choose a target skill and create a task analysis for that skill. Then have him/her decide whether to teach this skill using forward or backward chaining and explain their rationale.
- Have supervisee identify and describe the benefits and limitations of using both forward and backward chains. Have him/her list several behaviors/skills that they would use for each type of chaining procedure and why they chose that method.
- Have supervisee create a task analysis procedure for a skill they can demonstrate in the group supervision setting. Have him/her model the training procedure. Finally, have him/her role play being a teacher and the supervisor being the student as they demonstrate the steps of their task analysis chain.

Relevant Literature:

Cooper, J.O., Heron, T.E. & Heward W.L. (2007). *Applied Behavior Analysis* (2nd Ed.), Upper Saddle River, NJ. Pearson Prentice Hall. 435-453, 589.

Catania, A.C. (1998). *Learning* (4th Ed.), Upper Saddle River, NJ. Prentice-Hall, Inc. 44, 82, 124, 380.

Libby, M.E., Weiss, J.S., Bancroft, S., & Ahearn, W.A. (2008).A comparison of most-to-least and least-to-most prompting on the acquisition of solitary play skills. *Behavior Analytic Practices*, 1, 1, 37-43.

Kayser J. E, Billingsley F. F, & Neel R. S. (1986). A comparison of in-context and traditional instructional approaches: Total task, single trial versus backward chaining, multiple trials. *Journal of the Association for the Severely Handicapped.* 11, 28–38.

Spooner F. (1984). Comparisons of backward chaining and total task presentation in training severely handicapped persons. *Education and Training of the Mentally Retarded.* 19, 15–22.

Reynolds, G.S. (1975). *A primer of operant conditioning* (Rev. Ed.) Glenview, IL.:. Scott, Foresman.

McWilliams, R., Nietupski, J., & Hamre-Nietupski, S. (1990). Teaching complex activities to students with moderate handicaps through the forward chaining of shorter total cycle response sequences. *Education and Training in Mental Retardation*, 25, 3, 292-298.

Test, D.W., Spooner, F., Keul, P.K., & Grossi, T. (1990). Teaching adolescents with severe disability to use the public telephone. *Behavior Modification*, 14, 157-171.

Snell, M.E. & Brown, F. (2006). *Instruction of students with severe disabilities* (6th ed.) Upper Saddle River, NJ. Prentice Hall.

Related Lessons:

A-07: Measure trials to criterion.
D-03: Use prompts and prompt fading.
D-04: Use modeling and imitation training.
D-05: Use shaping.
E-01: Use interventions based on manipulation of antecedents, such as motivating operations and discriminative stimuli.
E-02: Use discrimination training procedures.
I-01: Define behavior in observable and measurable terms.
J-03: Select intervention strategies based on task analysis.
FK-10: Behavior, response, response class.

D-07 Conduct Task Analyses

Definition:

Task analysis - "The process of breaking a complex skill into smaller, teachable units, or the product of which is a series of sequentially ordered steps or tasks" (Cooper, Heron, & Heward, 2007, p. 706).

A task analysis can be taught using any of the following chaining procedures:

- Forward chaining - behaviors are taught in sequential order; reinforcement would occur once criteria for first behavior in the task analysis is achieved
- Backward chaining – all steps in the task analysis are done by trainer except for the final behavior; reinforcement would occur once criteria for last behavior in chain is achieved. Subsequent teaching trials would involve providing reinforcement after the next-to-last behavior is achieved, etc.
- Backward chaining with leaps- similar to backwards chaining, however, some steps are in the task analysis are not taught, and perhaps just probed in order to decrease the total amount of time spent teaching a skill. If there are some behaviors in the task analysis are mastered, a trainer could "leap" ahead a few steps to allow for more independence and maintenance of previously acquired skills.
- Total task presentation – prompting would occur at any point in the task analysis when a person is unable to complete any part of steps independently.

Examples:

- Accessing an iPhone 6
  1. Press home key (circle)
  2. Slide finger across bottom of screen, from left to right, over text that reads "slide to unlock"
  3. Enter passcode

- Washing a cup
  1. Turn on tap
  2. Pick up sponge and put dish soap on sponge
  3. Put down dish soap
  4. Pick up dirty cup, scrub outside rim, sides, and base of cup with sponge
  5. Scrub inside, base, and rim of cup with sponge
  6. Put sponge down
  7. Rinse cup with warm water
  8. Place cup in drainboard
  9. Rinse excess soap out of sponge
  10. Turn off tap
  11. Put sponge in holder/in sink

Assessment

- Ask your Supervisee to create a task analysis for a technology related task (e.g. faxing, scanning, etc.).
- Ask your Supervisee to create a task analysis for eating with a utensil.
- Have Supervisee create a task analysis on a skill that can be observed on the job. Once complete, have Supervisee observe an individual completing the task. Supervisee should make note of any differences in sequences of behavior or steps.
- Have Supervisee follow a task analysis for a task they are not familiar with.

Relevant Literature:

Cooper, J. O., Heron, T. E., & Heward, W. L. (2007). Applied behavior analysis.

Resnick, L. B., Wang, M. C., & Kaplan, J. (1973). Task analysis in curriculum design: a hierarchically sequenced introductory mathematics curriculum. *Journal of Applied Behavior Analysis*, 6(4), 679-709.

Bancroft, S. L., Weiss, J. S., Libby, M. E., & Ahearn, W. H. (2011). A comparison of procedural variations in teaching behavior chains: Manual guidance, trainer completion, and no completion of untrained steps. *Journal of applied behavior analysis*, *44*(3), 559-569.

Jerome, J., Frantino, E. P., & Sturmey, P. (2007). The effects of errorless learning and backward chaining on the acquisition of internet skills in adults with developmental disabilities. *Journal of applied behavior analysis*, *40*(1), 185-189.

Slocum, S. K., & Tiger, J. H. (2011). An assessment of the efficiency of and child preference for forward and backward chaining. *Journal of applied behavior analysis*, *44*(4), 793-805.

Related Lessons:
D-03 Use prompts and prompt fading
D-05 Use shaping
D-06 Use chaining

D-08 Use discrete-trials and free-operant arrangements

<u>Definitions:</u>
Free operant - " behaviors that have discrete beginning and ending points, require minimal displacement of the organism in time and space, can be emitted at nearly any time, do not require much time for completion, and can be emitted over a wide range of response rates." (Cooper, Heron, & Heward, 2007, p. 696)

Rate of responding is typically used to measure behavior considered to be free operant. Rate of responding is typically used because it uses count per unit of time. (i.e., a person can type 50 words per minute). However, rate of responding is not typically used to measure behavior that occurs within discrete trials. These responses can occur only within limited or restricted situations.

Discrete trial responses include responses to flash cards, answering teacher's questions, and choosing an answer from an array.

Discrete trial- "Any operant whose response rate is controlled by a given opportunity to emit the response. Each discrete response occurs when an opportunity to respond exists" (Cooper et al., 2007, p. 694).

<u>Assessment:</u>
- Have supervisee create a simple discrete trial program to teach a skill. Have him/her run conduct a trial using this program and identify the parts of a discrete trial.
- Have supervisee identify the differences between a discrete trial and a free operant trial. Have him/her list pros and cons for each method.
- Have supervisee identify what type of measurement procedures and data you would take for free operant trials as well as discrete trials. Have him/her describe why they would use that measurement system for each.

<u>Relevant Literature:</u>
Cooper, J.O., Heron, T.E. & Heward W.L. (2007). *Applied Behavior Analysis* (2nd Ed.), Upper Saddle River, NJ. Pearson Prentice Hall. 77-78, chapters 11-23, 25-28.
Otto, J. (2003). Discrete trial procedures vs. free-operant procedures. Retrieved from http://old.dickmalott.com/students/undergradprogram/psy3600/discrete_vs_free.html.
Malott, R.W., & Trojan, E.A. (2003). *Principles of Behavior.* (5th Ed.), Upper Saddle River, NJ. Pearson Prentice Hall. Chapter 17.
Mazur, J.E. (2002). *Learning and Behavior (5th Ed.).* Upper Saddle River, NJ. Pearson Prentice Hall.

<u>Related Lessons:</u>
A-01: Measure frequency (i.e., count).
A-02: Measure rate (i.e., count per unit time).
A-07: Measure trials to criterion.
D-03: Use prompts and prompt fading.
E-01: Use interventions based on manipulation of antecedents, such as motivating operations and discriminative stimuli.
E-12: Use errorless learning procedures.
H-01: Select a measurement system to obtain representative data given the dimensions of the behavior and the logistics of observing and recording.
FK-10: Behavior, response, response class.
FK-11: Environment, stimulus, stimulus class
FK-47: Identify the measurable dimensions of behavior (e.g., rate, duration, latency, inter-response time).

D-09 Use the verbal operants as a basis for language assessment

In the field of applied behavior analysis extensive research has been done on the development of verbal behavior.

"Verbal behavior involves social interactions between speakers and listeners, whereby speakers gain access to reinforcement and control their environment through the behavior of listeners" (Sundberg as cited in Cooper, Heron, & Heward, 2007, p. 529). Verbal operants are the basic units of this exchange.

In 1957 B.F. Skinner identified six elementary verbal operants in his book on *Verbal Behavior*. These included mands, tacts, intraverbals, echoics, textuals, and transcription. "Skinner's analysis suggests that a complete verbal repertoire is composed of each of the different elementary operants, and separate speaker and listener repertoires" (Sundberg as cited in Cooper, et al., 2007, p. 541).

Since Skinner described these operants, those in the field have applied these concepts to both language assessment and training. In order to evaluate whether or not specific language training is necessary, a variety of standardized tools have been used to test an individual's receptive and expressive language abilities. These include but are not limited to: the Peabody Picture Vocabulary Test III (Dunn & Dunn, 1997), the Comprehensive Receptive and Expressive Vocabulary Test (Hammill & Newcomer, 1997), the Assessment of Basic Language and Learning Skills (ABLLS) (Partington & Sundberg, 1998), the Verbal Behavior Milestones Assessment and Placement Program (VB-MAPP) and the CELF-4 Semel, Wiig, & Secord, 2003).

Not all of these tests will identify deficits in one or more of the verbal operants Some children who may be proficient in tacting (such as labeling things in their environment such as letters and numbers) may fail to make appropriate mands for desired items (Cooper, et al., 2007). In this case it is important for behavior analysts to use a combination of approaches or less standardized methods to assess these

needs. It may be helpful to observe the individual in their natural environment and take data on their verbal interactions. It will be important to ask questions such as:

- What is the frequency of and complexity of mands?
- What it the frequency and complexity of tacting behavior?
- Will the child or individual demonstrate echoic behavior when prompted?
- Does the child or individual engage in intraverbal behavior with known caregivers?
- Can or will the child or individual read words that are written down for him?
- Can or will the child or individual write down words that are said to him?

Assessment:

- Ask the supervisee to name the basic unit of language
- Ask the supervisee to name all 6 of the elementary verbal operants
- Ask the supervisee to name some of the standardized tests often used to assess language
- Ask the supervisee to explain why these standardized tests may not provide adequate information
- Ask the supervisee to describe how one might assess an individual's use of verbal operants if testing fails to yield enough information.

Relevant Literature:
Cooper J.O, Heron T.E., Heward W.L. (2007). *Applied behavior analysis* (2nd ed.) Upper Saddle River, NJ: Pearson
Hammill, D., & Newcomer, P.L. (1997). *Test of language development-3*. Austin, TX: Pro-Ed.

Partington, J. W., & Sundberg, M. L. (1998). *Assessment of basic language and learning skills. (The ABLLS): An assessment for language delayed students.* Pleasant Hill, CA: Behavior Analysts, Inc.

Semel, E, Wiig, E. H. & Second, W A. (2003) *Clinical evaluation of language fundamentals, fourth edition (CELF-4).* Toronto, Canada: The Psychological Corporation/A Harcourt Assessment Company.

Skinner, B.F. (1957). *Verbal Behaior.* New York: Appleton-Century.

Sundberg, M. L. (2008) *Verbal behavior milestones assessment and placement program: The VB-MAPP.* Concord, CA: AVB Press.

Sundberg, M.L. & Partington, J.W. (1998). *Teaching language to children with autism or other developmental disabilities.* Pleasant Hill, CA: Behavior Analysts, Inc.

Related Lessons:

D-10 Use echoic training.

D-11 Use mand training.

D-12 Use tact training.

D-13 Use intraverbal training.

D-14 Use listener training.

FK-43 Echoics

FK-44 Mands

FK-45 Tacts

FK-46 Intraverbals

D-10 Use Echoic Training

Echoics are units of verbal behavior that are, "evoked by a verbal discriminative stimulus that has point-to point correspondence and formal similarity with the response" (Cooper, Heron, & Heward, 2014, p. 694).

Repeating words, phrases, or other auditory verbal units is common for all speakers in day-to-day speech (Sundberg, 2008).

Echoic training, sometimes referred to as vocal imitation training, is a procedure in which a caregiver or teacher emits a sound and a listener echoes or repeats what has been said (Skinner, 1957). Reinforcement (either social, tangible or other) is often delivered after the correct utterance is given.

Echoic training can be used to teach a variety of skills such as:
- Mands-such as when you give a child a full verbal model of the appropriate way to ask for another cup of milk "I want milk" and he repeats this phrase.
- Tacts- such as telling a classroom full of Spanish students that the word for dog is "perro" and asking them to repeat this word back to you.
- Intraverbal behavior- such as an elementary school teaching modeling the fill in of the word "star" after saying "Twinkle, twinkle little _____" and pausing (Skinner, 1957).

When using echoic training, the trainer should:
1. Deliver the verbal discriminative stimulus (the word, sound or phrase you intend them to repeat).
2. Provide positive reinforcement for responses that have point-to-point similarity to the target response.

Assessment:
- Ask the supervisee to state what echoic training can be used to teach.
- Ask the supervisee to give examples of echoic training.
- Ask the supervisee to discuss how echoic training should be delivered.

Relevant Literature:
Drash, P. W., High, R. L., & Tudor, R. M. (1999). Using mand training to establish an echoic repertoire in young children with autism. *The Analysis of Verbal Behavior*, 16, 29–44.

Cooper J.O, Heron T.E, Heward W.L. (2014). *Applied behavior analysis*. Upper Saddle River, NJ: Pearson.

Kodak, T., & Clements, A. (2009). Acquisition of Mands and Tacts with Concurrent Echoic Training. *Journal of Applied Behavior Analysis*, 42(4), 839–843.

Mirenda, P. (2008). A Comparison of Stimulus-Stimulus Pairing, Standard Echoic Training, and Control Procedures on the Vocal Behavior of Children with Autism. *The Analysis of Verbal Behavior*, 24(1), 123–133.

Sundberg, M. L. (2008). *Verbal Behavior Milestones Assessment and Placement Program*. Concorde, CA: AVB Press

Skinner, B.F. (1957). *Verbal Behavior*. New York: Appleton-Century

Related Lessons:
D-01 Use positive and negative reinforcement.
D-04 Use modeling and imitation training.
FK-43 Echoics

D-11 Use Mand Training

Mands are important in the development of language in children. The development of a mands allows an individual to communicate their wants and needs, including basic needs such as food and water, to those around them. When an early learner fails to develop a mand repertoire, they may not be able to effectively communicate with others and may not be able to access these reinforcers. This can lead to frustration, learned helplessness, or a variety of other maladaptive behaviors such aggression, self-injurious behavior social withdrawal or tantrums (Cooper, Heron, & Heward, 2007).

When mands fail to develop typically, it is crucial begin language training. Cooper, Heron and Heward (2007) suggest teaching mands before all other types of verbal behavior as manding allows an individual to gain access to their wants and needs. During early training a variety of mands should be taught so that the child learns to differentiate their response based on their current needs and MO. Instructors should focus on teaching bids for edibles and tangibles before making other requests. Sundberg & Partington (1998) suggest that teachers should use a combination of "prompting, fading and differential reinforcement to transfer control from stimulus variables to motivative variables" (as cited in Cooper, Heron, & Heward, 2007, p. 541). It is important that both the echoic prompt and the non-verbal stimulus be faded out for mand training to be effective.

When using mand training, the trainer should:
1. Establish a likely MO (motivating operation). This may be done formally through preference assessment procedures or more informally through observations or caregiver report. It is important that a child be motivated to make a request for mand training to be effective. *Note: It may be helpful to ensure that a reinforcer has been withheld prior to training to ensure that it is potent. For instance a child who has just recently eaten is not as likely to be motivated to request food.*
2. Enrich the environment with potential reinforcers (things that the child generally seems to prefer such as foods and toys).
3. Wait for the child to initiate or show interest in the non-verbal stimulus (the child reaches for an item, emits some sort of vocalization, points to it, etc.).
4. Use an echoic prompt to label the non-verbal stimulus. Successively reinforce closer and closer approximations to the target verbal response and follow with specific reinforcement (the requested item).
5. Once the client is able to imitate the verbal model in the presence of the stimulus, gradually fade out the echoic prompt to establish the response "under the multiple control of the MO and the nonverbal stimulus" Sundberg, as cited in Cooper, Heron, & Heward, 2007, pp. 541-542).
6. Finally the presentation of the non-verbal stimulus should also be faded out so that the response is only under the control of the MO. This helps to ensure that the individual can make the request regardless of whether or not the item is physically present within the environment.
7. Gradually increase the verbal requirement over time so that the child is making more complex and specific requests ("I want the chocolate cookie.").

Assessment:
- Ask the supervisee to state what mand training can be used to teach.
- Ask the supervisee to give examples of mand training.
- Ask the supervisee to state why it is important to fade the non-verbal stimulus and the echoic prompt.

Relevant Literature:

Cooper J.O, Heron T.E, Heward W.L. (2007). *Applied behavior analysis* (2nd ed.) Upper Saddle River, NJ: Pearson

Drash, P. W., High, R. L., & Tudor, R. M. (1999). Using mand training to establish an echoic repertoire in young children with autism. *The Analysis of Verbal Behavior, 16*, 29–44.

Skinner, B.F. (1957). *Verbal Behavior*. New York: Appleton-Century.

Sundberg, M. L., Loeb, M., Hail, L., & Eigenheer, P. (2002). Contriving establishing operations to teach mands for information. The Analysis of Verbal Behavior, 18, 14-28

Sundberg, M.L., & Partington, J.W. (1998). *Teaching language to children with autism or other developmental disabilities.* Pleasant Hill, CA: Behavior Analysts, Inc.

Related Lessons:
FK-44 Mands

D-12 Use Tact Training

Practitioners may use a variety of techniques to teach language when working with clients. Tact training is one such technique in which a consumer may be taught to label "objects, actions, properties of objects and actions, prepositional relations, abstractions, private events, and so on" (Sundberg as cited in Cooper, Howard, & Heron, 2007, p. 544). "The goal of teaching is to bring a verbal response under nonverbal stimulus control" (Sundberg as cited in Cooper, Howard, & Heron, 2007, p.544).

Initially, a practitioner pairs a nonverbal stimulus (such as snow falling outside of one's window) with an echoic model "snow." The imitation of this verbal model is differentially reinforced. Over time this echoic is faded out so that only the presence of the nonverbal stimulus (the snow) sets the occasion for the consumer to label "snow" in the absence of a verbal model. A time delay procedure, in which the practitioner gradually delays the presentation of the echoic model after the nonverbal stimulus appears, may be helpful in fading out the verbal model.

When using tact training, the trainer should:

1. Ensure that the listener is attending. Make sure that they are looking in your direction, are making eye contact and that the environment isn't too noisy or distracting.
2. Pair the presentation of nonverbal stimulus that you would like to train with an echoic model.
3. Pause to allow the listener to process the information and wait for a response.
4. Provide differential reinforcement for responses that are closer and closer approximations to the verbal model. *Note: It may be difficult to differentially reinforce the tacting of events that cannot be shared by both instructor and student, such as private events like pain, as the instructor may not be able to adequately*

able to label them (Cooper, Howard, & Heron, 2007). *For this reason it is recommended that initial tact training be done with objects or actions that can be directly observed.*

5. Once the client is able to imitate the verbal model in the presence of the stimulus, gradually fade out the verbal model so that only the stimulus itself sets the occasion for the response.

Assessment:
- Ask the supervisee to state what tact training can be used to teach.
- Ask the supervisee to give examples of tact training.
- Ask the supervisee to discuss how tact training should be delivered.
- Ask the supervisee to state how the verbal model can be successfully faded out.

Relevant Literature:
Cooper J.O, Heron T.E, Heward W.L. (2007). *Applied behavior analysis* (2nd ed.) Upper Saddle River, NJ: Pearson
Skinner, B.F. (1957). *Verbal Behavior.* New York: Appleton-Century.
Sundberg, M. L., & Michael, J. (2001). The value of Skinner's analysis of verbal behavior for teaching children with autism. *Behavior Modification*, 25, 698-724.
Sundberg, M.L.,& Partington, J.W. (1998). *Teaching language to children with autism or other developmental disabilities.* Pleasant Hill, CA: Behavior Analysts, Inc.

Related Lessons:
D-12 Use Tact Training
FK-45 Tacts

D-13 Use Intraverbal Training

"Many children with autism, developmental disabilities, or other language delays suffer from defective or nonexistent intraverbal repertoires, even though some can emit hundreds of mands, tacts, and receptive responses" (Sundberg, as cited in Cooper, Heron, & Heward, 2007, p. 545).

Although typically developing children generally acquire this type of language on their own, some learners may not acquire this type of language without specific training in the skill. In such cases, intraverbal training may be recommended. Prior to starting intraverbal training, the learner must have a acquired a variety of pre-requisite skills such as being able to mand, tact, engage in echoic behavior or imitation, to receptively identify stimuli, and to do match to sample tasks (Sundberg & Partington, 1998). The goal is not to teach new language, but to bring words or phrases that are currently under nonverbal stimulus control entirely under verbal stimulus control (Cooper, Heron, & Heward, 2007). For instance, a child who has previously learned to tact or echo the word "cow" when they see a picture of a cow, may learn to then say "cow" when his teacher has asked, "What says moo?"

It is recommended that simple intraverbal interactions that are appropriate to the child's developmental age be taught before more complicated responses. Fill in the blank relations are often the easiest to teach first (Cooper et al., 2007). For instance, a learner may be taught to fill in the word "star" after someone has delivered the line "Twinkle, twinkle little _____." A teacher may start by using visual stimuli and then gradually fade out these prompts as the child is successful so that only the verbal stimulus is presented.

Since intraverbal behavior is reinforced by generalized conditioned reinforcement (i.e.,

social reinforcement via praise, eye contact, body language, etc.) it may be challenging to motivate some students initially to engage in the desired response. Trainers may need to initially pair specific reinforcement (such as a crayon after the child has responded "crayon" when asked, "What do you color with?") initially and then fade this over time (Cooper et al., 2007).

Varying both the verbal stimuli and the verbal responses over time will help to strengthen these responses (Cooper et al., 2007). For instance a child who has learned to respond "bear" when asked, "What is your favorite toy?" may then learn to respond with more complexity such as "blue bear" or "my blue bear with the purple hat." The teacher can also vary the verbal prompt such as asking, "What toy do you like the most?" which is simply another way of phrasing "what is your favorite toy," and is a part of the same stimulus class.

When using intraverbal training, the trainer should:

1. Be sure that the desired verbal responses are already in the child's or individual's repertoire

2. Ensure that the listener is attending. Make sure that they are looking in your direction, are making eye contact and that the environment isn't too noisy or distracting.

3. Deliver the verbal stimulus (i.e. "The itsy bitsy _____.") and pause. Initially pair the verbal response with a nonverbal stimulus that can be faded out over time (such as a picture of a spider or spider puppet).

4. Provide reinforcement for correct responding. Specific reinforcement

such as providing edibles, access to the spider puppet, etc. should be faded over time so that social reinforcement becomes the reinforcing consequence.

5. Once simple intraverbal relations have been established, teach the child to respond to variations to the verbal stimulus ("Who went up the water spout?") or respond with more complexity.

Assessment:

- Ask the supervisee to state what intraverbal training can be used to teach.
- Ask the supervisee to state the prerequisite skills that are needed to teach intraverbal behavior.
- Ask the supervisee to give examples of intraverbal training.
- Ask the supervisee to discuss how intraverbal training should be delivered.

- Ask the supervisee to state why nonverbal stimuli should be faded out.

Relevant Literature:

Cooper, J.O, Heron T.E, Heward W.L. (2007). *Applied behavior analysis* (2nd ed.) Upper Saddle River, NJ: Pearson

Partington, J. W., & Bailey, J. S. (1993). Teaching intraverbal behavior to preschool children. *The Analysis of Verbal Behavior, 11,* 9–18.

Skinner, B.F. (1957). *Verbal Behavior.* New York: Appleton-Century.

Sundberg, M.L. & Partington, J.W. (1998). *Teaching language to children with autism or other developmental disabilities.* Pleasant Hill, CA: Behavior Analysts, Inc.

Vedora, J., Meunier, L., & Mackay, H. (2009). Teaching Intraverbal Behavior to Children with Autism: A Comparison of Textual and Echoic Prompts. *The Analysis of Verbal Behavior, 25*(1), 79–86.

Related Lessons:

D-13 Use Intraverbal Training
FK-46 Intraverbals

D-14 Use listener training

<u>Definition:</u>

Listener – "someone who provides reinforcement for verbal behavior" (Cooper,
Heron, & Heward, 2007, p. 698)

Part of being involved in a verbal community
is reinforcing the behavior of speakers. There
are several methods for training someone to
respond as a listener. Skills such as vocal imitation (echoic), following instructions, answering questions (intraverbal), conversation
skills (intraverbal), indicating objects, etc., all
require listener behavior.

Sundberg discusses a distinction between intraverbal and listener responding. "If the
child's response were verbal, then it would
classified as intraverbal... but if the response
were nonverbal it would be classified as listener behavior (or often termed receptive language or receptive labeling)" (Sundberg, 2008,
pp. 11-12).

There are multiple protocols for receptive language training (cf., Fabrizio & Moors, 2001;
Leaf & McEachin, 1999; Lovaas, 2003; Maurice, Green, & Luce, 1996). In a review of
teaching receptive language to children with
autism, Pelios and Sucharzewski (2004) point
out that one must consider antecedent manipulations (e.g., within-stimulus prompts, keeping stimulus short, using topographically dis-
similar responses) and consequence manipulations (e.g., rich reinforcement schedules, token economies, performance based breaks).
Also, they recommend systematically programming specific antecedent and consequence manipulations and requiring specific
response requirements.

<u>Examples:</u>

- A teacher conducting receptive language training tells her student "sit

down" the student sits down and the
teacher praises the student. The
teacher then says "clap hands" the
student claps hands and the teacher
praises the student.
- A teacher presents an array of fruit
  and says to the student, "give me the
  apple." The student gives the teacher
  the apple and the teacher gives the
  student a token.

<u>Assessment:</u>

- Have supervisee read relevant literature on receptive language/listener
  training.
- Role play with your supervisee
  teacher (speaker) and student (listener) examples of receptive language training protocols.

<u>Relevant Literature:</u>

Cooper, J. O., Heron, T. E., & Heward, W. L.
(2007). *Applied behavior analysis.* Upper
Saddle River, NJ: Pearson Education.

Fabrizio, M. S. (2001). *A Brief Overview of Fluency-Based Instruction for Learners with Autism.* Fabrizio/Moors Consulting, Seattle, Washington.

Leaf, R., & McEachin, J. (1999). *A work in progress: Behavior management strategies and a
curriculum for intensive behavioral treatment of
autism.* New York: DRL Books, LLC.

Lovaas, O. I. (2003). *Teaching individuals with developmental delays: Basic intervention techniques.* Austin, TX: Pro-Ed.

Maurice C, Green G, Luce S, editors. Behavioral intervention for young children
with autism: A manual for parents and
professionals. Austin, TX: Pro-Ed;
1996.

Pelios, L. V., & Sucharzewski, A. (2004).
Teaching receptive language to children

with autism: A selective overview. *The Behavior Analyst Today*, *4*(4), 378.

Schlinger, H. D. (2008). Listening Is Behaving Verbally. *The Behavior Analyst*, *31*(2), 145–161.

Sundberg, M. L. (2008). VB-MAPP Verbal Behavior Milestones Assessment and Placement Program: a language and social skills assessment program for children with autism or other developmental disabilities: guide. Concord, CA: AVB Press.

Related Lessons:

D-10 Use echoic training.
D-13 Use intraverbal training.
FK-43 Echoics
FK-44 Mands
FK-45 Tacts
FK-46 Intraverbals

D-15 Identify punishers

Definition:
Punisher – "A stimulus change that decreases the future frequency of behavior that immediately precedes it" (Cooper, Heron, & Heward, 2007, p. 702).

Punishers can be categorized as unconditioned or conditioned. Unconditioned punishers, or unlearned punishers, are stimuli whose presentation functions as punishment without previous pairing with any other punishers. Such punishers consist of stimulation such as pain, intense odors, visual stimulation, taste, sound, or extreme temperatures (Cooper, Heron, & Heward, 2007). Conditioned punishers, or learned punishers, are stimuli whose presentation has previously been paired with an unconditioned punisher or a previously conditioned punisher (Cooper, Heron, & Heward, 2007). For example, if a person eats yogurt and immediately gags or vomits, yogurt may become a conditioned aversive and thereby a conditioned punisher by decreasing the behavior of eating yogurt and possibly other food with a similar consistency to yogurt. As the above examples of conditioned and unconditioned punishers show, the process of punishment is a naturally occurring phenomenon that causes behavior change. However, punishment procedures can also be an effective means for decreasing challenging behavior that is life threatening or resistant to other forms of intervention in an ethical manner. Iwata (1988) recommends that behavior analysts view the use of punishers as a default technology to be used when other interventions have failed.

Regarding the selection of a punisher to use in an intervention, it is important to note that punishers are idiosyncratic. A punisher for one person maybe a reinforcer for someone else, and perhaps a neutral stimulus to another. For this reason, a punisher assessment can assist in identifying stimuli that will likely function as punishers by measuring avoidance and escape behavior following the presentation with each stimulus (Fisher et al., 1994). Once potential punishers have been identified there are some factors to consider when choosing a stimulus to use in the treatment of challenging behavior. Research has indicated that the magnitude, or amount of the punisher, should be delivered at the optimum level at the outset of the intervention (Azrin & Holz, 1966; Thompson et al., 1999). Furthermore, in keeping with ethical considerations the selection of the least intrusive punisher(s) is recommended. Typically intrusiveness is outlined by hierarchically arranging interventions according to the degree to which the intervention limits individual freedom, intrudes into the child's life, or produces discomfort, pain, or distress (Luiselli, 2008). Pairing procedures may be beneficial in assisting with the identification of less intrusive punishers by establishing less intrusive conditioned punishers (Vorndran & Lerman, 2006). Lastly, it should be noted that Lerman and Vorndran (2002) highlighted the need for further basic and applied research on punishment due to a need for identifying strategies to enhance the effectiveness of least intrusive punishment procedures.

Assessment:
- Ask supervisee to give examples of an unconditioned punisher
- Ask supervisee to give examples of a conditioned punisher
- Ask supervisee to identify ethical considerations regarding the use of punishment and selecting punishers
- Ask supervisee to list the characteristics that should be considered when selecting a punisher

Relevant Literature:
Azrin, N. H., & Holz, W. C. (1966). Punishment. *Operant behavior: Areas of research and application*, 380-447.
Behavior Analyst Certification Board (BACB) Behavior Analyst Certification

Board professional and ethical compliance code for behavior analysts. 2014. Retrieved from http://www.bacb.com/Download-files/BACB_Compliance_Code.pdf.

Cooper, J. O., Heron, T. E., & Heward, W. L. (2007). *Applied behavior analysis (2nd ed.).* Upper Saddle River, NJ: Pearson.

Fisher, W. W., Piazza, C. C., BowMAN, L. G., Kurtz, P. F., Sherer, M. R., & Lachman, S. R. (1994). A preliminary evaluation of empirically derived consequences for the treatment of pica. *Journal of Applied Behavior Analysis, 27*(3), 447-457.

Iwata, B. A. (1988). The development and adoption of controversial default technologies. *The Behavior Analyst, 11*(2), 149.

Lerman, D. C., & Vorndran, C. M. (2002). On the status of knowledge for using punishment: Implications for treating behavior disorders. *Journal of Applied Behavior Analysis, 35*(4), 431-464.

Luiselli, J. K. (Ed.). (2008). *Effective practices for children with autism: Educational and behavior support interventions that work.* Oxford University Press.

Thompson, R. H., Iwata, B. A., Conners, J., & Roscoe, E. M. (1999). Effects of reinforcement for alternative behavior during punishment of self-injury. *Journal of Applied Behavior Analysis, 32*(3), 317.

Vorndran, C. M., & Lerman, D. C. (2006). Establishing and maintaining treatment effects with less intrusive consequences via a pairing procedure. *Journal of applied behavior analysis, 39*(1), 35-48.

Related Lessons:

D-16 Use positive and negative punishment.

D-17 Use appropriate parameters and schedules of punishment.

J-02 Identify potential interventions based on assessment results and the best available scientific evidence.

J-10 When a behavior is to be decreased, select an acceptable alternative behavior to be established or increased.

FK-19 Unconditioned punishment

FK-20 Conditioned punishment

FK-21 Schedules of reinforcement and punishment

FK-23 Automatic reinforcement and punishment

D-16 Use positive and negative punishment

Definitions:

Punishment - "Occurs when stimulus change immediately follows a response and decreases the future frequency of that type of behavior in similar conditions" (Cooper, Heron, & Heward, 2007, p. 702).

Positive Punishment: "A behavior is followed immediately by the presentation of a stimulus that decreases the future frequency of the behavior" (Cooper, Heron, & Heward, 2007, p. 701).*

Example: Albert is learning to drive. Albert drives fast and speeds along the highway. His mother provides a firm reprimand directly following the speeding. Albert no longer speeds when his mother is in the car.

Negative Punishment -"A…behavior is followed immediately by the removal of a stimulus (or a decrease in the intensity of the stimulus), that decreases the future frequency of similar responses under similar conditions" (Cooper Heron, & Heward, 2007, p. 700). *

Example: Albert is learning to drive. Albert drives fast and speeds along the highway. His mother removes Albert's driving privilege for a week following the speeding. Albert no longer speeds.

Assessment:

- Ask your supervisee what the behavioral process behind "time-out" is.
- Ask your supervisee to create an example of both positive and negative punishment
- Ask supervisee to explain the difference between negative reinforcement and negative punishment
- Have the supervisee provide labels in the boxes

Relevant Literature:

Bailey, J., & Burch, M. (2011). *Ethics for Behavior Analysts: 2nd Expanded Edition*. Taylor & Francis.

	Remove or Decrease intensity of Stimulus	Remove or Decrease intensity of Stimulus
Frequency of Behavior	?	?
	?	?

Cooper, J. O., Heron, T. E., & Heward, W. L. (2007). Applied behavior analysis: 2nd Edition. Pearson Education, Inc.

Foxx, R. M. (1982). *Decreasing behaviors of severely retarded and autistic persons*. Champaign, IL: Research Press.

Houten, R., Axelrod, S., Bailey, J. S., Favell, J. E., Foxx, R. M., Iwata, B. A., & Lovaas, O. I. (1988). The right to effective behavioral treatment. *Journal of Applied Behavior Analysis, 21*(4), 381-384.

Related Lessons:

D-01 Use positive and negative reinforcement
D-17 Use appropriate parameters and schedules of punishment
D-19 Use combinations of reinforcement with punishment and extinction
E-11 Use pairing procedures to establish new conditioned reinforcers and punishers
G-07 Practice within one's limits of professional competence in applied behavior analysis, and obtain consultation, supervision, and training, or make referrals as necessary
J-10 When a behavior is to be decreased, select an acceptable alternative behavior to be established or increased
FK-19 Unconditioned punishment
FK 20 Conditioned punishment

Footnotes:

Alternatively Fox (1982) described positive and negative punishment as Type I punishment (contingent stimulation) and Type II punishment (contingent withdrawal of a stimulus).

An emphasis on the ethical considerations of using punishment should be introduced when punishment is first discussed.

D-17 Use appropriate parameters and schedules of punishment

Definitions:

Punishment - "Occurs when stimulus change immediately follows a response and decreases the future frequency of that type of behavior in similar conditions" (Cooper, Heron, & Heward, 2007, p. 702).*

Legislation and agency policies limit the use of punishment. Lerman and Vorndran (2002) suggested that punishment may be considered if:

1. The challenging behavior produces serious physical harm and has to be suppressed quickly
2. Reinforcement based treatments have not reduced the problem behavior to socially acceptable levels or
3. The reinforcer maintaining the challenging behavior cannot be identified or withheld

BACB Labels specific considerations regarding punishment in the ethical guideline 4.08:

4.08 Considerations Regarding Punishment Procedures:

(a) Behavior analysts recommend reinforcement rather than punishment whenever possible.

(b) If punishment procedures are necessary, behavior analysts always include reinforcement procedures for alternative behavior in the behavior-change program.

(c) Before implementing punishment-based procedures, behavior analysts ensure that appropriate steps
have been taken to implement reinforcement-based procedures unless the severity or dangerousness of the behavior necessitates immediate use of aversive procedures.

(d) Behavior analysts ensure that aversive procedures are accompanied by an increased level of training, supervision, and oversight. Behavior analysts must evaluate the effectiveness of aversive procedures in a timely manner and modify the behavior-change program if it is ineffective. Behavior analysts always include a plan to discontinue the use of aversive procedures when no longer needed. (BACB, 2014, pp.12-13)

Ethical Considerations Related to Punishment as outlined by Cooper, Heron, and Heward (2007):

1. The right to safe and humane treatment
2. Least restrictive alternative
3. Right to effective treatment

Appropriate Use of Punishment as outlined by Cooper, Heron, and Heward (2007):

1. Conduct a functional assessment
2. Attempt reinforcement based strategies (behavior as above does not reach socially acceptable levels)
3. Conduct punisher assessment
4. Ensure informed consent is given
5. Include reinforcement based strategies with punishment procedures
6. Ensure all staff are trained in the procedure and monitored closely
7. Use punishers of sufficient quality and magnitude
8. Use varied punishers
9. Deliver punisher at the beginning of a behavioral sequence
10. Punish each instance of the behavior Initially
11. Shift to intermittent schedule gradually
12. If delay in punishment use mediation
13. Supplement punishment with complementary interventions
14. Be prepared for negative side effects
15. Collect data, graph and evaluate daily
16. Discontinue procedure if a decrease in behavior is not observed

Assessment:

- Provide scenarios in which clients would not qualify for a punishment procedure (e.g., behavior does not cause physical harm, reinforcement based strategies have not been attempted, or consent was not obtained.)

- Ask Supervisee to list the four considerations the BACB lists when considering punishment
- Ask the Supervisee to list the side effects of punishment
- Ask the Supervisee to outline the recommendation for a client who had been receiving a punishment procedure for 2 months and head hitting remained consistent at 10 times a day. (should discontinue)
- Have the supervisee list all of the things that must happen prior to a punishment procedure beginning (functional assessment, reinforcement based program ineffective, consent obtained, staff trained)

Relevant Literature:

Bailey, J., & Burch, M. (2011). *Ethics for Behavior Analysts: 2nd Expanded Edition.* Taylor & Francis.

Behavior Analyst Certification Board (BACB) Behavior Analyst Certification Board professional and ethical compliance code for behavior analysts. 2014. Retrieved from http://www.bacb.com/Download-files/BACB_Compliance_Code.pdf.

Cooper, J. O., Heron, T. E., & Heward, W. L. (2007). Applied behavior analysis: 2nd Edition. Pearson Education, Inc.

Foxx, R. M. (1982). *Decreasing behaviors of severely retarded and autistic persons.* Champaign, IL: Research Press.

Houten, R., Axelrod, S., Bailey, J. S., Favell, J. E., Foxx, R. M., Iwata, B. A., & Lovaas, O. I. (1988). The right to effective behavioral treatment. *Journal of Applied Behavior Analysis, 21*(4), 381-384.

Lerman, D. C., & Vorndran, C. M. (2002). On the status of knowledge for using punishment: Implications for treating behavior disorders. *Journal of Applied Behavior Analysis, 35*(4), 431-464.

Iwata, B. A. (1988). The development and adoption of controversial default technologies. *The Behavior Analyst, 11*(2), 149.

Related Lessons:
D-16 Use positive and negative punishment
D-15 Identify punishers
D-19 Use combinations of reinforcement with punishment and extinction
E-11 Use pairing procedures to establish new conditional reinforcers and punishers
G-07 Practice within one's limits of professional competence in applied behavior analysis, and obtain consultation, supervision, and training, or make referrals as necessary
J-10 When a behavior is to be decreased, select an acceptable alternative behavior to be established or increased
FK-19 Unconditioned punishment
FK 20 Conditioned punishment
FK 21 Schedules of reinforceement and punishment
FK 38 Behavioral contrast

Footnotes
- Positive punishment may also be described as a type of aversive control. Negative side effects include: emotional or aggressive reactions, behavioral contrast, escape and avoidance of the punisher, modeling of inappropriate behavior and the overuse associated with negative reinforcement of the person presenting the punisher (Cooper, Heron, & Heward, 2007)

D-18 Use Extinction

Extinction "involves eliminating the reinforcement contingency maintaining a response" and has "been used successfully to reduce the frequency of a variety of behavioral disorders" (Lerman & Iwata, 1995, p. 93). To use it effectively, determine the reinforcer and prevent the behavior from contacting reinforcement. Extinction occurs when the behavior no longer produces reinforcement such as:

- Social Positive
- Social Negative
- Automatic reinforcement

Extinction may have unwanted side effects:
1. Extinction bursts
2. Initial increases in target behavior as the individual engages in an increased rate of behavior to access previous reinforcers
3. Extinction-induced aggression
4. Increased unwanted novel behavior

To use extinction effectively, withhold all reinforcers maintaining the problem behavior and provide frequent opportunities for the individual's behavior to contact new reinforcement contingencies (e.g. problem behavior no longer produces reinforcement while replacement behavior produces does produce reinforcement). It may not work if the client aggresses for attention (e.g., response blocking may reinforce aggression).

Extinction is not advised in environments where peers are likely to imitate problem behaviors (e.g., classroom settings). Use of extinction for severe aggression or self-injury behaviors may result in harm to client or peers. Extinction is not selected to manage severely disruptive high-frequency behavior.

Do not use extinction as a singular intervention. Unwanted effects of extinction are reduced when coupled with differential reinforcement strategies (Athens & Vollmer, 2010).

Example:
Teach client to raise hand for attention (differential reinforcement strategy) while putting spitting for attention on extinction. Give client access to previous reinforcers to minimize aversive effects of extinction.

Assessment:
- Provide hypothetical scenarios and have supervisee determine what type of extinction procedure should be utilized and what appropriate replacement behavior should be reinforced.
- Have supervisee explain 3 scenarios in which extinction should not be utilized.
- Have supervisee describe additional treatment components which can increase the efficacy of treatment.

Relevant Literature:
Lerman, D.C., & Iwata, B.A., (1995). Prevalence of the extinction burst and its attenuation during treatment. *Journal of Applied Behavioral Analysis, 28(1)*, 93-94.
Athen, E.S., & Vollmer, T.R., (2010). An investigation of differential reinforcement of alternative behavior without extinction. *Journal of Applied Behavioral Analysis, 43(4)*, 569-589.

Related Lessons:
C-03 State and plan for unwanted effects of extinction
D-18. Use Extinction.
D-19 Use combinations of reinforcement with punishment and extinction
J-06 Select intervention strategies based on supporting environments
J-07 Select intervention strategies based on environmental and resource constraints
J-09 Identify and address practical and ethical considerations when using experimental designs to demonstrate program effectiveness.
J-10 When a behavior is to be decreased, select an acceptable alternative behavior to be established or increased.

D-19 Use combinations of reinforcement with punishment and extinction

A guideline for using extinction effectively is the simultaneous use of reinforcement procedures. Extinction used alone may result in a temporary increase in the target behavior known as extinction burst (Cooper, Heron, & Heward, 2007). Teaching an alternative behavior may decrease the extinction burst effects and other possible side effects such as aggressive behavior (Lerman, Iwata, & Wallace, 1999). Similarly, several studies have found that differential reinforcement procedures are most effective when used in conjunction with extinction (e.g., Fisher, Piazza, Cataldo, Harrell, Jefferson, & Conner, 1993; Hagopian, Fisher, Sullivan, Acquisto, & LeBlanc, 1998; Piazza, Patel, Gulotta, Sevin, & Layer, 2002). Using extinction with differential reinforcement ensures that concurrent access to reinforcement for inappropriate behavior is not favored, thereby increasing the likelihood of allocation to the alternative behavior targeted for increase.

Likewise, punishment procedures are most effective when used in conjunction with reinforcement-based procedures (Millenson, 1967). The main rationale for use of reinforcement with punishment procedures is that punishment is considered an intrusive treatment procedure. In addition, punishment procedures do not teach the individual any appropriate skills. Teaching appropriate skills helps to solve these problems. Reinforcing an alternative behavior makes it more likely that punishment procedures can then be faded out as the appropriate behavior replaces the inappropriate behavior. A study conducted by Holz, Azrin and Ayllon (1963) even found that punishment was ineffective without the use of reinforcement contingencies. Several studies have illustrated the benefits of using reinforcement in conjunction with punishment procedures (e.g., Fisher et al., 1993; Hagopian et al., 1998; Thompson, Iwata, Conners, & Roscoe, 1999).

Assessment:

- Provide the supervisee with articles from the relevant literature and discuss the findings and their considerations for clinical application.
- Ask the supervisee to list the problems associates with using extinction procedures alone
- Ask supervisee to list the benefits of using reinforcement based procedures with extinction
- Ask the supervisee to list the problems associates with using punishment procedures alone
- Ask supervisee to list the benefits of using reinforcement based procedures with punishment

Relevant Literature:

Cooper, J. O., Heron, T. E., & Heward, W. L. (2007). Applied behavior analysis (2nd ed.). Upper Saddle River, NJ: Pearson.

Fisher, W., Piazza, C., Cataldo, M., Harrell, R., Jefferson, G., & Conner, R. (1993). Functional communication training with and without extinction and punishment. Journal of Applied Behavior Analysis, 26(1), 23–36.

Hagopian, L. P., Fisher, W. W., Sullivan, M. T., Acquisto, J., & LeBlanc, L. A. (1998). Effectiveness of functional communication training with and without extinction and punishment: A summary of 21 inpatient cases. Journal of Applied Behavior Analysis, 31(2), 211-235.

Holz, W. C., Azrin, N. H., & Ayllon, T. (1963). Elimination of behavior of mental patients by response-produced extinction. Journal of the Experimental Analysis of Behavior, 6(3), 407.

Lerman, D. C., Iwata, B. A., & Wallace, M. D. (1999). Side effects of extinction: prevalence of bursting and aggression during the treatment of self-injurious behavior. Journal of applied behavior analysis, 32(1), 1-8.

Millenson, J. R., & Leslie, J. C. (1967). *Principles of behavioral analysis* (pp. 43-44). New York: Macmillan.

Piazza, C. C., Patel, M. R., Gulotta, C. S., Sevin, B. M., & Layer, S. A. (2002). On the relative contributions of positive reinforcement and escape extinction in the treatment of food refusal. *Journal of applied behavior analysis*, *36*(3), 309-324.

Thompson, R. H., Iwata, B. A., Conners, J., & Roscoe, E. M. (1999). Effects of reinforcement for alternative behavior during punishment of self-injury. *Journal of Applied Behavior Analysis*, *32*(3), 317.

Related Lessons:

B-10 Conduct a component analysis to determine the effective components of an intervention package.

C-01 State and plan for the possible unwanted effects of reinforcement.

C-02 State and plan for the possible unwanted effects of punishment.

C-03 State and plan for the possible unwanted effects of extinction.

D-01 Use positive and negative reinforcement.

D-02 Use appropriate parameters and schedules of reinforcement.

D-15 Identify punishers.

D-16 Use positive and negative punishment.

D-17 Use appropriate parameters and schedules of punishment.

D-18 Use extinction.

D-20 Use response-independent (time-based) schedules of reinforcement (i.e., noncontingent reinforcement).

D-21 Use differential reinforcement (e.g., DRO, DRA, DRI, DRL, DRH).

I-06 Make recommendations regarding behaviors that must be established, maintained, increased, or decreased.

I-07 Design and conduct preference assessments to identify putative reinforcers.

J-02 Identify potential interventions based on assessment results and the best available scientific evidence.

J-10 When a behavior is to be decreased, select an acceptable alternative behavior to be established or increased.

D-20 Use response-independent (time-based) schedules of reinforcement (i.e., non-contingent reinforcement)

Definition:

Noncontingent reinforcement (NCR) – "A procedure in which stimuli with known reinforcing properties are presented on fixed-time (FT) or variable time (VT) schedules completely independent of behavior; often used as an antecedent intervention to reduce problem behavior" (Cooper, Heron & Heward, 2007, p. 700).

Noncontingent reinforcement is sometimes used in applied research in an experimental design called the NCR reversal technique. This design involves a baseline phase, NCR phase (where a potential reinforcer is delivered on a fixed or variable time schedule independent of the target behavior), and a phase where the reinforcer is delivered contingent on a set behavioral criteria. The phases are repeated as necessary to indicate experimental control over the dependent variable. The NCR and baseline conditions function as a comparative measure to validate the independent variable in these studies.

Differential reinforcement procedures may limit access to reinforcement if appropriate behavior occurs at low rates. NCR gives consistent access to reinforcement.

Example:

A DRO program was trialed for 3 weeks to decrease Jimmy's verbal protesting during group activities. Based on data collected, the DRO program was deemed ineffective for decreasing Jimmy's verbal protesting. Mr. Jones took data and found that Jimmy could quietly engage in group activities for 3 minutes before starting to protest. Mr. Jones decided to implement a 2 minute NCR program in which he would give Jimmy a sticker every 2 minutes regardless of the presence of interfering behaviors.

Non- Example:

Mr. Michael was concerned with Barry's aggressive behavior during group activities. He decided to give him a sticker for every 2 minutes that he did not engage in aggressive behavior.

Assessment:

- Have supervisee create an NCR program and explain procedures to other supervisees.

- Have Supervisee identify the difference between differential reinforcement and noncontingent reinforcement and give examples of both.
- Have supervisee give examples of NCR used in his/her professional and nonprofessional life.

Relevant Literature:

Cautela, J. R. (1984). General level of reinforcement. *Journal of Behavior Therapy and Experimental Psychiatry*, 15, 109-114.

Cooper, J.O., Heron, T.E. & Heward W.L. (2007). *Applied Behavior Analysis* (2nd Ed.), Upper Saddle River, NJ. Pearson Prentice Hall.

Hagopian, L. P., Fisher, W. W., & Legacy, S. M. (1994). Schedule effects of noncontingent reinforcement on attention-maintained destructive behavior in identical quadruplets. *Journal of Applied Behavior Analysis*, 27, 317-325.

Ingvarsson, E.T., Kahng, S., Hausman, N.L. (2008). Some effects of noncontingent positive reinforcement on multiply controlled Problem behavior and compliance in a demand context. *Journal of Applied Behavior Analysis*. 41, 3, 435-440.

Wilder, D. A., Normand, M., & Atwell, J. (2005). Noncontingent reinforcement as treatment for food refusal and associated self-injury. *Journal of Applied Behavior Analysis*, 38, 549-553.

Related Lessons:
B-04: Use withdrawal/reversal designs.
C-01: State and plan for the unwanted effects of reinforcement.
D-02: Use appropriate parameters and schedules of reinforcement.
D-21: Use differential reinforcement (e.g., DRO, DRA, DRI, DRL, DRH)
J-02: Identify potential interventions based on assessment results and the best available scientific evidence.

D-21 Use differential reinforcement (e.g., DRO, DRA, DRI, DRL, DRH)

Definitions:

Differential Reinforcement - "Reinforcing only those responses within a response class that meet a specific criterion along some dimension(s) (i.e., frequency, topography, duration, latency or magnitude) and placing all other behaviors in the class on extinction" (Cooper, Heron, & Heward, 2007, p. 693).
Five common variations of differential reinforcement are:

Differential reinforcement of other behavior (DRO) is a procedure that provides reinforcement for the absence of problem behavior during a period of time (interval) or at a specific time (momentary) (Cooper, Heron, & Heward, 2007).

Differential reinforcement of alternative behavior (DRA) is the reinforcement of a response that is an appropriate alternative to problem behavior (Cooper, Heron, & Heward, 2007).

Differential reinforcement of incompatible behavior (DRI) is the reinforcement of a response that is physically incompatible with the target problem behavior (Cooper, Heron, & Heward, 2007).

Differential reinforcement of high rates (DRH) is reinforcement contingent upon a behavior occurring at a set high rate used to increase the overall rate of a behavior (Cooper, Heron, & Heward, 2007).

Differential reinforcement of low rates of behavior (DRL) is reinforcement contingent upon behavior occurring at a set reduced rate used to decrease the overall rate of a behavior but not to eliminate it completely (Cooper, Heron, & Heward, 2007).

Examples:
- DRO: Providing a toy following the absence of inappropriate vocalizations for 5 minutes which decreases inappropriate vocalizations.
- DRA: Providing a break for handing over a break card which increases the use of the break card in the future.
- DRI: Providing social attention for having hands in their own pant pockets which subsequently decreases scratching at caregivers hands.
- DRH: A student typically only completes one math worksheet per class period. Providing a break with a preferred item contingent on finishing three math worksheets, which increases the number of worksheets completed by a student. The student only gets the preferred item when they complete three worksheets.
- DRL: Providing attention when a student says "excuse me" 2 times every 10 minutes and not providing attention if the behavior occurs more frequently within that 10 minute period which maintains low rates of the behavior

Assessment:
- Provide the supervisee with several target behaviors and their respective function. Have him/her select which differential reinforcement procedure(s) would be the most appropriate for each and why. Review it and provide feedback.
- Have the supervisee describe the benefits of each differential reinforcement procedure.
- Have the supervisee list the conditions in which the use of each variation would not be desirable.
- Provide supervisee with an article from the relevant literature regarding DRA or DRI and discuss the alternative or in-

compatible behavior the authors selected. In addition, ask them to come up with other alternative or incompatible behaviors which could have been used in the study.

- Provide supervisee with an article from the relevant literature and discuss if the reinforcer selected by the authors is functional or arbitrary. In addition, ask the supervisee to come up with other putative reinforcers which the study could have used. Finally, discuss the pros and cons of using an arbitrary reinforcer and functional reinforcers.

Relevant Literature:

Cooper, J. O., Heron, T. E., & Heward, W. L. (2007). Applied behavior analysis (2nd ed.). Upper Saddle River, NJ: Pearson.

Cowdery, G. E. (1990). Effects and Side Effects of DRO as Treatment for Self-Injurious Behavior. Journal of Applied Behavior Analysis, 23(4), 497-506.

Deitz, S. M. (1977). An analysis of programming DRL schedules in educational settings. Behaviour Research and Therapy, 15(1), 103-111.

Deitz, D. E., & Repp, A. C. (1983). Reducing Behavior through Reinforcement. Exceptional Education Quarterly, 3(4), 34-46.

Hanley, G. P., Iwata, B. A., & Thompson, R. H. (2001). Reinforcement schedule thinning following treatment with functional communication training. Journal of Applied Behavior Analysis, 34(1), 17-38.

Kahng, S. W., Abt, K. A., & Schonbachler, H. E. (2001). Assessment and treatment of low-rate high-intensity problem behavior. Journal of Applied Behavior Analysis, 34(2), 225.

Lalli, J. S., Casey, S., & Kates, K. (1995). Reducing escape behavior and increasing task completion with functional communication training, extinction and response chaining. Journal of Applied Behavior Analysis, 28(3), 261-268.

Lindberg, J. S., Iwata, B. A., Kahng, S., & DeLeon, I. G. (1998). DRO contingencies: an analysis of variable-momentary schedules. Journal of applied behavior analysis, 32(2), 123-35.

Mazaleski, J. L. (1993). Analysis of the Reinforcement and Extinction Components in DRO Contingencies with Self-Injury. Journal of Applied Behavior Analysis, 26(2), 143-56.

Petscher, E. S., Rey, C., & Bailey, J. S. (2009). A review of empirical support for differential reinforcement of alternative behavior. Research in Developmental Disabilities, 30(3), 409-425.

Rehfeldt, R. A., & Chambers, M. R. (2003). Functional analysis and treatment of verbal perseverations displayed by an adult with autism. Journal of Applied Behavior Analysis, 36(2), 259-261.

Seys, D. M., & Duker, P. C. (1978). Improving residential care for the retarded by differential reinforcement of high rates of ward-staff behaviour. Behavioural Analysis and Modification, 2, 203-210.

Vollmer, T. R., & Iwata, B. A. (1992). Differential reinforcement as treatment for behavior disorders: Procedural and functional variations. Research in Developmental Disabilities, 13(4), 393-417.

Vollmer, T. R., Roane, H. S., Ringdahl, J. E., & Marcus, B. A. (1999). Evaluating treatment challenges with differential reinforcement of alternative behavior. Journal of Applied Behavior Analysis, 32(1), 9-23.

Related Lessons:

C-01 State and plan for the possible unwanted effects of reinforcement.

D-02 Use appropriate parameters and schedules of reinforcement.

D-19 Use combinations of reinforcement with punishment and extinction.

F-07 Use functional communication training.

I-07 Design and conduct preference assessments to identify putative reinforcers.

J-02 Identify potential interventions based on assessment results and the best available scientific evidence

E-01 Use interventions based on manipulation of antecedents, such as motivating operations and discriminative stimuli

While it is commonly known that behaviors are maintained by consequences, including antecedent interventions within an individual's treatment package can often expedite positive behavioral change and mitigate negative effects of consequent strategies (e.g. extinction bursts). Some antecedent strategies include motivating operations, discriminative stimuli, non-contingent reinforcement and usage of high probability request sequences.

Michael (1982, p. 149) describes motivating operations as "a stimulus change which, (1) given the momentary effectiveness of some particular type of reinforcement (2) increases the frequency of a particular type of response (3) because that stimulus change has been correlated with an increase in the frequency with which that type of response has been followed by that type of reinforcement."

Skinner first explored this concept, describing deprivation and satiation to be motivating variables that govern behavior. Simply put, reinforcers obtain most of their reinforcing value depending on the individual's drive to obtain that reinforcer, which is a direct result of deprivation-satiation contingencies. The motivating operation for one's behavior that has run three miles in the heat is to quench their thirst increasing the value of water as a reinforcer. Having no money to put into a vending machine to get a bottle of water is the motivating operation to ask friends for loose change. Similarly, after the person drinks an entire bottle of water, water may no longer function as a reinforcer. Behavior analysts can thereby affect behavioral change by manipulating motivating operations (e.g. challenging behavior maintained by escape from non-preferred tasks may be mitigated by giving the individual frequent breaks).

Another antecedent strategy is effectively programming for discriminative stimuli. Skinner claimed that virtually all operant behavior falls under stimulus control, asserting that "if all behavior were equally likely to occur on all occasions, the result would be chaotic" (Skinner, 1953, p. 108). It is therefore important for individuals to learn to discriminate between conditions in which specific responses will be reinforced and when these responses will not. Discriminative stimuli evoke behavior because they have been correlated with increased probability of accessing a reinforcer. For instance, teaching a student to mand for a break can be problematic if the student mands for a break continuously throughout the day, thereby yielding very little on-task behavior. However, this can be possibly remedied by the availability of a break is represented by the presence of a break icon (e.g. break icon is the discriminative stimulus, signaling that if the student asks for a break, a break will be granted).

Other antecedent strategies include usage of non-contingent reinforcement and usage of high-probability request sequences. Non-contingent reinforcement is "an antecedent intervention in which stimuli with known reinforcing properties are delivered on a fixed-time or variable-time schedule independent of the learner's behavior" (Cooper, Heron & Heward, 2007, p. 489). This operates on the principle of motivating operations. By satiating an individual with wants/needs, the individual is no longer motivated to engage in responses that used to generate that want/need (e.g. giving attention to a student every five minutes may abolish attention as a reinforcer, thereby reducing the need to engage in inappropriate attention-seeking behavior).

Assessment:

- Have your supervisee list and describe applicable antecedent interventions.
- In a clinical setting or during role-play, have your supervisee describe what motivating operations may be affecting the client's behavior.
- Describe a scenario and have the supervisee lists some potential antecedent strategies that can be used and have them describe why they chose these strategies.

Relevant Literature:

Michael, J. (1982). Distinguishing between discriminative and motivational functions of stimuli. *Journal of Experimental Analysis of Behavior, 37(1)*, 149-155.

Skinner, B. F. (1953). *Science and human behavior.* New York: Macmillan.

Smith, R.G. & Iwata, B.A. (1997). Antecedent influences on behavior disorders. *Journal of Applied Behavior Analysis, 30(2)*, 343-375.

Related Lessons:

E-09: Arrange high probability request sequences

FK-26: Unconditioned motivating operations

FK-27: Conditioned motivating operations

FK-29: Distinguish between the discriminative stimulus and the motivating operation

E-02 Use discrimination training procedures

Discrimination training procedures involve "reinforcing or punishing a response in the presence of one stimulus and extinguishing it or allowing it to recover in the presence of another stimulus" (Malott &Trojan Suarez, 2004, p. 485). There are typically two competing contingencies when discrimination training occurs. The first contingency involves an S-delta (i.e., signals that a specified response will not be reinforced or punished when in the presence of a specified stimulus). The second contingency involves a discriminative stimulus (i.e., signals that a specified response will be reinforced in the presence of a specific stimulus condition). When discrimination training occurs, a specified response will no longer be reinforced in the presence of an S-delta, however, that same response will be reinforced in the presence of a discriminative stimulus. The goal of discrimination training is to reinforce responses in certain stimulus conditions so that they occur more frequently when those stimulus conditions are present and over time, the response will no longer occur in the presence of the S-delta. When discrimination training is successful, the learner can discriminate which antecedent stimulus conditions will result in greater reinforcement for a given response.

Example:
Discrimination training can be used to teach an individual appropriate times to take breaks, when or where it is acceptable to engage in self-stimulatory behaviors, what items in the kitchen can be accessed without asking for permission, and so on. Discrimination training procedures are evident in basic instructional lessons such as teaching a child to identify colors to seemingly natural situations such as only scheduling clients on days allowed by funding sources because this results in you being paid for your services.

Carl's teacher determines attention is reinforcing his speaking out in class. Carl's teacher teaches Carl to ask questions when there is a green card present on the board, and not to ask questions when there is a red card on the board. She does this by only delivering attention to Carl when the green card is present on the board, and ignoring Carl when the red card is present.

Assessment:
- Ask supervisee to provide examples of how discrimination procedures can be used with a specific client or to teach a specific skill.
- Ask supervisee to clearly operationalize the S-delta and discriminative stimulus contingencies that will be utilized during a specific discrimination training procedure.
- Observe supervisee describe discrimination procedures to a client, colleague, etc.

Relevant Literature:
Cooper, J. O., Heron, T. E., & Heward, W. L. (2007). Stimulus Control. *Applied Behavior Analysis* (pp. 392-409). Upper Saddle River, NJ: Pearson Prentice Hall.
Malott, R. W., & Trojan Suarez, E.A. (2004). Discrimination. *Principles of Behavior* (pp. 206-225). Upper Saddle River, NJ: Pearson Prentice Hall.
Taylor-Santa, C., Sidener, T. M., Carr, J. E., & Reeve, K. F. (2014). A discrimination training procedure to establish conditioned reinforcers for children with autism. *Behavioral Intervention, 29,* 157-176.

Related Lessons:
D-08 Use discrete-trial and free-operant arrangements
E-01 Use interventions based on manipulation of antecedents, such as motivating operations and discriminative stimuli
E-03 Use instructions and rules
E-13 Use matching-to-sample procedures
J-11 Program for stimulus and response generalization
FK-11 Environment, stimulus, stimulus class
FK-24 Stimulus control
FK-25 Multiple functions of a single stimulus
FK-35 Stimulus discrimination

E-03 Use instructions and rules

Rules are descriptions of behavioral contingencies (e.g., "Putting a sweater on when it is cold outside will help you stay warm"). When rules are followed, behavior can come under the control of delayed or indirect consequences therefore resulting in rule-governed behavior. Malott and Trojan-Suarez (2004) suggest that all instructions involve rules. For example, incomplete rules (e.g., "Stop it") provide minimal instruction (e.g., stop) and imply an outcome (e.g., you might get in trouble). It is argued that rules function as reinforcement-based or punishment-based discriminative stimuli (Malott & Trojan-Suarez, 2004). Skinner (1969) referred to rules, instructions, advice, and laws as contingency-specifying stimuli, describing the $S^D \cdot R \rightarrow S^r$ relations of everyday life.

Evidence that behavior is the result of instructional control or rule following is provided if: (1) there is no obvious or immediate consequence of the behavior; (2) the delivery of the consequence following the behavior exceeds 30 seconds; (3) behavior changes without reinforcement; (4) a substantial increase in the rate of behavior occurs following one instance of direct contact with reinforcement; and (5) the rule exists but no consequence (including automatic reinforcement) exists following the behavior (Cooper, Heron, & Heward, 2007).

Assessment:
- Ask supervisee to discriminate between direct-acting contingencies and rule-governed behavior.
- Ask supervisee to provide examples of rules.
- Ask supervisee to identify rules that may be governing a client's behavior.

- If a rule exists, ask supervisee to describe how a direct-acting contingency can be used instead and vice versa.

Relevant Literature:
Cooper, J. O., Heron, T. E., & Heward, W. L. (2007). Positive reinforcement. *Applied Behavior Analysis* (pp. 256-290). Upper Saddle River, NJ: Pearson Prentice Hall.

Hayes, S. C. (2004). *Rule-Governed Behavior: Cognition, Contingencies & Instructional Control.* Oakland, CA: Context Press.

Malott, R. W., & Trojan Suarez, E.A. (2004). Analogs to reinforcement and avoidance part 1. *Principles of Behavior* (pp. 377-393). Upper Saddle River, NJ: Pearson Prentice Hall.

Malott, R. W., & Trojan Suarez, E.A. (2004). Analogs to reinforcement and avoidance part 2. *Principles of Behavior* (pp. 394-409). Upper Saddle River, NJ: Pearson Prentice Hall.

Skinner, B. F. (1969). *Contingencies of reinforcement: A theoretical analysis.* New York: Appleton-Centrury-Crofts.

Related Lessons:
D-01 Use positive and negative reinforcement.

D-16 Use positive and negative punishment.

K-02 Identify the contingencies governing the behavior of those responsible for carrying out behavior-change procedures and design interventions accordingly.

FK-30 distinguish between motivating operation and reinforcement effects

FK-31 behavioral contingencies

FK-33 functional relations

FK-41 contingency-shaped behavior

FK-42 rule-governed behavior

E-04 Use Contingency Contracting

Definition:

Contingency contract - "…also called a behavioral contract, is a document that specifies a contingent relationship between the completion of a specified behavior and access to, or delivery of, a specified reward such as free time, a letter grade or access to a preferred activity" (Cooper, Heron & Heward, 2007, p. 551).

Contingency contracts have several components:

- Outlines the task to be completed- includes an objective definition of the task, who must complete the task and when the task must be completed.
- Specifies the reward contingent on task completion- includes description of the reward, who will deliver the reward, who will measure, whether the task has been completed to criterion, and when the reward will be received.
- Outlines how performance will be measured and what data will be taken.

Contingency contracts can be highly effective if used properly because the individual whose behavior is to be changed is involved in the process from the start. Studies have shown that contingency contracting "…has been identified as an important step toward self-management of behavior" (Miller & Kelley, 1994, p. 74) because by helping to determine the parameters of the task and outlining what and when rewards should be given, reinforcer assessments have already been identified and the individual is already motivated to engage in the target behavior, which can greatly increase compliance. However, Cooper, Heron and Heward (2007) caution against using contingency contracts with all populations. There

must be set criteria that the individual must already possess in order for contingency contracts to be effective. The target behavior must already be in the individual's repertoire and the individual must already be able to discriminate when and which environments are appropriate for the response to occur. Additionally, the individual's behavior must be able to "come under the control of the visual or oral statements (rules) of the contract" (Cooper, Heron, & Heward, 2007, p. 558). The individual does not need to be proficient in reading so long as the contract is adapted using symbols, icons, photographs, etc. and the individual thoroughly understands the reinforcement contingency.

Assessment:

- Have the supervisee design a contingency contract.
- Have the supervisee describe each component of the contract.

Relevant Literature:

Cooper, J. O., Heron, T. E., & Heward, W. L. (2007). *Applied behavior analysis* (2nd ed.). Upper Saddle River, NJ: Prentice Hall.

Miller, D.L., & Kelley, M.L. (1994). The use of goal setting and contingency contracting for improving children's homework performance. *Journal of Applied Behavioral Analysis 27(10)*, 73-84.

Related Lessons:

K-02 Identify the contingencies governing the behavior of those responsible for carrying out behavior-change procedures and design the interventions accordingly

FK-42 Rule-governed behavior

E-05 Use independent, interdependent, and dependent group contingencies

The three group contingencies as defined by Cooper, Heron, & Heward (2007):

"An independent group contingency is an arrangement in which a contingency is presented to all members of a group, but reinforcement is delivered only to those group members who meet the criterion outlined in the contingency." (Cooper et al., 2007, p. 568)

"An interdependent group contingency is one in which all members of a group must meet the criterion of the contingency (individually and as a group) before any member earns the reward." (Cooper et al., 2007, p. 569)

"Under a dependent group contingency the reward for the whole group is dependent on the performance of an individual student or small group." (Cooper et al., 2007, p. 568)

These three contingencies use the principles of reinforcement to change the behavior of a group of individuals. They involve "a common consequence (usually, but not necessarily, a reward intended to function as reinforcement) contingent on the behavior of one member of the group, the behavior of part of the group, or the behavior of everyone in the group." (Cooper et al., 2007, p. 567)

Examples:
- Independent Group Contingency
  o *Each student was given a math worksheet and received a special sticker if they completed the work without engaging in disruptive behavior. Billy, Johnny, and Sam finished their work quietly and earned stickers, but Danny was disruptive and only finished half his worksheet so he did not earn a sticker.*
- Interdependent Group Contingency
  o *Each student in Mrs. Kelly's class had to complete their math worksheets before they were allowed to go outside for recess.*

The students who finished first were allowed to help any of the struggling students. Sam was the last one working and Roger came over to help him complete his work. Once Sam was finished the whole class earned recess time.
- Dependent Group Contingency
  o *At the end of football practice, Mr. Bill told the team that they could stop running wind sprints if Roger caught a long pass from the coach. Roger caught that pass and the team cheered as they went to shower and practice ended.*

Assessment:
- Have supervisee identify and describe group contingencies he/she has encountered in his/her professional career.
- Give examples of various contingencies and ask supervisees to identify which of the three group contingencies is exhibited in each example.
- Have supervisee choose a group contingency and create guidelines for a program to change the behavior of a group using the designated contingency.

Relevant Literature:
Cooper, J.O., Heron, T.E. & Heward W.L. (2007). *Applied Behavior Analysis* (2nd Ed.), Upper Saddle River, NJ. Pearson Prentice Hall. 567-573.

Kamps, D., Howard, W., Heitzman-Powell, L., Laylin, J., Szoke, C., Petrillo, T., & Culey, A. (2011). Class-Wide Function-Related Intervention Teams: Effects of Group Contingency Programs in Urban Classrooms. *Journal of Positive Behavior Interventions*, 13, 154-167.

Litow, L. & Pumroy, D. K. (1975). A brief review of classroom group-oriented contingencies. *Journal of Applied Behavior Analysis*, 8(3), 341-347.

Nevin, A., Johnson, D., & Johnson, R. (1982). Effects of group and individual contingencies on academic performance and social relations of special needs students. *Journal of School Psychology*. 116, 1, 41-59.

Theodore, L.., Bray, M., Kehle, T., & Jenson, W. (2001). Randomization of Group Contingencies and Reinforcers to Reduce Classroom Disruptive Behavior. *Journal of School Psychology*. 39, 3, 267-277.

Related Lessons:

C-01: State and plan for the unwanted effects of reinforcement.

D-01: Use positive and negative reinforcement.

D-02: Use appropriate parameters and schedules of reinforcement.

D-19: Use combinations of reinforcement with punishment and extinction.

D-21: Use differential reinforcement (e.g., DRO, DRA, DRI, DRL, DRH)

E-04: Use contingency contracting

F-02: Use token economies and other conditioned reinforcement systems

E-06 Use Stimulus Equivalence Procedures

In the field of applied behavior analysis, a number of procedures have been used to teach new concepts. One of these procedures is known as stimulus equivalence. In 1971, Murray Sidman discovered that a previously untaught, unreinforced stimuli could come under stimulus control through its pairing with other stimuli which were explicitly taught (Sidman, 1971). This concept revolutionized the field as it demonstrated a new way of teaching that could potentially reduce the amount of time needed to teach a new class of stimuli. "Behavior analysts define stimulus equivalence by testing stimulus-stimulus relations. A positive demonstration of all three behavioral tests (i.e. reflexivity, symmetry, and transitivity) is necessary to meet the definition of an equivalence relation among a set of arbitrary stimuli" (Cooper, Heron, & Heward, 2007, p. 398).

• Reflexivity describes the action of selecting a stimulus that is matched to itself in the absence of training and reinforcement (A=A). For instance an individual is shown three pictures; a penny, a nickel, and a dime. When given an identical picture of a penny, he matches it to the identical picture of a penny in the array (Sidman, 1994).

• Symmetry describes the reversibility of the sample stimulus and a comparison stimulus (A=B and B=A). For instance an individual who is taught to select the picture of a penny (out of an array of 3), when the word penny is given, would also be able to choose the comparison spoken word *penny* shown the picture of the penny without being previously taught this correlation (Sidman, 1994).

• Transitivity is the most crucial test for demonstrating stimulus equivalence. A third, untrained relation emerges as a result of being taught the first two relations. (A=C and C=A) "…emerges as a product of training two other stimulus-stimulus relations" (Cooper, Heron, & Heward, 2007, p. 399).

The following equation demonstrates the basic principals of stimulus equivalence:
1. If A = B, and
2. B = C, then
3. A = C

Sidman and Tailby (1982)

When using stimulus equivalence, decide what relations are to be taught (i.e. spoken word to picture, picture to written word, drawing to real-life picture, etc.). Decide which order the conditional relations are to be taught. Teach the relations A=B and B=C to mastery criteria. Once mastery criteria are met for the first two relations, test for reflexivity, symmetry, and transitivity using the same criteria. If the participant demonstrates these relations without having been previously been taught them, they will have acquired the third relation C=A that demonstrates the most important test for stimulus equivalence.

Assessment:

• Ask the supervisee to explain the concept of stimulus equivalence.
• Ask the supervisee to name the three tests that demonstrate the basic principles of stimulus equivalence and describe each of these.
• Ask the supervisee to give examples of some new concepts that might be taught through stimulus equivalence

Relevant Literature:

Cooper J.O., Heron T.E., Heward W.L. (2007). *Applied behavior analysis* (2nd ed.) Upper Saddle River, NJ: Pearson
Sidman, M. (1971) Reading and auditory-visual equivalences. *Journal of Speech & Hearing Research*, Volume 14(1), 5-13.
Sidman, M. (1994). *Equivalence Relations and Behavior: A Research Story.* Boston: Author's Cooperative.
Sidman, M. and Tailby, W. (1982). Conditional Discrimination vs. Matching to Sample: An Expansion of the Testing Paradigm. *Journal of Experimental Analysis Behavior*, 37: 5–22.

Related Lessons:
E-06 Use stimulus equivalence procedures.
E-13 Use matching-to-sample procedures.
FK-11 environment, stimulus, stimulus class
FK-12 stimulus equivalence
FK-13 reflexive relations (US-UR)
FK-24 stimulus control
FK-28 transitive, reflexive, surrogate motivating operations
FK-35 stimulus discrimination

E-07 Plan for behavioral contrast effects

What is behavioral contrast?

- George Reynolds first presented behavioral contrast in 1961. He defined behavioral contrast as "an increase in the rate of responding in one component of a multiple schedule when certain changes occur in the other component" (p. 60).

- Cooper, Heron and Heward (2007) state that behavioral contrast "can occur as a function of a change in reinforcement or punishment density on one component of a multiple schedule" (p. 337).

Example of Behavioral Contrast

- Cooper, Heron and Heward (2007) give a good example of behavioral contrast to illustrate the concept; "...a pigeon pecks a backlit key, which alternates between blue and green, reinforcement is delivered on the same schedule on both keys, and the bird pecks at approximately the same rate regardless of the key's color." (p. 337). However, this changes so that responses on one component of the schedule are punished, i.e., pecks on the blue key are punished because reinforcement is not delivered, but pecks on the other (green) key continue to produce reinforcement. As a result, rate of responding decreases on the blue key and rate of responding on the green key increases, even though no more reinforcement is delivered from the green key than before.

Plan for the effects of behavioral contrast

- It is important to consider *prior* to beginning an intervention, whether behavioral contrast may occur as a result of that planned intervention. If behavioral contrast is a possibility; then planning for its occurrence is crucial.

- Cooper, Heron and Heward (2007, p. 338) suggest that one way to minimize or completely prevent the contrast effects of punishment is to plan the intervention so that the consequence is consistently applied to the target behavior across all relevant environments and stimulus conditions. All those involved in the client's life that may be required to deliver the consequence, will need to be thoroughly trained to ensure its consistent implementation.

- Additionally, reinforcement will need to be minimized, or where possible, withheld, when the target behavior has occurred. Similarly, training will need to be provided to all those involved so that the client isn't receiving reinforcement when the target behavior is emitted.

Assessment:

- Ask your Supervisee to define behavioral contrast.
- Ask your Supervisee to describe what will happen in this example if behavioral contrast is in effect:
  - A child has been playing with two musical toys, allocating an equal amount of time playing with each toy. One of the musical toys is yellow and one of the musical toys is red. The red toy's battery begins to give out so that when the child presses the button, sometimes the music is not produced. However, the yellow musical toy continues to work well and music is produced each time the child pushes the button. What will happen to the rate of responding for each of the musical toys? **(Answer = the rate of responding on the red musical toy will decrease and the rate**

of responding on the yellow toy will increase, even though there isn't any additional reinforcement being produced from the yellow toy).

Relevant Literature:

Cooper, J. O., Heron, T. E., & Heward, W. L. (2007). Applied Behavior Analysis, 2nd ed. Upper Saddle River, New Jersey: Pearson Prentice Hall.

Fagan, J. W. (1978). Behavioral contrast in infants. *Infant behavior and development, 2*, 101-112.

Hantula, D. A., & Crowell, C. R. (1994). Behavioral contrast in a two-option analogue task of financial decision making. *Journal of Applied Behavior Analysis, 27*, 607-617.

McSweeney, F. K., & Weatherly, J. N. (1998). Habituation to the reinforcer may contribute to multiple-schedule behavioral contrast. *Journal of the Experimental Analysis of Behavior, 69*, 199-221.

Reynolds, G. S. (1961a). Behavioral contrast. *Journal of Experimental Analysis of Behavior, 4*, 57 – 71.

Reynolds, G. S. (1963). Some limitations on behavioral contrast and induction during successive discrimination. *Journal of Experimental Analysis of Behavior, 6*, 131-139.

Tarbox, J., & Parrott Hayes, L. (2005). Verbal behavior and behavioral contrast in human subjects. *The Psychological Record, 55*, 419-437.

Weatherly, J. N., Melville, C. L., & McSweeney, F. K. (1996). Picking, pecking, and pressing: A cross-species demonstration of behavioral contrast. *The Psychological Record, 46*, 351-372.

Weatherly, J. N., King, B. M., Arthur, E. I. L. (2002). Rats' level pressing for 1% sucrose and food-pellet reinforcement: In search of negative behavioral contrast. *The Psychological Record, 52*, 507-529.

Related Lessons:
C-02: State and plan for the possible unwanted effects of punishment
D-15: Identify punishers
D-16: Use positive and negative punishment
D-17: Use appropriate parameters and schedules of punishment
D19: Use combinations of reinforcement with punishment and extinction
J-10: When a behavior is to be decreased, select an acceptable alternative behavior to be established or increased
K-02: Identify the contingencies governing the behavior of those responsible for carrying out behavior-change procedures and design interventions accordingly
FK-38: Behavioral contrast
FK-40: Matching law

E-08 Use the matching law and recognize factors influencing choice

<u>Definitions:</u>

Matching Law - "When two or more concurrent-interval schedules are available, the relative rate of response matches (or equals) the relative rate of reinforcement. More generally, the matching law states that the distribution of behavior between (or among) alternative sources of reinforcement is equal to the distribution of reinforcement for these alternatives" (Pierce & Cheney, 2013, p. 260).

Choice - "...the emission of one of two or more alternative and, usually, incompatible responses" (Catania, 2007, p.431).

Organisms are constantly confronted with making choices; the allocation of responding is based upon the probability of reinforcement for that response. There are also other variables known to effect response allocation such as magnitude of reinforcement, quality of reinforcement, delay to reinforcement, and duration of reinforcement (Baum, 1974). If a variable that is affecting responding on a particular option cannot be identified, this is known as *bias*. An example of bias might be a right-handed person responding on an option to the right side. This variable and others are accounted for using different coefficients in the matching law.

Multiple basic and applied studies with humans and non-humans have demonstrated that behavior is allocated to response options based on reinforcement schedules available on those options (Baum, 1974; Borrero & Vollmer, 2002; Epling & Pierce, 1983).

There is debate about the status of the matching law as a convenient description vs. a fundamental property of behavior (c.f., Catania, 1981; Killeen, 2015, Rachlin, 1971)

<u>Assessment:</u>
- Have supervisee define choice and describe the matching law.
- Have supervisee describe variables known to influence response allocation among alternatives.

- Have supervisee set up and conduct an experiment involving concurrent schedules with different magnitudes/qualities/delays/duration of reinforcement on different options.
- Have supervisee use the equation for the matching law to investigate matching for two different responses.

<u>Relevant Literature:</u>

Baum, W. M. (1974). On two types of deviation from the matching law: Bias and undermatching. *Journal of the experimental analysis of behavior, 22*(1), 231.

Baum, W. M. (1979). Matching, undermatching, and overmatching in studies of choice. *Journal of the experimental analysis of behavior, 32*(2), 269.

Borrero, J. C., & Vollmer, T. R. (2002). An application of the matching law to severe problem behavior. *Journal of Applied Behavior Analysis, 35*(1), 13-27.

Catania, A. C. (2007). Learning (Interim. *4ª. Ed.)* USA: Sloan Publishing.

Catania, A. C. (2012). Discussion: The flight from experimental analysis. *EUROPEAN JOURNAL OF BEHAVIOR ANALYSIS, 13*, 165-176.

Cooper, J. O., Heron, T. E., & Heward, W. L. (2007). *Applied behavior analysis.* Upper Saddle River, NJ: Pearson Education.

Epling, W. F., & Pierce, W. D. (1983). Applied behavior analysis: New directions from the laboratory. *The Behavior Analyst, 6*(1), 27.

Herrnstein, R. J. (1961). Relative and absolute strength of response as a function of frequency of reinforcement. *Journal of the experimental analysis of behavior, 4*(3), 267.

Killeen, P. R. (2015), The logistics of choice. Journal of the Experimental Analysis Behavior. doi: 10.1002/jeab.156

Pierce, W. D., & Cheney, C. D. (2013). *Behavior analysis and learning.* (5th ed.) New York, NY: Psychology Press.

Rachlin, H. (1971). On the tautology of the matching law. *Journal of the Experimental Analysis of Behavior, 15*(2), 249-251.

<u>Related Lessons:</u>
A-14 Design and implement choice measures.

E-09 Arrange high-probability request sequences

Using a high-probability (high-p) request sequence involves presenting a series of requests that the individual has a history of following before presenting a target request (low-p). The following is recommended in order to maximize the effectiveness of the high-p request sequence: (1) tasks/requests should already be in the learner's repertoire (i.e., the skill is considered mastered); (2) high-p requests should be presented rapidly; (3) the first low-p request should be presented immediately after reinforcement for high-p compliance; and (4) and salient reinforcers should be used for low-p requests (Cooper, Heron, & Heward, 2007). It is also recommended to avoid using low-difficulty tasks immediately after a maladaptive behavior that was triggered by a high-difficulty task (Sailors, Guess, Rutherford, & Baer, 1968). In the initial stages of acquisition of a low-p request, increasing the number of high-p requests increases the effectiveness of the high-p request sequence (Mace, 1996). High-p request sequences may be helpful in reducing the reinforcing value of escape from requests and the maladaptive behaviors that often occur when low-p requests are presented. (Cooper, Heron, & Heward, 2007)

There is a common misconception that the effects of the high-p sequence are related exclusively to the repeated delivery of the high-p demands. The dense schedule of reinforcement is also a necessary component for this procedure. Zuluaga & Normand (2008) tested the effects of the high-p sequence without reinforcement versus the high-p sequence with reinforcement. Compliance with low-p demands increased only when reinforcers were delivered after the high-p requests.

There are some discussions in the field about whether the high-p request sequence and behavioral momentum should be considered synonymous. In 1996, Nevin describes his concerns by suggesting that "translating the terms of the metaphor into the high-p procedure, or indeed any other application, encounters some uncertainties and entails a fair amount of speculation; thus, alternative accounts are surely possible" (p.554).

Assessment:

- Ask supervisee to demonstrate implementing a high-p request sequence with a client. Supervisor should provide modeling and feedback as necessary.

- Require that the supervisee reads and summarizes Zululaga & Normand (2008).

- Ask supervisee to describe why Nevin suggests that the high-p request sequence and behavioral momentum should not be considered synonymous.

Relevant Literature:

Cooper, J. O., Heron, T. E., & Heward, W. L. (2007). Antecedent interventions. *Applied Behavior Analysis* (pp. 486-499). Upper Saddle River, NJ: Pearson Prentice Hall.

Davis, C. A., & Reichle, J. (1996). Variant and invariant high-probability requests: Increasing appropriate behaviors in children with emotional-behavioral disorders. *Journal of Applied Behavior Analysis, 29*, 471-482.

Mace, F. C. (1996). In pursuit of general behavioral relations. *Journal of Applied Behavior Analysis, 29*, 557-514.

Mace, F. C., & Belfiore, P. (1990). Behavioral momentum in the treatment of escape-motivated stereotypy. *Journal of Applied Behavior Analysis, 23*(4), 507.

Nevin, J. A. (1996). The Momentum of Compliance. Journal of Applied Behavior Analysis, 29(4), 535–547.

Sailor, W., Guess, D., Rutherford, G., & Baer, D. M. (1968). Control of tantrum behavior by operant techniques during experimental verbal training. *Journal of Applied Behavior Analysis, 1*(3), 237-243.

Related Lessons:

D-01 Use positive and negative reinforcement.
D-02 Use appropriate parameters and schedules of reinforcement.
E-01 Use interventions based on manipulation of antecedents, such as motivating operations and discriminative stimuli.
E-10 Use the Premack principle.

E-10 Use the Premack principle

Definition:

The Premack principle - ..."a principle of reinforcement which states that an opportunity to engage in more probable behaviors (or activities) will reinforce less probable behaviors (or activities)."(Barton, 2013, p. 2345).

"For example, if a child often plays computer games (more probable) and avoids completing math problems (less probable), we might allow her to play the computer after (contingent upon) completing 15 math problems. Prior to the introduction of the Premack principle, systems of reinforcement were viewed as the contingency between a stimulus and behavior. The Premack principle expanded the existing reinforcement contingency of stimulus behavior to include contingencies between two behaviors. This principle is often referred to as 'grandma's rule' because grandmothers (or any caregivers) often apply this principle: 'you have to eat your vegetables (less probable) before you can have dessert (more probable)'" (Barton, 2013, p. 2345).

In education, the Premack principle is the basis for "first/then" strategies. "First/then" strategies consist of a teacher telling a student "First *X*, then *Y*" with *X* being a less preferred activity or task demand and *Y* being a more preferred activity contingent on the completion of *X*.

Premack principles use preferred activities as reinforcers to help increase engagement in less preferred activities or demands.

Example:
A father tells his teenage son, "When you have finished washing the dishes, you can watch TV."

Assessment:
- Have supervisee give examples of Premack's principle in his/her daily life.
- Have supervisee create a role play scenario in which he/she demonstrates the use of the Premack principle.
- Have supervisee find an article on the use of the Premack principle, summarize, and discuss benefits and limitations of use.

Relevant Literature:

Azrin, N. H., Vinas, V., & Ehle, C. T. (2007). Physical activity as reinforcement for classroom calmness of ADHD children: A preliminary study. *Child & Family Behavior Therapy, 29, 2,* 1-8.

Barton, E.E. (2013). Premack's Principle. In *Encyclopedia of Autism Spectrum Disorders.* Volkmar, F.R. (Ed.) (p. 2345) Springer New York: New York, NY.

Cooper, J.O., Heron, T.E. & Heward W.L. (2007). *Applied Behavior Analysis* (2nd Ed.), Upper Saddle River, NJ. Pearson Prentice Hall. 271-273, 277.

Mazur, J.E. (1975). The Matching Law and Quantifications Related to Premack's Principle. *Journal of Experimental Psychology: Animal Behavior Processes,* 1, 4, 374-386.

Sigafoos, J. (2005). From Premack to PECS: 25 Years of Progress in Communication Intervention for Individuals with Developmental Disabilities. *Educational Psychology,* 25, 6, 601-607.

Welsh, D.H., Bernstein, D.J., & Luthans, F. (1992). Application of the Premack Principle of Reinforcement to the Quality Performance of Service Employees. Journal of Organizational Behavior Management, 13, 1, 9.

Related Lessons:
D-01: Use positive and negative reinforcement
D-02: Use appropriate parameters and schedules of reinforcement.
I-07: Design and conduct preference assessments to identify putative reinforcers.

E-11 Use pairing procedures to establish new conditioned reinforcers

"Stimulus events or conditions that are present or that occur just before or simultaneous with the occurrence of other reinforcers (or punishers) may acquire the ability to reinforce (or punish) behavior when they later occur on their own as consequences. Called conditioned reinforcers or conditioned punishers, these stimulus changes function as reinforcers and punishers only because of their prior pairing with other reinforcers or punishers" (Cooper et al., 2007, p. 40).

Definition:
Conditioned reinforcer – "…a previously neutral stimulus change that has acquired the capability to function as a reinforcer through stimulus-stimulus pairing with one or more unconditioned or conditioned reinforcers" (Cooper et al., 2007, p. 269).

Some common conditioned reinforcers include social praise, tokens, and money because they are often paired with other reinforcers.

Conditioned reinforcers become stronger the more they are paired with other known reinforcers. For instance, paper money will likely not function as a reinforcer until he/she buy toys, candy, and other things that he enjoys with it. The more the child uses money to buy items that are appetitive, the more the paper money becomes a conditioned reinforcer.

The more items the conditioned reinforcer can "buy", the less sensitive to motivating operations they become. This is called generalized conditioned reinforcement. The more reinforcers that have been paired with the stimulus, the more generalized the conditioned reinforcer is.

Assessment:
- Have supervisee create a token economy and explain how it would be used as a conditioned reinforcer in their professional setting.
- Have supervisee create a list of conditioned and unconditioned reinforcers and explain the difference between the two.
- Have supervisee explain the concept of a generalized conditioned reinforcer and how this is different from typical conditioned reinforcers.

Relevant Literature:
Cooper, J.O., Heron, T.E. & Heward W.L. (2007). *Applied Behavior Analysis* (2nd Ed.), Upper Saddle River, NJ. Pearson Prentice Hall. 40-41, 269-270.
Williams, B.A. & Fantino, E. (1978). Effects on choice of reinforcement delay and conditioned reinforcement. *Journal of Experimental Analysis of Behavior*, 29, 1, 77-86.
Engelmann, S. (1975). *Your child can succeed.* New York, NY: Simon and Schuster. (pp. 98-100).
Morse, W.H. & Kelleher, R.T. (1977). Determinants of reinforcement and punishment. In W.K. Honig & J.E.R. Staddon (Eds.), *Handbook of operant behavior* (pp. 174-200). Upper Saddle River, NJ: Prentice Hall.

Related Lessons:
C-01: State and plan for the possible unwanted effects of reinforcement.
D-01: Use positive and negative reinforcement.
D-02: Use appropriate parameters and schedules of reinforcement.
E-02: Use discrimination training procedures.
F-02: Use token economies and other conditioned reinforcement systems.
I-07: Design and conduct preference assessments to identify putative reinforcers.
J-04: Select intervention strategies based on client preferences.
J-11: Program for stimulus and response generalization.
FK-14: Respondent conditioning (CS-CR)
FK-16: Respondent-operant interactions
FK-18: Conditioned reinforcement
FK-21: Schedules of reinforcement and punishment
FK-27: Conditioned motivating operations
FK-34: Conditional discriminations

E-12 Use Errorless Learning Procedures

Definition:

Errorless learning - an "approach whereby the task is manipulated to eliminate/reduce errors. Tasks are executed in such a way that the subject is unlikely to make errors" (Fillingham, Hodgson, Sage, & Ralph, 2003, p. 339).

Errorless learning techniques include most-to-least prompt fading or stimulus shaping/fading techniques. Prompts are removed gradually as the individual becomes more adept with the skill, thereby reducing the likelihood of errors. To apply errorless learning, behavioral strategies utilized may include: response prevention (e.g. only S+ is presented allowing for only correct responding or physical guidance is provided with instruction so incorrect responses are not possible); verbal prompt fading; modeling; stimulus fading (e.g. emphasizing a physical dimension of the stimuli to evoke a correct response such as by illuminating the correct selection, S+, and presenting the incorrect selection, S-, in a dimmer format); or stimulus shaping (e.g. increasing likelihood of correct responding by gradually changing the shape of the stimulus to maintain correct responding).

The advantages of errorless learning include that it removes negative side effects involved with trial-and-error learning and that it is proven particularly effective among individuals that suffer from brain damage or have a developmental disorder. The disadvantages include cost, time-intensity, and maybe considered less natural than trial-and-error learning (Mueller, Palkovic & Maynard, 2007).

Trial-and-error learning, being presented with stimuli in which both the correct selection

(S+) and incorrect selection (S-) are available, can lead to adverse side effects due to the possibility of incorrect responding and failure to access reinforcers. Research has shown that this can result in aggression, negative emotional responses and stimulus overselectivity (Mueller et al., 2007).

Assessment:

- Have supervisee demonstrate the difference between trial-and-error learning and errorless learning on the job or during role-play.
- Have supervisee describe how and when prompts will be faded to promote independent responding.

Relevant Literature:

Fillingham, J.K,, Hodgson, C., Sage, K., & Ralph, M.A. (2003). The application of errorless learning to aphasic disorders: A review of theory and practice. *Neuropsychological Rehabiliation, 13*(3), 337-363.

Mueller, M.M., Palkovic, C.M., & Maynard, C.S. (2007). Errorless learning: review and practical application for teaching children with pervasive developmental disorders. *Psychology in the Schools, 44*(7), 691-700.

Terrace, H.S. (1963). Discrimination learning with and without "errors". *Journal of the Experimental Analysis of Behavior, 6*(1), 1-27.

Related Lessons:

D-03 Use prompts and prompt fading
D-04 Use modeling and imitation training
FK-24 Stimulus control

E-13 Use matching-to-sample procedures

Definition:

Matching-to-sample - "A procedure for investigating conditional relations and stimulus equivalence. A matching-to-sample trial begins with the participant making a response that presents or reveals the sample stimulus; next, the sample stimulus may or may not be removed, and two or more comparison stimuli are presented. The participant then selects one the comparison stimuli. Responses that select a comparison stimulus that matches the sample stimulus are reinforced, and no reinforcement is provided for responses selecting the nonmatching comparison stimuli" (Cooper, Heron, & Heward, 2007, p. 699).

Example:

A teacher presents a student with a picture of an apple. The teacher then lays out three other picture cards away from the original picture of an apple. One picture card depicts an apple, the second picture card depicts a banana, and the final picture card depicts an orange. The teacher holds up the initial picture card depicting an apple and states, "match". The student takes the picture of an apple and places it on top of the corresponding picture of an apple. The teacher says, "Great job" and gives the student a high five.

Assessment:

- Have supervisee create a mock lesson displaying match-to-sample task. He/she must create a match-to-sample program, a data sheet to record responses, and task materials needed to complete the task. Have him/her role-play this task scenario with supervisor. Supervisor will play the role of the client and supervisee will play the role of the teacher or therapist.
- Have supervisee create a lesson that demonstrates stimulus equivalence. He/she must start with match-to-sample task and then use other topographies of sample stimulus to display stimulus equivalence.
- Have supervisee describe the match-to-sample procedure and stimulus equivalence. Have him/her discuss how match-to-sample procedures can be implemented to test for stimulus equivalence.

Relevant Literature:

Cooper, J.O., Heron, T.E. & Heward W.L. (2007). *Applied Behavior Analysis* (2nd Ed.), Upper Saddle River, NJ. Pearson Prentice Hall. 398-401.

Cumming, W.W. & Berryman, R. (1965). The complex discriminated operant: Studies of matching-to-sample and related problems. In D.I. Mostofsky (Ed.), *Stimulus Generalization* (pp. 284-333). Palo Alto, CA: Stanford University Press.

Fields, L., Garrutto, M., & Watanabe, M. (2010). Varieties of stimulus control in matching-to-sample: A kernel analysis. *The Psychological Record*, 60, 3-26.

Sidman, M., Wilson-Morris, M., & Kirk, B. (1986). Matching-to-sample procedures and the development of equivalence relations: The role of naming. *Analysis and Interventions in Developmental Disabilities*, 6, 1, 1-19.

Related Lessons:

D-03: Use prompts and prompt fading.
D-08: Use discrete-trials and free-operant arrangements.
E-02: Use discrimination training procedures.
E-06: Use stimulus equivalence procedures.
E-12: Use errorless learning procedures.

F-01 Use self-management strategies

Definition:

Self-management - "...behavior that a person emits to influence another behavior" (Cooper, Heron, & Heward, 2007, p. 577).

Skinner (1953) first outlined the idea of self-management with his theories on self-control. He defined self-control as, "When a man controls himself, chooses a course of action, thinks out the solution to a problem, or strives towards an increase in self-knowledge, he is behaving. He controls himself precisely as he would control the behavior of anyone else- through the manipulation of variables of which behavior is a function" (pp. 228-229).

"All self-control- or self-management- tactics can be operationalized in terms of two behaviors: (a) the target behavior a person wants to change (Skinner's controlled response) and (b) the self-management behavior (Skinner's controlling response) emitted to control the target behavior" (Cooper et al., 2007, p. 577).

Applications include "helping a person be more effective and efficient in his daily life, replacing bad habits with good ones, accomplishing difficult tasks, and achieving personal goals" (Cooper et al., 2007, p. 579).

Example:
- Skipping lunch (controlling behavior) to enjoy all three courses of your dinner (controlled behavior).
- Leaving a bag of garbage near the front door (controlling behavior) to remind you to take it to the dumpster next time you leave the house (controlled behavior).

Assessment:
- Have supervisee identify and define a personal target behavior they would like to increase or decrease. (i.e., exercising more, eating less, studying more, swearing less, etc...).
- Have him/her research various self-management studies relevant to the target behavior they want to decrease.
- Have supervisee create guidelines and criteria for their self-management project to be reviewed by supervisor.

Relevant Literature:

Agran, M. (Ed.) (1997). *Self-directed learning: Teaching self-determination skills.* Pacific Grove, CA. Brooks/Cole.

Baum, W.M. (2005). *Understanding behaviorism: Science, behavior, and culture* (2nd ed.). Malden, MA. Blackwell Publishing.

Cooper, J. O., Heron, T. E., & Heward, W. L. (2007). *Applied behavior analysis.* (2nd ed.) Upper Saddle River, NJ: Pearson Education, 576-612, 646, 648-650.

Epstein, R. (1997). Skinner as self-manager. *Journal of Applied Behavior Analysis, 30,* 545-568.

Kazdin, A.E. (2001). *Behavior modification in applied settings* (6th ed.). Belmont, CA. Wadsworth.

Skinner, B.F. (1953). *Science and human behavior.* New York: MacMillan, pp. 228-240.

Thoreson, C.E., & Mahoney, M.J. (1974). *Behavioral self-control.* New York: Holt, Rinehart, & Winston.

Watson, D.L., & Tharp, R.G. (2007). *Self-directed behavior: Self-modification for personal adjustment* (9th ed.). Belmont, CA. Wadsworth/Thompson Learning.

Related Lessons:

B-03: Systematically arrange independent variables to demonstrate their effects on dependent variables.

F-02: Use token economies and other conditioned reinforcement systems.

I-01: Define behavior in observable and measurable terms.

I-06: Make recommendations regarding behaviors that must be established, maintained, increased, or decreased.

J-01: State intervention goals in observable and measurable terms.

J-02: Identify potential interventions based on assessment results and the best available scientific evidence.

J-10: When a behavior is to be decreased, select an acceptable alternative behavior to be established or increased.

FK-18: Conditioned reinforcement.

FK-20: Conditioned punishment.

FK-31: Behavioral contingencies.

F-02 Use token economies and other conditioned reinforcement systems

Definition:

Conditioned Reinforcer - "A stimulus change that functions as a reinforcer because of prior pairing with one or more other reinforcers" (Cooper, Heron, & Heward, 2007, p. 692).

"Token economies are used as a method of strengthening a behavior, or increasing its frequency, because the tokens are a way of 'paying' children for completing tasks and the children can then use these tokens to buy desired activities or items" (Miltenberger, 2008, p. 513).

A token economy uses a conditioned reinforcer, or token, as currency for a student to exchange for a backup reinforcer (i.e., tangible items, edibles, activities, etc…) based on earning a certain amount of tokens for desired target behaviors.

The strength of the token is derived from its being paired with other reinforcers (also referred to as a backup reinforcer). If the backup reinforcer loses value due to satiation, the token will subsequently lose its effectiveness.

Miltenberger (2008) listed seven components that need to be defined before implementing a token economy. These include: identifying the desired target behavior to be strengthened, identifying tokens to be used as conditioned reinforcement, identifying backup reinforcers, outlining a reinforcement schedule for token delivery, identifying the amount of tokens needed to exchange for reinforcers, identifying the time and place to exchange tokens, and identifying if a response cost contingency would be necessary for the individual.

Assessment:

- Have supervisee review literature on token economies and present a brief literature review on the topic. Have him/her identify strengths and weaknesses of token economies, define any key terms, and discuss future research directions.
- Have supervisee develop a token economy and present this program. Have him/her identify and create tokens and a token board, identify a list of backup reinforcers, and create guidelines on the implementation of this program.

- Have supervisee define cost response and discuss how it relates to token economies.

Relevant Literature:

Ayllon, T. & Azrin, N. (1968). *The Token Economy: A Motivational System for Therapy and Rehabilitation.* New York: Appleton Century Crofts.

Cooper, J., Heron, T., & Heward, W. (2007). *Applied Behaviour Analysis.* New Jersey: Pearson Education.

Foxx, R. (1998). A comprehensive treatment program for inpatient adolescents. *Behavioural Interventions, 13,* 67-77.

Hackenberg, T. (2009). Token Reinforcement: A Review and Analysis. *Journal of the Experimental Analysis of Behaviour, 91,* 257-286.

Kazdin, A. (1982). The Token Economy: A Decade Later. *Journal of Applied Behaviour Analysis, 15,* 431-445.

Kazdin, A., & Bootzin, R. (1972). The Token Economy: An Evaluative Review. *Journal of Applied Behaviour Analysis, 5,* 343-372.

Malott & Trojan-Suarez, (2006). *Principles of Behaviour.* New Jersey: Pearson Prentice Hall.

Matson, J. & Boisjoli (2009). The token economy for children with intellectual disability and/or autism: A review. *Research in Developmental Disabilities, 30,* 240-248.

Miltenberger, R. (2008). *Behaviour Modification.* Belmont, CA. Wadsworth Publishing.

Tarbox, R., Ghezzi, P., & Wilson G. (2004). The effects of token reinforcement on attending in a young child with autism. *Behavioural Interventions, 21,* 156-164.

Related Lessons:

C-01: State and plan for the possible unwanted effects of reinforcement.
D-01: Use positive and negative reinforcement.
D-02: Use appropriate parameters and schedules of reinforcement.
D-19: Use combinations of reinforcement with punishment and extinction.
D-21: Use differential reinforcement
E-04: Use contingency contracting.
E-05: Use independent, interdependent, and dependent group contingencies.
I-07: Design and conduct preference assessments to identify putative reinforcers.
FK-18: Conditioned reinforcement.
FK-21: Schedules of reinforcement and punishment.
FK-31: Behavioral contingencies.
FK-41: Contingency-shaped behavior

F-03 Use Direct Instruction

Definition:

Direct instruction - a teaching method "…emphasizing the use of specified teacher directions, programmed instruction and presentation of materials, examples, and prompts, the use of reinforcement and mastery learning principles, regular and direct assessment, and teaching prerequisite skills." (Callahan, Shukla-Mehta, & Wie, 2010, p. 78).

Direct instruction was developed to improve academic skills of elementary school students with learning challenges. This model of instructional design was proposed by Engelmann and Becker (Becker, et al., 1975). Direct instruction relies on scripted lessons implemented by a directly trained teacher provided to small-group of learners. These scripted lessons include a lot of examples and non-examples. Students respond in unison when asked by a teacher and practice skills in groups until reaching a mastery level. Students and teachers systematically measure and teachers analyze students' performance. Those who follow the DI model believe that the learner knows better; that all children can be taught. If a student fails, this is teacher's fault. Additionally, the process of teaching includes hierarchy of instruction complexity: basic skills should be taught before advancing to more complex skills.

Assessment:
- Have supervisee define direct instruction. Have him/her identify and explain the characteristics and methodology associated with the curriculum.
- Have supervisee identify the differences between direct instruction and other teaching methodologies.
- Have supervisee list the pros and cons of implementing direct instruction. Have him/her describe if they would use direct instruction over other methodologies and curricula and why.

Relevant Literature:

Callahan, K., Shukla-Mehta, S., MaGee, S., & Wie, M. (2010). ABA vs. TEACCH: The case for defining and validating comprehensive treatment models in autism. *Journal of Autism and Developmental Disorders*, 40, 1, 74-88.

Cooper, J. O., Heron, T. E., & Heward, W. L. (2007). *Applied behavior analysis.* (2nd ed.). Upper Saddle River, NJ: Pearson Education.

Moran, D.J. & Mallot, R.W. (2004). *Evidence Based Educational Methods.* (1st ed.). San Diego, CA: Elsevier Academic Press. pp. 81-91.

Ledford, J.R., Lane, J.D., Elam, K.L., & Wolery, M. (2012). Using response-prompting procedures during small group direct-instruction: Outcomes and procedural variations. *American Journal on intellectual and Developmental Disabilities*, 117, 5, 413-434.

Gersten, R., & Keating, T. (1987). Long-term benefits from direct instruction. *Educational Leadership*, 44, 6, 28-31.

Gersten, R., Keating, T., & Becker, W. (1988). The continued impact of the direct instruction model: Longitudinal studies of follow through students. *Education and Treatment of Children*, 11, 4, 318-327.

Gersten, R., Woodward, J., & Darch, C. (1986). Direct instruction: A research-based approach to curriculum design and teaching. *Exceptional Children*, 53, 1, 17-31.

Graves, A. W. (1986). Effects of direct instruction and meta-comprehension training on finding main ideas. *Learning Disabilities Research*, 1, 2, 90-100.

Related Lessons:
A-07: Measure trials to criterion.
D-03: Use prompts and prompt fading.
D-08: Use discrete trials and free-operant arrangements.
J-02: Identify potential interventions based on assessment results and the best available scientific evidence.
J-11: Program for stimulus and response generalization.
J-12: Program for maintenance.
J-14: Arrange instructional procedures to promote generative learning (i.e., derived learning).

F-04 Use precision teaching

Precision teaching is a methodology of teaching which involves measuring performance of a learner and making changes based on these data. Precision teaching was proposed by Ogden Lindsley in 1964 in an article "Direct Measurement and Prosthesis of Retarded Behavior".

There are four steps of precision teaching process:

1. **Pinpoint** - means to describe an actual movement which a learner needs to perform in a specific time interval to show an improvement on learning behavior.
2. **Record** - means that a learner or a teacher collect data on pinpointed behavior regularly and display these data graphically using the Standard Celeration Chart (the SCC).
3. **Change** - means that the teacher analyzes the data using guidelines of analyzing the SCC (Graf & Lindsley, 2002) and quickly makes changes in a current instructional method if needed.
4. **Try Again** - means that the teacher keeps exploring the best instructional methods for those learners who need more help and provides the learners with the opportunities to practice until the mastery level.

Precision teaching follows four principles described by Kubina (2012): "(i) a focus on observable behavior, (ii) the use of frequency as data metric, (iii) graphing student performance data on a Standard Celeration Chart, and (iv) making decisions based on performance data" (As cited in Cooper, Heron, Heward, 2007, p. 142).

Example:

- A teacher's objective is to teach a student to say and write an answer when vocally asked simple math problems questions. The teacher will record how many times a student answers correctly in one minute interval. These data will be collected over the next several weeks and progress will be charted using a Standard Celebration Chart. Decisions about the teaching procedure will be made depending on the performance data.

Non- example:

- A teacher's objective is to teach students to solve simple math problems. Percent correct are collected across the quarter. At the end of the quarter a report card will be sent to the student's home.

Assessment:

- Have supervisee identify the benefits of adding precision teaching to a curriculum.
- Have supervisee identify and describe the key features of precision teaching.
- Have supervisee describe the parts of a Standard Celeration Chart. Have him/her discuss the benefits of using this graphic display to track data.

Relevant Literature:

Cooper, J. O., Heron, T. E., & Heward, W. L. (2007). *Applied behavior analysis*. Upper Saddle River, NJ: Pearson Education, 139-144.

Cooper, J.O. (2000). Tutoring Joe: Winning with the precision teaching team. In W.L. Heward (ed.) *Exceptional Children: An introduction to special education* (6th ed.) Upper Saddle River, NJ: Merrill, 268-270.

Kerr, K.P., Smyth, P., & McDowell, C. (2003). Precision teaching children with autism: Helping design effective programmes.

Early Childhood Development and Care, 173, 4, 399-410.

Hughes, J.C., Beverley, M., & Whitehead, J. (2007). Using precision teaching to increase the fluency of word reading with problem readers. *European Journal of Behavior Analysis*, 8, 221-238.

Kubina, R. M. (2012). *Precision teaching book.* [S.l.]: Greatness Achieved Pub Co.

Kubina, R.M., Morrison, R., & Lee, D.L. (2002). Benefits of adding precision teaching to behavioral interventions for students with autism. *Behavioral Interventions*, 17, 233-246.

Potts, L., Eshleman, J.W., & Cooper, J.O. (1993). Ogden R. Lindsley and the historical development of precision teaching. *The Behavior Analyst*, 2, 16, 177-189.

Related Lessons:

A-01: Measure frequency (i.e., count)

A-07: Measure trials to criterion.

F-03: Use Direction Instruction

H-01: Select a measurement system to obtain representative data given the dimensions of the behavior and the logistics of observing and recording.

H-02: Select a schedule of observation and recording periods.

H-03: Select a data display that effectively communicates relevant quantitative relations.

H-04: Evaluate changes in level, trend, and variability.

H-05: Evaluate temporal relations between observed variables (within and between sessions, times series).

J-15: Base decision-making on data displayed in various formats.

FK-33: Functional relations.

F-05 Use personalized systems of instruction (PSI)

Personalized system of instruction (PSI) was created by Fred S. Keller. PSI uses self-paced modules with study guides to help direct students' learning. Proctors are used to help students with the material and lectures are not as common compared to traditional teaching formats. PSI focuses on self-paced learning by the student rather than teacher directed instruction. Specific criteria on mastery tests are required before moving on to the next module. Keller (1968) summarized his writings from 1967 describing features of this type of training:

1. The go-at-your-own-pace component
2. The unit-perfection requirement for advancement
3. The use of lectures and demonstrations sparingly but not for critical information
4. The promotion of written word in teacher-student communication
5. The use of proctors for repeated testing, immediate scoring, answering questions, and personal-social part of the educational process

Assessment:

- Have supervisee identify the key components of personalized Systems of Instruction (PSI).

- Have supervisee provide benefits and drawbacks for instruction using PSI.

- Have supervisee choose a topic and create a mock PSI curriculum on that topic. Include modules, competency exams, and guidelines for other considerations when using PSI for that topic.

Relevant Literature:

Axelrod, S. (1992). Disseminating an effective educational technology. *Journal of Applied Behavior Analysis*, 1, 25, 31-35.

Buskist, W., Cush, D., & DeGrandpre, R. J. (1991). The life and times of PSI. *Journal of Behavioral Education*, 1, 215–234.

Keller, F. S. (1994). The Fred S. Keller School: CABAS at work. *The Current Repertoire*, 10, 3–4.

Keller, F. S. (1968). Goodbye, teacher. *Journal of Applied Behavior Analysis*, 1, 79–89.

Keller, F. S., & Sherman, G. (1982). *The PSI handbook*. Lawrence, KS: TRI Publications.

Twyman, J.S. (1992). The Fred S. Keller School. *Journal of Applied Behavior Analysis*, 4, 31, 695-701.

Eyre, H.L. (2007) Keller's personalized system of instruction: Was it fleeting fancy or is there a revival on the horizon? The Behavior Analyst, 8, 3, 317-324.

Related Lessons:

F-01: Use self-management strategies.

F-04: Use precision teaching.

J-14: Arrange instructional procedures to promote generative learning (i.e., derived relations).

F-06 Use incidental teaching

Definition:

Incidental teaching - When the "instructor assesses the child's ongoing interests, follows the child's lead, restricts access to high interest items, and constructs a lesson within the natural context, with a presumably more motivated child." (Anderson & Romanczyk, 1999, p. 169)

Incidental teaching requires an instructor to use moments in the natural environment as teaching opportunities. It can be used to teach language based skills, social skills, play skills, or other skills as well.

Example:

- Todd often struggles to initiate play with his peers during recess. His teacher decided to go over and prompt Todd to introduce himself to Mike and ask him to play a game.

Non-example:

Rich wanted to help teach Todd multiplication, so he gave him a worksheet and sat down with him to go through the problems one by one.

Assessment:

- Have supervisee define and describe incidental teaching.
- Have supervisee describe how they use incidental teaching at work to teach various skills.
- Have supervisce describe the pros and cons of incidental teaching.

Relevant Literature:

Anderson, S. R., & Romancyzk, R. G. (1999). Early intervention for young children with autism: Continuum-based behavioral models. *Journal of the Association for Persons with Severe Handicaps*, 24, 162–173.

Cooper, J. O., Heron, T. E., & Heward, W. L. (2007). *Applied behavior analysis*. Upper Saddle River, NJ: Pearson Education, 448, 542, 634.

Hart, B. & Risley, T.R. (1975) Incidental teaching of language in the preschool. *Journal of Applied Behavior Analysis*, 8, 4, 411-420.

McGee, G.G., & Daly, T. (2007). Incidental Teaching of Age-Appropriate Social Phrases to Children with Autism. *Research and Practice for Persons with Severe Disabilities*, 32, 112-123.

McGee, G.G., Morrier, M.J., & Daly, T. (1999) An Incidental Teaching Approach to Early Intervention for Toddlers with Autism. *Research and Practice for Persons with Severe Disabilities*, 24, 133-146.

McGee, G. G., Krantz, P. J., Mason, D., & McClannahan, L. E. (1983). A modified incidental-teaching procedure for autistic youth: acquisition and generalization of receptive object labels. Journal of Applied Behavior Analysis, 16(3), 329–338.

Related Lessons:

B-03: Systematically arrange independent variables to demonstrate their effects on dependent variables.

D-04: Use modeling and imitation training.

D-05: Use shaping.

D-11: Use mand training.

J-06: Select intervention strategies based on supporting environments.

J-11: Program for stimulus and response generalization.

FK-44: Mands.

F-07 Use functional communication training

Definition:

Functional communication training (FCT) - "…an application of differential reinforcement of alternative behaviors (DRA) because the intervention develops an alternative communicative response as an antecedent to diminish the problem behavior" (Fisher, Kuhn, & Thompson, 1998, p. 543).

The alternative response can include vocalizations, sign language, communication boards and devices, picture cards, or gestures.

Carr and Durand (1985) used a two-step process to demonstrate how to deliver FCT. First they completed a functional behavior assessment to identify the stimuli with known reinforcing properties that maintain the problem behavior, and second, they used those stimuli as reinforcers to develop an alternative behavior to replace the problem behavior.

Guidelines for the effective use of functional communication training include providing a dense schedule of reinforcement, fading prompts, and the appropriate reinforcement schedule thinning after the response is at strength.

Example:

Rob was throwing books at his teacher every time he was asked to do a math worksheet. After completing a functional analysis, Rob's teacher found throwing books was maintained by access to escape. Rob was taught to ask for a break when he was doing math instead of throwing something at his teacher. This response, paired with pre-teaching and prompt fading, helped replace the problematic behavior.

Assessment:

- Have supervisee identify the advantages and disadvantages of functional communication training.
- Have supervisee identify some common guidelines for using FCT.
- Have supervisee describe instance when he/she used FCT in a professional setting.

- Have supervisee describe how functional behavior assessment (FBA) and differential reinforcement of alternative behaviors (DRA) relate to the use of FCT.

Relevant Literature:

Cooper, J. O., Heron, T. E., & Heward, W. L. (2007). *Applied behavior analysis.* Upper Saddle River, NJ: Pearson Education, 494-496.

Durand, V.M. (1999). Functional communication training using assistive devices: Recruiting natural communities of reinforcement. *Journal of Applied Behavior Analysis*, 32, 247-267.

Carr, E.G., & Durand, V.M. (1985). Reducing behavior problems through functional communication training. *Journal of Applied Behavior Analysis*, 18, 111-126.

Durand, V.M, & Carr, E.G. (1992). An analysis of maintenance following functional communication training. *Journal of Applied Behavior Analysis*, 25, 777-794.

Fisher, W.W., Kuhn, D.E., & Thompson, R.H. (1998). Establishing discriminative control of responding using functional and alternative reinforcers during functional communication training. *Journal of Applied Behavior Analysis*, 31, 543-560.

Hanley, G.P., Iwata, B.A., & Thompson, R.H. (2001). Reinforcement schedule thinning following treatment with functional communication training. *Journal of Applied Behavior Analysis*, 34, 17-38.

Related Lessons:

D-02: Use appropriate parameters and schedules of reinforcement.

D-03: Use prompts and prompt fading.

D-04: Use modeling and imitation training.

D-05: Use shaping.

D-10: Use echoic training.

D-11: Use mand training.

D-21: Use differential reinforcement

E-01: Use interventions based on manipulation of antecedents

I-03: Design and implement individualized behavioral assessment procedures.

I-04: Design and implement the full range of functional assessment procedures.

F-08 Use augmentative communication systems

"A set of procedures and processes by which an individual's communication skills (i.e., production as well as comprehension) can be maximized for functional and effective communication. It involves supplementing or replacing natural speech and/or writing with aided (e.g. picture communication symbols, line drawing, Blissymbols, and tangible objects) and/or unaided symbols (e.g. manual signs, gestures, and finger spelling)" (American Speech-Language-Hearing Association, 2002).

Augmentative communication includes any modality that supplements a person with difficulties engaging in spoken language. This can include gestures, sign language, PECS, electronic devices, picture books, etc…

The use of augmentative communication should be considered as a way to allow the user to access reinforcement from the natural environment. Often functionally equivalent responses can be taught to replace problematic behavior therefore leading to a decrease in that behavior (Durand, 1999).

Teaching of functional communication using augmentative communication devices should be taught using the same strategies to teach other skills (prompt fading, reinforcement considerations, generalization considerations, etc.)

Augmentative communication systems should not be confused with the long-discredited "facilitated communication" which is a pseudoscientific attempt at getting people with developmental disabilities to communicate.

Example:
- Bill uses pictures to tell his teachers when he wants.

- Ralph is eating snack and signs "more" to his teacher after running out of crackers to eat. She gladly hands him more and praises him for using his words.
- Hillary uses an app on a tablet device that generates speech sounds so others respond to her.

Non-examples:
- Bill wants more crackers so tells his teacher, "I want some more, please." using spoken word.
- Bill wants more crackers so he hits his fist on the table and screams. His teacher says, "oh, you're still hungry? Here are a few more crackers".

Assessment:
- Have supervisee research various augmentative communication systems. Have him/her choose a system and describe it in detail.
- Have supervisee identify the benefits of using alternative communication systems for non-vocal-verbal students.
- Have supervisee describe situations where they would seek the advice of speech-language professionals for more information regarding the pros and cons of each system.

Relevant Literature:
American Speech-Language-Hearing Association. (2002). Augmentative and alternative communication: knowledge and skills for service delivery [Knowledge and Skills]. Available from www.asha.org/policy.
Charlop-Christy, M. H., Carpenter, M., Le, L., LeBlanc, L. A., & Kellet, K. (2002). Using the picture exchange communication

system (PECS) with children with autism: Assessment of PECS acquisition, speech, social-communicative behavior, and problem behavior. *Journal of applied behavior analysis, 35*(3), 213-231.

Dattilo, J., & Camarata, S. (1991). Facilitating conversation through self-initiated augmentative communication treatment. *Journal of Applied Behavior Analysis, 24*(2), 369-378.

Jacobson, J. W., Mulick, J. A., & Schwartz, A. A. (1995). A history of facilitated communication: Science, pseudoscience, and antiscience science working group on facilitated communication. *American Psychologist, 50*(9), 750.

Durand, V. M. (1999). Functional communication training using assistive devices: recruiting natural communities of reinforcement. *Journal of Applied Behavior Analysis, 32*(3), 247.

Mirenda, P., Iacono, T., & Williams, R. (1990). Communication options for persons with severe and profound disabilities: State of the art and future directions. *Journal of the Association for Persons with Severe Handicaps.*

Related Lessons:
D-03: Use prompts and prompt fading.
D-04: Use modeling and imitation training.
D-05: Use shaping.
F-07: Use functional communication training.

G-01 Review records and available data at the outset of the case

An important part of understanding the client you are working with is to take time to review the treatment history of this individual. There are records related to a medical history that would be beneficial to see. This would include medical procedures, medications, and any current health concerns. It's also important to get the history of treatment related to psychological/behavioral intervention as well.

Gresham, Watson, Steuart, & Skinner in 2001 recommend that FBAs should include a record review to understand more about the history of the client as well as information regarding previous interventions.

Matson (2010) summarized this position by saying "The behavior analyst should carefully review records relating to previous attempts to change potential target behaviors. Records indicating previous success with related target behaviors or a history of limited impact on a behaviour despite well-planned and faithfully implemented change programmes may be useful in selecting change targets which can be achieved within meaningful timescales" (p. 35).

Assessment:

- Have the supervisee describe where he/she would go to get access to these records. Pick a client and have him/her actually show you where the information is located.

- Have the supervisee describe the reasons why it's important to do a records review when getting a new client or starting a new behavioral intervention.

Relevant Literature:

Gresham, F. M., Watson, T. S., Steuart, T., & Skinner, C. H. (2001). Functional Behavioral Assessment: Principles, Procedures, and Future Directions. School Psychology Review, 30(2), 156–172.

Matson, J. L. (Ed.). (2010). *Applied Behavior Analysis for Children with Autism Spectrum Disorders* (2009 edition). New York: Springer.

Related Lessons:

G-01 Review records and available data at the outset of the case.

G-02 Consider biological/medical variables that may be affecting the client.

G-03 Conduct a preliminary assessment of the client in order to identify the referral problem.

G-04 Explain behavioral concepts using non-technical language.

G-05 Describe and explain behavior, including private events, in behavior-analytic (non-mentalistic) terms.

G-06 Provide behavior-analytic services in collaboration with others who support and/or provide services to one's clients.

G-07 Practice within one's limits of professional competence in applied behavior analysis, and obtain consultation, supervision, and training, or make referrals as necessary.

I-03 Design and implement individualized behavioral assessment procedures.

I-04 Design and implement the full range of functional assessment procedures.

K-01 Provide for ongoing documentation of behavioral services.

G-02 Consider biological/medical variables that may be affecting the client

The Behavior Analyst Certification Board (BACB) instructs that a "behavior analyst recommends seeking a medical consultation if there is any reasonable possibility that a referred behavior influenced by medical or biological variables" in section **3.02 Medical Consultation, of the BACB** professional and ethical compliance code for behavior analysts **(2014)**

This is relevant both in research and practice. Therefore, the first step in the assessment process should be to determine whether the problem may be due to a medical/biological issue and whether a medical evaluation has been completed (Cooper, Heron & Heward, 2007). Failure to rule out medical needs would be unethical as it would delay potentially necessary medical treatment that may even prove life threatening dependent on the medical concerns or the severity of the challenging behavior.

Possible pain related disorders or other medical/biological disorders that restrict an individual's ability to engage in appropriate behavior should be investigated. Some relevant behavioral topics correlated with a high likelihood of medical and biological causes are feeding disorders, toileting challenges (e.g., encopresis and incontinence), sleep problems and self-injury. Take self-injury for example; studies have shown that self-injurious behavior (SIB) has been maintained by pain attenuation which, can be categorized as automatic negative reinforcement behavior (Carr & Smith, 1995; O'Reilly, 1997). In detail, an increase in painful stimulation is an establishing operation (EO), thereby increasing behavior that has been reinforced by pain reduction.

Aside from the common examples presented above, it is possible that any form of challenging behavior could be a result of an underlying medical or biological issue. For example, aggressive behavior may also be related to pain related disorders which act as an EO (Carr et al., 2003; Skinner, 1953). The argument has also been made that aggressive behavior in response to painful stimulation may be respondent behavior (Ulrich & Azrin, 1962). Furthermore, Kennedy and Meyer (1996) found that the occurrence of allergy symptoms and sleep deprivation were correlated with an increase in escape maintained challenging behavior.

Assessment:

- Ask the supervisee what the first part of assessment should be regarding specific situations that would require collaboration with medical professionals to rule out any underlying medical issues. Have them give a rationale as to why this is important.

- Ask the supervisee to list a few possible medical/biological considerations that should be ruled out when treating a feeding disorder, toileting issue or sleep problem.

- Provide supervisee with examples such as this one: A student in a school setting is engaging in severe tooth picking and the classroom teacher is calling you for advice on what to do. Then ask the supervisee what the first step of assessment should be to treating this challenging behavior.

Relevant Literature:

Behavior Analyst Certification Board (BACB) Behavior Analyst Certification Board professional and ethical compliance code for behavior analysts. 2014. Retrieved from http://www.bacb.com/Download-files/BACB_Compliance_Code.pdf.

Carr, E. G., Smith, C. E., Giacin, T. A., Whelan, B. M., & Pancari, J. (2003). Menstrual discomfort as a biological setting event for severe problem behavior: Assessment and intervention. *Journal Information, 108*(2).

Carr, E. G., & Smith, C. E. (1995). Biological setting events for self-injury. *Mental Retardation and Developmental Disabilities Research Reviews, 1*(2), 94-98.

Cooper, J. O., Heron, T. E., & Heward, W. L. (2007). *Applied behavior analysis (2nd ed.). Upper Saddle River, NJ: Pearson.*

Kennedy, C. H., & Meyer, K. A. (1996). Sleep deprivation, allergy symptoms, and negatively reinforced problem behavior. *Journal of Applied Behavior Analysis, 29*(1), 133-135.

O'Reilly, M. F. (1997). Functional analysis of episodic self-injury correlated with recurrent otitis media. *Journal of Applied Behavior Analysis, 30*(1), 165-167.

Skinner, B. F. (1953). *Science and human behavior.* Simon and Schuster.

Ulrich, R. E., & Azrin, N. H. (1962). Reflexive fighting in response to aversive stimulation. *Journal of the Experimental Analysis of Behavior, 5*(4), 511.

Related Lessons:

G-01 Review records and available data at the outset of the case.

G-03 Conduct a preliminary assessment of the client in order to identify the referral problem.

G-06 Provide behavior-analytic services in collaboration with others who support and/or provide services to one's clients.

G-07 Practice within one's limits of professional competence in applied behavior analysis, and obtain consultation, supervision, and training, or make referrals as necessary.

FK-13 Reflexive relations (US-UR)

FK-26 Unconditioned motivating operations

G-03 Conduct a preliminary assessment of the client in order to identify the referral problem

Definition:

Behavioral assessment - "A form of assessment that involves a full range of inquiry methods (observation, interview, testing, and the systematic manipulation of antecedent or consequent variables) to identify probable antecedent and consequent controlling variables. Behavioral assessment is designed to discover resources, assets, significant others, competing contingencies, maintenance and generality factors, and possible reinforcers and/or punishers that surround the potential target behavior" (Cooper, Heron, & Heward, 2007, p. 691).

Five Phases of a Behavioral Assessment
Hawkins (1979) described behavioral assessment as being funnel shaped, beginning with a broad scope and then moving to a narrow focus.

1. Screening and general disposition
2. Defining and quantifying problems or goals
3. Pinpointing the target behavior
4. Monitoring progress
5. Follow-up

The preliminary assessment consists of the first 3 phases of this model. It is the broad gathering of information needed in order to pinpoint the target behavior. Once the target behavior is selected, a formal functional behavioral assessment is required.

Preliminary Assessment
Assessment Methods*

1. Interviews (client and significant others)
2. Checklists
3. Standardized Tests
4. Direct Observations

Social Significance
Before selecting a target behavior, it is important to reflect on how important the behavior change is for the client, not to others around the client. The rational for the behavior change must be critically analyzed. Cooper Heron, and Heward (2007) suggest the following methods for determining the social significance of the target behavior

- Is the behavior likely to produce reinforcement in the natural environment?
- Is the skill useful?
- Will it increase the individual's access to new reinforcing environments?
- Will it allow more social interaction?
- Is it a pivotal behavior?
- Is it a behavior cusp?
- Is it age-appropriate?
- If it is a behavior to be eliminated?
- What is the replacement skill?
- Is the identified behavior actually problematic?
- Is this the identified behavior just reports or is it real?

Prioritizing Target Behaviors
If a number of target behaviors are selected which are socially significant, it is then important to prioritize the target behavior ensuring dangerous behavior is targeted first. Other guidelines are listed by Cooper, Heron, and Heward (2007) as the following:

- Pose a danger to client or others?
- How often does it occur?
- How longstanding is the problem?
- Will changing the behavior produce higher rates of reinforcement?
- What is the importance related to overall independence?
- Will changing the behavior reduce negative attention?
- Will changing the behavior produce positive attention?
- How likely is success of changing the behavior?

- How much will it cost to change the behavior?

Defining the Target Behavior

Before beginning, the target behavior must be objectively and concisely defined in a clear concrete observable manner.

Setting the Criteria for Behavior Change

Goals must be socially meaningful to the person's life.

Assessment:

- Ask supervisee what assessment tools can be used to do a preliminary assessment.

- Provide examples of targets, which are and are not socially significant and ask the supervisee to determine if these behaviors are appropriate target behaviors. Have supervisee explain why.

- Provide a list of five target responses and have the supervisee prioritize them, justifying their decisions using the guidelines provided by Cooper, Heron and Heward (2007).

Relevant Literature:

Bailey, J., & Burch, M. (2011). *Ethics for Behavior Analysts: 2nd Expanded Edition.* Taylor & Francis.

Cooper, J. O., Heron, T. E., & Heward, W. L. (2007). Applied behavior analysis: 2nd Edition. Pearson Education, Inc.

Hawkins, R. P. (1979). The functions of assessment: Implications for selection and development of

devices for assessing repertoires in clinical, educational, and other settings. *Journal of Applied*

Behavior Analysis, 12(4), 501-516.

Linehan, M. M. (1977). Issues in behavioral interviewing. *Behavioral assessment: New directions in clinical psychology. New York: Brunner/Mazel.*

Houten, R. V. (1979). Social validation: The evolution of standards of competency for target behaviors. *Journal of Applied Behavior Analysis, 12*(4), 581-591.

Related Lessons:

I-01 Define behavior in observable and measurable terms

I-02 Define environmental variables inobservable and measurable terms

J-01 State intervention goals in observable and measurable terms

G-04 Explain behavioral concepts using nontechnical language

It is important for a behavior analyst to have a strong verbal repertoire when speaking about the science of behavior analysis. Jargon used in journals, universities, and with other behavior analysts is valuable to promote effective action on the part of the listener with precise discriminative control.

That being said, Skinner wrote that we should choose words for the effects they have on the listener (Skinner, 1957) and unless that listener has extensive training in behavior analysis, our use of technical language will "fall on deaf ears" and not produce effective action. When speaking with client family members, friends, or professionals from other closely related fields, it is important to remember that your verbal behavior is for the benefit of your audience. Bailey (1991) describes this phenomenon well:

"In our zeal to be scientific, we have stressed the need to match the requirements of science in our writing and publishing. Although this has given us much-needed academic credibility (faculty can be promoted and tenured by publishing in JABA) it doesn't help at all in selling our technology to the masses" (p. 446)

During the supervision process, spend considerable amounts of time, working on precise definitions for technical terms. This benefits the supervisee in several ways. It allows him/her to behave effectively as a listener and speaker when interacting with other behavior analysts in the field. It will also promote accurate translations to nontechnical language. If a precise definition is practiced, a less technical, more layperson-friendly definition will be easier to describe and it will be more likely to be accurate.

Assessment:
- Ask Supervisee to give a precise definition of a behavioral term from a textbook. Then ask Supervisee to accurately describe the term in nontechnical language. Work on this for the most commonly used terms. Provide feedback after, when in a supervision meeting.
- Observe the Supervisee describing a behavior analytic concept to another person (client, colleague, etc.) The Supervisee should be able to answer basic questions related to the topic using nontechnical language. Provide feedback after, when in a supervision meeting.

Relevant Literature:
Bailey, J. S. (1991). Marketing behavior analysis requires different talk. *Journal of Applied Behavior Analysis, 24*(3), 445-448.
Lindsley, O. R. (1991). From technical jargon to plain English for application. *Journal of Applied Behavior Analysis, 24*(3), 449-458.
Malott, R. W. (1992). Should we train applied behavior analysts to be researchers?. *Journal of applied behavior analysis, 25*(1), 83-88. Skinner B.F. Verbal behavior. New York: Appleton-Century-Crofts; 1957.

Related Lessons:
G-06 Provide behavior-analytic services in collaboration with others who support and/or provide services to one's clients.
I-06 Make recommendations regarding behaviors that must be established, maintained, increased, or decreased.
J-06 Select intervention strategies based on supporting environments.
J-07 Select intervention strategies based on environmental and resource constraints.
K-01 Provide for ongoing documentation of behavioral services.
K-03 Design and use competency-based training for persons who are responsible for carrying out behavioral assessment and behavior-change procedures.
K-08 Establish support for behavior-analytic services from direct and indirect consumers.
K-09 Secure the support of others to maintain the client's behavioral repertoires in their natural environments.

G-05 Describe and explain behavior, including private events, in behavior-analytic (non-mentalistic) terms

Behavior analysts must have a strong verbal repertoire when speaking about behavior analysis. This includes using behavior-analytic language when describing and explaining behavior, including private events.

Skinner's radical behaviorism rejected psychological models of behavior that relied on mentalistic explanations. Mentalistic approaches attributed the origination and cause of behavior to "inner" dimensions or mental entities (i.e., hypothetical constructs and explanatory fictions such as the unconscious or psyche). Mentalistic explanations of behavior often neglect the consideration and analysis of controlling variables in the environment and use circular reasoning to explain the cause and effect of behavior. Understanding the philosophy of radical behaviorism and the principles of behavior can assist behavior analysts in explaining behavior in behavior-analytic terms.

For example, you are conducting a functional behavior assessment in a school setting for a student who engages in high rates of aggression in the classroom. The teacher tells you that the student's aggression occurs because the student is frustrated and lives in an unpleasant environment at home. This is a mentalistic explanation. After several observations, you have determined that when academic demands are placed, the student engages in aggression and their aggression is reinforced by escape (i.e., academic demands are removed). This is a behavior-analytic explanation of behavior that accounts for behavior as it is a function of environmental variables.

Using behavior-analytic language to explain and describe behavior can be difficult as we are often exposed to mentalistic explanations (e.g., "wanting to" or "felt like it" as causes of behavior). Read Malott and Trojan-Suarez (2004) for a discussion about circular reasoning and talking about behavior.

Assessment:

- Ask supervisee to explain and describe behavior in behavior-analytic terms.
- Provide supervisee with examples of mentalistic explanations of behavior and ask supervisee to provide behavior-analytic explanations.
- Observe supervisee explain behavior in behavior-analytic terms to a colleague or client.

Relevant Literature:

Cooper, J. O., Heron, T. E., & Heward, W. L. (2007). Definition and characteristics of applied behavior analysis. *Applied Behavior Analysis* (pp. 1-23). Upper Saddle River, NJ: Pearson Prentice Hall.

Malott, R. W., & Trojan Suarez, E.A. (2004). Reinforcement. *Principles of Behavior* (pp. 28-35). Upper Saddle River, NJ: Pearson Prentice Hall.

Moore, J. (2008). *Conceptual Foundations of Radical Behaviorism.* Cornwall-on-Hudson, NY: Sloan Publishing.

Related Lessons:

FK-07 Environmental (as opposed to mentalistic) explanations of behavior
FK-08 Distinguish between radical and methodological behaviorism.
FK-31 Behavioral contingencies
FK-33 Functional relations
G-04 Explain behavioral concepts using nontechnical language.
I-01 Define behavior in observable and measurable terms.
I-02 Define environmental variables in observable and measurable terms.

G-06 Provide behavior analytic services in collaboration with others who support and/or provide services to one's clients

Content area 2.03 (a) (Behavior Analysts' Responsibility to Clients) of the professional and ethical compliance code for behavior analysts states that, "When indicated and professionally appropriate, behavior analysts cooperate with other professionals, in a manner that is consistent with the philosophical assumptions and principles of behavior analysis, in order to effectively and appropriately serve their clients." In other words, it is our ethical responsibility to collaborate and communicate with all service providers and other individual stakeholders if it will best service our clients.

Example:
Mary has been exhibiting aggression during sessions with her occupational therapist whenever a novel task is presented. The BCBA has come up with a general behavior support plan for all staff working with Mary to decrease these behaviors. The plan involves multiple options that all are relevant to the addressing the function of the aggression. The BCBA sets up a training to discuss and explain the proper implementation of these intervention strategies, and get feedback from other service providers such as the occupational therapist to increase the social validity of the treatment and increase the likelihood of treatment fidelity.

Assessment:
- Have supervisee identify and list all caregivers and professionals who may provide services to the individuals on their case load. Have supervisee list ways that they can increase communication with these individuals to ensure the most effective interventions and treatment of their clients.
- Have supervisee discuss how to effectively disseminate intervention information and train others on behavior analytic techniques, while using non-technical language that other service providers can comprehend and will be able to implement.
- Discuss behavioral skills training and how this could be an effective tool to train others in the implementation of behavior analytic procedures.

Relevant Literature:
Cooper, J.O., Heron, T.E. & Heward W.L. (2007). *Applied Behavior Analysis* (2nd Ed.), Upper Saddle River, NJ. Pearson Prentice Hall. 641-642, 675-676.
Kelly, A. & Tincani, M. (2013). Collaborative training and practice among applied behavior analysts who support individuals with autism spectrum disorder, *Education and Training in Autism and Developmental Disabilities*. 48, 1, 120-131.
Professional and Ethical Compliance Code for Behavior Analysts. Copyright © 2014 by the Behavior Analysis Certification Board®, Inc. ("BACB"), all rights reserved. (Content list items 2.02-2.03).

Related Lessons:
G-04: Explain behavioral concepts using non-technical language.
G-07: Practice within one's limits of professional competence in applied behavior analysis, and obtain consultation, supervision, training, or make referrals as necessary.
G-08: Identify and make environmental changes that reduce the need for behavior analysis services.
I-06: Make recommendations regarding behaviors that must be established, maintained, increased, or decreased.
J-11: Program for stimulus and response generalization.
J-14: Arrange instructional procedures to promote generative learning (i.e., derived relations).
K-03: Design and use competency-based training for persons who are responsible for carrying out behavioral assessment and behavior-change procedures.
K-08: Establish support for behavior-analytic services from direct and indirect consumers.
K-09: Secure the support of others to maintain the client's behavioral repertoires in their natural environments.

G-07 Practice within one's limits of professional competence in applied behavior analysis, and obtain consultation, supervision, and training, or make referrals as necessary

Behavior analysts follow guidelines related to boundaries of competence in 1.02 of the Behavior Analyst Certification Board professional and ethical compliance code for behavior analysts:

1.02 Boundaries of Competence.
(a) All behavior analysts provide services, teach, and conduct research only within the boundaries of their competence, defined as being commensurate with their education, training, and supervised experience.
(b) Behavior analysts provide services, teach, or conduct research in new areas (e.g., populations, techniques, behaviors) only after first undertaking appropriate study, training, supervision, and/or consultation from persons who are competent in those areas… (BACB, 2014, p.4).

Practicing within your area of competence, training and experience
If, for example, a senior therapist working within an intensive behavior intervention program for preschoolers suddenly began working with adults with phobias then they would be in violation of this ethical guideline. Cooper, Heron, and Heward (2007) go on further to say that even within one's competence area, if a situation exceeds your training or experience then a referral to another behavior analyst should be made. If there is a gap in expertise, available then workshops and conferences may be accessed. Mentors, supervisors and colleagues can provide additional training.

Bailey and Burch (2011) relate this ethical boundary to the Hippocratic Oath, "*Do no harm*". The guideline addresses the responsible conduct of behavior analysts, ensures the safety of clients, and protects the integrity of the field.

Assessment:
- Discuss case examples from Bailey and Burch (2011).
- Have the supervisee come up with five fictitious examples of situations where the ethical guideline 1.02 was broken and provide creative solutions to the situation.
- Use behavior skills training to teach your supervisee how to respond to a client asking your supervisee to provide services within an area in which they had no experience.

Relevant Literature:
Bailey, J., & Burch, M. (2011). *Ethics for Behavior Analysts: 2nd Expanded Edition.* Taylor & Francis.
Behavior Analyst Certification Board (BACB) Behavior Analyst Certification Board professional and ethical compliance code for behavior analysts. 2014. Retrieved from www.bacb.com/Download-files/BACB_Compliance_Code.pdf.
Cooper, J. O., Heron, T. E., & Heward, W. L. (2007). Applied behavior analysis: 2nd Edition. Pearson Education, Inc.
Houten, R., Axelrod, S., Bailey, J. S., Favell, J. E., Foxx, R. M., Iwata, B. A., & Lovaas, O. I. (1988). The right to effective behavioral treatment. *Journal of Applied Behavior Analysis, 21*(4), 381-384.

Related Lessons:
B-02: Review and interpret articles from the behavior analytic literature.
G-02: Consider biological/medical variables that may be affecting the client.
G-06: Provide behavior analytic services in collaboration with others who support and/or provide services to one's clients.
K-08: Establish support for behavior analytic services from direct and indirect consumers.
K-09: Secure the support of others to maintain the client's behavioral repertoires in their natural environment.

G-08 Make environmental changes that reduce the need for behavior analysis services

"Behavior analysis is a science of studying how we can arrange our environments so they make very likely the behaviors we want to be probably enough, and they make unlikely the behaviors we want to be improbable" (Cooper, Heron, & Heward, 2007, p. 15). The behavior analyst assesses the nature of the fit between an individual and the environment in which he/she functions using a three-part contingency (antecedent, behavior, consequences) structure of events. In this process, the analyst identifies motivating operations associated with antecedent events and the consequences that maintain problem behaviors or prevent adequate development of adaptive behaviors. This information can be used to identify relatively uncomplicated proactive environmental changes that will improve the functioning of the individual. As a result of the individual's increased access to positive reinforcement, more intrusive behavior interventions may be less necessary.

Examples:

- Parents found it difficult to get their daughter ready for the school bus on time. They decided they would try giving her time to shower at night instead of in the morning. They added showering to her regular nighttime routine and the daughter not only got to the school bus on-time but began to go to sleep earlier after the expanded nighttime routine.
- A student refused to sit in his seat at school. An occupational therapist suggested a gel filled wedge for the student's chair and the student not only remained seated in one class, but chose to use the wedge in all of his classes.

Assessment:

- If a student screams and covers his ears when moderate noises occur in the classroom, what would the supervisee suggest as the simplest environmental arrangement that might be considered for that student?
- A client throws objects at staff and pounds the wall when they sit and watch the staff's favorite television shows at night in the client's apartment. What might the staff be told to change at night before the analyst

designs a program for reinforcing the client's appropriate television behavior or punishing his inappropriate behavior?

- If an analyst determines that attention is a major positive reinforcer for problem behaviors for a client, what would the supervisee consider to be an important consequence to increase following appropriate behavior?

Relevant Literature:

Cooper, J.O., Heron, T.E. & Heward W.L. (2007). *Applied Behavior Analysis* (2nd Ed.), Upper Saddle River, NJ. Pearson Prentice Hall.

Related Lessons:

B-02 Review and interpret articles from the behavior-analytic literature.

D-21 Use differential reinforcement

E-01 Use interventions based on manipulation of antecedents, such as motivating operations and discriminative stimuli.

E-03 Use instructions and rules.

I-03 Design and implement individualized behavioral assessment procedures.

I-05 Organize, analyze, and interpret observed data.

I-06 Make recommendations regarding behaviors that must be established, maintained, increased, or decreased.

J-04 Select intervention strategies based on client preferences.

J-05 Select intervention strategies based on the client's current repertoires.

J-06 Select intervention strategies based on supporting environments.

J-07 Select intervention strategies based on environmental and resource constraints.

J-08 Select intervention strategies based on the social validity of the intervention.

J-10 When a behavior is to be decreased, select an acceptable alternative behavior to be established or increased.

J-12 Program for maintenance.

K-09 Secure the support of others to maintain the client's behavioral repertoires in their natural environments.

FK-05 Parsimony

FK-06 Pragmatism

FK-23 automatic reinforcement and punishment

FK-26 unconditioned motivating operation

FK-33 functional relations

H-01 Select a measurement system to obtain representative data given the dimensions of the behavior and the logistics of observing and recording

Assessment and treatment decisions of behavior analysts rely on data. A behavior analyst can design and implement effective treatments only when the data accurately represent the behavior of interest (validity) and have been reliably recorded as they are observed. To accomplish this goal, behavior analysts choose behaviors and dimensions of those behaviors to facilitate accurate and consistent recording within a given context for each client. Behavior analysts measure "three fundamental properties, or dimensional quantities" (Cooper et al., 2007, p. 75) of behavior:

- Repeatability--Behavior can be counted in the same way each time it occurs.
- Temporal extent--Behavior can be measured in relation to time.
- Temporal locus—Behavior occurs in relation to other behaviors.

First, identify which of these three properties will provide the most accurate method for quantifying behavior. Then, decides what dimension of behavior to measure, such as a count of occurrences, frequency of behavior per unit of time, duration, latency, or other. Last, decide who will record the behavior and in what context. If a preferred measurement system is unlikely to be effectively implemented, then the analyst has to reconsider definitions or recording circumstances in order to obtain adequate and accurate data for decision-making.

Examples:
- A teacher is asked to record the number of times a student yells out inappropriate language in class each day. Since the time the student spends in class varies widely during the week, the behavior analyst designed a measurement system to record rate (number of occurrences divided by time in class) of yelling out inappropriate language. With these data, the behavior analyst can compare the student's behavior across time of unequal durations.
- A parent is committed to accurately recording data to show duration of a child's tantrums, but found that she was not always in close proximity with the child when the behavior begins. The behavior analyst identifies two conditions during the day when the mother can accurately record duration of each tantrum (the first 30 minutes after school and the last 30 minutes before bedtime). The mother records duration of total tantruming behavior during each 30 minute-observation twice a day.

Assessment:
- Have supervisee list and describe each measurable unit of behavior.
- Have supervisee list and describe each of the three fundamental properties of behavior.
- Provide the supervisee with a number of scenarios. Have the supervisee design/describe a data collection procedure to measure target behavior.

Relevant Literature:
Cooper, J.O., Heron, T. E., & Heward, W. L. (2007). *Applied behavior analysis.* Upper Saddle River, NJ: Pearson Education.

Gast, D. L. (2010). *Single subject research methodology in behavioral sciences*. New York: NY: Routledge.

Related Lessons:

A-01 Measure frequency

A-02 Measure rate (i.e., count per unit time).

A-03 Measure duration

A-04 Measure latency

A-09 Evaluate the accuracy and reliability of measurement procedures.

A-10 Design, plot, and interpret data using equal-interval graphs.

D-05 Use shaping.

H-02 Select a schedule of observation and recording periods.

H-03 Select a data display that effectively communicates relevant quantitative relations.

H-04 Evaluate changes in level, trend, and variability.

H-05 Evaluate temporal relations between observed variables (within & between sessions, time series).

I-01 Define behavior in observable and measurable terms.

I-05 Organize, analyze, and interpret observed data.

K-07 Evaluate the effectiveness of the behavioral program.

FK-33 functional relations

FK-41 contingency-shaped behavior

FK-47 Identify the measurable dimensions of behavior (e.g. rate, duration, latency, interresponse time)

FK-48 State the advantages and disadvantages of using continuous measurement procedures and discontinuous measurement procedures (e.g. partial- and whole-interval recording, momentary time sampling.)

H-02 Select a schedule of observation and recording periods

BCBAs select the most appropriate forms of measurement. The target behavior should have a clear and observable operational definition so that it can be recorded during a period of observation. Using a consistent measurement procedure and schedule of observation will help ensure that the data are truly reflective of the target behavior you want to measure. Specify a time interval (or observation period) for recording data. Additionally, time intervals used in interval recording should remain consistent across observations (e.g., if you collect data on a target behavior during a 15 minute observation using 30-second partial intervals then you should use the same procedure on subsequent observations). If you change any aspect of the operational definition, observational period, or measurement procedures, explain the change when presenting data.

Example:
- If your client's parent reported that aggression only happens when the client is asked to brush their teeth, then you want to ensure that you can observe the client during times they are asked to brush their teeth.
- An instructor wanted to use the PLA-CHECK measurement procedure to record his students' involvement in an in-class group assignment. It would be appropriate to collect these data when students separate into groups and start the assignment. Recording data during the lecture or a test would not be an appropriate observation period.

Assessment:
- Provide supervisee with a target behavior and ask supervisee to explain what measurement procedure should be used and observation periods should occur.

- Provide supervisee with various scenarios of target behaviors, measurement procedure, and observation period and ask supervisee to determine the appropriateness of the measurement procedure and observation.
- Ask supervisee to develop procedures for observing and recording a target behavior in a client's behavior intervention program.

Relevant Literature:
Cooper, J. O., Heron, T. E., & Heward, W. L. (2007). Measuring behavior. *Applied Behavior Analysis* (pp. 72-101). Upper Saddle River, NJ: Pearson Prentice Hall.
Bailey, J. & Burch, M. (2010). *25 Essential Skills and Strategies for the Professional Behavior Analyst: Expert Tips for Maximizing Consulting Effectiveness*. New York, NY: Routledge.

Related Lessons:
A-01 Measure frequency (i.e., count).
A-02 Measure rate (i.e., count per unit time).
A-03 Measure duration.
A-04 Measure latency.
A-05 Measure interresponse time (IRT).
A-06 Measure percent of occurrence.
A-07 Measure trials to criterion.
A-12 Design and implement continuous measurement procedures (e.g., event recording).
A-13 Design and implement discontinuous measurement procedures (e.g., partial & whole interval, momentary time sampling).
A-14 Design and implement choice measures.
FK-47 Identify the measurable dimensions of behavior (e.g., rate, duration, latency, interresponse time).
FK-48 State the advantages and disadvantages of using continuous measurement procedures and discontinuous measurement procedures (e.g., partial- and whole-interval recording, momentary time sampling).

H-03 Select a data display that effectively communicates relevant quantitative relations

Behavior change is an ongoing process that must be continuously evaluated. This evaluation occurs through an analysis of data that reflects the quantifiable form of the behavior of interest. However, understanding the extent of behavior change can be difficult if one is looking at raw data alone. As such, behavior analysts use graphic displays to analyze, interpret, and communicate the results of behavior interventions (Cooper, Heron, & Heward, 2007). The most common graphic displays include line graphs, bar graphs, cumulative records, Standard Celeration charts, and scatterplots. The clinical utility of each graphic display varies so it is important to select the graphic display that will most accurately illustrate what the behavior analyst wants to understand.

Cooper et al. (2007) outlines the following purposes for the different graphic displays.

Line graphs are the most common form of graphic display and can be used to (1) show multiple dimensions of one behavior, (2) two or more different behaviors, (3) a behavior under different conditions, (4) changes in the target behavior relative to the manipulation of an independent variable, (5) and the behavior of multiple learners.

Bar graphs are typically used to (1) display discrete data that cannot be captured by an underlying dimension reflected on a horizontal axis and (2) provide an easy comparison of variables during different conditions.

Cumulative records are useful when the behavior analyst wants to (1) illustrate the total number of responses made over time, (2) the graph is used as a means to provide feedback to the learner, (3) the behavior of interest can only occur once during the specified measurement period, and (4) an analysis of a specific instance during an experiment is warranted.

The Standard Celeration Chart is a semilogarithmic chart that is used to reflect a linear measure of change across time. Lastly, scatterplots illustrate the comparative distribution of discrete measures in a data set and can be useful to uncover relationships across different subsets of data.

Example:
- If you want to see data paths across three behaviors and different intervention conditions,

then a line graph is the most appropriate graphic display.
- Your client has rapidly acquired several language targets. A cumulative record can illustrate acquisition and is more efficient than creating a line graph for each acquired language target.

Assessment:
- Ask supervisee to explain the utility of each type of graphic display.
- Provide supervisee with examples of graphs and ask supervisee to identify which type of display is used and interpret the data presented in the display.
- Ask supervisee to create at least one of each type of graphic display.
- Provide examples of different measures of behavior and what information is desired from each set of data and ask supervisee to identify which graphic display would be most appropriate to communicate the results.

Relevant Literature:
Cooper, J. O., Heron, T. E., & Heward, W. L. (2007). Constructing and interpreting graphic displays of behavioral data. *Applied Behavior Analysis* (pp. 126-157). Upper Saddle River, NJ: Pearson Prentice Hall.
Parsonson, B. S., & Baer, D. M. (1978). The analysis and presentation of graphic data. In T. R. Kratochwill (Ed.), *Single subject research: Strategies for evaluating change* (pp. 101-165). New York, NY: Academic Press.

Related Lessons:
A-10 Design, plot, and interpret data using equal-interval graphs.
A-11 Design, plot, and interpret data using a cumulative record to display data.
A-12 Design and implement continuous measurement procedures (e.g., event recording).
FK-47 Identify the measurable dimensions of behavior (e.g., rate, duration, latency, interresponse time).
B-03 Systematically arrange independent variables to demonstrate their effects on dependent variables.
H-04 Evaluate changes in level, trend, and variability.
H-05 Evaluate temporal relations between observed variables (within &between sessions, time series).

H-04 Evaluate changes in level, trend and variability

Definitions:

Level - "The value on the vertical axis scale around which a set of behavioral measures converge is called **level**. In the visual analysis of behavioral data, level is examined within a condition in terms of its absolute value (mean, median, and/or range) on the *y*-axis scale, the degree of stability or variability, and the extent of change from one level to another... The mean level of a series of behavioral measures within a condition can be graphically illustrated by the addition of a mean level line: a horizontal line drawn through a series of data points within a condition at that point on the vertical axis equaling the average value of the series of measures" (Cooper, Heron & Heward, 2007, pp. 150-151).

Trend - "The overall direction taken by a data path is its **trend**" (Cooper, Heron & Heward, 2007, p. 151). Trends can be described in terms of their direction, i.e., ascending, descending or zero/no trend. They can also be described in terms of their degree or magnitude, and the extent of variability, the data points around the trend have. The direction and degree of trend shown in a series of data points can be visually represented on a graph by drawing a straight line through the data. This is called a *trend line* or *line of progress* (Cooper, Heron & Heward, 2007).

Variability - "How often and the extent to which multiple measures of behavior yield different outcomes is called **variability**" (Cooper, Heron & Heward, 2007, p. 150).

Assessment:
- Ask your Supervisees to define level/trend/variability.
- Ask your Supervisee to graph a set of data and describe the level/trend/variability shown in the data.

Relevant Literature:

Cooper, J. O., Heron, T. E., & Heward, W. L. (2007). Applied Behavior Analysis, 2nd ed. Upper Saddle River, New Jersey: Pearson Prentice Hall.

Keohane, D. D., & Greer, R. D. (2005). Teachers' use of a verbally governed algorithm and student learning. *International Journal of Behavioral and Consultation Therapy, 1,* 249-268.

Lindsley, O. R. (1985). *Quantified trends in the results of behavior analysis.* Presidential address at the Eleventh Annual Convention of the Association for Behavior Analysis, Columbus, OH.

McCain, L. J., & McCleary, R. (1979). The statistical analysis of the simple interrupted time series quasi-experiment. In T. D. Cook & D. T. Campbell (Eds.), *Quasi-experimentation: Design and analysis issues for field settings.* Chicago: Rand McNally.

White, O. (2005). Trend lines. In G. Sugai & R. Horner (Eds.), *Encyclopedia of behavior modification and cognitive behavior therapy, Volume 3: Educational applications.* Pacific Grove, CA; Sage Publications.

Related Lessons:
A-10: Design, plot, and interpret data using equal-interval graphs
A-11: Design, plot, and interpret data using a cumulative record to display data
H-03: Select a data display that effectively communicates relevant quantitative relations
H-04: Evaluate changes in level, trend, and variability
I-01: Define behavior in observable and measurable terms
I-05: Organize, analyze, and interpret observed data
FK-47: Identify the measurable dimensions of behavior (e.g., rate, duration, latency, interresponse time)

H-05 Evaluate temporal relations between observed variables (within & between sessions, time series)

Behavior analysts can analyze data across several **temporal relations** prior to visual inspection. "The manner in which data are aggregated before transforming them into a visual display serves an equally influential role in data analysis" (Fahmie & Hanley, 2008, p. 320). Such aggregation occurs with the use of within-session, between-session in time series data.

Between-session analysis involves plotting total number of occurrences of a dependent variable within some unit of time (i.e., sessions) and visually inspecting point-by-point (i.e., session-by-session). Another prevalent type of aggregation occurrences of behavior is **within-session data** (likely due to its universal application).

Within-sessing data can be analyzed via the observation of data as it changes throughout the duration of the session or at specific times during the session. Fahmie and Hanley (2008) outlined eight conditions under which within-session data are valuable:

1. Description of naturally occurring behavioral relations (descriptive assessment)
2. Determination of behavioral function (functional analyses)
3. Detection of within-session trends
4. Safeguard clients from any risks associated with prolonged session exposure
5. Creation of sufficient data for analysis following abbreviated data collection
6. Determination of observation session duration
7. Clarification of counterintuitive response patterns
8. Understanding behavioral processes

There are several methods of within-session data analysis. In the descriptive assessment literature, within-session data are calculated via conditional probabilities to determine possible temporal relations between behavior and environmental events (e.g., occurrence/nonoccurrence of putative reinforcer delivery) (Vollmer, Borrero, Wright, Camp, & Lalli, 2001). In the functional analysis literature, within-session data have been used to compare the utility of two types of functional analyses (e.g., trial-based versus multi-element) (Kahng & Iwata, 1999; LaRue et al., 2010). Moreover, within-session data have been used in an effort to further analyze unclear results following an unclear analysis of full session data (Call & Mevers, 2014; Kahng & Iwata, 1999; Payne et al., 2014; Roane, Lerman, Kelley, & VanCamp, 1999; Vollmer, Marcus, Ringhdahl & Roane, 1995; Vollmer et. al., 1993). For example, Kahng & Iwata (1999) compared full 15-minute functional analysis session data with within-session data by plotting the first session of each condition into a minute-by-minute observation period. One of their findings was that within-session data clarified unclear (absence of function) results of the full session data.

In another example, Payne et al., (2014) analyzed within-session data in different manner by comparing data when the putative establishing operation (EO) was present versus when the putative EO was absent across the last five 10-minute sessions of each condition. The results generated from the within-session data analysis was used to develop a second experimental analysis that clarified the function of the behavior for the two participants.

Assessment:
- Have the supervisee read the Fahmie & Hanley (2008) article. Then provide the supervisee with examples of different data analysis units along the

continuum the authors display in Figure 1. Have them place the scenarios along the continuum and discuss.

- Have the supervisee describe different methods of within session data collection (e.g. minute-by-minute, event based observation period comparisons) and their utility (a review of the methods used in the relevant literature will assist with this task)

Relevant Literature:

Call, N. A. and Lomas Mevers, J. E. (2014), The Relative Influence of Motivating Operations for Positive and Negative Reinforcement on Problem Behavior During Demands. *Behavioral Interventions*, 29: 4–20. doi: 10.1002/bin.1374

Fahmie, T. A., & Hanley, G. P. (2008). Progressing Toward Data Intimacy: A Review of Within-Session Data Analysis. *Journal of Applied Behavior Analysis*, *41*(3), 319.

Hartmann, D. P., Gottman, J. M., Jones, R. R., Gardner, W., Kazdin, A. E., & Vaught, R. S. (1980). Interrupted time-series analysis and its application to behavioral data. *Journal of Applied Behavior Analysis*, *13*(4), 543-559.

Iwata, B. A., Wallace, M. D., Kahng, S., Lindberg, J. S., Roscoe, E. M., Conners, J., & Worsdell, A. S. (2000). Skill acquisition in the implementation of functional analysis methodology. *Journal of Applied Behavior Analysis*, *33*(2), 181-194.

Krause, T. R., Seymour, K. J., & Sloat, K. C. M. (1999). Long-term evaluation of a behavior-based method for improving safety performance: a meta-analysis of 73 interrupted time-series replications. *Safety Science*, *32*(1), 1-18.

LaRue, R. H., Lenard, K., Weiss, M. J., Bamond, M., Palmieri, M., & Kelley, M. E. (2010). Comparison of traditional and trial-based methodologies for conducting functional analyses. *Research in Developmental Disabilities*, *31*(2), 480-487.

Payne, S. W., Dozier, C. L., Neidert, P. L., Jowet, E. S., & Newquist, M. H. (2014). Using Additional Analyses to Clarify the Functions of Problem Behavior: An Analysis of Two Cases. *Education and Treatment of Children*, *37*(2), 249-275.

Roane, H. S., Lerman, D. C., Kelley, M. E., & Van Camp, C. M. (1999). Within-session patterns of responding during functional analyses: The role of establishing operations in clarifying behavioral function. *Research in Developmental Disabilities*, *20*(1), 73-89.

Tryon, W. W. (1982). A simplified time-series analysis for evaluating treatment interventions. *Journal of applied behavior analysis*, *15*(3), 423-429.

Vollmer, T. R., Borrero, J. C., Wright, C. S., Camp, C. V., & Lalli, J. S. (2001). Identifying possible contingencies during descriptive analyses of severe behavior disorders. *Journal of Applied Behavior Analysis*, *34*(3), 269-287.

Vollmer, T. R., Iwata, B. A., Zarcone, J. R., Smith, R. G., & Mazaleski, J. L. (1993). Within-session patterns of self-injury as indicators of behavioral function. *Research in Developmental Disabilities*, *14*(6), 479-492.

Vollmer, T. R., Marcus, B. A., Ringdahl, J. E., & Roane, H. S. (1995). Progressing from brief assessments to extended experimental analyses in the evaluation of aberrant behavior. *Journal of Applied Behavior Analysis*, *28*(4), 561-576.

Related Lessons:

H-01 Select a measurement system to obtain representative data given the dimensions of the behavior and the logistics of observing and recording.

H-04 Evaluate changes in level, trend, and variability.

I-05 Organize, analyze and interpret observed data

J-15 Base decision-making on data displayed in various formats

FK-47 Identify the measurable dimensions of behavior (e.g., rate, duration, latency, interresponse time).

I-01 Define behavior in observable and measurable terms

The importance of defining behavior in observable and measurable terms:

- As Baer, Wolf and Risley said in 1968, "since the behavior of an individual is composed of physical events, its scientific study requires their precise measurement" (p. 93). In order to be scientific in our study of behavior, we must be very clear about what behavior it is we are actually studying. Therefore, the target behavior must be observable and measurable. Cooper, Heron and Heward (2007) also make the point that one of the most basic tenets of science is replication. In order for other scientists to replicate an experiment or study, the definition of the behavior under investigation and how it was measured must be transparent enough, that future replication is possible.

Technically-sound written definitions of target behaviors

- Cooper, Heron, and Heward, (2007), suggest that a good behavioral definition is:
- **Operational** (it allows the practitioner to obtain complete information about a behavior's occurrence/non-occurrence and allows the accurate application of the procedures.)
- Cooper, Heron and Heward (2007) also state that good definitions increase the likelihood that an accurate *evaluation* of the effectiveness of a study or experiment will be conducted.

Two types of target behavior definitions

- Cooper, Heron, and Heward (2007, p. 65) suggest that there are two types of target behavior definitions:
- **Functional** (These types of definition label responses as part of the target behavior's response class if they have the same effect upon the environment.)

- **Topographical** (These types of definition look at the shape or form of the target behavior.)

How to write behavioral definitions

- Cooper, Heron, and Heward (2007) cite Hawkins and Dobes (1977) as giving three characteristics of good written target behavior definitions:
- Objective (should refer only to observable characteristics of the behavior and environment and shouldn't utilize inferential terms, such as "feeling angry".)
- Clear (the definition should be readable and unambiguous.)
- Complete (it should outline the boundaries of what is included as an instance of a response and what is not included.)

Assessment:

- Ask your supervisee to give you examples of behavior that is not observable or measurable.
- Ask your Supervisees to write target behavioral definitions for the following behaviors:
- Hand flapping (Answer = Any repetitive, rapid motor movement of the hands in a back and forth motion which lasts at least 1 second)
- Vocal Manding (Answer = Any occurrence of requesting access to a preferred item/action/event using a vocalization such as "cookie please")
- Throwing (Answer = picking up an item and throwing it at least a 30 cm distance from the body)
- Being angry (Answer = this is not an observable or measurable behavior)

Relevant Literature:

Baer, D. M., Wolf, M. M., & Risley, T. R. (1968). Some current dimensions of applied behavior analysis. *Journal of Applied Behavior Analysis, 1*, 91-97.

Cooper, J. O., Heron, T. E., & Heward, W. L. (2007). Applied Behavior Analysis, 2nd ed. Upper Saddle River, New Jersey: Pearson Prentice Hall.

Hawkins, R. P., & Dobes, R. W. (1977). Behavioral definitions in applied behavior analysis: Explicit or implicit? In B. C. Etzel, J. M. LeBlanc, & D. M. Baer (Eds.), New developments in behavioral research: Theory, method, and application (pp. 167-188).

Van Houten, R. (1979). Social Validation: The evolution of standards of competency for target behaviors. *Journal of Applied Behavior Analysis, 26*, 197-203.

Related Lessons:

H-01: Select a measurement system to obtain representative data given the dimensions of the behavior and the logistics of observing and recording

H-02: Select a schedule of observation and recording periods.

I-02: Define environmental variables on observable and measurable terms

J-01: State intervention goals in observable and measurable terms

FK-47: Identify the observable dimensions of behavior (e.g., rate, duration, latency, interresponse time)

I-02 Define environmental variables in observable and measurable terms

The importance of defining environmental variables in observable and measurable terms

- As Cooper, Heron, and Heward (2007) state, in order to achieve a high level of treatment integrity in an experiment, it is of utmost importance to "develop complete and precise operational definitions of the treatment procedures" (Cooper, Heron, & Heward, 2007, p. 235). In the same way that it is critical to define target behavior in observable and measurable terms, so is the case with defining environmental variables.

- Baer, Wolf, and Risley (1968) stress that the "technological" dimension of Applied Behavior Analysis refers simply to the fact that "the techniques making up a particular behavioral application are completely identified and described"(Baer, Wolf, & Risley, 1968, p. 95). As such, the techniques, or environmental variables being manipulated, must be defined in observable and measurable terms to meet the technological dimension of applied behavior analysis (Cooper, Heron, & Heward, 2007).

- However, historically, operationally defining independent variables has not been conducted to the standard required for a science of behavior that seeks to achieve the technological dimension of applied behavior analysis*. It has also not been done to the same standard as that of the dependent variables (Johnston & Pennypacker, 1980; Peterson, Homer & Wonderlich, 1982; Gresham, Gansle & Noell, 1993). In 1982 Peterson, Homer and Wonderlich called for researchers to measure the independent variables in a more stringent manner. Unfortunately, an assessment of this area later on by Gresham, Gansle and Noell (1993) found that this had not been accomplished.

- Defining environmental variables in observable and measurable terms

- It is believed that environmental variable definitions should be written to meet the same standards as those required to be met by *target behavior* definitions (Gresham, Gansle & Noell, 1993). They should be "clear, concise, unambiguous, and objective" (Cooper, Heron & Heward, 2007, p. 235).

- Gresham *et al.* (1993, p. 261) suggest that independent variable definitions can be made along four dimensions: spatial, verbal, physical and temporal.

Example Definition

- Gresham *et al.* (1993, pp. 261-262) give an example of an adequate definition of an independent variable, a time-out procedure, provided by Mace, Page, Ivancic and O'Brien (1986).

  o Immediately following the occurrence of a target behavior (temporal dimension), (b) the therapist said, "No, go to time-out" (verbal dimension), (c) led the child by the arm to a prepositioned time-out chair (physical dimension), and (d) seated the child facing the corner (spatial dimension). (e) If the child's buttocks were raised from the time-out chair or if the child's head was turned more than 45° (spatial dimension), the therapist used the least amount of force necessary to guide compliance with the time-out procedure (physical dimension). (f) At the end of 2 min (temporal dimension), the therapist turned the time-out chair 45° from the corner (physical and spatial dimensions) and walked away (physical dimension).

- Gresham *et al.*, (1993, p. 262) argued that a failure to define operational variables along these four dimensions, as done so by Mace, Page, Ivancic and O'Brien (1986), makes "replication and external validation of behavior-analytic investigations difficult."

Assessment:

- Ask your Supervisee to explain why it's important as a behavior analyst to define environmental variable in observable and measurable terms.
- Ask your Supervisee to write an operational definition for the following independent variable:
  - Verbal Praise (Answer = (a) Immediately following the occurrence of a target behavior (temporal dimension), (b) the therapist delivered verbal praise, for example, "great job/nice work/well done" (verbal dimension), (c) but did not provide any physical contact such as a hi-five or pat on the back (physical dimension). The therapist was within 2 to 20 feet of the client at all times during the intervention (spatial dimension).

Relevant Literature:

Baer, D. M., Wolf, M. M., & Risley, T. R. (1968). Some current dimensions of applied behavior analysis. *Journal of Applied Behavior Analysis, 1,* 91-97.

Cooper, J. O., Heron, T. E., & Heward, W. L. (2007). *Applied Behavior Analysis,* 2nd ed. Upper Saddle River, New Jersey: Pearson Prentice Hall.

Gresham, F. M., Gansle, K. A. & Noell, G. H. (1993). Treatment integrity in applied behavior analysis with children. *Journal of Applied Behavior Analysis, 26,* 257-263.

Johnston, J., & Pennypacker, H. S. (1980). *Strategies and tactics of human behavioral research.* Hillsdale, N.J.: Erlbaum.

Peterson, L., Homer, A. L., Wonderlich, S. A. (1982). The integrity of independent variables in behavior analysis. *Journal of Applied Behavior Analysis, 15,* 477-492.

Related Lessons:

B-11: Conduct a parametric analysis to determine the effective values of an independent variable
I-01: Define behavior in observable and measurable terms
I-04: Design and implement the full range of functional assessment procedures
J-01: State intervention goals in observable and measurable terms
FK-07: Environmental (as opposed to mentalistic explanations of behavior)
FK-11: Environment, stimulus, stimulus class
FK-33: Functional relations

Footnotes

* See Baer, Wolf & Risley (1968) for more information on the seven dimensions of Applied Behavior Analysis.

I-03 Design and implement individualized behavioral assessment procedures

"Behavioral assessment involves a variety of methods including direct observations, interviews, checklists, and tests to identify and define targets for behavior change" (Cooper, Heron, & Heward, 2007, p. 49).

"Applied behavior analysis uses the methods of FBA to identify antecedent and consequent events and to use this information in designing interventions to change socially significant behaviors (Gresham, Watson, & Skinner, 2001, p. 157)."

"FBA is designed to obtain information about the purpose (function) a behavior serves for a person....FBA is used to identify the type and source of reinforcement for challenging behaviors as the basis for intervention efforts… (Cooper et al., 2007, p. 501)."

"Once the function of behavior is determined, this information is used to design interventions to reduce problem behaviors and to facilitate positive behaviors" (Gresham et al., 2001, p. 158).

The first step in the process is to define the target behaviors that the assessment will focus on. These behaviors are typically identified by teachers, therapists, or caregivers due to their interference with learning, adaptive functioning, and overall quality of life. In following the principles of ABA, the behaviors targeted for assessment must be socially significant.

Another direct method of determining the function of a behavior is to conduct a functional analysis. This involves systematic manipulation of the environment, while controlling variables to evoke the target behavior under conditions representing each possible function. The typical functions of behavior include access to attention, access to tangible items, escape from demands, and automatic reinforcement. During a functional analysis, each function is assessed to determine if they

are maintaining the target behavior. FA is considered to be the most reliable source for determining the function of a behavior, but may not be feasible in some settings due to the time it takes to conduct, safety implications (depending on the severity of the target behavior), and resources needed to conduct each experimental phase.

Other methods used to gather information about the function of target behaviors in a behavioral assessment include a thorough review of the client's previous records (academic reports, past evaluations, behavior support plans, IEP's, etc.), the use of behavioral rating scales such as the FAST (functional analysis screening tool), MAS (Motivational Assessment Scale), or PBQ (Problem Behavior Questionnaire)), structured interviews with caregivers (i.e., functional assessment interview form), direct observation in the target environment (i.e., home, school, community), behavior data collection and analysis, and A-B-C data collection and analysis. These indirect assessments should be used to inform an experimental functional analysis. They are not designed to determine the function of a response on their own.

Once the direct and indirect assessments are completed, this information is analyzed and the BCBA makes recommendations for intervention based on the results of assessments.

Example:
Rich is completing an FBA on the aggression of one of his students. After teacher interviews, the completion of rating scales, and several observations in various settings, Rich hypothesizes that the function of aggression is escape from demands. He uses this information to create an intervention plan to decrease aggression at school.

Assessment:
- Have supervisee complete a behavior rating scale on an individual based on one of their behaviors.

This can include the FAST, MAS, PBQ, or another common rating scale used in behavioral assessments. Once the supervisee has completed the rating scale, have them score the form and present the results.

- Supervisor will create role plays in which each supervisee will collect ABC data on specific topography of problem behavior. After a number of instances have been recorded, supervisee will analyze the data and formulate a hypothesized function of the problem behavior.

- Have supervisee read Iwata, Dorsey, Slifer, Bauman, & Richman (1982/1994) and describe the experimental conditions of a functional analysis.

Relevant Literature:

Carr, E. (1993). Behavior analysis is not ultimately about behavior. *The Behavior Analyst*, 16, 47-49.

Cooper, J.O., Heron, T.E. & Heward W.L. (2007). *Applied Behavior Analysis* (2nd Ed.), Upper Saddle River, NJ. Pearson Prentice Hall. 49-71, 300, 335-336, 364-366, 457, 459-460, 499-524.

Gresham, F., Watson, T.S., & Skinner, C.H. (2001). *Functional Behavioral Assessment: Principals, Procedures, and Future Directions.* School Psychology Review, 30, 2, 156-172.

Iwata, B. A., Dorsey, M. F., Slifer, K. J., Bauman, K. E., & Richman, G. S. (1994). Toward a functional analysis of self-injury. *Journal of applied behavior analysis,* 27(2), 197-209.

O'Neill, R., Horner, R., Albin, R., Storey, K., & Sprague, J. (1997). *Functional assessment and program development for problem behaviors.* Pacific Grove, CA: Brooks/Cole.

Sprague, J., Sugai, G. & Walker, H. (1998). *Antisocial Behavior in Schools.* In T.S. Watson & F.M. Gresham (Eds). *Handbook of child behavior therapy* (pp. 451-474). New York: Pleunum Press.

Witt, J., Daly, E., & Noell, G.H. (2000). *Functional Assessment: A step by step guide to solving academic and behavior problems.* Longmont, CO. Sopris West.

Related Lessons:

B-03: Systematically arrange independent variables to demonstrate their effects on dependent variables.

E-01: Use interventions based on manipulation of antecedents, such as motivating operations and discriminative stimuli.

G-01: Review records at the outset of a case.

G-04: Conduct a preliminary assessment of the client in order to identify the referral problem.

G-05: Describe and explain behavior, including private events, in behavior-analytic (non-mentalistic) terms.

G-08: Identify and make environmental changes that reduce the need for behavior analysis services.

H-02: Select a schedule of observation and recording periods.

I-01: Define behavior in observable and measurable terms.

I-02: Define environmental variables in observable and measurable terms.

I-04: Design and implement the full range of functional assessment procedures.

I-06: Make recommendations regarding behaviors that must be established, maintained, increased, or decreased.

J-01: State intervention goals in observable and measurable terms.

J-02: Identify potential interventions based on assessment results and the best available scientific evidence.

J-10: When a behavior is to be decreased, select an acceptable alternative behavior to be established or increased.

I-04 Design and implement the full range of functional assessment procedures

Definitions:

Functional behavior assessment (FBA) - "A systematic method of assessment for obtaining information about the purposes (functions) a problem behavior serves for a person; results are used to guide the design of an intervention for decreasing the problem behavior and increasing appropriate behavior" (Cooper, Heron, & Heward, 2007, p. 696).

Functional analysis (FA) - "An analysis of the purposes of problem behavior, wherein antecedents and consequences representing those in the person's natural routines are arranged within an experimental design so that their separate effects on problem behavior can be observed and measured" (Cooper, Heron, & Heward, 2007, p. 696).* The FA is considered to be best practice standard in conducting a functional assessment (Hanley, Iwata, & McCord 2003).

Descriptive assessment - "Direct observation of problem behavior and the antecedent and consequent events under naturally occurring conditions" (Cooper, Heron, & Heward, 2007, p. 693).* The advantages are that the information yields what happens in the individual's natural environment, does not disrupt the individual's routine, and provides information for designing a functional analysis. The disadvantages of these assessments are false positives due to behavior maintained by intermittent reinforcement or the presence of antecedent and consequent events which are often present but have no functional relation, the time required in taking data, and inaccurate data collection. Also, there is little correspondence between descriptive analysis outcomes being compared to functional analysis outcomes (Pence, Roscoe, Bourret, and Ahearn, 2009)

Indirect assessment - "Structured interviews, checklists, rating scales, or questionnaires used to obtain information from people who are familiar with the person exhibiting the problem behavior" (Cooper, Heron, & Heward, 2007, p. 697). The advantages of indirect assessments are that the forms can yield valuable information and are convenient. The disadvantage is the lack of research supporting the reliability of these measurements.

The ethical guidelines of BACB requires BCBAs to conduct a functional assessment according to 3.01 Behavior-Analytic Assessment. RBT

(a) Behavior analysts conduct current assessments prior to making recommendations or developing behavior-change programs. The type of assessment used is determined by clients' needs and consent, environmental parameters, and other contextual variables. When behavior analysts are developing a behavior-reduction program, they must first conduct a functional assessment.

(b) Behavior analysts have an obligation to collect and graphically display data, using behavior-analytic conventions, in a manner that allows for decisions and recommendations for behavior-change program development (BACB, 2014, p.8).

Role of Functional Behavior Assessment as outlined by Cooper, Heron, and Heward (2007).

• Identifies antecedent variables that may be altered to prevent problem behaviors.
• Identifies reinforcement contingencies which can be altered so problem behavior no longer receives reinforcement.
• Identifies reinforcers for alternative replacement behavior.
• Reduces the reliance on default technologies such as punishment.

Conducting a functional behavior assessment as outlined by Cooper, Heron, and Heward (2007).

• Conduct indirect assessments
• Conduct a descriptive assessment
• Analyze data from the indirect and descriptive assessment and create a hypotheses
• Test conditions the data suggest may be contributing to the behavior using a functional analysis
• Develop intervention strategies based on the results.

Assessment:

- Have supervisee list in order the process of completing a functional assessment.
- Have supervisee describe the benefits and limitations of each of the assessment procedures.
- Use behavior skills training techniques to teach your supervisee how to conduct an indirect assessment. Accompany the supervisee in completing their first indirect assessment and provide reinforcement and feedback following the session.
- Use behavior skills training techniques to teach your supervisee how to collect ABC data. Explain the process, model and then practice using you tube videos of challenging behaviors. Provide reinforcement and feedback and continue practicing until the supervisee clearly demonstrates skills in collecting ABC data. Accompany the supervisee in completing live ABC data, take interrater reliability and compare scores providing reinforcement and feedback.
- Use behavior skills training techniques to teach your supervisee how to complete an FA. Practice until the supervisee clearly demonstrates skills in the control condition and some test conditions of an FA. Accompany the supervisee in completing live FAs, prompting and providing reinforcement and feedback. Continue to monitor supervisee in this process until they have demonstrated the completion of multiple FA's accurately and are able to set up individualized FAs based on the descriptive data.

Relevant Literature:

Baer, D. M., Wolf, M. M., & Risley, T. R. (1987). Some still-current dimensions of applied behavior analysis. *Journal of Applied Behavior Analysis*, *20*(4), 313-327.

Behavior Analyst Certification Board (BACB) Behavior Analyst Certification Board professional and ethical compliance code for behavior analysts. 2014. Retrieved from http://www.bacb.com/Download-files/BACB_Compliance_Code.pdf.

Cooper, J. O., Heron, T. E., & Heward, W. L. (2007). Applied Behavior Analysis: 2nd Edition. Pearson Education, Inc..

Hanley, G. P., Iwata, B. A., & McCord, B. E. (2003). Functional analysis of problem behavior: A review. *Journal of Applied Behavior Analysis*, *36*(2), 147-185.

Iwata, B. A., Pace, G. M., Dorsey, M. F., Zarcone, J. R., Vollmer, T. R., Smith, R. G. Willis, K. D. (1994). The functions of self-injurious behavior: An experimental-epidemiological analysis. *Journal of Applied Behavior Analysis*, *27*(2), 215–240.

Pence, S. T., Roscoe, E. M., Bourret, J. C., & Ahearn, W. H. (2009). Relative contributions of three descriptive methods: Implications for behavioral assessment. *Journal of Applied Behavior Analysis*, *42*(2), 425-446.

Sasso, G. M., Reimers, T. M., Cooper, L. J., Wacker, D., Berg, W., Steege, M. & Allaire, A. (1992). Use of descriptive and experimental analyses to identify the functional properties of aberrant behavior in school settings. *Journal of Applied Behavior Analysis*, *25*(4), 809-821.

Related Lessons:
B-03 Systematically arrange independent variables to demonstrate their effects on dependent variables
B-05 Use alternating treatment designs
E-01 Use interventions based on manipulation of antecedents, such as motivating operations and discriminative stimuli
H-01 Select a measurement system to obtain representative data given the dimensions of the behavior and the logistics of observing and recording
H-03 Select a data display that effectively communicates relevant quantitative relations
H-05 Evaluate temporal relations between observed variables
I-03 Design and implement individualized behavioral assessment procedures

Footnotes:
*Functional analysis may also be called an analog analysis or experimental analysis.
*Descriptive analysis may also be called direct assessment.

I-05 Organize, analyze and interpret observed data

Organize the data

- Once data have been collected in their raw format, it is then important to organize the data into a format that is easy to analyze (Cooper, Heron & Heward, 2007). The most effective way to do this, and the most common method utilized by Behavior Analysts, is to visually display the data in a **graph** (Cooper, Heron, & Heward, 2007).
- As Parsonson and Baer (1978, p. 134) said "the function of the graph is to communicate…..in an attractive manner, descriptions and summaries of the data that enable rapid and accurate analysis of the facts" (cited from Cooper, Heron & Heward, 2007, p. 128).
- The visual formats most often used by behavior analysts are line graphs, bar graphs, cumulative records, semilogarithmic charts and scatterplots* (Cooper, Heron & Heward, 2007).

Analyze and interpret observed data

- Behavior analysts use a systematic form of assessing graphically displayed data called **visual analysis** (Cooper, Heron & Heward, 2007).
- Visual analysis encompasses examining each of three characteristics in a graphic display of data, both within and across the different conditions and phases of an experiment. These three characteristics are:
  - ○ The level of the data
  - ○ The extent and type of variability in the data
  - ○ The trends in the data
- Johnston and Pennypacker (1993b, p. 320) recommend that the viewer should carefully examine the graph's overall construction, paying attention to details such as the axis labels and the scaling of each axis, prior to attempting to interpret the data. They argue "it's impossible to interpret graphic data without being influenced by various characteristics of the graph itself" (cited from Cooper, Heron & Heward, 2007, p. 149).

Visual analysis within conditions

- Within given conditions, examination needs to occur to determine a few relevant factors (Cooper, Heron & Heward, 2007):
  - ○ The number of data points in each condition (in general, the more measurements of the dependent variable there are per unit of time, the more confidence one can have in the data).
  - ○ Variability (A high degree of variability usually indicates little control has been achieved over the factors influencing behavior).
  - ○ Level (examined in terms of its absolute value within a condition, the degree of stability/variability and the extent of change from one level to another).
  - ○ Trend (the trend indicates whether a particular behavior has increased, decreased or has neither increased nor decreased within a condition).

Visual analysis between conditions

- After examining the data within each condition or phase of a study, visual analysis now proceeds to examining the data between conditions (Cooper, Heron & Heward, 2007):
  - ○ Comparison needs to be made between the different conditions of the level, trend and variability of the data (Cooper, Heron & Heward, 2007, p. 154).

○   The data are examined in terms of the overall level of performance between conditions; generally when there is no overlap of data points between the highest values in one condition and the lowest values in another condition, there is a strong likelihood that the behavior changed from one condition to the next (Cooper, Heron & Heward, 2007, p. 154).

Once an "examination and comparison of changes in level, trend and variability between conditions has occurred, a comparison needs to be made of performance across *similar* conditions" (Cooper, Heron & Heward, 2007, p. 155). If a behavior change is found to have occurred over the course of an intervention, the next question to be asked is, "was the behavior change a result of the intervention?" (Cooper, Heron & Heward, 2007, p. 155).

Assessment:

• Ask your Supervisee to explain why it's important as a behavior analyst to organize and interpret observed data.

• Ask your Supervisee to organize a set of data and display it graphically in the most appropriate way.

Relevant Literature:

Cooper, J. O., Heron, T. E., & Heward, W. L. (2007). *Applied Behavior Analysis*, 2nd ed. Upper Saddle River, New Jersey: Pearson Prentice Hall.

Fisher, W. W. Piazza, C. C. & Roane, H. S. (2011). *Handbook of Applied Behavior Analysis*. New York: The Guildford Press.

Johnston, J., & Pennypacker, H. S. (1993b). *Readings for Strategies and tactics of behavioral research* (2nd ed.). Hillsdale, NJ: Erlbaum.

Parson, B. S. & Baer, D. M. (1978). The analysis and presentation of graphic data. In T. R. Kratochwill (Ed.), *Single subject research: Strategies for evaluating change* (p. 101 – 165). New York: Academic Press.

Related Lessons:

A-10: Design, plot and interpret data using equal-interval graphs

A-11: Design, plot and interpret data using a cumulative record to display data

B-04: Use withdrawal/reversal designs

B-05: Use alternating treatments (i.e., multielement) designs

B-06: Use changing criterion designs

B-07: Use multiple baseline designs

B-08: Use multiple probe designs

B-09: Use combinations of design elements

J-15: Base decision-making on data displayed in various formats

Footnotes

* See Cooper, Heron & Heward (2007), pages 129 – 154 for more information on these graphic displays.

I-06 Make recommendations regarding behaviors that must be established, maintained, increased, or decreased.

Hawkins (1984, p. 284) (cited from Cooper, Heron & Heward, 2007, p. 56) defined habilitation as "the degree to which the person's repertoire maximizes short and long term reinforcers for that individual and for others, and minimizes short and long term punishers."

When determining what behaviors to target, one can use the relevance of behavior rule (Ayllon and Azrin, 1968) as a guide. This rule states that a target behavior should only be selected if it is likely to produce reinforcement for the client in their natural environment. Another key factor is deciding if the behavior will generalize to other settings and be sustainable once the behavior change program has ended.

Cooper et al. (2007) provide some considerations when choosing a target behavior to increase, decrease, or maintain. These include:

1. Does this behavior pose any danger to the client or others?
2. How many opportunities will the person have to use this new behavior? Or how often does this problem behavior occur?
3. How long-standing is the problem or skill deficit?
4. Will changing the behavior produce higher rates of reinforcement for the person?
5. What will be the relative importance of this target behavior to the future skill development and independent functioning?
6. Will changing this behavior reduce negative attention from others?
7. Will the new behavior produce reinforcement for significant others?
8. How likely is success in changing this target behavior?
9. How much will it cost to change this behavior?

Example:
Dave has decided to implement an intervention to increase a student's compliance. He chose this because lack of compliance interferes with the student's ability to learn new skills and access reinforcement by completing their work and daily routines.

Assessment:
- Write a list of potential target behaviors. Have supervisee rank the behaviors in order of social significance and give rationale for their decisions.
- Have supervisee present a case study on a client they are familiar with, including the maladaptive behaviors in their repertoire. Have the supervisee choose two behaviors to target for intervention and state why they chose those behaviors.

Relevant Literature:
Ayllon, T. & Azrin, N.H. (1968). *The token economy: A motivational system for therapy and rehabilitation.* New York: Appleton-Century-Crofts.
Cooper, J.O., Heron, T.E. & Heward W.L. (2007). *Applied Behavior Analysis* (2nd Ed.), Upper Saddle River, NJ. Pearson Prentice Hall. 55-65, 237-238.
Hawkins, R.P. (1984) What is "meaningful" behavior change in a severely/profoundly retarded learner: The view of a behavior analytic parent. In W.L. Heward, T.E. Heron, D.S. Hill, & J. Trap-Porter (Eds.) *Focus on behavior analysis in education.* (pp. 282-286). Upper Saddle River, NJ: Prentice-Hall/ Merrill.
Hawkins, R.P. (1986) Selection of target behaviors. In R.O. Nelson & S.C. Hayes (Eds.), *Conceptual foundations of behavioral assessment* (pp. 331-385). New York: Guilford Press.
Rosales-Ruiz, J. & Baer, D.M. (1997). Behavioral cusps: A developmental and pragmatic concept for behavior analysis. *Journal of Applied Behavior Analysis*, 30, 533-544.

Related Lessons:

B-01: Use the dimensions of applied behavior analysis (Baer, Wolf, & Risley, 1968) to evaluate whether interventions are behavior analytic in nature.

G-03: Conduct a preliminary assessment of the client in order to identify the referral problem.

G-05: Describe and explain behavior, including private events, in behavior analytic (non-mentalistic) terms.

I-01: Define behavior in observable and measurable terms.

J-01: State intervention goals in observable and measurable terms.

J-05: Select intervention strategies based on the client's current repertoires.

J-08: Select intervention strategies based on the social validity of the intervention.

J-10: When a behavior is to be decreased, select an acceptable alternative behavior to be established or increased.

J-13: Select behavioral cusps as goals for intervention when appropriate.

FK-10: Behavior, response, response class.

I-07 Design and conduct preference assessments to identify putative reinforcers.

Definition:

Stimulus preference assessment-"a variety of procedures used to determine (a) the stimuli that the person prefers, (b) the relative preference values of those stimuli, (c) the conditions under which those preference values change when task demands, deprivation states, or schedules of reinforcement are modified." (Cooper, Heron, & Heward, 2007, pp. 275-276)

Preference assessments allow for one to evaluate a large number of stimuli in a brief period of time (Hagopian, Long, & Rush, 2004). These stimuli are likely to function as reinforcers for a client/participant. Preference assessments also take into account care provider options (Green et al. 1988).

Example:

- Example: Marvin is working to teach a student to make requests for preferred edibles using a picture exchange communication system. Unfortunately, the child is not demonstrating a preference and is equally likely to choose either of the two cards presented. He is equally likely to consume any edible that is associated with one of two cards. Marvin decides to do a preference assessment to see if he can identify an edible that the boy does *not* like. He conducts a paired stimulus preference assessment with eight items he thinks the student will potentially not prefer. He notices that initially the boy chooses the black licorice but then spits it out. Over several presentations the child's selection avoids this item. It is not consumed on any of the presentations scoring it as 0% or "not preferred."
- Example: The Zippadeedooda Perfume Company is testing a new line of products. They hire ten women to rate their new line of fragrances. They ask the ladies to smell each of the 8 samples provided and use a Likert type scale to have them rate each of the fragrances; *really like, somewhat like, neutral, somewhat dislike, and really dislike.* Those that

score the overall lowest ratings according to the test group are not marketed, as it is unlikely that their client base will find them appealing either.

- • Non-example: Marvin's student has worked hard on his schoolwork and has earned a choice of an edible. Marvin takes a box of candies out of his desk containing eight different types of sweets and tells his student that he can pick one. The boy chooses a chocolate candy over all the other options and eats it. He cannot assume that the child dislikes the rest of the candies because he did not observe the boy eating any of the others.

Assessment:

- Ask your supervisee to define a putative reinforcement assessment
- Ask your supervisee to state the purpose of a putative reinforcement assessment
- Require your supervisee to run a couple different types of reinforcer assessments. Provide feedback during role play and other observations.

Relevant Literature:

Cooper J.O, Heron T.E, Heward W.L. (2007). *Applied behavior analysis* (2nd ed.) Upper Saddle River, NJ: Pearson

Green, C.W., Reid, D. H., White, L. K., Halford, R. C., Brittain, D. P., & Gardner, S. M. (1988). Identifying reinforcers for persons with profound handicaps: Staff opinion versus systematic assessment of preferences. *Journal of Applied Behavior Analysis, 21,* 31-43.

Hagopian, L. P., Long, E. S., & Rush, K. S. (2004). Preference assessment procedures for individuals with developmental disabilities. *Behavior Modification, 28*(5), 668-677.

Related Lessons:

D-01-Use positive and negative reinforcement
I-07-Design and conduct preference assessments to identify putative reinforcers
J-04-Select intervention strategies based on client preferences

J-01 State intervention goals in observable and measurable terms

"Target behaviors are selected for study in applied behavior analysis because of their importance to the people involved. Applied behavior analysts attempt to increase, maintain, and generalize adaptive, desirable behaviors and decrease the occurrence of maladaptive, undesirable behaviors" (Cooper, Heron, & Heward, 2007, p. 69).

Van Houten (1979) cited in Cooper et al. (2007, p. 69) suggests "two basic approaches to determining socially valid goals: (a) Assess the performance of people judged to be highly competent, and (b) experimentally manipulate different levels of performance to determine empirically which produces optimal results. Regardless of the method used, specifying treatment goals before intervention begins providing a guideline for continuing or terminating treatment. Further, setting objective, predetermined goals helps to eliminate disagreements or biases among those involved in evaluating a program's effectiveness."

Examples:
- The intervention goal: Client's aggression will decrease by 80% of baseline levels across 5 consecutive school days. Staff will record every instance of hitting across the school day on the data collection sheet.
- The intervention goal: Client will expressively identify 10 different colors with 80% accuracy, across 3 consecutive days. Staff will record data on correct and incorrect responses.

Assessment:
- Have supervisee create a sample intervention goal that targets a response for increase.
- Have supervisee create a sample intervention goal that targets a response for decrease.
- Have supervisee explain why it's important to have objective predetermined intervention goals.

Relevant Literature:
Cooper, J. O., Heron, T. E., & Heward, W. L. (2007). *Applied behavior analysis*. Upper Saddle River, NJ: Pearson Education.
Houten, R. V. (1979). Social validation: The evolution of standards of competency for target behaviors. *Journal of Applied Behavior Analysis, 12*(4), 581-591

Related Lessons:
B-01 Use the dimensions of applied behavior analysis (Baer, Wolf, & Risley, 1968) to evaluate whether interventions are behavior analytic in nature.
I-01 Define behavior in observable and measurable terms.
I-02 Define environmental variables in observable and measurable terms.
FK-07 Environmental (as opposed to mentalistic) explanations of behavior

J-02 Identify potential interventions based on assessment results and the best available scientific evidence.

"Interventions should be functionally equivalent to problem behavior" (Cooper, Heron, & Heward, 2007, p. 513). In other words, the intervention should serve as a more appropriate way of accessing a specific function than the interfering behavior. "One effective way to design interventions is to review confirmed hypotheses to determine how the ABC contingency can be altered to promote more positive behavior" (Cooper, et al., 2007, p. 513). In other words if you can change the antecedents or consequences associated with a problem behavior, you may be able to decrease occurrences of that behavior.

Wolf (1978) recommended that interventions should be assessed based on appropriateness and the potential social significance of the outcomes. Specific social validity assessments can be conducted "to help choose and guide (behavior change) program developments and applications" (Baer & Schwartz, 1991, p. 231).

Results of an FBA can help determine which interventions would not be appropriate to decrease the target behavior. Once assessments are completed, monitor the progress of the interventions put in place and conduct follow up assessments regularly. Any intervention program should be based on techniques found in behavior analytic literature. This ensures that the intervention is a proven technology and has stood up to experimental manipulation and decreased or increased similar types of behavior.

In regard to assessments that are not based on the function of the behavior, (i.e., adaptive assessments, verbal behavior assessments, cognitive assessments) a profile of strengths and weaknesses as well as standard scores and rankings are typically provided once the assessment is completed. The areas that present as weaknesses should typically be addressed first based on their social significance to the client. Once these areas have been identified, appropriate interventions can be put into place to build the client's missing repertoires and skill base.

Example:
George completed an FBA on Sam's instances of aggression in the classroom. The hypothesized function for this behavior was escape from demands. George created an intervention plan that would allow Sam to functionally ask for breaks to briefly escape work demands.

Assessment:
- Assign a specific behavior as well as a hypothesized function of that behavior. Have supervisee research and identify 3 potential interventions to decrease the target behavior based on the hypothesized function.
- Have supervisee explain under what circumstances they would use each intervention.

Relevant Literature:
Baer, D.M. & Schwartz, I.S. (1991). If reliance on epidemiology were to become epidemic, we would need to assess its social validity. *Journal of Applied Behavior Analysis*, 24, 321-334.

Cooper, J.O., Heron, T.E. & Heward W.L. (2007). *Applied Behavior Analysis* (2nd Ed.), Upper Saddle River, NJ. Pearson Prentice Hall. 55-65, 237-240, 513-523, 623-624.

Gresham, F., Watson, T.S., & Skinner, C.H. (2001). *Functional Behavioral Assessment: Principals, Procedures, and Future Directions.* School Psychology Review, 30, 2, 156-172.

Lerman, D.C., Iwata, B.A., Smith, R.G., Zincone, J.R., & Vollmer, T.R. (1994). Transfer of behavioral function as a contributing factor in treatment relapse. *Journal of Applied Behavior Analysis*, 27, 357-370.

Related Lessons:
E-01: Use interventions based on manipulation of antecedents, such as motivating operations and discriminative stimuli.

I-01: Define behavior in observable and measurable terms.

I-02: Define environmental variables in observable and measurable terms.

I-04: Design and implement the full range of functional assessment procedures.

I-06: Make recommendations regarding behaviors that must be established, maintained, increased, or decreased.

J-01: State intervention goals in observable and measurable terms.

J-02: Identify potential interventions based on assessment results and the best available scientific evidence.

J-10: When a behavior is to be decreased, select an acceptable alternative behavior to be established or increased.

J-03 Select intervention strategies based on task analysis

What are the options for intervention strategies when it comes to teaching a chain of behavior through a task analysis?

- Once a person's baseline level has been assessed (through the single or multiple-opportunity method*) to determine what components of the task analysis he/she can perform, the appropriate intervention strategy needs to be selected. Cooper, Heron & Heward (2007) suggest there are four appropriate intervention strategies which practitioners can choose from; forward chaining, total-task chaining, and backward chaining.
- Cooper, Heron and Heward (2007, p. 446) argue that research to date does not suggest a clear answer to the question "which chaining strategy to use?" As such, it is very important to examine the results of the baseline level assessment, to consider the client and how they learn best, and what the different intervention strategies can offer in different situations, in order to select the most appropriate method.

Total-task chaining

- If the client performs quite a few steps in the task analysis but is not performing them in the correct sequence, the most appropriate method to choose would probably be total-task chaining.
- Total-task chaining would also be an appropriate intervention strategy to select when the client has generalized motor imitation and moderate to severe disabilities (Test et al., 1990, cited from Cooper, Heron & Heward, 2007).
- When the chain is quite short and not too complex, this may also be an appropriate teaching method to utilize (Cooper, Heron & Heward, 2007).

Forward chaining

- This approach may be more appropriate to use when the client has demonstrated more proficiency with the *first* couple of steps in the chain and/or the last steps in the chain are more complex to complete.
- It may also be useful to use this approach when it is necessary to link smaller chains into larger ones. For example, if you have a skill such as bed making and this is made up of perhaps

four/five skill clusters, forward chaining is a useful method to link the skill clusters altogether (Cooper, Heron & Heward, 2007).

Backward chaining

- Backward chaining may be more appropriate to use when the client has demonstrated more proficiency with the *last* couple of steps in the chain and/or steps that appear earlier in the chain are more complex to complete.

Assessment:

- Ask your Supervisee to identify situations in which he/she might suggest forward chaining
- Ask your Supervisee to identify situations in which he/she might suggest backward chaining
- Ask your Supervisee to identify situations in which he/she might suggest total-task chaining

Relevant Literature:

Cooper, J. O., Heron, T. E., & Heward, W. L. (2007). *Applied Behavior Analysis*, 2nd ed. Upper Saddle River, New Jersey: Pearson Prentice Hall.

Kazdin, A. E. (2001). *Behavior Modifications in applied settings* (6th ed). Belmont, CA: Wadsworth.

Miltenberger, R. G. (2001). *Behavior Modification: Principles and procedures* (2nd ed). Belmont, CA: Wadsworth/Thomson Learning.

Test, D. W., Spooner, F. Keul, P. K., & Grossi, T. (1990). Teaching adolescents with severe disability to use the public telephone. *Behavior Modification, 14*, 157-171. Cited from, Cooper, J. O., Heron, T. E., & Heward, W. L. (2007, p. 446). *Applied Behavior Analysis*, 2nd ed. Upper Saddle River, New Jersey: Pearson Prentice Hall.

Related Lessons:

D-06: Use chaining
D-07: Conduct task analyses
J-02: Identify potential interventions based on assessment results & best scientific evidence.
J-05: Select intervention strategies based on the client's current repertoire

Footnotes

* Please see task list item D-07 for more information on conducting task analyses
* Please see task list item D-06 for a more detailed description of the different chaining procedures.

J-04 Select intervention strategies based on client preferences

The importance and ethical necessity of basing intervention strategies on client preferences

- As behavior analysts, it is our ethical responsibility to continually put our client's needs first, and this includes, considering which type of intervention may be more preferred by the clients we serve. As Bailey and Burch (2011) state, one of our core ethical principles is treating others with care and compassion and this encompasses giving our clients choices (Bailey & Burch, 2011).

- Historically, consideration of client preferences is an area that within behavior analysis, perhaps has not been given as much attention as it deserves. In one area of study, Hanley, Piazza, Fisher, Contrucci & Maglieri (1997) reported that, "few if any studies have examined the social acceptability of or consumer preferences" for the relevant treatment options but had instead given more weight to the opinions of the caregivers as opposed to those of the client (Hanley *et al.*, 1997, p. 460). Another interesting train of thought has been that "choice making is often not taught" (Bannerman, Sheldon, Sherman, & Harchik, 1990, p. 81).

- Another reason for considering clients' preferences over treatment options is it may make the intervention more *successful*. Data from Miltenberger, Suda, Lennox and Lindeman (1991) indicated it was very important for successful treatment, to consider client preferences when selecting interventions. Findings from many other studies have also supported this premise (e.g., Berk, 1976; Hanley, Piazza, Fisher, & Maglieri, 2005; Mendonca & Brehm, 1983; Perlmuter & Montry, 1973).

Selecting interventions based on client preferences

- There are methods reported in the literature for determining which treatment method is more preferred by a client*. As such, once it has been established that an intervention is necessary to treat a behavior, it is imperative then to consider assessing a client's preference for one treatment option over others to assist with the behavior change program. In this way, treatment is more likely to be successful, will likely have more social validity (Schwartz & Baer, 1991) and will be meeting more of our ethical standards as behavior analysts.

Assessment:
- Ask your Supervisee to explain why it's important as behavior analysts to select interventions based on client preferences.
- Ask your Supervisee to investigate what different methods are available for evaluating clients' preferences for different interventions and report them back to you, along with advantages and disadvantages of each method.

Relevant Literature:
Bailey, J. & Burch, M. (2011). *Ethics for Behavior Analysts*, 2nd ed. New York, London: Routledge/Taylor & Francis Group.
Bannerman, D. J., Sheldon, J. B., Sherman, J. A., & Harchik, A. E. (1990). Balancing the right to habilitation with the right to personal liberties: The rights of people with developmental disabilities to eat too many doughnuts and take a nap. *Journal of Applied Behavior Analysis, 23*, 79–89.
Berk, R. A. (1976). Effects of choice of instructional methods on verbal learning tasks. *Psychological Reports, 38*, 867-870.

Hanley, G. P., Piazza, C. C., Fisher, W. W., Contrucci, S. A. & Maglieri, K. A. (1997). Evaluation of client preferences for function-based treatment packages. *Journal of Applied Behavior Analysis, 30*, 459-473.

Hanley, G. P., Piazza, C. C., Fisher, W. W. & Maglieri, K. A. (2005). On The Effectiveness of And Preference For Punishment And Extinction Components Of Function-Based Interventions. *Journal of Applied Behavior Analysis, 38*, 51-65.

Mendonca, P. J. & Brehm, S. S. (1983). Effects of choice on behavioral treatment of overweight children. *Journal of Social and Clinical Psychology, 1*, 343-358.

Miltenberger, R. G., Suda, K. T., Lennox, D. B. & Lindeman, D. P. (1991). Assessing the acceptability of behavioral treatments to persons with mental retardation. *American Journal on Mental Retardation, 96*, 291–298.

Perlmuter, L. C. & Montry, R. A. (1973). Effect of choice of stimulus on paired-associate learning. *Journal of Experimental Psychology, 99*, 120-123.

Related Lessons:
E-08: Use the matching law and recognize factors influencing choice
I-07: Design and conduct preference assessments to identify putative reinforcers
J-02: Identify potential interventions based on assessment results and the best available scientific evidence.
J-05: Select intervention strategies based on the client's current repertoire
J-06: Select intervention strategies based on supporting environments
J-07: Select intervention strategies based on environmental and resource constraints
J-08: Select intervention strategies based on the social validity of the intervention

Footnotes
*1 See Hanley, Piazza, Fisher, Contrucci & Maglieri (1997) and Miltenberger, Suda, Lennox & Lindeman (1991) for more information about how to test clients' preferences for different interventions.

J-05 Select intervention strategies based on the client's current repertoires

The importance of considering the client's current repertoires

- Basing intervention strategies on the client's current repertoires is a key foundation of what behavior analysts do. It is imperative that prior to implementing any type of intervention or strategy with a client, the behavior analyst is extremely clear about what the client already does and can therefore, consider possible intervention strategies. Noell, Call, and Ardoin (2011) state that "one of the considerable challenges in teaching arises from identifying not only the behaviors that are prerequisites for the target response, but also the level of skill proficiency needed to set the occasion for teaching the target skill" (Noell, Call, & Ardoin, 2011, cited from Fisher, Piazza, & Roane, 2011, p. 251).

The importance of accurate assessments

- In order to assess a client's current repertoires, it is imperative that these repertoires are properly assessed. For example, assessments to evaluate the presence of a particular skill or repertoire should take place in a variety of different environments, with many different examples of stimuli, with the antecedent presented in a variety of different ways, and with many different people presenting the skill. Novel examples of the skill should also be tested. Noell *et al.* (2011) emphasize this point by suggesting that "assessment of behavior under varied conditions in a manner that tests consequences should be an element of any pre-teaching assessment" (Noell, Call & Ardoin, 2011, cited from Fisher, Piazza & Roane, 2011, p. 255).

Once assessments of the client's current repertoires are complete

- Once the assessment stage is complete, it is then appropriate to select possible intervention strategies. As Noell *et al.* (2011) propose it is important at this point that behavior analysts "keep the long-term view in mind" (Noell, Call & Ardoin, 2011, cited from Fisher, Piazza &Roane, 2011, p. 266). We should be attempting to "not bring individual operants under stimulus control" but instead "help clients and students develop the complex, flexible repertoires that are adaptive, that remain in contact with reinforcement, and that confer adaptive advantage and endure" (Noell, Call & Ardoin, 2011, cf. Fisher, Piazza & Roane, 2011, p. 266).

Assessment:

- Ask your Supervisee to explain why it's important as a behavior analyst to select interventions based on the client's current repertoires.
- Ask your Supervisee to conduct an assessment with a client, if possible, and design potential interventions or strategies. Give feedback as appropriate.
- Have you Supervisee take the lead on assessing and developing interventions with your supervision.

Relevant Literature:

Fisher, W. W., Piazza, C. C., & Roane, H. S. (Eds.). (2011). *Handbook of applied behavior analysis.* Guilford Press.

Noell, G. H., Call, N. A. & Ardoin, S. P. (2011). Building complex repertoires from discrete behaviors by establishing stimulus control, behavioral chains, and strategic behavior.

Shapiro, E. S. (1996). *Academic skills problems: Direct assessment and intervention* (2nd ed.). New York: Guildford Press.

Related Lessons:

D-09: Use the verbal operants as a basis for language assessment.

G-03: Conduct a preliminary assessment of the client in order to identify the referral problem.

I-03: Design and implement individualized behavioral assessment procedures.

J-03: Select intervention strategies based on task analysis.

I-04: Design and implement the full range of functional assessment procedures.

J-02: Identify potential interventions based on assessment results & best scientific evidence.

J-06: Select intervention strategies based on supporting environments

J-07: Select intervention strategies based on environmental and resource constraints

J-08: Select intervention strategies based on the social validity of the intervention

J-06 Select intervention strategies based on supporting environments.

"Achieving optimal generalized outcomes requires thoughtful, systematic planning. This planning begins with two major steps: (1) selecting target behaviors that will meet natural contingencies of reinforcement, and (2) specifying all desired variations of the target behavior and the settings/situations in which it should (and should not) occur after instruction has ended" (Cooper, Heron, & Heward, 2007, p. 623). In other words, an intervention must be selected that will allow the client to access reinforcement in a specific environment. If that is not possible, then alternative interventions should be explored.

Ayllon and Azrin (1968) state that an important rule of thumb is to choose interventions that will help produce reinforcement after the intervention is discontinued. The intervention should support the student until they can access naturally existing contingencies (i.e., verbal praise from a teacher) and then more intensive, contrived contingencies should be systematically faded. The goal of most intervention programs is to teach a skill and then fade support so the client can implement that skill across settings.

Cooper, Heron, & Heward (2007, p. 626) identify 5 strategic approaches to promote generalized behavior change.

1. Teach the full range of relevant stimulus conditions and response requirements (i.e., teaching sufficient stimulus and response examples based on the setting)
2. Make the instructional setting similar to the generalization setting. (i.e., program common stimuli and teach loosely)
3. Maximize the target behavior's contact with reinforcement in the generalization setting. (i.e., ask people in the generalization setting to reinforce the target behavior, teach the learner to recruit reinforcement, and teach the target behavior to levels of performance required by natural existing contingencies of reinforcement.)
4. Mediate generalization (i.e., teach self-management skills & contrive mediating stimulus)
5. Train to generalize. (i.e., reinforce response variability and instruct learner to generalize)

Example:

George set up a token economy for Bill that systematically increased the number of responses needed to earn a token. After some time, Bill was earning tokens for completing an entire worksheet rather than earning a token for each question answered. This allowed Bill to independently complete worksheets in his general education classroom without a paraprofessional by his side giving him tokens after each answer.

Assessment:

- Give supervisee a reinforcement program. Have him/her create a fading procedure for this program to increase the number of responses required to earn a token.

- Have supervisee list the five strategies for promoting generalized behavior change and have him/her give examples of each.

- Have supervisee describe and differentiate between contrived contingencies and naturally existing contingencies and give several examples of each.

Relevant Literature:

Ayllon, T., & Azrin, N.H. (1968). *The token economy: A motivational system for therapy and rehabilitation.* New York: Appleton-Century-Crofts.

Baer, D.M. (1999). *How to plan for generalization* (2ⁿᵈ ed.). Austin, TX.: Pro-Ed.

Cooper, J.O., Heron, T.E. & Heward W.L. (2007). *Applied Behavior Analysis* (2ⁿᵈ Ed.), Upper Saddle River, NJ. Pearson Prentice Hall. 55-65, 623-624, 652.

Snell, M.E., & Brown. F. (2006). *Instruction of students with severe disabilities* (6ᵗʰ ed.). Upper Saddle River, NJ: Prentice Hall.

Stokes, T.F., & Baer, D.M. (1977). An implicit technology of generalization. *Journal of Applied Behavior Analysis*, 10, 349-367.

Stokes, T.F., & Osnes, P.G. (1989). An operant pursuit of generalization. *Behavior Therapy*, 20, 337-355.

Related Lessons:

G-08: Identify and make environmental changes that reduce the need for behavior analysis services.

J-07: Select intervention strategies based on environmental and resource constraints.

J-08: Select intervention strategies based on the social validity of the intervention.

J-11: Program stimulus & response generalization

J-12: Program for maintenance.

K-07: Evaluate the effectiveness of the behavioral program.

K-09: Secure the support of others to maintain the client's behavioral repertoires in their natural environments.

J-07 Select intervention strategies based on environmental and resource constraints.

"The independent variable should be evaluated not only in terms of its effects on the dependent variable, but also in terms of its social acceptability, complexity, practicality, and cost" (Cooper, Heron, & Heward, 2007, p. 250).

One method for determining the feasibility of an intervention is by asking consumers (parents, teachers, administrators) to rate the social validity of the client's performance. Questions that are typically posed to consumers before interventions are implemented include asking the consumer how reasonable they feel the intervention is, asking the consumer's willingness to implement the intervention strategies, asking if the consumer would be willing to change the environment to implement the intervention, asking how disruptive the intervention may be to the natural environment, asking how costly it would be to implement the intervention, asking if there will be any discomfort in the client when implementing these procedures, and asking if carrying out the intervention will fit with the classroom or setting routines (Reimers & Wacker, 1988 cited from Cooper et al., 2007, pp. 238-239).

Example:
Rob has decided to implement a reinforcement program based on appropriate responses rather than a fixed time DRO program. He understands that there is no paraprofessional in the classroom to help run the program and the teacher has other educational duties so she cannot run a timer and deliver reinforcement consistently enough for a rigorous DRO.

Assessment:
- Have supervisee come up create a list of appropriate questions to ask consumers when determining an interventions appropriateness and acceptability. Have each supervisee create his/her own treatment acceptability rating form.
- Have supervisee list and describe various extraneous factors that must be taken into consideration before implementing an intervention. Have supervisee explain why it is important to have consumer satisfaction with an intervention program.

Relevant Literature:
Cooper, J.O., Heron, T.E. & Heward W.L. (2007). *Applied Behavior Analysis* (2nd Ed.), Upper Saddle River, NJ. Pearson Prentice Hall. 240 (Figure 10.5), 250, 652, 674-676.

Hawkins, R.P. (1984). What is "meaningful" behavior change in a severely/ profoundly retarded learner: The view of a behavior analytic parent. In W.L. Heward, T.E. Heron, D.S. Hill, & J. Trap-Porter (Eds.), Focus on behavior analysis in education (pp. 282-286). Upper Saddle River, NJ: Prentice-Hall/Merrill.

Reimers, T.M., & Wacker, D.P. (1988). Parent's ratings of the acceptability of behavior treatment recommendations made in an outpatient clinic: A preliminary analysis of the influence of treatment effectiveness. *Behavioral Disorders*, 14, 7-15.

Wolf, M.M. (1978). Social Validity: The case for subjective measurement or how applied behavior analysis is finding its heart. *Journal of Applied Behavior Analysis*, 11, 203-214.

Related Lessons:
C-01: State and plan for the possible unwanted effects of reinforcement.
G-06: Provide behavior-analytic services in collaboration with others who support and/or provide services to one's clients.
G-08: Identify and make environmental changes that reduce the need for behavior analysis services.
I-01: Define behavior in observable and measurable terms.
I-02: Define environmental variables in observable and measurable terms.
J-06: Select intervention strategies based on supporting environments.
J-08: Select intervention strategies based on the social validity of the intervention.
K-07: Evaluate the effectiveness of the behavioral program.
K-09: Secure the support of others to maintain the client's behavioral repertoires in their natural environments.
FK-11: Environment, stimulus, stimulus class.

J-08 Select intervention strategies based on the social validity of the intervention

A distinguishing characteristic of applied behavior analysis is assessing an individual's functioning within the context of natural environments. This applied aspect focuses the behavior analyst on identifying meaningful goals and acceptable methods for intervention that will increase the individual's independence and level of functioning in natural settings. The behavior analyst sets intervention goals that comply with stated preferences of the individual client, goals of those who live and work with the individual, and consider how typical individuals function in similar environments. Analysts seek goals that are socially valid and intervention methods that are not only scientifically validated strategies for accomplishing those goals, but strategies that can be expected to be implemented consistently and with fidelity by those who will apply the strategies. Although an intervention might be effective in a clinical, controlled setting, the behavior analyst must consider intervention limitations related to "social acceptability, complexity, practicality, and cost. Regardless of their effectiveness, treatments that are perceived by practitioners, parents, and/or clients as unacceptable or undesirable for whatever reason are unlikely to be used" (Cooper et al, 2007, p. 250).

Examples:
A child hits her six month-old sister even when their parents model and reinforce appropriate behaviors toward the baby. The parents find it difficult to avoid explaining to the child, at the same time that they block her physically, reasons her behaviors are unkind and even dangerous. The behavior analyst talks to the parents about how the parent's explanations might be reinforcing the big sister aggression. The parents and the analyst increase the opportunities they have to individually attend to the child during appropriate play throughout the day. The parents ask the analyst to help them design a structured plan to teach appropriate sibling behaviors through language, modeling, literature, role play, movies, and increased reinforcement for appropriate behaviors of the sister toward her younger sibling.

A man hits his head and pulls at his ears with such force that he has required emergency medical care. At the beginning of treatment, the behavior analyst recommends that the man be given access to a helmet to prevent significant injury when he is not adequately staffed to stop his behavior. His family is against the man appearing in public with a protective helmet. The behavior analyst explains the reasons such equipment might be important for protecting the man from harm when his 1:1 staff person is distracted by driving a car or interacting with clerks or others in the community. The analyst and the family agree that until interventions stops the severe self-injury, the man will participate in community activities with a helmet unless a family member accompanies staff in the community with him.

Assessment:
A behavior analyst wants to increase a nonverbal teenager's independent functioning during daily care routines by teaching him to dress, brush teeth, and bathe independently. The boy's mother says she doesn't mind physically prompting her son through those daily care routines, but states that she hates his screaming while she does it.

The analyst completes a functional assessment and learns the following: The boy can complete most of the steps for dressing, brushing teeth, and bathing independently, but has not learned a consistent chain of steps for each skill. The boy screams at other times during the day when his mother uses physical prompting. Ask the supervisee to consider the social validity of the behavior analyst's goals and the preferences expressed by the boy's mother.

1. Ask the supervisee to write at least one hypothesis to explain, based on the information above, what might be the relations between the self-care skills and the screaming behavior.

2. Ask the supervisee to explain to the mother why teaching the son chained steps for each skill is important for ending the screaming behavior in non-technical language in order to gain her support for teaching self-care routines.

Relevant Literature:

Cooper, J.O., Heron, T. E., & Heward, W. L. (2007). *Applied behavior analysis.* Upper Saddle River, NJ: Pearson Education.

Fawcett, S. B. (1991). Social validity: A note on methodology. *Journal of Applied Behavior Analysis, 24*(2), 235-239.

Wolf, M. M. (1978). Social validity: The case for subjective measurement or how applied behavior analysis is finding its heart. *Journal of applied behavior analysis, 11*(2), 203-214.

Related Lessons:

G-06 Provide behavior-analytic services in collaboration with others who support and/or provide services to one's clients

G-08 Identify and make environmental changes that reduce the need for behavior analysis services.

I-06 Make recommendations regarding behaviors that must be established, maintained, increased, or decreased.

J-04 Select intervention strategies based on client preferences.

J-05 Select intervention strategies based on the client's current repertoires.

J-06 Select intervention strategies based on supporting environments.

J-12 Program for maintenance.

K-02 Identify the contingencies governing the behavior of those responsible for carrying out behavior-change procedures and design interventions accordingly.

K-03 Design and use competency-based training for persons who are responsible for carrying out behavioral assessment and behavior-change procedures.

K-09 Secure the support of others to maintain the client's behavioral repertoires in their natural environments.

J-09 Identify and address practical and ethical considerations when using experimental designs to demonstrate treatment effectiveness

The general goal of behavioral research is "to demonstrate that measured changes in the target behavior occur because of experimentally manipulated changes in the environment" (Cooper, 2007, p. 160). Without a controlled research design, practitioners cannot claim a causal relation between intervention and behavior change. Practical and ethical concerns limit practitioner's use of experimental designs in most settings. Typical risks associated with controlled research include the need to delay treatment while collecting baseline data or to withdraw interventions that are successful. Each research design has specific risks to participants associated with its application. In applied practice, meaningful, socially valid, and lasting change is the goal. Clients, parents, staff, and teachers prefer the most efficient and effective path toward treatment goals. For such reasons, practitioners seek to show evidence of a correlation rather than a causal relation between changes in a client's behavior and an intervention by providing comparison of patterns of baseline (A) and intervention (B) responding over time. The AB design has poor experimental control but strong practical and ethical value in natural settings.

Examples:

A researcher-practitioner designed a multiple baseline study for a woman who hit and scratched herself. The researcher's review of the first three days of baseline data showed that occurrences of the behavior were highly variable without an obvious pattern of responding. The researcher concluded that further delay of treatment that might decrease a dangerous behavior was not ethical. The researcher knew that the strength of the results of his research would be threatened if he began treatment before he had a clear pattern in

baseline responding, but his responsibility to his client, and those close to her, was his primary concern. He regretted not anticipating this possibility by choosing a research design that could have demonstrated experimental control without depending on highly stable baseline responding.

A student's teacher did not want the student to participate in a graduate supervisee's study because the supervisee planned to work with the student during classroom reading instruction. Even though the research study was designed to provide a benefit to the student by increasing sight-word reading, the boy's parent refused to sign permission for his participation. The supervisee realized that social validity was threatened by his original plan and he would have to arrange to work with the student after school or exclude him from the study.

Assessment:

1. Ask the supervisee to explain what baseline logic is and why it is important for showing causal (experimentally controlled research) or correlational (change over time) relations between an intervention and an individual's behavior change.

2. A graduate student supervisee was planning to conduct single subject research using a withdrawal (ABAB) design. The supervisee wanted to test for a causal relation between a gel-filled wedge pillow and the fidgety, out-of-seat behavior of a middle school student in his class. His supervisor warned that removing an effective treatment might have long-lasting results on the student's performance. What design might the supervisee recommend that would show repetitive positive effects of the gel-filled pillow intervention

without requiring the supervisee to withdraw a beneficial treatment? Ask the supervisee to demonstrate his decision by drawing a rough line graph showing both designs with the gel-filled pillow as the intervention and explain why one design is a better choice ethically while still meeting practical goals for the supervisee and student.

Relevant Literature:

Cooper, J.O., Heron, T. E., & Heward, W. L. (2007). *Applied behavior analysis*. Upper Saddle River, NJ: Pearson Education.

Gast, D. L. (2010). *Single subject research methodology in behavioral sciences*. New York: NY: Routledge.

Related Lessons:

B-03 Systematically arrange independent variables to demonstrate their effects on dependent variables.

G-08 Identify and make environmental changes that reduce the need for behavior analysis services.

H-03 Select a data display that effectively communicates relevant quantitative relations.

J-02 Identify potential interventions based on assessment results and the best available scientific evidence.

06 Select intervention strategies based on supporting environments.

J-07 Select intervention strategies based on environmental and resource constraints.

J-08 Select intervention strategies based on the social validity of the intervention.

J-10 When a behavior is to be decreased, select an acceptable alternative behavior to be established or increased.

K-02 Identify the contingencies governing the behavior of those responsible for carrying out behavior-change procedures and design interventions accordingly.

K-07 Evaluate the effectiveness of the behavioral program

J-10 When a behavior is to be decreased, select an acceptable alternative behavior to be established or increased.

Definition:

Differential reinforcement of alternative behavior (DRA) - "a procedure for decreasing problem behavior in which reinforcement is delivered for a behavior that serves as desirable alternative to the behavior targeted for reduction and withheld following instances of the problem behavior" (Cooper, Heron & Heward, 2007, p. 693).

When choosing a replacement behavior, look at behavior that would serve the same function or would meet the same reinforcers for the problem behavior. This response could be using vocal-verbal behavior, exchanging a symbol, using sign language, etc. Consider the pros and cons of each mode. How quickly can the response be taught? Is it likely to be less or more effortful than the problem behavior? Will the new response meet reinforcement in natural settings?

Initially, the response to be taught should be reinforced on a continuous reinforcement schedule to ensure that the individual makes steady contact with the reinforcer and that this new replacement behavior occurs often and becomes strengthened in the individual's repertoire. Once the new response is at strength, the DRA schedule should be thinned to reflect reinforcement rates that occur in the natural environment (e.g., a child learning to request for a break in lieu of eloping will not likely be granted a break every time he/she asks for one in a typical classroom environment).

Challenging behavior may resurge when DRA schedules are thinned. There are several techniques that can be utilized to decrease this occurrence: increase the response requirement of the alternative response (e.g., if the alternate response is to ask for a break, allow a break only after completion of a set amount of work), provide a delay for reinforcement for the alternative response (e.g., provide a break after several minutes), decrease availability of alternative response materials (e.g. if break is requested utilizing a break card, limit amount of breaks or decrease presentation), and use of a multiple schedule of reinforcement such as providing more reinforcement for completing work than asking for a break (Sweeney & Shahan, 2013).

Assessment:
- At a job or during role-play, ask supervisee what would be an appropriate alternative behavior that would allow the individual to access same or similar reinforcer. Ask about alternative responses for a variety of reinforcer types.
- Have your supervisee list considerations when selecting an appropriate alternative replacement behavior
- At a job or during role-play, have your supervisee design criteria for when DRA schedule should be thinned and what that process should look like.

Relevant Literature:
Athen, E.S., & Vollmer, T.R., (2010). An investigation of differential reinforcement of alternative behavior without extinction. *Journal of Applied Behavioral Analysis, 43(4)*, 569-589.

Cooper, J. O., Heron, T. E., & Heward, W. L. (2007). *Applied behavior analysis* (2nd ed.). Upper Saddle River, NJ: Prentice Hall.

Sweeney, M.M., & Shahan, T.A., (2013). Effects of high, low, and thinning rates of alternative reinforcement on response elimination and resurgence. *Journal of the Experimental Analysis of Behavior, 100(1)*, 102-116.

Vollmer, T. R., Roane, H. S., Ringdahl, J. E., & Marcus, B. A. (1999). Evaluating treatment challenges with differential reinforcement of alternative behavior. *Journal of Applied Behavior Analysis, 32*(1), 9-23.

Related Lessons:
D-02 Use appropriate parameters and schedules of reinforcement.
D-18. Use Extinction.
D.-19 Use combinations of reinforcement with punishment and extinction.
I-06 Make recommendations regarding behaviors that must be established, maintained, increased or decreased.
J-06 Select intervention strategies based on supporting environments.
J-07 Select intervention strategies based on environmental and resource constraints.

J-11 Program for stimulus and response generalization

Behavior analysts teach socially significant skills to help clients function where they work or live. Program interventions for the client behavior to contact naturally occurring reinforcement contingencies in their typical environments using new skills. Generalization might result in a "a great deal of generalized behavior change; that is, after all components of an intervention have been terminated, the learner may emit the newly acquired target behavior, as well as several functionally related behaviors not observed previously in his repertoire, at every appropriate opportunity in all relevant settings, and he may do so indefinitely" (Cooper, Heron, & Heward, 2007, p. 621).

To increase stimulus generalization, the behavior analyst systematically varies where intervention is implemented, conditions under which it is implemented, and people who implement it in a gradual manner from acquisition through practicing stages. To develop a response class of functionally equivalent skills, the behavior analyst trains using a variety of responses that eventually may include incorrect responses and novel correct responses.

Assessment:
- Have supervisee read Stokes and Baer (1977).
- Have supervisee list and describe the ways one might program for generalization.
- Provide examples of skills that may be taught to an individual. Have supervisee describe how they can program for generalization and indicate which type of generalization (stimulus or response) they will be training.

Example:

Stimulus generalization strategies Teach:	Response generalization strategies Teach:
A range of appropriate situations and people to greet socially: Teacher; peer; parent; sibling; or stranger passing on sidewalk.	A range of appropriate responses: "Hello"; "HI"; head nod; or "How are you?"
A range of appropriate math addition sentences: Two plus two equals four; $2 + 2 = 4$	A range of appropriate behaviors to show the math problem total: written number 4; saying "four;" or holding up four fingers.
A range of ways for others to ask for a choice: "Tell me what you want"; "point to what you want"; "take one".	A range of behaviors for appropriately making choices: point; take; sign; or tell.

Relevant Literature:
Cooper, J.O., Heron, T. E., & Heward, W. L. (2007). *Applied behavior analysis*. Upper Saddle River, NJ: Pearson Education.
Stokes, T. F., & Baer, D. M. (1977). An implicit technology of generalization. *Journal of Applied Behavior Analysis, 10*(2), 349-367.

Related Lessons:
E-02 Use discrimination training procedures.
I-06 Make recommendations regarding behaviors that must be established, maintained, increased, or decreased.
J-02 Identify potential interventions based on assessment results and the best available scientific evidence.
J-12 Program for maintenance.
FK-11 environment, stimulus, stimulus class
FK-12 stimulus equivalence
FK-24 Stimulus control
FK-36 response generalization

J-12 Program for Maintenance

Response maintenance refers to "the extent to which a learner continues to perform the target behavior after a portion or all of the intervention responsible for the behavior's initial appearance in the learner's repertoire has been terminated" (Cooper, Heron & Heward, 2007, p. 703). Rusch and Kazdin (1981) note that withdrawing or gradually fading components of an individual's treatment package can support response maintenance.

Program for behavior learned in structured environments to be maintained with contingencies in the client's natural environment. Thin reinforcement schedules so that the natural environment can support and continue to maintain similar rates in behavior (e.g. While learning to mand, a child may be given a chip every time she asks for a chip. However, as she becomes more adept with this goal, the schedule of reinforcement should move from a continuous schedule to an intermittent schedule because the child will not always be given a chip upon request in her natural environment.)

Response maintenance can often be confused with generalization across multiple exemplars. The key difference is that response maintenance is said to occur if the response can be maintained in settings and situations in which it was previously exhibited, *after* generalization to that setting and/or situation has already occurred at least once in the past. For instance, if an individual was taught how to purchase items at a store and did so successfully at some point at Starbucks, McDonald's and Target but did not exhibit this skill at Starbucks a month later, a lack of response maintenance is said to occur. If, however, the individual did not exhibit the skill at Macy's where the individual has never performed the skill, a lack of generalization is said to occur (Cooper, Heron, & Heward, 2007).

Assessment:
- Have supervisee give examples of response maintenance.
- In a role-play or on the job, ask supervisee how he/she would program for response maintenance.

Relevant Literature:
Cooper, J. O., Heron, T. E., & Heward, W. L. (2007). *Applied behavior analysis* (2nd ed.). Upper Saddle River, NJ: Prentice Hall.
Rusch, F. R. & Kazdin, A.E. (1981). Toward a methodology of withdrawal designs for the assessment of response maintenance. *Journal of Applied Behavioral Analysis, 14 (2),* 131-140.

Related Lessons:
J-06 Select intervention strategies based on supporting environments
J-07 Select intervention strategies based on environmental and resource constraints
J-08 Select intervention strategies based on social validity of intervention
J-11 Program for stimulus and response generalization

J-13 Select behavioral cusps as goals for intervention when appropriate.

"A behavior that has consequences beyond the change itself, some of which may be considered important…What makes a behavior change a cusp is that it exposes the individual's repertoire to new environments, especially new reinforcers and punishers, new contingencies, new responses, new stimulus controls, and new communities of maintaining or destructive contingencies. When some or all of these events happen, the individual's repertoire expands; it encounters a differentially selective maintenance of the new as well as some old repertoires, and perhaps that leads to some further cusps." (Rosales-Ruiz & Baer, 1997, p. 534).

Bosch and Fuqua (2001) cited 5 criteria for a behavior to be considered a behavioral cusp. "They stated that a behavior might be a cusp if it meets one or more of five criteria: "(a) access to new reinforcers, contingencies, and environments; (b) social validity; (c) generativeness; (d) competition with inappropriate responses; and (e) number and the relative importance of people affected." (Bosch & Fuqua, 2001, p. 125 via Cooper et al., 2007, p. 59).

Examples:
Common behavioral cusps include crawling, reading, imitation skills, walking, talking, and writing. These skills set the stage for the client to develop and learn many other skills (i.e., reading allows a client to access leisure material, access information, and is necessary in regards to reading street and safety signs, and accessing various other forms of reinforcement).

Assessment:
- Have supervisee identify 5 behaviors that he/she feels are behavioral cusps. Have him/her describe why the behavior is a behavioral cusp.
- Have supervisee read Rosales-Ruiz & Baer (1997) article on behavioral cusps. Have him/her summarize the main points of this article.

Relevant Literature:
Cooper, J.O., Heron, T.E. & Heward W.L. (2007). *Applied Behavior Analysis* (2nd Ed.), Upper Saddle River, NJ. Pearson Prentice Hall. 58-59.
Rosales-Ruiz, J., & Baer, D. M. (1997). Behavioral cusps: A developmental and pragmatic concept for behavior analysis. *Journal of Applied Behavior Analysis*, 30, 533–544.
Bosch, S. & Fuqua, R.W. (2001). Behavioral cusps: a model for selecting target behaviors. *Journal of Applied Behavior Analysis*, 34(1), 123-125.

Related Lessons:
G-08: Identify and make environmental changes that reduce the need for behavior analysis services.
I-01: Define behavior in observable and measurable terms.
I-06: Make recommendations regarding behaviors that must be established, maintained, increased, or decreased.
J-01: State intervention goals in observable and measurable terms.
J-08: Select interventions based on the social validity of the intervention.
J-14: Arrange instructional procedures to promote generative learning (i.e., derived relations).
FK-10: Behavior, response, response class.

J-14 Arrange instructional procedures to promote generative learning (i.e., derived relations).

Generative learning involves applying learning to novel contexts without being explicitly taught and is related to language and cognition. Deriving relations is based on the stimulus equivalence paradigm and procedures (Sidman, 1971). A small number of taught relations among stimuli may generate numerous derived relations (Wulfert & Hayes, 1988). Readers are encouraged to understand stimulus equivalence prior to arranging instructional procedures to promote generative learning. Experimental procedures often utilize matching-to-sample tasks or a computerized program called Implicit Relational Assessment Procedure (IRAP) to teach derived relations. It has been extensively studied in children with autism (Kilroe, Murphy, Barnes-Holmes, & Barnes-Holmes, 2014). The general instructional procedure involves providing explicit reinforcement for a series of conditional discriminations, after which untrained relations (i.e., derived relations) will emerge and can be subsequently reinforced.

Stimulus equivalence is one of several empirically supported examples of derived relations, as relations can be derived based on opposition, temporality, analogy, comparison, and distinction (Stewart, McElwee, & Ming, 2013). Relational Frame Theory (RFT) was developed as a behavior analytic account of human language and cognition (Hayes, Barnes-Holmes, & Roche, 2001) and addresses the need for a theoretical explanation for generative learning, Resources for learning RFT are included in the relevant literature section.

Example:
- A learner is taught that spoken word "apple" = picture of an apple = written word "apple" = picture of an apple. These two relations are directly taught. However, through this explicit training, the learner can derive that the spoken word "apple" = written word "apple." In this example, reinforcement should occur for successful matching of the two trained relations. Once the third relation is derived, the response should be reinforced.

Assessment:
- Ask supervisee to provide a definition of derived relations.
- Ask supervisee to provide examples of derived relations.
- Supervisor should ensure that supervisee thoroughly understands stimulus equivalence, matching-to-sample procedures, and conditional discriminations, in order to arrange instructional procedures to promote generative learning. Once this foundational learning has occurred, supervisor can ask supervisee to demonstrate teaching procedures that will facilitate generative learning.

Relevant Literature:
Hayes, S. C., Barnes-Holmes, D., & Roche, B. (2001). *Relational frame theory: A post-skinnerian account of human language and cognition.* New York, NY: Plenum Press.

Sidman, M. (1994). Equivalence relations and behavior: A research story. Boston, MA: Author's Cooperative.

Stewart, I., McElwee, J., & Ming, S. (2013). Language generativity, response generalization, and derived relational responding. *Analysis of Verbal Behavior, 29,* 137-155.

Torneke, N. (2010). *Learning RFT: An introduction to relational frame theory and its clinical application.* Oakland, CA: Context Press.

Wulfert, E., & Hayes, S. C. (1988). Transfer of a conditional ordering response through conditional equivalence classes. *Journal of the Experimental Analysis of Behavior, 50,* 125-144.

Related Lessons:
E-06 Use stimulus equivalence procedures.
FK-11 environment, stimulus, stimulus class.
FK-24 stimulus control.
FK-34 conditional discriminations.

J-15 Base decision-making on data displayed in various formats

Behavior analysts make decisions during assessment and intervention based on data. Graphic displays (e.g., line graphs, bar graphs, and cumulative graphs) aid accurate and efficient interpretation of quantitative data and facilitate communication with others. "The primary function of a graph is to communicate without assistance from the accompanying text" (Spriggs & Gast, 2010, p. 167). Line graphs are most often used by behavior analysts to show effects and possible functional relations between intervention (independent variable) and a defined behavior (dependent variable). Bar graphs are often used by behavior analysts to summarize or compare discrete aspects of recorded behavior. Cumulative graphs show the rate of change in responding across time. Although they may be used with duration or latency data, they are most often used to show frequency data. Behavior analysts often use tables to summarize data or other information. "An informative table supplements—rather than duplicates—the text" (APA, 2010). As with graphs, a table should communicate efficiently but include enough information to be understood alone without explanations in the text.

Examples:

Example 1: A behavior analyst interprets the effectiveness of a constant time delay procedure for teaching a student 10 sight words using the following line graph:

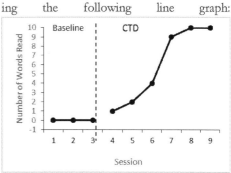

2: A behavior analyst uses a table to summarize the number of times a child chose a specific toy during seven sessions of free-play with four toys available.

Toy	Chosen 1st	Chosen 2nd	Chosen 3rd	Chosen 4th	Frequency of toy as 1st or 2nd choice
Car	5	2	0	0	7
Blocks	0	3	4	0	3
Bubbles	1	1	3	2	2
Doll	1	1	0	5	2

Assessment:

Example 1 data display: Ask the supervisee to interpret results of the constant time delay intervention using only the graphic data. Would the supervisee recommend CTD for teaching discrete skills to this student? Ask the supervisee to write a title for this graph.

Example 2 data display: Ask the supervisee to interpret information in the table to decide which toys she would place in a free time area for this child to enjoy. Would the supervisee consider adding different types of any one toy to the playtime area based on this data? If so, which type? If not, why not? Ask the supervisee to write a title for this table.

Relevant Literature:

American Psychological Association. (2010). *Publication manual of the American Psychological Association* (6th ed.). Washington, DC: Author.

Cooper, J. O., Heron, T. E., & Heward, W. L. (2007). *Applied behavior analysis.* Upper Saddle River, NJ: Pearson Education.

Spriggs, A. D., & Gast, D. L. (2010). Visual representation of data. In D. L. Gast (Ed.), *Single subject research methodology in behavioral sciences (pp 166-198).* New York, NY: Routledge.

Related Lessons:

A-10 Design, plot, and interpret data using equal-interval graphs.

A-11 Design, plot, and interpret data using a cumulative record to display data.

A-12 Design and implement continuous measurement procedures (e.g., event recording).

A-14 Design and implement choice measures.

B-03 Systematically arrange independent variables to demonstrate their effects on dependent variables.

H-01 Select a measurement system to obtain representative data given the dimensions of the behavior and the logistics of observing and recording.

H-03 Select a data display that effectively communicates relevant quantitative relations.

H-04 Evaluate changes in level, trend, and variability.

I-05 Organize, analyze, and interpret observed data.

I-07 Design and conduct preference assessments to identify putative reinforcers.

J-01 State intervention goals in observable and measurable terms.

K-04 Design and use effective performance monitoring and reinforcement systems.

FK-33 functional relations

K-01 Provide for Ongoing Documentation of Behavioral Services

Behavior analysts follow guidelines related to documentation in 2.10 and 2.11 of the Behavior Analyst Certification Board professional and ethical compliance code for behavior analysts Boundaries of Competence:

2.10 Documenting Professional Work and Research.

(a) Behavior analysts appropriately document their professional work in order to facilitate provision of services later by them or by other professionals, to ensure accountability, and to meet other requirements of organizations or the law.
(b) Behavior analysts have a responsibility to create and maintain documentation in the kind of detail and quality that would be consistent with best practices and the law.

2.11 Records and Data.

(a) Behavior analysts create, maintain, disseminate, store, retain, and dispose of records and data relating to their research, practice, and other work in accordance with applicable laws, regulations, and policies; in a manner that permits compliance with the requirements of this Code; and in a manner that allows for appropriate transition of service oversight at any moment in time.
(b) Behavior analysts must retain records and data for at least seven (7) years and as otherwise required by law. (BACB, 2014, p.9)

Written documentation of work products (such as raw data sheets, reports and spreadsheets) must be kept be kept in secure locations in the event that this information may need to be transferred to other professionals that are also supporting the client. Ongoing documentation and record-keeping also ensures accountability for services rendered. Documentation should be thorough and well-maintained; should the behavioral analysts'

professional services be involved in legal proceedings, documentation must be detailed and comprehensive enough to meet judicial scrutiny (Bailey & Burch, 2011).

Record disposal must sufficiently eliminate all confidential records that may reveal client's private health information. Electronic transfer of client's identifying information and records under any insecure medium (e.g. public areas, fax and email) are prohibited by the Health Insurance Portability and Accountability Act (Cooper, Heron, & Heward, 2007).

Assessment:

- Provide hypothetical scenarios and ask your supervisee if documentation of behavioral services was sufficient.
- Ask your supervisee where current work products are stored. Request to see written documentation of work products assess to see if documentation is thorough and well-maintained.
- Use behavioral skills training to practice documenting sessions with clients or observations of staff members.

Relevant Literature:

Bailey, J., & Burch, M. (2011). *Ethics for Behavior Analysts: 2nd Expanded Edition.* Taylor & Francis.

Behavior Analyst Certification Board (BACB) Behavior Analyst Certification Board professional and ethical compliance code for behavior analysts. 2014. Retrieved from www.bacb.com/Download-files/BACB Compliance Code.pdf.

Cooper, J. O., Heron, T. E., & Heward, W. L. (2007). *Applied behavior analysis* (2nd ed.). Upper Saddle River, NJ: Prentice Hall.

K-02 Identify the contingencies governing the behavior of those responsible for carrying out behavior-change procedures and design interventions accordingly.

Behavior is understood to be a product of the environment in which it occurs. This is the same for all organisms, including the client, the caretakers, the professionals working with the client, and ourselves. A well trained behavior analyst accounts for the environmental arrangement for all of the individuals involved in the behavior change process.

For instance, if a procedure is very effortful and will not produce an effect for several weeks, what will reinforce the behavior of the family member/teacher who will be implementing it? If a procedure produces lots of aggression or screaming, it should be considered that these are often aversive stimuli to the people implementing it.

"Treatment drift occurs when the application of the independent variable during later phases of an experiment differs from the way it was applied at the outset of the study." (Cooper et al., 2007, p. 235).This is often the result of a practitioner's behavior meeting competing contingencies after having followed the plan for a period of time.

High treatment integrity can be achieved by creating a thorough and precise definition for the independent variables, simplifying the treatment procedures, providing ample training and practice to all individuals responsible for treatment, and assessing the contingencies each person's behavior will meet while following through with these interventions.

Other factors that can help improve treatment integrity and regulate the behavior of those involved in the experiment include using less expensive and less intrusive procedures, seeking help and input from the participants family members and other people close to them, setting socially significant but easy-to-meet criterion for reinforcement, eliminat-

ing reinforcement gained outside of performing the target response, and contrive contingencies that will compete with natural contingencies.

Example:
Don has been asked to help deliver a new differential reinforcement program to decrease his student's self-injury. However, he has been short of staffing lately and cannot do this consistently throughout the day. This has caused the program to be run without integrity and the self-injury to remain at the same rates. Rick, the BCBA who designed the program, started observing the classroom to see why the program was not working. After noticing that Don was only delivering the reinforcers intermittently and missing opportunities for reinforcement, Rick decided to retrain Don and ask the principal for extra staff when someone calls out sick.

Non-example:
Roger is implementing a new response cost program to decrease verbal protesting for one of his students. However, even though the program has been run as designed for several weeks, there has been no effect on the verbal protesting of the student. The supervisor collected integrity data and found that the plan had been run as prescribed. The problem is likely related to the procedure itself and not its implementation.

Assessment:
- Make sure the supervisee makes considerations about the effort and practicality of the treatment they attempt to get other people to implement.
- Have supervisee identify several strategies for increasing treatment integrity.

Have him/her describe how they would use these strategies in an applied setting.

- Have supervisee read several articles in which an intervention was implemented to decrease or increase a target behavior. Have him/her identify the strategies the researcher used to increase treatment integrity.

- Have supervisee define and describe treatment drift. Have him/her describe how they would account for the occurrence of treatment drift and adjust an intervention or experiment accordingly.

Relevant Literature:

Cooper, J.O., Heron, T.E. & Heward W.L. (2007). *Applied Behavior Analysis* (2nd Ed.), Upper Saddle River, NJ. Pearson Prentice Hall. 235-236, 603-604, 607-609, 652, 659-678.

Fryling, M.F., Wallace, M.D., & Yassine, J.N. (2012). Impact of treatment integrity on intervention effectiveness. *Journal of Applied Behavior Analysis*, 45, 2, 449-453.

DiGennaro-Reed, F.D, Reed, D.D, Baez, C.N, & Maguire, H. (2011) A parametric analysis of errors of commission during discrete-trial training. *Journal of Applied Behavior Analysis*, 44,611–615.

Wheeler, J.J, Baggett, B.A, Fox, J., & Blevins, L. (2006). Treatment integrity: A review of intervention studies conducted with children with autism. *Focus on Autism and Other Developmental Disabilities*, 21, 45–54.

Wilder, D.A, Atwell, J., & Wine, B. (2006). The effects of varying levels of treatment integrity on child compliance during treatment with a three-step prompting procedure. *Journal of Applied Behavior Analysis*, 39, 369–373.

McIntyre, L.L, Gresham, F.M, DiGennaro, F.D, & Reed, D.D. (2007). Treatment integrity of school-based interventions with children in the Journal of Applied Behavior Analysis 1991–2005. *Journal of Applied Behavior Analysis*, 40, 659–672.

Peterson, L, Homer, A.L, & Wonderlich, S.A.(1982). The integrity of independent variables in behavior analysis. *Journal of Applied Behavior Analysis*, 15, 477–492.

St. Peter Pipkin, C, Vollmer, T.R, & Sloman, K.N. (2010). Effects of treatment integrity failures during differential reinforcement of alternative behavior: A translational model. *Journal of Applied Behavior Analysis*, 43, 47–70.

Related Lessons:

J-01: State intervention goals in observable and measurable terms.

K-03: Design and use competency-based training for persons who are responsible for carrying out behavioral assessment and behavior-change procedures.

K-04: Design and use effective performance monitoring and reinforcement systems.

K-05: Design and use systems for monitoring procedural integrity.

K-06: Provide supervision for behavior-change agents.

K-08: Establish support for behavior-analytic services from direct and indirect consumers.

K-03 Design and use competency-based training for persons who are responsible for carrying out behavioral assessment and behavior change procedures

Rationale
In order for staff and family members to collect accurate data and to carry out a behavior intervention plan effectively and consistently, all staff must receive training. Inconsistent applications of procedures may lead to slow improvement or have effects that make behavior worse than before treatment.

Training models
Much research has studied competency based training for staff, teachers and parents. Parsons and Reed (1995) increased staff performance by using classroom-based instruction, observation, and feedback on the work site. Shore et al. (1995) provided training in data collection, calculation, and review of treatment procedure, followed by training in treatment implementation in-situ with feedback and assistance. A third phase of instructing supervisors how to train direct service providers was implemented. Sarokoff and Sturmey (2004) provided staff with a written definition of the plan, feedback regarding their baseline performance, rehearsal with reinforcement and corrective feedback, and in-situ modeling and rehearsal for 10 minutes. Miles and Wilder (2009) used Behavior Skills Training (BST) that involved providing a written description, reviewing baseline performance, rehearsal and feedback, and then repeating modeling and rehearsal until the staff completed three trials accurately.

BST has also been used to train individuals to conduct behavioral assessments such as functional analyses. For example, Iwata et al. (2000) and Lambert, Bloom, Clay, Kunnavatanna, and Collins (2014) trained participants to conduct functional analysis conditions with adequate fidelity.

Elements of competency-based training
- Clear instructions
- Modeling
- Rehearsal
- Feedback
- Repetition until skills mastered
- Treatment Integrity data monitored

Threats to accuracy and reliability
Poor staff training can lead to inaccurate baseline, functional assessment and treatment data. Systematic training of occurrence and nonoccurrence and other critical data collection information and providing booster training will help to minimize the following challenges:
- Observer drift
- Observer reactivity

Assessment:
- Ask your supervisee to list elements of competency-based training.
- Ask your supervisee to create an example curriculum for training staff to collect ABC data collection.
- Use behavior skills training to teach your supervisee to teach a treatment procedure to staff.

Relevant Literature:
Cooper, J. O., Heron, T. E., & Heward, W. L. (2007). Applied Behavior Analysis: 2ⁿᵈ Edition. Pearson Education, Inc..

Iwata, B. A., Wallace, M. D., Kahng, S., Lindberg, J. S., Roscoe, E. M., Conners, J., ... & Worsdell, A. S. (2000). Skill acquisition in the implementation of functional analysis methodology. *Journal of Applied Behavior Analysis*, *33*(2), 181-194.

Lambert, J. M., Bloom, S. E., Clay, C. J., Kunnavatana, S. S., & Collins, S. D. (2014). Training residential staff and supervisors to conduct traditional functional analyses. *Research in developmental disabilities*, *35*(7), 1757-1765.

Miles, N. I., & Wilder, D. A. (2009). The effects of behavioral skills training on caregiver implementation of guided compliance. *Journal of applied behavior analysis*, *42*(2), 405-410.

Parsons, M. B., & Reid, D. H. (1995). Training residential supervisors to provide feedback for maintaining staff teaching skills with people who have severe disabilities. *Journal of Applied Behavior Analysis*, *28*(3), 317-322.

Sarokoff, R. A., & Sturmey, P. (2004). The effects of behavioral skills training on staff implementation of discrete-trial teaching. *Journal of Applied Behavior Analysis*, *37*(4), 535-538.

Shore, B. A., Iwata, B. A., Vollmer, T. R., Lerman, D. C., & Zarcone, J. R. (1995). Pyramidal staff training in the extension of treatment for severe behavior disorders. *Journal of Applied Behavior Analysis*, *28*(3), 323-332.

Related Lessons:
D-04 Use modeling and imitation training
D-05 Use shaping
E-03 Use instructions and rules
F-03 Use direct instruction
K-02 Identify the contingencies governing the behavior of those responsible for carrying out behavior-change procedures and design interventions accordingly

K-04 Design and use effective performance monitoring and reinforcement systems

Rationale
Staff performance in the application of behavioral strategies is critical to the success of the behavior intervention plan. Developing a system to monitor staff performance and motivate staff performance is just as important as developing an effective intervention plan.

Staff performance models
Richman, Riordan, Reiss, Pyles, and Bailey (1988) found that self-monitoring and supervision feedback increased staff performance.

Arco (2008) found that defining the process before training, providing on-the job supervisory feedback, and having staff provide self-generated outcome feedback before and after training was effective at increasing and maintaining the performance in behavioral treatment programs.

Codding, Feinberg, Dunn, and Pace (2004) found that treatment integrity increased following a one hour performance feedback session every other week. Social validity ratings provided favorable feedback for the frequent supervisions.

Iwata, Bailey, Brown, Foshee, and Alpern (1976) found that performance-based lottery improved the performance of institutional staff.

Elements of providing effective performance based monitoring and reinforcement systems
- Provide clear instructions and objectives in observable measurable terms
- Develop treatment integrity checklist
- Train the supervisor to provide supervision and frequent on the job feedback (both corrective and positive)
- Train staff to collect a self-monitoring system for their performance
- Train the supervisor to provide social or tangible reinforcement based on performance of the staff
- Teach the supervisor to graph and monitor staff performance while looking for trend lines

Assessment:
- Ask your supervisee to list elements of providing effective performance based monitoring and reinforcement systems.

- Ask your supervisee to create an example of performance based monitoring and a reinforcement system for a current intervention plan.
- Use behavior skills training to teach your supervisee to implement the approved procedure with staff.

Relevant Literature:
Arco, L. (2008). Feedback for improving staff training and performance in behavioral treatment programs. *Behavioral Interventions*, *23*(1), 39-64.

Codding, R. S., Feinberg, A. B., Dunn, E. K., & Pace, G. M. (2005). Effects of immediate performance feedback on implementation of behavior support plans. *Journal of Applied Behavior Analysis*, *38*(2), 205-219.

Iwata, B. A., Bailey, J. S., Brown, K. M., Foshee, T. J., & Alpern, M. (1976). A performance-based lottery to improve residential care and training by institutional staff. *Journal of Applied Behavior Analysis*, *9*(4), 417-431.

Richman, G. S., Riordan, M. R., Reiss, M. L., Pyles, D. A., & Bailey, J. S. (1988). The effects of self-monitoring and supervisor feedback on staff performance in a residential setting. *Journal of Applied Behavior Analysis*, *21*(4), 401-409.

Related Lessons:
D-01 Use positive reinforcement
F-01 Use self-management strategies
F-02 Use token economies and other conditioned reinforcement systems
F-03 Use direct instruction
H-03 Select a schedule of observation and recording periods
H-04 Select a data display that effectively communicates relevant qualitative relations
H-04 Evaluate changes in level, trend and variability
I-01 Define behavior in observable measurable terms
K-03 Design and use competency-based training for persons responsible for carrying out behavioral assessment & behavior-change procedures
K-05 Design and use systems for monitoring procedural integrity

K-05 Design and use systems for monitoring procedural integrity

Definitions:

Procedural Integrity - "The extent to which the independent variable is applied exactly as planned and described and no other unplanned variables are administered inadvertently along with the planned treatment" (Cooper Heron, & Heward, 2007, pp. 706-707).

Treatment Drift - "An undesirable situation in which the independent variable of an experiment is applied differently during later stages than it was at the outset of the study" (Cooper Heron, & Heward, 2007, p. 706).

Low treatment integrity is not only bad for research (confounding, cannot interpret the results) but can also lead to inconsistencies and poor outcomes in treatments. These can be related to many factors such as experimenter bias (unfair advantage to see positive results), staff implementing only procedures they favor, treatment too difficult to implement, poor staff training, or staff turnover.

Systems to Avoid Treatment Drift
- Precise operational definition
- Make behavioral plan simple and easy to administer
- Provide competency-based training (use behavior skills training)
- Assess treatment integrity

Assessing Treatment Integrity
- Provide a brief checklist of each of the components in the treatment plan
- May be self-monitored but important to conduct inter-rater reliability
- Establish a schedule to complete the treatment integrity
- Graph the percent of treatment integrity and monitor to ensure treatment drift does not occur

Assessment:
1. Ask supervisee to describe why procedural integrity is important.
2. Ask supervisee to create a procedural integrity checklist for a behavioral program.
3. Ask supervisee to collect data using the procedural integrity checklist in the natural environment and take inter-rater reliability measurement with yourself, discuss discrepancies, repeat if necessary.

Relevant Literature:
Cooper, J. O., Heron, T. E., & Heward, W. L. (2007). Applied behavior analysis: 2nd Edition. Pearson Education, Inc.
Johnston, J. M., & Pennypacker, H. S. (2011). *Strategies and tactics of behavioral research*. Routledge.
Wolery, M. (1994). Procedural fidelity: A reminder of its functions. *Journal of Behavioral Education, 4*(4), 381-386.

Related Lessons:
F-01 Use self-management strategies
H-03 Select a schedule of observation and recording periods
H-04 Select a data display that effectively communicates relevant qualitative relations
H-04 Evaluate changes in level, trend and variability
K-03 Design and use competency-based training for persons who are responsible for carrying out behavioral assessment and behavior-change procedures
K-04 Design and use effective performance monitoring and reinforcement systems

Footnotes:
Also called procedural fidelity, treatment integrity, procedural reliability, or treatment adherence

K-06 Provide supervision for behavior-change agents

Smith, Parker, Taubman, and Lovaas (1992) found that knowledge transfer from a staff training workshop did not generalize to the group home. Research suggests that training is most effective if there is training and ongoing supervision in the environment where the behavior change program is occurring (Parsons & Reed, 1995; Sarokoff & Sturmey, 2004; Miles & Wilder, 2009)

Codding, Feinberg, Dunn and Pace (2004) found that treatment integrity increased following a one hour performance feedback session every other week. Social validity ratings provided favorable feedback for the frequent supervisions.

Cooper, Heron and Heward (2007) suggest that supervision of data takers and booster training is necessary to avoid observer drift.

Observing and graphing data will provide immediate feedback on the participant's performance. This can lead to quick decisions, modifications if necessary, or the termination of ineffective programs. This supervision is necessary to create the most effective interventions and troubleshoot areas for improvement. It is also important to observe the intervention in the natural environment in order to determine if the intervention is realistic and practical in the natural environment.

Summary of Rationale for Supervision of Behavior Change Agents

- Provides effective knowledge transfer for individuals implementing the intervention
- Increases motivation and treatment integrity
- Reduces error associated with data collection
- Allows for quick clinical decisions to modify or terminate programs which ensures the most effective treatment

Assessment:

- Ask supervisee to describe why it is important to provide supervision of behavior change agents.
- Look at data with supervisee and ask them to discuss what modification they may consider
- Have supervisee observe intervention in the home environment and ask them to write down suggestions to increase the effectiveness of the plan.

Relevant Literature:

Codding, R. S., Feinberg, A. B., Dunn, E. K., & Pace, G. M. (2005). Effects of immediate performance feedback on implementation of behavior support plans. *Journal of Applied Behavior Analysis, 38*(2), 205-219.

Cooper, J. O., Heron, T. E., & Heward, W. L. (2007). *Applied Behavior Analysis: 2nd Edition.* Pearson Education, Inc.

Miles, N. I., & Wilder, D. A. (2009). The effects of behavioral skills training on caregiver implementation of guided compliance. *Journal of Applied Behavior Analysis, 42*(2), 405-410.

Parsons, M. B., & Reid, D. H. (1995). Training residential supervisors to provide feedback for maintaining staff teaching skills with people who have severe disabilities. *Journal of Applied Behavior Analysis, 28*(3), 317-322.

Sarokoff, R. A., & Sturmey, P. (2004). The effects of behavioral skills training on staff implementation of discrete-trial teaching. *Journal of Applied Behavior Analysis, 37*(4), 535-538.

Smith, T., Parker, T., Taubman, M., & Ivar Lovaas, O. (1992). Transfer of staff training from workshops to group homes: A failure to generalize across settings. *Research in Developmental Disabilities, 13*(1), 57-71.

Related Lessons:

H-03 Select a schedule of observation and recording periods.
H-04 Select a data display that effectively communicates relevant qualitative relations
H-04 Evaluate changes in level, trend and variability.
K-02 Identify the contingencies governing the behavior of those responsible for carrying out behavior-change procedures and design interventions accordingly.
K-03 Design and use competency-based training for persons who are responsible for carrying out behavioral assessment and behavior-change procedures.
K-04 Design and use effective performance monitoring and reinforcement systems.

K-07 Evaluate the effectiveness of the behavioral program

In the field of applied behavior analysis, it is crucial to have ongoing evaluation of the effectiveness of behavior programs. This helps to ensure that the most effective treatments are being offered to a client based on ethical practices, the most current research, and the individual's needs.

Birnbrauer (1999) lists the following steps for evaluating the effectiveness of treatment:

1. Describe the exact purposes of the treatment —what is it intended to achieve?
2. Describe exactly how the treatment is conducted —there should be no mystery or secrecy about the methods and procedures being used.
3. Describe how treatment effects were measured —what numerical data were collected and how were they collected?
4. Show before and after data collected by independent, unbiased evaluators
5. Show follow up data —do the persons maintain gains? Do they continue to improve? Do they regress?

"The data obtained throughout a behavior change program or a research study are the means for that contract; they form the empirical basis for every important decision: to continue with the present procedure, to try a different intervention, or to reinstitute a previous condition" (Cooper, Heron, & Heward, 2007, p. 167). It is important that if there is evidence of behavioral regression or that the treatment package is ineffective, that the team re-evaluate, make changes or adjustments, or discontinue a behavioral program entirely. It is unethical to continue a behavioral program that is deemed ineffective.

Assessment:

- Ask the supervisee to state why ongoing evaluation of a behavioral program is important.
- Ask the supervisee to state what all important program decisions should be driven by.
- Ask the supervisee to state who should be evaluating data.
- Ask the supervisee under which conditions to discontinue a behavioral program.

Relevant Literature:

Bailey, J., & Burch, M. (2011). *Ethics for Behavior Analysts: 2nd Expanded Edition.* Taylor & Francis.

Birnbrauer, J.S (1999). How to Evaluate Intervention Programs. Cambridge Center for Behavioral Studies, Inc.

Cooper J.O, Heron T.E, Heward W.L. (2007). *Applied behavior analysis* (2nd ed.) Upper Saddle River, NJ: Pearson.

Related Lessons:

B-01 Use the dimensions of applied behavior analysis (Baer, Wolf, &Risley, 1968) to evaluate whether interventions are behavior analytic in nature.

FK-47 Identify the measurable dimensions of behavior (e.g., rate, duration, latency, interresponse time).

G-01 Review records and available data at the outset of the case.

H-01 Select a measurement system to obtain representative data given the dimensions of the behavior and the logistics of observing and recording.

I-01 Define behavior in observable and measurable terms.

I-05 Organize, analyze, and interpret observed data.

I-06 Make recommendations regarding behaviors that must be established, maintained, increased, or decreased.

J-01 State intervention goals in observable and measurable terms.

K-07 Evaluate the effectiveness of the behavioral program.

K-08 Establish support for behavior analytic services from direct and indirect consumers

As a behavior analyst, it is important to conduct yourself with professionalism to your clients and their family and also to individuals from other disciplines that may support your client. You must enlist a circle of care around your client, which will help you to better understand your client through the lenses of another discipline. For example if you have a child who has feeding refusal, taking the time to enlist information from the nutritionist, speech pathologist, doctors and occupational therapists will help you to provide safe and effective treatment.

In addition, when providing treatment having help from people within the client's family, the community, and from the circle of care around your client will enable you to generalize skills to new environments, new people and new activities. These individuals can be a great asset in troubleshooting and providing additional data as well.

Additionally, when your goals are met, you will leave. In order for the continued support of your client and the maintenance of the goals, it is important to enlist individuals who will be with the client for a longer period.

Bailey and Burch (2010) provide a useful book on professional strategies. He provides several suggestions on how to establish a working relationship in the best interest of the client. Establishing yourself as a positive reinforcer for your colleagues by demonstrating integrity, basic meeting etiquette, providing a professional image, using nontechnical language, listening to others, and bringing their opinions into the assessment.

Assessment:
1. Ask supervisee to describe the importance of enlisting the help of direct and indirect consumers.
2. Use behavior skill tracking to teach and practice describing interventions in nontechnical terms.
3. Discuss challenges in dealing with colleagues within different fields and strategies to help.

Relevant Literature:

Bailey, J. S., & Burch, M. R. (2009). *25 Essential Skills & Strategies for the Professional Behavior Analyst: Expert Tips for Maximizing Consulting Effectiveness.* Taylor & Francis.

Bailey, J., & Burch, M. (2011). *Ethics for Behavior Analysts: 2nd Expanded Edition.* Taylor & Francis.

Behavior Analyst Certification Board (BACB) Behavior Analyst Certification Board professional and ethical compliance code for behavior analysts. 2014. Retrieved from http://www.bacb.com/Download-files/BACB_Compliance_Code.pdf.

Related Lessons:

G-07 Practice within one's limits of professional competence in applied behavior analysis, and obtain consultation, supervision, training, or make referrals as necessary.

K-09 Secure the support of others to maintain the client's behavioral repertoires in their natural environments.

K-10 Arrange for the orderly termination of services when they are no longer required.

K-09 Secure the support of others to maintain the client's behavioral repertoires in their natural environments.

Foxx (1996, p. 230) stated that in programming successful behavior change interventions, "10% is knowing what to do; 90% is getting people to do it…Many programs are unsuccessful because these percentages have been reversed." (Cooper et al., 2007, p. 652).

Being explicit yet simplistic in describing programs and protocols will help secure support from other individuals in a client's environment. If a behavior change procedure or program is too difficult, technical, or places unreasonable demands on the other individuals involved, they are less likely to implement these programs. In addition, adequate training of behavior procedures should be provided to ensure proper implementation by those interacting with the client in the natural environment. Specifically, training pertaining to the delivery of reinforcers, which maintain the individual's newly acquired behavioral repertoires.

Jarmolowicz et al. (2008) compared the effectiveness of conversational language instructions and technical language instructions when explaining how to implement a treatment to caregivers. They found that the caregivers that were given conversational language instruction implemented the treatment more accurately.

Example:
Richard is trying to generalize skills learned in the special education classroom for one of his students. He went to each teacher to explain how this will help the student in their class and answered any questions they may have about the programs. In addition, he conducted a training on the specific program and offered to consult with each teacher in order to make sure generalization was successful and the repertoire was maintained.

Assessment:
- Have supervisee identify ways they can build a rapport with other service providers and help support them when they have a student who needs to generalize and maintain skills in new settings.
- Have supervisee choose a particular behavior change program or strategy. Have him/her describe and explain this program to an individual who does not have a background in applied behavior analysis.
- Have supervisee choose a specific behavior change program. Have him/her practice explaining the benefits of this program to others in order to get them on board with implementing this program.
- Give supervisee a complex behavior change program. Have him/her simplify this program and create guidelines and instructions that they could give to an individual who does not have knowledge of applied behavior analytic strategies and techniques.

Relevant Literature:
Cooper, J.O., Heron, T.E. & Heward W.L. (2007). *Applied Behavior Analysis* (2nd Ed.), Upper Saddle River, NJ. Pearson Prentice Hall. 641-642, 652.

David P. Jarmolowicz, SungWoo Kahng, Einar T. Ingvarsson, Richard Goysovich, Rebecca Heggemeyer, Meagan K. Gregory, and Steven J. Taylor (*2008*) Effects of Conversational Versus Technical Language on Treatment Preference and Integrity. Intellectual and Developmental Disabilities: June 2008, Vol. 46, No. 3, pp. 190-199.

Stokes, T.F., Baer, D.M., & Jackson, R.L. (1974). Programming the generalization of a greeting response in four retarded children. *Journal of Applied Behavior Analysis*, 7, 599-610.

Related Lessons:
H-01: Select a measurement system to obtain…

J-01: State intervention goals in observable and measurable terms.

K-03: Design and use competency-based training for persons responsible for carrying out behavioral assessment & behavior-change procedures.

K-04: Design and use effective performance monitoring and reinforcement systems.

K-06: Provide supervision for behavior-change agents.

K-08: Establish support for behavior-analytic services from direct and indirect consumers

K-10 Arrange for the orderly termination of services when they are no longer required

Behavior analysts follow guidelines related to arranging for termination of services in 2.15 of the Behavior Analyst Certification Board professional and ethical compliance code for behavior analysts:

2.15 Interrupting or Discontinuing Services.

(d) Discontinuation only occurs after efforts to transition have been made. Behavior analysts discontinue a professional relationship in a timely manner when the client: (1) no longer needs the service, (2) is not benefiting from the service, (3) is being harmed by continued service, or (4) when the client requests discontinuation.

(e) Behavior analysts do not abandon clients. Prior to discontinuation, for whatever reason, behavior analysts: discuss the client's views and needs, provide appropriate pre-termination services, suggest alternative service providers as appropriate, and take other reasonable steps to facilitate timely transfer of responsibility to another provider if the client needs one immediately, upon client consent. (BACB, 2014, P. 10).

Before services are terminated, behavior analysts must discuss the client's needs with all pertinent parties (e.g. client's parents, legal guardians, school administrators). The client's welfare should be prioritized above all else and a transition plan should be put in place well before services are discontinued. Referrals to other professionals should be given if appropriate. (Bailey & Burch, 2005)

Assessment:

- Ask supervisee to describe conditions under which services should be discontinued for a client
- Ask supervisee what steps they should undergo before discontinuing a client's services

Relevant Literature:

Bailey, J., & Burch, M. (2011). *Ethics for Behavior Analysts: 2nd Expanded Edition.* Taylor & Francis.

Behavior Analyst Certification Board (BACB) Behavior Analyst Certification Board professional and ethical compliance code for behavior analysts. 2014. Retrieved from http://www.bacb.com/Download-files/BACB_Compliance_Code.pdf.

Related Lessons:

G-07 Practice within one's limits of professional competence in applied behavior analysis and obtain consultation, supervision, and training, or make referrals as necessary.

K-09 Secure the support of others to maintain the client's behavioral repertoires in their natural environments.

FK-01 Lawfulness of behavior

Definition:

Lawfulness of behavior – "behavior is the result of some condition that has *caused* it to happen" (Malott, 2012, p. 168)

The lawfulness of behavior makes a science of behavior possible. "Science is, of course, more than a set of attitudes. It is a search for order, for uniformities, for lawful relations among the events in nature" (Skinner, 1953, p.13).

If behavior did not follow universal laws related to the environment that hosts it, it would not be possible to predict or control responding in a scientific way. Skinner describes the necessity for lawfulness of behavior in this quote: "If we are to use the methods of science in the field of human affairs, we must assume that behavior is lawful and determined. We must expect to discover that what a man does is the result of specifiable conditions and that once these conditions have been discovered, we can anticipate and to some extent determine his actions" (Skinner, 1953, p. 6).

Assessment:

- Ask your supervisee to describe why an understanding of lawfulness of behavior is important when designing treatments for their client.

- Ask your supervisee to role-play a scenario in which he/she discusses lawfulness of behavior with a caretaker or teacher of a client.

Relevant Literature:

Malott, R. (2012). *Issues in the Analysis of Behavior.* Behaviordelia.

Skinner, B. F. (1953). *Science and human behavior.* New York: Macmillan.

Related Lessons:

B-03 Systematically arrange independent variables to demonstrate their effects on dependent variables.

FK-02 Selectionism (phylogenic, ontogenic, cultural)

FK-03 Determinism

FK-04 Empiricism

FK-05 Parsimony

FK-06 Pragmatism

FK-02 Selectionism (phylogenic, onto-genic, cultural)

Definition:

Selectionism - refers to selection by consequences, a scientific paradigm, which asserts that all forms of operant behavior evolve as a result of the consequences that occurred during one's lifetime.

Skinner (1981) wrote:
"Human behavior is the joint product of (i) the contingencies of survival responsible for the natural selection of the specific and (ii) the contingencies of reinforcement responsible for the repertoires acquired by its members, including (iii) the special contingencies maintained by the social environment. (Ultimately, of course, it is all a matter of natural selection, since operant conditioning is an evolved process, of which cultural practices are special applications.)" (p. 502).

Skinner's paradigm emphasizes the role of function and draws on evolutionary theory and natural selection (phylogeny). Ontogeny refers to the learning history of an individual. Skinner viewed cultural practices as an evolved process maintained by operant conditioning. Variation in behavior is required for selection by consequences, meaning the most adaptive behavioral repertoire persists because it serves a valuable function for the organism (Cooper, Heron, & Heward, 2007). Maladaptive, unhealthy, and harmful behavior can persist because it serves a function for the individual (e.g., substance abuse, non-suicidal self-harm, etc.).

Example:
- In evolutionary history, our ancestors ate certain foods because it had an adaptive value as it helped ensure survival (natural selection of behavior; phylogenic selection). The food did not necessarily need to be a reinforcer but was necessary for survival. However, in modern times, we all have food preferences and may eat food that has no nutritional value or health benefits, indicating that specific foods are eaten because of their reinforcing value (ontogenic selection). This type of eating habit is not adaptive (e.g., think about overeating, binge eating, obesity and the subsequent health problems that can emerge from this type of eating behavior) but it is strengthened and maintained by operant conditioning, thus reflecting selection by consequences (Skinner, 1981).
- Cultural Selection: Pennypacker (1992) provides examples of how selection by consequences is observed in education, economics, and politics and social organization.

Assessment:
- Ask supervisee to define selectionism.
- Ask supervisee to read and summarize the relevant literature, while highlighting examples that reflect selectionism.
- Ask supervisee to provide an example of behavior maintained by selectionism.

Relevant Literature:
Cooper, J. O., Heron, T. E., & Heward, W. L. (2007). Measuring behavior. *Applied Behavior Analysis* (pp. 72-101). Upper Saddle River, NJ: Pearson Prentice Hall.
Pennypacker, H. S. (1992). Is behavior analysis undergoing selection by consequences? *American Psychologist, 47,* 1491-1498.
Skinner, B. F. (1981). Selection by consequences. *Science, 212,* 501-504.

Related Lessons:
FK-15 operant conditioning
FK-31 behavioral contingencies
FK-33 functional relations
FK-41 contingency-shaped behavior
FK-42 rule-governed behavior

FK-03 Determinism

Definition:

Determinism - the assumption that "the universe is a lawful and orderly place in which all phenomena occur as the result of other events" (Cooper, Heron, & Heward, 2007, p.5).

The implication here is that events don't just occur by accident; they occur as the result of something else happening. This is an important attitude of science because if the behavior of organisms was *not* orderly or lawful, scientists would be unable to identify why a behavior was occurring and therefore modify it. (Fisher, Piazza, & Roane, 2011, p. 9)

Example:

A window banging

A window does not just randomly bang shut; it bangs shut because a gust of wind has blown it and this has exerted enough force upon the window to close it.

Example:

A pipe bursting

A water pipe does not just spontaneously burst; it bursts because there is a fault somewhere in the system, which has caused a build up of water in the pipes, resulting in so much pressure within the system that the pipe has burst.

Example:

Self-injurious behavior (SIB)

A client's self-injurious behavior does not just suddenly decrease after days of high rates of SIB. It decreases because the sensory-blocking procedure that's in place has begun to extinguish the behavior.

Assessment:

- Ask your Supervisee to give an explanation to the scenarios below as they align with determinism.
  o A glass breaks. (Possible answers could include = someone knocks it over causing it to break, the wind blows through the window and knocks it over causing it to smash, the dog kicks the glass as he runs past it, resulting in it breaking).

  o A client begins to emit correct responses when tacting the colors purple and green, which he has previously had a low rate of correct responses for. (Possible answers could include = the intervention which is in place has resulted in the appropriate stimulus control being acquired for purple and green, leading to an increased rate of correct responding; the client's Mother has been working on the colors green and purple at home with him; the client has been observing a peer tact the colors purple and green during play).

  o A client's sleep pattern changes and he begins to refuse to go to bed at 10 pm but instead will not go to bed until 3 am. (Possible answers could include = the client has been reinforced when he has been up late as his Mother has permitted him to watch TV; the client has not been woken until 4 pm in the afternoon after not going to bed until 3.30 am the night before; a client's medication has been changed and this results in disturbed sleep and periods of insomnia).

Relevant Literature:

Cooper, J. O., Heron, T. E., & Heward, W. L. (2007). *Applied Behavior Analysis*, 2nd ed. Upper Saddle River, New Jersey: Pearson Prentice Hall.

Delprato, D. J., & Midgley, B. D. (1992). Some fundamentals of B.F. Skinner's behaviorism. *American Psychologist, 48*, 1507-1520.

Fisher, W.W., Piazza, C. C., Roane, H. S. (2011). *Handbook of Applied Behavior Analysis*. The Guildford Press, New York London.

Related Lessons:

FK-01: Lawfulness of behavior
FK-04: Empiricism
FK-05: Parsimony
FK-06: Pragmatism

Footnotes

* Please refer to FK04-FK06 for a description of the other attitudes of science

FK-04 Empiricism

Definition:

Empiricism - "the practice of objective observation of the phenomena of interest" (Cooper et al., 2007, p. 5).

According to Fisher (2011), scientists make observations about the world by using information available to the senses. Sensory evidence is the primary source of information and should maintain the attitude of empiricism by believing what they observe the world to be and not what they have been taught that it should be.

Example:

Mr. Johnson, a BCBA, conducts a functional analysis to determine the function of Billy's aggressive behavior in class. He completes rating scales, interviews, and other indirect assessment procedures, but doesn't use these to guess the reinforcer for Billy's aggression. Mr. Johnson uses the indirect assessment procedures to inform his experiment. He designs a pairwise functional analysis and runs out several phases of direct observation until results are conclusive. He concludes that Billy's aggressive behavior is sensitive to attention as a maintaining variable. At the IEP meeting, Billy's parents applaud Mr. Johnson's empiricism for completing such a thorough assessment and analyzing all the possible factors before determining a function.

Non-example:

Mr. Riley is a district BCBA and has been asked to conduct a functional behavior assessment for Mary in regards to her aggressive behavior. Mr. Riley hypothesizes that Mary is engaging in aggressive behavior to get access to her dolls because all little girls like dolls. Based on his reasoning he has already decided that Mary's aggression is maintained by access to dolls. Since he already has a strong hypothesis for the function of aggression, Mr. Riley writes a report and creates a treatment for Mary.

Assessment:

- Have supervisee describe the term empiricism and how it relates to applied behavior analysis. Have him/her identify ways that they can make sure that their work is empirically based.

- Have supervisee read an article on decreasing problematic behavior. Have him/her identify what makes this article empirically sound.

- Have supervisee list practices that are not empirically based and then identify what the individual could do to make sure that they were practicing appropriate empiricism.

Relevant Literature:

Cooper, J.O., Heron, T.E. & Heward W.L. (2007). *Applied Behavior Analysis* (2nd Ed.), Upper Saddle River, NJ. Pearson Prentice Hall. 5, 22, 159.

Baer, D.M., Wolf, M.M., & Risley, T.R. (1968). Some Current Dimensions of Applied Behavior Analysis. *Journal of Applied Behavior Analysis,* 1, 1, 91-97.

Fisher, W.W., Piazza, C. C., Roane, H. S. (2011). *Handbook of Applied Behavior Analysis.* The Guildford Press, New York London.

Schmidt, F.L. (1992). What do data really mean? Research findings, meta-analysis, and cumulative knowledge in psychology. *American Psychologist*, 47, 10, 1173-1181.

Related Lessons:

B-01: Use the dimensions of applied behavior analysis (Baer, Wolf, & Risley, 1968) to evaluate whether interventions are behavior analytic in nature.

H-01: Select a measurement system to obtain representative data given the dimensions of the behavior and the logistics of observing and recording.

H-03: Select a data display that effectively communicates relevant quantitative relations.

I-01: Define behavior in observable and measurable terms.

I-03: Design and implement individualized behavioral assessment procedures.

I-05: Organize, analyze, and interpret observed data.

J-01: State intervention goals in observable and measurable terms.

J-15: Base decision making on data displayed in various formats.

K-07: Evaluate the effectiveness of the behavioral program.

FK-10: Behavior, response, response class.

FK-05 Parsimony

Definition:

Parsimony - The concept "that "simple, logical explanations must be ruled out, experimentally or conceptually, before more complex, or abstract experimentations are considered" (Cooper, Heron, & Heward, p. 22).

Behavior analysts attempt to identify the simplest explanation for an individual's observed responses and then apply the least complex intervention that results in improved behavior.

Examples:
* A non-verbal client hits her head repeatedly for a period of days each month. Although the analyst considered multiple environmental antecedent and consequent factors that might influence the client's behavior, she first looked at the calendar to see if the client's head hitting each month corresponded to her monthly menstrual cycle. She found that head-hitting occurred the last days immediately before her period began and the first day of her period. The analyst asked a nurse to review the data and recommend a medical intervention before the analyst continued to assess the influence of external environmental factors.
* An analyst was asked to design strategies for staff when responding to a client's aggressive behavior after asking him to brush his teeth. He reviewed the data staff had recorded about self-care behaviors and saw that aggression was a relatively new behavior during teeth-brushing. He learned that the client became aggressive toward staff shortly after they began buying a discounted toothpaste instead of the client's usual brand. When the analyst offered the client a choice between the two brands, the client chose his old brand and aggression did not occur after asking him to brush his teeth.

Assessment:
* Give the supervisee 3 scenarios and ask the supervisee to consider what might be a parsimonious (simplest that works) first approach for each situation.
* Example of a scenario for assessment: An adult client sometimes asks to go outside before breakfast. He screams and refuses to eat when he is made to sit at the table instead of going outside. Staff believe he should eat a good breakfast as part of his regular morning routine before he begins activities. A parsimonious response from the analyst might be to suggest that staff add a choice step before breakfast in which staff ask the client if he would like to go outside for 5 minutes before he eats.

Relevant Literature:
Cooper, J.O., Heron, T.E. & Heward W.L. (2007). *Applied Behavior Analysis* (2nd Ed.), Upper Saddle River, NJ. Pearson Prentice Hall. 113-122.
Etzel, B. C., & LeBlanc, J. M. (1979). The simplest treatment alternative: The law of parsimony applied to choosing appropriate instructional control and errorless-learning procedures for the difficult-to-teach child. *Journal of Autism and Developmental Disorders, 9*(4), 361-382.

Related Lessons:
* FK-01: Lawfulness of behavior.
* FK-02: Selectionism (phylogenic, ontogenic, cultural)
* FK-03: Determinism
* FK-04: Empiricism
* FK-06: Pragmatism

FK-06 Pragmatism

Definition:

Pragmatism – "a reasonable and logical way of doing things or of thinking about problems that is based on dealing with specific situations instead of on ideas and theories" (*Merriam-Webster.com, 2015*).

ABA is an inclusive approach that is easily replicable for socially significant effects by a variety of individuals that may benefit from its methodology. Jon Bailey (2000, p. 477) stated that "It seems to me that applied behavior analysis is more relevant than ever before and that it offers our citizens, parents, teachers, and corporate and government leaders advantages that cannot be matched by any other psychological approach…"

"Classroom teachers, parents, coaches, workplace supervisors, and sometimes the participants themselves implemented the interventions found effective in many ABA studies. This demonstrates the pragmatic element of ABA. Although doing ABA requires far more than learning to administer a few simple procedures, it is not prohibitively complicated or arduous." (Cooper et al., 2007, p. 19).

In other words, the pragmatism of ABA is in its *practicality* and *justification* of methods that give it appeal to a wider audience compared to other sciences searching for "truth".

Example:

Gloria was looking for a reinforcement program for her classroom because her students were not turning their homework in on time. She consulted with the district BCBA and was able to come up with an effective and simple class-wide reinforcement program that helped her students to turn their homework on time.

Non-example:

Richard was a first grade teacher and wanted to represent his student's data using a scatterplot graph. However, he did not have previous training in this area and was unable to accomplish this task. He felt that this method for graphical display was too difficult to figure out.

Assessment:

- Have supervisee explain reinforcement, punishment, mand, and tact in simple, pragmatic terms that a layperson could apply.
- Have supervisee identify and describe some common ABA practices and techniques that are used by professionals who have not been directly trained in ABA. Have him/her describe why these approaches represent the pragmatic nature of applied behavior analysis.

Relevant Literature:

Bailey, J.S. (2000). A futurist perspective for applied behavior analysis. In J. Austin & J.E. Carr (Eds.), *Handbook of applied behavior analysis* (pp. 473-488). Reno, NV: Context Press.

Cooper, J.O., Heron, T.E. & Heward W.L. (2007). *Applied Behavior Analysis* (2nd Ed.), Upper Saddle River, NJ. Pearson Prentice Hall. 19, 22.

Heward, W.L. (2005). Reasons applied behavior analysis is good for education and why those reasons have been insufficient. In W.L. Heward, T.E. Heron, N.A. Neef, S.M. Peterson, , D.M. Sainato, G. Cartledge, R. Gardner, III, L.D. Peterson, S.B. Hersh, & J.C. Dardig (Eds.), *Focus on behavior analysis in education: Achievements, challenges, and opportunities* (pp. 316-348). Upper Saddle River, NJ: Merrill/Prentice Hall.

Related Lessons:

B-01: Use the dimensions of applied behavior analysis (Baer, Wolf, & Risley, 1968) to evaluate whether interventions are behavior analytic in nature.

G-04: Explain behavioral concepts using nontechnical language.

G-06: Provide behavior analytic services in collaboration with others who support and/or provide services to one's clients.

K-08: Establish support for behavior-analytic services from direct and indirect consumers.

K-09: Secure the support of others to maintain the client's behavioral repertoires in their natural environments.

FK-07 Environmental (as opposed to mentalistic) explanations of behavior

Definition:

Mentalism-"An approach to explaining behavior that assumes that a mental, or 'inner,' dimension exists that differs from a behavioral dimension and that phenomena in this dimension either directly cause or at least mediate some forms of behavior, if not all" (Cooper, Heron, Heward, 2007, p. 699).

An environmental explanation of behavior can be described by physical events in the phylogenetic or ontogenetic history of the organism that cause behavior to occur. A behavior analyst believes that all behavior is a result of these physical events and that there is no reason to believe that there are some causes of behavior outside of physical dimensions.

It can be difficult sometimes, as we learn behavior analysis, to describe behavior without the use of mentalistic explanations (e.g., the hit me because he's frustrated). This is because in non-behavior analytic cultures, where many behavior analysts spend most of their lives, behavior is described this way and there is reinforcement available from that verbal community to perpetuate mentalistic explanations of behavior. For instance, it is common for people to believe that we each are responsible for our own actions and that the choices we make are done so with "free-will". Johnston (2014) mentions that, "After a lifetime of explaining behavior in terms of such apparent freedom, it is understandably difficult to accept what appears to be a helpless or passive role…" (p.5)

Much of behavior in society is controlled by consequences. Johnston (2014) says "…we assign the responsibility for behavior not to the individual but to sources of control in the physical environment. From this perspective, holding individuals responsible for their behavior by specifying the consequences for certain actions remains an important contingency because it helps manage those tendencies to act in one way or another" (p.11).

Assessment:

- Provide scenarios for a supervisee describing repetitive problem behaviors that might lead to a conclusion that internal events are controlling variables for behavior. Tell the supervisee to write a mentalistic explanation that might explain the behavior and then identify a radical behaviorist approach to explaining the same response.

- Present a scenario in which a supervisee is working with parents or staff who insist that their child is hitting them because she is angry or frustrated. Ask the supervisee to role play explaining to care givers that behavior analysts look at anger and frustration a different way.

Relevant Literature:

Cooper, J. O., Heron, T. E., & Heward, W. L. (2007). *Applied behavior analysis.* Upper Saddle River, NJ: Pearson Education.

Skinner, B. F. (1953). Emotion. In *Science and human behavior (pp.160-170).* New York: Macmillan.

Related Lessons:

B-01 Use the dimensions of applied behavior analysis (Baer, Wolf, & Risley, 1968) to evaluate whether interventions are behavior analytic in nature.

G-04 Explain behavioral concepts using nontechnical language.

G-05 Describe and explain behavior, including private events, in behavior-analytic (non-mentalistic) terms.

I-01 Define behavior in observable and measurable terms.

I-02 Define environmental variables in observable and measurable terms.

K-02 Identify the contingencies governing the behavior of those responsible for carrying out behavior-change procedures and design interventions accordingly.

FK-01 Lawfulness of behavior

FK-03 Determinism

FK-07 Environmental (as opposed to mentalistic) explanations of behavior

FK-08 Distinguish between radical and methodological behaviorism

<u>Definition:</u>
Radical behaviorism – "the philosophy of a science of behavior treated as a subject matter in its own right apart from internal explanations, mental or physiological" (Skinner, 1989, p. 122).

Methodological behaviorism – "represents a formal and strategic agreement to regard the relation between publicly observable stimulus variables and publicly observable behavior as the appropriate subject matter for psychology as a science" (Moore, 2008, p. 385).

The distinction between radical and methodological behaviorism can be summed up by the views on private events. Private events, or events observable by only the individual engaging in the response, are not included in the analysis of behavior by a methodological behaviorist position. Radical behaviorists consider private events to be no different than any other behavior, therefore, allowing it to be understood within the same conceptual framework understood for overt behavior.

<u>Assessment:</u>
- Ask your supervisee to describe the distinction between radical and methodological behaviorism.
- Have your supervisee describe the advantages of the methodological behaviorist's view.
- Have your supervisee describe the advantages of the radical behaviorist's view.

<u>Relevant Literature:</u>
Baum, W. M. (2011). What is radical behaviorism? A review of Jay Moore's Conceptual Foundations of Radical Behaviorism. *Journal of the experimental analysis of behavior, 95*(1), 119-126.

Cooper, J. O., Heron, T. E., & Heward, W. L. (2007). *Applied behavior analysis.* Upper Saddle River, NJ: Pearson Education.

Moore, J. (2011). A review of Baum's review of Conceptual Foundations of Radical Behaviorism. *Journal of the experimental analysis of behavior, 95*(1), 127-140.

Moore, J. (2009). Why the radical behaviorist conception of private events is interesting, relevant, and important. *Behavior and Philosophy,* 21-37.

Moore, Jay (2008). *Conceptual Foundations of Radical Behaviorism.* Sloan Pub.

Skinner, B. F. (1989). *Recent issues in the analysis of behavior.* Prentice Hall. Chicago.

<u>Related Lessons:</u>
B-01 Use the dimensions of applied behavior analysis (Baer, Wolf, & Risley, 1968) to evaluate whether interventions are behavior analytic in nature.

G-04 Explain behavioral concepts using nontechnical language.

G-05 Describe and explain behavior, including private events, in behavior-analytic (nonmentalistic) terms.

FK-01 Lawfulness of behavior

FK-07 Environmental (as opposed to mentalistic) explanations of behavior

FK-09 Distinguish between the conceptual analysis of behavior, experimental analysis of behavior, applied behavior analysis, and behavioral service delivery.

The conceptual analysis of behavior is a combination of philosophical, theoretical, and historical investigations behind the science of behavior. The modern philosophy of behavior analysis is specifically referred to as Radical Behaviorism and was coined by B.F. Skinner. Radical Behaviorism is rooted in the idea that the science of behavior is a natural science encompassed by behavioral events that happen due to the way the universe is arranged (determinism) and explained by other natural events (Baum, 1995) like the phenomenon of gravity. These behavioral events are analyzed in relation to the past and present environment (ontogenic and cultural contingencies) and evolutionary history (phylogenic contingencies). This approach sets itself apart from other behavioral philosophies (e.g., methodological behaviorism) by including overt behavior as an important variable but also acknowledging unobserved behavior (i.e., private events) (Skinner, 1953). Moreover, internal states, intervening variables and hypothetical constructs (mentalistic explanations) are not used to understand or analyze behavior (Baum, 2011). This philosophy sets the foundation for the other three domains described below.

The experimental analysis of behavior (EAB) is a natural science approach to the study of behavior. The methodology includes rate of response as a basic dependent variable, repeated or continuous measurement of clearly defined response classes, within subject comparisons, visual analysis of data and an emphasis on describing functional relations between behavior and controlling variables. EAB methodology was founded by B.F. Skinner and first publicly presented in his book *The Behavior of Organisms* (1938/1966) (Cooper, Heron, & Heward, 2007). EAB is often referred to as basic research.

Applied behavior analysis (ABA) is a science that develops its technology based on the principles of behavior and applies them systematically to produce socially significant behavior change. Furthermore, experimentation is used to identify the independent variables responsible for behavior change. Lastly, the adequacy of ABA work is determined by the seven characteristics (applied, behavioral, analytic, technological, conceptually systematic effective and generalizable) set forth by Baer, Wolf and Risley (1968) (Cooper, Heron, & Heward, 2007).

Behavioral service delivery consists of putting ABA principles that have been experimentally validated into practice. Behavioral service providers design, implement an evaluate behavior change procedures applied to socially significant behavior (Cooper, Heron, & Heward, 2007). It is important that behavioral service providers apply a conceptual framework in order to offer a thorough explanation of the causes of behavior that are consistent with the established science of behavior. However it is also important that they can explain these concepts to non-behavioral service providers and families in everyday language by essentially, strengthening two verbal repertoires (Johnston, 2013).

The four above mentioned domains have been described as an overlapping continuum that includes similarities and differences between each domain. This view emphasizes the fact that the four domains should be dependent on each other and mutually influenced by developments in each of the other domains (Cooper, Heron, & Heward 2007; Moore & Cooper, 2003). Moore and Cooper (2003) argue that students of behavior analysis be offered a balanced approach by incorporating all four domains into their training experience.

Assessment:
- Ask the supervisee to define each of the domains and then state how each influences the other domains.
- Throughout the course of supervision, when reading behavior analytic articles have the supervisee describe the implications of the article in terms of its relation to each of the four domains
- Require the supervisee to speak in technical dialect but also provide the supervisee with opportunities to practice restating their precise understanding of behavioral concepts in everyday language that can be understood by families and non-behavioral providers while retaining the underlying philosophy of behavior.
- Have a discussion with the supervisee about how the four domains are interrelated and why it is important that the domains influence each other and not operate in isolation.

Relevant Literature:

Baer, D. M., Wolf, M. M., & Risley, T. R. (1968). Some current dimensions of applied behavior analysis. *Journal of applied behavior analysis*, *1*(1), 91-97.

Baum, W. M. (1995). Radical behaviorism and the concept of agency. *Behaviorology*, *3*, 93-106.

Baum, W. M. (2011). What is radical behaviorism? A review of Jay Moore's Conceptual Foundations of Radical Behaviorism. *Journal of the experimental analysis of behavior*, *95*(1), 119-126.

Cooper, J. O., Heron, T. E., & Heward, W. L. (2007). *Applied behavior analysis (2nd ed.)*. *Upper Saddle River, NJ*: Pearson

Johnston, J.V. (2013). *Radical Behaviorism for ABA Practitioners*. Publisher Sloan Publishing

Moore, J., & Cooper, J. O. (2003). Some proposed relations among the domains of behavior analysis. *The Behavior Analyst*, *26*(1), 69.

Skinner, B. F. (1953). *Science and human behavior*. Simon and Schuster.

Related Lessons:

B-01 Use the dimensions of applied behavior analysis (Baer, Wolf, & Risley, 1968) to evaluate whether interventions are behavior analytic in nature.

G-04 Explain behavioral concepts using non-technical language

G-05 Describe and explain behavior, including private events, in behavior-analytic (non-mentalistic) terms.

G-06 Provide behavior-analytic services in collaboration with others who support and/or provide services to one's clients.

FK-01 Lawfulness of behavior

FK-02 Selectionism (phylogenic, ontogenic, cultural)

FK-03 Determinism

FK-04 Empiricism

FK-05 Parsimony

FK-06 Pragmatism

FK-07 Environmental (as opposed to mentalistic) explanations of behavior

FK-08 Distinguish between radical and methodological behaviorism

FK-10 Behavior, response, response class

Definitions:

Behavior - "The activity of living organisms; human behavior includes everything that people do" (Cooper, Heron, & Heward, 2007, p. 25).

Response - A single instance or occurrence of a specific class or type of behavior" (Cooper, Heron, & Heward, 2007, p. 703).

Response Class - "A group of responses of varying topography, all of which produce the same effect on the environment" (Cooper, Heron, & Heward, 2007, p. 703).

Example:

Opening a door

 a.   Example (behavior): Beezus stands up from her chair, heads towards a closed door, and pushes on it. The door is now open.

 b.   Example (response): When encountering a closed door, Beezus extends an open palm and pushes on it. The door is now open.

 c.   Example (response class): Beezus encounters many doors during her day. Sometimes she opens them with an open palm and sometimes with a closed palm. Some times she opens them with her left hand and at other times with her right hand. No matter which way she chooses to open a door, the result is always the same.

Assessment:

 •   Ask your supervisee to define behavior, response, and response class.

 •   Ask your supervisee to identify the behavior(s), responses, and response class from the above examples.

 •   Ask your supervisee to create other examples and non-examples of his/her own.

 •   Have your supervisee describe how these three terms are related.

Relevant Literature:

Cooper J.O, Heron T.E, Heward W.L. (2007). *Applied behavior analysis* (2nd ed.) Upper Saddle River, NJ: Pearson

Johnston, J.M., & Pennypacker, H.S. (1993a). *Strategies and Tactics for Human Behavioral Research (2nd ed.).* Hillsdale, NJ: Erlbaum.

Michael, J. (2004). *Concepts and Principles of Behavior Analysis (*rev. ed.). Kalamazoo, MI: Society for the Advancement of Behavior Analysis.

Skinner, B.F. (1969). *Contingencies of Reinforcement: A Theoretical Analysis.* New York: Appleton-Century-Crofts.

Related Lessons:

FK-36 Response Generalization

G-05 Describe and explain behavior, including private events, in behavior-analytic (non-mentalistic) terms.

I-01 Define behavior in observable and measurable terms

FK-11 Environment, Stimulus, Stimulus Class

Definitions:

Environment - "The conglomerate of real circumstances in which the organism or reference part of the organism exists; behavior cannot occur in the absence of environment" (Cooper, Heron, & Heward, 2007, p. 694).

Stimulus - "Any physical event, combination of events, or relation among events" (Catania, 2013, p. 466).

Stimulus class - "A group of stimuli that share specified common elements along formal (e.g. size, color), temporal (e.g. antecedent or consequent), and/or functional (e.g., discriminative stimulus) dimensions" (Cooper, Heron, & Heward, 2007, p. 705).

- "Any group of stimuli sharing a predetermined set of common elements in one or more of these dimensions" (Cooper, Heron, & Heward, 2007, p. 27).

Example: A trip to the mall

- Environment: Willis is shopping at the local mall. The local mall would be an environment.
- Stimulus: Willis is walking through the food court. He smells some pizza cooking from one of the establishments and suddenly his stomach starts growling. He stops and gets some food. All of the things in the food court, including the smells, the changes in his stomach, and the food are stimuli.
- Stimulus class: At the food court, Willis will buy items that will all function as reinforcers for eating behavior. In this case, the burger, the

fries, and the cookie he bought are in the same stimulus class.

Assessment:

- Ask your supervisee to define environment, stimulus, and stimulus class.
- Ask your supervisee to identify the environment, the stimulus (stimuli), and the stimulus class(es) from the above examples. Use examples of stimulus classes related to the formal, temporal, and functional dimensions.
- Ask your supervisee to create other examples and a non-examples of his/her own.
- Have your supervisee to compare and contrast these terms.

Relevant Literature:

Catania, A. C. (2013). *Learning* (5th ed.). Cornwall-on-Hudson, NY: Sloan.

Cooper J.O, Heron T.E, Heward W.L. (2007). *Applied behavior analysis* (2nd ed.) Upper Saddle River, NJ: Pearson

Johnston, J.M., & Pennypacker, H.S. (1993a). *Strategies and Tactics for Human Behavioral Research (2nd ed.).* Hillsdale, NJ: Erlbaum.

Michael, J. (2004). *Concepts and Principles of Behavior Analysis* (rev. ed.). Kalamazoo, MI: Society for the Advancement of Behavior Analysis.

Related Lessons:

FK-11 environment, stimulus, stimulus class

FK-12 Stimulus Equivalence

Definition:

Stimulus equivalence - "The emergence of accurate responding to untrained and nonreinforced stimulus-stimulus relations following the reinforcement of responses to some stimulus-stimulus relations. A positive demonstration of reflexivity, symmetry and transitivity is necessary to meet the definition of equivalence" (Cooper, Heron & Heward, 2007, p. 705)".

Related definitions:

Reflexivity - "A type of stimulus-to-stimulus relation in which the student, without any prior training or reinforcement for doing so, selects a comparison stimulus that is the same as the same stimulus" (Cooper, Heron & Heward, 2007, p. 702).

- Example: Without prior reinforcement or training, when shown a picture of a dog and given a picture of the same dog, a rat, and a cow, student matches the picture of the two dogs (e.g. A=A).

Symmetry - "A type of stimulus-to-stimulus relationship in which the learner, without prior training or reinforcement for doing so, demonstrates the reversibility of matched sample and comparison stimuli" (Cooper, Heron & Heward, 2007, p. 705).

- Example: Student is taught that when given the written word *dog* to select the picture of a dog. Without further reinforcement or training, when given the picture of the dog, student selects the written word *dog* (e.g. If A=B, then B=A).

Transitivity - "A derived stimulus-stimulus relation that emerges as a product of training two other stimulus-stimulus relations" (Cooper, Heron & Heward, 2007, p. 706).

- Example: Student is taught that when given the written word *dog* to select the picture of the dog (e.g. A=B). Student is also taught to select the picture of the dog when hearing the spoken word *dog* (e.g.

B=C). Without further reinforcement or training, student selects the written word *dog* after hearing the spoken word *dog* (e.g. C=A).

Example of Stimulus Equivalence:

- When learner responds without prior reinforcement and training that A=A (exhibiting reflexivity) and if A=B, then B must also = A (exhibiting symmetry) and finally that if A=B and B=C, then C must also equal A (exhibiting transitivity).

Non-Example of Stimulus Equivalence:

- When learner responds without prior reinforcement and training that A=A (exhibiting reflexivity) and if A=B, then B must also equal A (exhibiting symmetry) but cannot show that if A=B and B=C, then C must also equal A (failure to exhibit transitivity).

Assessment:

- Have supervisees display equivalence with respect to the words "reflexivity", "transitivity", and "symmetry" in the spoken form, written form, and written definitions.
- Have supervisee assess for stimulus equivalence on the job or during role-play
- Have supervisee demonstrate an example of stimulus equivalence during role-play

Relevant Literature:

Cooper, J. O., Heron, T. E., & Heward, W. L. (2007). *Applied behavior analysis* (2nd ed.). Upper Saddle River, NJ: Prentice Hall.

Sidman, M. (1997). Equivalence relations. Journal of the Experimental Analysis of Behavior, 68(2), 258-266.

Sidman, M. (2009). Equivalence relations and behavior: An introductory tutorial. *The Analysis of verbal behavior, 25*(1), 5.

FK-13 Reflexive relations (US-UR)

Definition:

Unconditioned stimulus (US) - is a "stimulus change that elicits respondent behavior (i.e., unconditioned response) in the absence of prior learning. The UR is typically regarded as a built-in bodily mechanism that exists through natural evolution" (Cooper, Heron, & Heward, 2007, pp. 30, 39).   The US-UR relation is an unconditioned reflex.

Example:

- Air blowing in eye (US) → blinking (UR)
- Cold/low temperature (US) → shivering (UR)
- Hot/high temperature (US) → sweating (UR)
- Food in mouth (US) → salivation (UR)
- Hot surface (US) → move hand away (UR)

Assessment:

- Ask supervisee to provide examples of US-UR relations.
- Ask supervisee to discriminate between respondent behavior and operant behavior.

Relevant Literature:

Bijou, S. W., & Baer, D. M. (1961). *Child Development: Volume 1. A Systematic and Empirical Theory*. New York, NY: Appleton-Century-Crofts.

Cooper, J. O., Heron, T. E., & Heward, W. L. (2007). Basic concepts. *Applied Behavior Analysis* (pp. 24-46). Upper Saddle River, NJ: Pearson Prentice Hall.

Pavlov, I. P. (1927). *Conditioned Reflexes: An Investigation of the Physiological Activity of the Cerebral Cortex*. London: Oxford University Press.

Related Lessons:

FK-14 Respondent conditioning (CS-CR)
FK-15 Operant conditioning
FK-16 Respondent-operant interaction

FK-14 Respondent Conditioning (CS-CR)

Definitions:

Reflex - "The reliable production of a response by a stimulus" (Catania, 1998, p. 8).

Respondent behavior - "behavior that is elicited by antecedent stimuli. Respondent behavior is induced, or brought out, by a stimulus that precedes the behavior; nothing else is required for the response to occur" (Cooper et al., 2007, p. 29).

"New stimuli can acquire the ability to elicit respondents. Called respondent conditioning, this type of learning is associated with Russian physiologist Ivan Petrovich Pavlolv…" (Cooper et al., 2007, p. 30).

Pavlov's experiments consisted of a group of dogs who were trained to salivate at the sound of a metronome started just prior to feeding them. Before initial training, the presence of food (US) elicited salivation (UR), but the metronome (NS) was not paired with this response. After numerous trials of food being paired with the sound of the metronome, the dogs began salivating whenever they heard the metronome. After being paired with the presentation of food for several trials, the metronome became a conditioned stimulus (CS) and a conditioned reflex (CR) was elicited.

Example:

Roger usually drinks soda every day for lunch. When drinking soda, the sugar (US) inside his blood elicits the release of insulin from his pancreas (UR). Now, when he opens the soda, the snap of the can (CS) starts to elicit the release of insulin (CR) before he takes a drink.

Assessment:

- Have supervisee list various examples of respondent behavior. Have him/her explain respondent conditioning and define stimulus-stimulus pairing, unconditioned stimulus, neutral stimulus, conditioned stimulus, and conditioned reflex.
- Have supervisee identify and describe an example of respondent conditioning (not an example from the Cooper et al. 2007 text or Pavlov's experiments).
- Have supervisee create an abstract for an experiment involving respondent conditioning. Have him/her describe how they would conduct the experiment to achieve respondent conditioning.
- Have supervisee compare and contrast respondent conditioning and operant conditioning.

Relevant Literature:

Catania, A.C. (1998). Learning (4th Ed.), Upper Saddle River, NJ. Prentice-Hall, Inc.

Cooper, J.O., Heron, T.E. & Heward W.L. (2007). *Applied Behavior Analysis* (2nd Ed.), Upper Saddle River, NJ. Pearson Prentice Hall. 29-31 (Figure 2.1), 33 (Table 2.3), 393, 606.

Skinner, B.F. (1984). The Evolution of Behavior. *Journal of the Experimental Analysis of Behavior*, 41, 2, 217-221.

Poling, A., & Braatz, D. (2001). Principles of learning: Respondent and operant conditioning and human behavior. *Handbook of organizational performance: Behavior analysis and management*, 23-49.

Skinner, B.F. (1938). The behavior of organisms: an experimental analysis. Oxford, England: Appleton-Century. (457 pp.)

Pavlov, I.P. (1928). Lectures on conditioned reflexes: Twenty-five years of objective study of the higher nervous activity (behaviour) of animals. (Horsley, G.W., Trans.). New York, NY, US: Liverwright Publishing Corporation. (414 pp.).

Related Lessons:

FK-10: Behavior, response, response class.
FK-13: Reflexive relations (US-UR).
FK-15: Operant conditioning
FK-16: Respondent-operant interactions
FK-17: Unconditioned reinforcement
FK-24: Stimulus control
FK-26: Unconditioned motivating operations
FK-35: Stimulus discrimination

FK-15 Operant Conditioning

Definition:

Operant Conditioning - "The basic process by which operant learning occurs; consequences (stimulus changes immediately following responses) result in an increased (reinforcement) or decreased (punishment) frequency of the same type of behavior under similar motivational and environmental conditions in the future" (Cooper, Heron & Heward, 2007, pp. 700-701).

Examples:
- A rat is deprived of food. The rat walks near a specific part of their cage and receives food. As a result, the future probability of the rat walking toward that area of the cage increases.
- A child hits their sibling when fighting over a toy. The child is sent to timeout. As a result, the future probability of hitting their sister decreases.

Assessment:
- Have supervisee provide examples of operant conditioning.
- Have supervisee describe ways of determining if operant conditioning is occurring (detect a reinforcing or punishing effect on behavior).

Relevant Literature:

Cooper, J.O., Heron, T. E., & Heward, W. L. (2007). *Applied behavior analysis.* Upper Saddle River, NJ: Pearson Education.

McAllister, L. W., Stachowiak, J. G., Baer, D. M., & Conderman, L. (1969). The application of operant conditioning techniques in a secondary school classroom. *Journal of Applied Behavior Analysis,2*(4), 277-285.

Related Lessons:
FK-15 Operant conditioning
FK-31 Behavioral contingencies
FK-33 Functional relations

FK-16 Respondent-operant interactions

Definitions:

Respondent behavior - "A response component of a reflex; behavior that is elicited, or induced, by antecedent stimuli" (Cooper, Heron, & Heward, 2007, p. 703).

Operant behavior – "Behavior that is selected, maintained, and brought under stimulus control as a function of its consequences" (Cooper, Heron, & Heward, 2007, p. 701).

Operant and respondent behavior interact very commonly. They may occur concurrently when a stimulus both evokes an operant response while at the same time elicits a respondent response on the part of the organism. The procedures involved with what we call operant or respondent conditioning are names of procedures for the ease of use of our field. There are respondent and operant interactions occurring whenever an organism behaves.

Pierce and Cheney (2013) describe it this way: "When biologically relevant stimuli such as food are contingent on an organism's operant behavior, species-characteristic, innate behavior is occasionally elicited at the same time" (p. 194). The presence of stimuli that have been paired with aversive or appetitive stimulation will elicit respondent behavior at the same time operant behavior is occurring to access or avoid those stimuli.

"The neural capacity for operant conditioning arose on the basis of species history; organisms that changed their behavior as result of life experience had an advantage over animals that did not do so" (Pierce & Cheney, 2013, p. 194).

Certain respondent behavior interacts with operant behavior. The effects are often described as motivating operations. For instance, behavior changes before and after meal times, with or without medications, after traumatic events, or disruptions in family life.

Examples:
- After a traumatic event involving physical abuse, every time a male walks into the room, your client "freezes" and does not follow instructions. This could be due to elicited behavior ("freezing" in the presence of conditioned aversive

stimuli) in competition with operant behavior (following instructions).
- A medication, when consumed, will elicit respondent behavior that makes certain things more or less aversive. Consider if your client starts taking a medication to decrease aggression maintained by access to toys. The effect of the medication may decrease the likelihood that toys function as a reinforcer in effect decreasing the amount of aggression. It may increase the likelihood that food functions as a reinforcer.

Assessment:
- Ask your supervisee to describe how respondent behavior can interact with operant behavior.
- Ask your supervisee to give an example of when this might occur with one of his/her clients during a specific treatment procedure.

Relevant Literature:

Cooper, J. O., Heron, T. E., & Heward, W. L. (2007). Applied behavior analysis (2nd ed). Upper Saddle River, N.J: Pearson/Merrill-Prentice Hall.

Cheney, C. D., & Pierce, W. D. (Eds.). (2013). Behavior analysis and learning (5th ed). New York, NY: Psychology Press.

Davis, H., & Hurwitz, H. M. B. (Eds.). (1977). Operant-Pavlovian interactions. Hillsdale, N.J. : New York: L. Erlbaum Associates ; distributed by the Halsted Press Division of J. Wiley.

Related Lessons:

G-02 Consider biological/medical variables that may be affecting the client.

G-05 Describe and explain behavior, including private events, in behavior-analytic terms.

FK-07 Environmental (as opposed to mentalistic) explanations of behavior

FK-13 reflexive relations (US-UR)

FK-14 respondent conditioning (CS-CR)

FK-15 operant conditioning

FK-17 Unconditioned reinforcement

Definition:

Unconditioned reinforcer - "A stimulus change that increases the frequency of any behavior that immediately precedes it irrespective of the organism's learning history with the stimulus. Unconditioned reinforcers are the product of the evolutionary development of the species (phylogeny) Also called primary or unlearned reinforcer" (Cooper, Heron, & Heward, 2007 p.707).

"...momentary effectiveness of an unconditioned reinforcer is a function of current motivating operations" (Cooper et al., 2007, p. 39).

Example:

- Food, water, oxygen, warmth, and sexual stimulation are some examples of unconditioned reinforcers.
- A teacher gives a child a pretzel after the child does a task. The child's engagement in the task increases in the future.
- This is an example of unconditioned reinforcement.

Assessment:

- Have supervisee create a list of unconditioned reinforcers. Have him/her define and describe the role satiation and deprivation plays in unconditioned reinforcement.
- Have supervisee give examples of unconditioned reinforcers. Have him/her describe the difference between conditioned and unconditioned reinforcement.
- Have supervisee explain the relationship between conditioned and unconditioned reinforcers and the role unconditioned reinforcers may play in creating conditioned reinforcers.

Relevant Literature:

Bijou, S.W., & Baer, D.M. (1965). *Child Development: Vol. 2. Universal Stage of infancy.* New York, NY. Appleton-Century-Crofts.

Cooper, J.O., Heron, T.E. & Heward W.L. (2007). *Applied Behavior Analysis* (2nd Ed.), Upper Saddle River, NJ. Pearson Prentice Hall. 38-40, 269-270, 295.

Gerwirtz, J. & Pelaez-Nogueras, M. (2000). Infant emotions under the positive-reinforcer control of caregiver attention and touch. In J.C. Leslie & D. Blackman (Eds.), *Issues in experimental and applied analyses of human behavior.* Reno, NV. Context Press. 271-291.

Malott, R.W., Tillema, M., & Glenn, S. (1978). *Behavior Analysis and Behavior Modification: An introduction.* Kalamazoo, MI. Behaviordelia. 9.

Pelaez-Nogueras, M., Gerwirtz, J.L., Field, T., Cigales, M., Malphurs, J., Clasky, S., & Sanchez, A. (1996). Infants' preference for touch simulation in face-to-face interactions. *Journal of Applied Developmental Psychology,* 17, 199-213.

Skinner, B.F. (1953). *Science and Human Behavior.* New York, NY. McMillan.

Related Lessons:

C-01: State and plan for unwanted effects of reinforcement.

D-01: Use positive and negative reinforcement.

D-02: Use appropriate parameters and schedules of reinforcement.

D-19: Use combinations of reinforcement with punishment and extinction.

FK-02: Selectionism (phylogenic, ontogenic, cultural)

FK-13: Reflexive relations (US-UR)

FK-16: Respondent-operant interactions

FK-19: Unconditioned punishment

FK-21: Schedules of reinforcement and punishment.

FK-26: Unconditioned motivating operations.

FK-30: Distinguish between motivating operations and reinforcement effects

FK-18 Conditioned reinforcement

Definition:

Conditioned reinforcer - "A stimulus change that functions as a reinforcer because of prior pairing with one or more other reinforcers; sometimes called secondary or learned reinforcers" (Cooper et al., 2007, p. 692).

Conditioned reinforcement – "the operation, or process, of a response producing a conditioned reinforcer that increases the likelihood that response occurs in the future" (Cooper et al., 2007, p. 40).

Example:

- Money, tokens, stickers.
- A teacher says "good job" after a student returns their homework. The student continues to return their homework in the future.

Assessment:

- Have supervisee explain the differences between conditioned and unconditioned reinforcers.
- Have supervisee explain the process of producing a conditioned reinforcer (i.e., token systems). Have him/her give an example from their professional experience.
- Have supervisee read and summarize a journal article on the topic of conditioned reinforcement.

Relevant Literature:

Alessi, G. (1992) Models of proximate and ultimate causation in psychology. *American Psychologist*, 48, 1359-1370.

Cooper, J.O., Heron, T.E. & Heward W.L. (2007). *Applied Behavior Analysis* (2nd Ed.), Upper Saddle River, NJ. Pearson Prentice Hall. 40-41, 269-270, 295.

Higgins, J.W., Williams, R.L., & McLaughlin, T.F. (2001). The effects of a token economy employing instructional consequences for a third grade student with learning disabilities: A data-based case study. *Education and Treatment of Children*, 24, 1, 99-106.

Michael, J. (2004) *Concepts and principles of behavior analysis* (rev. ed.). Kalamazoo, MI. Society for the Advancement of Behavior Analysis. 66.

Morse, W.H., & Kelleher, R.T. (1977). Determinants of reinforcement and punishment. In W.K. Honig & J.E.R. Staddon (Eds.), *Handbook of Operant Behavior*, Upper Saddle River, NJ. Prentice Hall. 176-177, 180.

Related Lessons:

C-01: State and plan for the unwanted effects of reinforcement.

D-01: Use positive and negative reinforcement.

D-02: Use appropriate parameters and schedules of reinforcement.

D-20: Use response-independent (time based) schedules of reinforcement (i.e., noncontingent reinforcement).

D-21: Use differential reinforcement (e.g., DRO, DRA, DRI, DRL, DRH)

F-02: Use token economies and other conditioned reinforcement systems

J-04: Select intervention strategies based on the client's preferences.

K-04: Design and use effective performance monitoring and reinforcement systems.

FK-02: Selectionism (phylogenic, ontogenic, cultural)

FK-14: Respondent conditioning (CS-CR)

FK-15: Operant conditioning

FK-16: Respondent-operant interactions.

FK-17: Unconditioned reinforcement

FK-21: Schedules of reinforcement and punishment

FK-26: Unconditioned motivating operations

FK-27: Conditioned motivating operations

FK-19 Unconditioned Punishment

Definition:

Unconditioned punisher – "A stimulus change that decreases the frequency of any behavior that immediately precedes it irrespective of the organism's learning history with the stimulus" (Cooper, Heron, & Heward, 2007, p. 707).*

Examples:
Bright lights, loud sounds, extreme temperatures, certain tastes (sour, bitter), physical restraint, loss of bodily support, extreme muscular efforts, etc.

Assessment:
- Ask the supervisee to describe an example of unconditioned punishment.
- Use the supervisee to describe the difference between unconditioned punishment and an unconditioned punisher.
- Ask the supervisee to list as many unconditioned punishers as possible in one minute.

Relevant Literature:
Cooper, J. O., Heron, T. E., & Heward, W. L. (2007). *Applied Behavior Analysis*: 2nd Edition.Pearson Education, Inc.

Herman, R. L., & Azrin, N. H. (1964). Punishment by noise in an alternative response situation. *Journal of the Experimental Analysis of Behavior*, 7(2), 185-188.

Related Lessons:
D-17 Use appropriate parameters and schedules of punishment
D-16 Use positive and negative Punishment
D-19 Use combinations of reinforcement with punishment and extinction
E-11 Use pairing procedures to establish new conditioned reinforcers and punishers
G-07 Practice within one's limits of professional competence in applied behavior analysis, and obtain consultation, supervision, and training, or make referrals as necessary
J-10 When a behavior is to be decreased, select an acceptable alternative behavior to be established or increased
FK 20 Conditioned punishment

Footnotes:
*Conditioned punishers are products of the evolutionary development of the species (Cooper, Heron, & Heward, 2007).
*Conditioned punishers are also called primary or unlearned punishers (Cooper, Heron, & Heward, 2007).

FK-20 Conditioned punishment

Definition:

Conditioned punisher – "a stimulus that functions as a punisher as the result of being paired with unconditioned or conditioned punishers" (Cooper, Heron, & Heward, 2007, p. 40).

Conditioned punishment as defined by Hake and Azrin (1965) is a process that "results when it can be shown (1) there is little or no punishment effect before the stimulus is paired with an unconditioned punisher, but (2) a punishment effect occurs after (3) the stimulus has been paired, or is being paired, with an unconditioned punisher" (p. 279). Evidence of conditioned punishment was suggested in early research when a reduction in a response was observed following the process of pairing a stimulus with an electric shock followed by discontinuing the shock and making the stimulus contingent upon a selected response (Hake & Azrin, 1965).

Example:

- Similar to classical conditioning, a tone (neutral stimulus) is repeatedly paired with an electric shock (unconditioned punisher) whenever a dog barks, in time the tone (conditioned punisher) suppresses the bark in the absence of the electric shock.
- A child engages in aggression. A parent responds to aggression by taking away their child's favorite video game contingent on every instance of aggression. The parent begins to pair removal of the video games with a reprimand. The reprimand may function as a conditioned punisher if aggression continues to decrease following the presentation of a reprimand without taking away the video games. This process illustrates conditioned punishment.
- Conditioned punishers may be referred to as learned or secondary punishers.

Assessment:

- Ask supervisee to explain the process of conditioned punishment.
- Ask supervisee to define a conditioned punisher.
- Ask supervisee to provide examples of conditioned punishment and a conditioned punisher.
- Ask supervisee to identify examples of conditioned punishment in a client's environment.

Relevant Literature:

Bailey, J., & Burch, M. (2011). *Ethics in Behavior Analysis* (2nd ed). New York, NY: Routledge.

Cooper, J. O., Heron, T. E., & Heward, W. L. (2007). Measuring behavior. *Applied Behavior Analysis* (pp. 72-101). Upper Saddle River, NJ: Pearson Prentice Hall.

Hake, D. F., & Azrin, N. H. (1965). Conditioned punishment. *Journal of the Experimental Analysis of Behavior, 8*, 279-293.

Iwata, B. A. (1988). The development and adoption of controversial default technologies. *The Behavior Analyst, 11,* 149-157.

Related Lessons:

C-02 State and plan for the possible unwanted effects of punishment.
D-15 Identify punishers.
D-16 Use positive and negative punishment.
D-17 Use appropriate parameters and schedules of punishment.
D-18 Use extinction.
D-19 Use combinations of reinforcement with punishment and extinction.
FK-14 respondent conditioning (CS-CR)
FK-17 unconditioned reinforcement
FK-18 conditioned reinforcement
FK-19 unconditioned punishment
FK-21 schedules of reinforcement and punishment

FK-21 Schedules of Reinforcement and Punishment

Definition:

Schedule of reinforcement/punishment – "rule that specifies the environmental arrangements and response requirements that will result in reinforcement or punishment" (Cooper, Heron & Heward, 2007, p. 703).

Related Definitions:
A continuous schedule of reinforcement: reinforcement is given for each occurrence of behavior

- Also known as a 1:1 schedule of reinforcement or (CRF)

A continuous schedule of punishment: punishment is given after each occurrence of behavior

- Also known as a 1:1 schedule of punishment

An intermittent schedule of reinforcement: reinforcement is given after some, but not all occurrences of behavior

- Types of intermittent schedules of reinforcement:
  o A fixed ratio schedule of reinforcement: Requires a completion of a specified number of responses to gain access to reinforcement
    ▪ Example: A student may have to complete 5 correct math problems on a computer game before progressing to the next level (this is a FR-5 schedule of reinforcement).
  o A variable ratio schedule of reinforcement: Requires the completion of a varied number of responses to gain access to reinforcement
    ▪ Example: A young girl may be called on when she raises her hand quietly in class on average once every 5 times. Sometimes, the teacher calls on her every 4 times she raises her hand. Other times the teacher calls on her every 6 times she raises her hand. The teacher provides attention on average every 5 times (this is a VR-5 schedule of reinforcement).

  o A fixed interval schedule of reinforcement: provides reinforcement for the first response after a fixed duration of time
    ▪ Example: An alarm clock is set for 7:00 am every morning. If an individual presses snooze, it will allow the individual to sleep in again for 10 minutes. The individual cannot press snooze before the alarm rings (this is a FI-10 minute schedule of reinforcement).
  o A variable interval schedule of reinforcement: produces reinforcement for the first response after a variable duration of time
    ▪ Example: A person goes to a fast food restaurant. Sometimes he has to stand in line, while other times, he may order immediately upon entering. This interval varies each time he goes to the restaurant.

Intermittent schedule of punishment: punishment is delivered after some but not all occurrences of behavior.

Assessment:
- During a job or during role-play, have your supervisee determine what schedule of reinforcement or punishment is being used
- Use SAFMEDS or flashcards to practice definitions related to the various types of schedules.

Relevant Literature:
Cooper, J. O., Heron, T. E., & Heward, W. L. (2007). *Applied behavior analysis* (2nd ed.). Upper Saddle River, NJ: Prentice Hall.

Related Lessons:
D-02 Use appropriate parameters and schedules of reinforcement
D-17 Use appropriate parameters and schedules of punishment

FK-22 Extinction

Definition:

Extinction - "The discontinuing of reinforcement of a previously reinforced behavior; the primary effect is a decrease in the frequency of the behavior until it reaches a pre-reinforced level or ultimately ceases to occur" (Cooper, Heron & Heward, 2007, p. 695).

Example:

Screaming to avoid/escape washing hands

- Example: A young woman at a group home was observed to scream loudly every time she was instructed to wash her hands. Each time she began screaming, she was allowed to avoid the task for an average of ten minutes or escape the task altogether. A behavioral analyst instructed group home staff to put this behavior on extinction. After being instructed to wash her hands, group home staff physically guided her to comply even if she began screaming. After a week, screaming decreased to near zero levels.

- Non-example: A young woman at a group home was observed to scream loudly every time she was instructed to wash her hands. Each time she began screaming, she was allowed to avoid the task for an average of ten minutes or escape the task altogether. When she engaged in screaming, group home staff would tell her that if she stopped screaming and complied she would be given chips, a preferred food.

Different types of extinction:

- Extinction of behavior maintained by positive reinforcement: This occurs when behavior to access tangibles, activities, and/or attention is no longer reinforced.

- Extinction of behavior maintained by negative reinforcement: This occurs when behavior to avoid/escape an aversive stimulus/event is no longer reinforced.

- Extinction of behavior maintained by automatic reinforcement: This occurs when behavior that provides a natural and automatic sensory consequence is no longer reinforced. (e.g., a child is blocked each time he raises both hands above his mid-line to engage in hand-flapping.)

Assessment:

- -Provide a hypothetical scenario and have your supervisee determine if an extinction procedure is in place. If so, have your supervisee define which type of extinction.

- -Have your supervisee give you 3 various examples of extinction.

- Describe the pros and cons of extinction procedures based on readings assigned.

Relevant Literature:

Cooper, J. O., Heron, T. E., & Heward, W. L. (2007). *Applied behavior analysis* (2nd ed.). Upper Saddle River, NJ: Prentice Hall.

Lerman, D. C., Iwata, B. A., & Wallace, M. D. (1999). Side effects of extinction: prevalence of bursting and aggression during the treatment of self-injurious behavior. *Journal of Applied Behavior Analysis, 32*(1), 1-8.

Magee, S. K., & Ellis, J. (2000). Extinction effects during the assessment of multiple problem behaviors. *Journal of Applied Behavior Analysis, 33*(3), 313-316.

Related Lessons:

C-03 State and plan for unwanted effects of extinction

D-18. Use Extinction.

D.-19 Use combinations of reinforcement with punishment and extinction.

FK-23 Automatic reinforcement and punishment

Definition:

Automatic reinforcement - "Reinforcement that occurs independent of the social mediation of others" (Cooper Heron, & Heward, 2007, p. 267).

Example:

- Scratching an insect bite removes an itch; eating food when hungry removes hunger, humming may be auditory reinforcement; nonfunctional movements such as hand flapping may produce a sensation, which is automatically reinforcing; some self-injurious behavior may produce a sensation, which the individual may enjoy.

- **Automatic punishment** - "Punishment that occurs independent of the social mediation by others"(Cooper Heron, & Heward, 2007, p. 534).

- Albert bites his canker sore, causing a shocking pain. Albert is becomes cautious as he eats with his canker sore until the canker disappears. A dog gets a thorn in his paw. He experiences pain when he steps down on his foot. He begins to walk on three legs.

Assessment:

- Ask your supervisee to come up with several examples of automatic punishment and automatic reinforcement.

- Ask your supervisee provide examples of how extinction of the following automatically reinforced behavior may occur: child making sounds by tapping the table, child receiving kinesthetic stimulation by flapping his arms, child throws up and eats vomit for the taste, child scratching surface for tactile stimulation on fingers, child flipping light switch on and off to gain a visual sensation

- Ask supervisee if they will likely have to treat clients with an automatic punishment function (yes-many food refusal behavior may have an automatic punishment for example).

Relevant Literature:

Cooper, J. O., Heron, T. E., & Heward, W. L. (2007). *Applied Behavior Analysis*. 2nd Edition.Pearson Education, Inc.

Vollmer, T. R. (1994). The concept of automatic reinforcement: Implications for behavioral research in developmental disabilities. *Research in Developmental Disabilities, 15*(3), 187-207.

Related Lessons:

FK-17 Unconditioned reinforcement
FK-19 Unconditioned punishment
FK-22 Extinction

FK-24 Stimulus control

Definitions:

Stimulus control - "A situation in which the frequency, latency, duration, or amplitude of a behavior is altered by the presence or absence of an antecedent stimulus" (Cooper, Heron, & Heward, 2007, p. 705).

Example: When the telephone rings, George picks up the receiver. Picking up the receiver is under the stimulus control of a ringing phone.

Discriminated operant - "An operant that occurs more frequently under some antecedent conditions than under others" (Cooper, Heron, & Heward, 2007, p.694).

Example: In the above example, picking up the receiver is the discriminated operant.

Discriminative stimulus (S^D) - "A stimulus in the presence of which responses of some type have been reinforced and in the absence of which the same type of responses have occurred and not been reinforced" (Cooper, Heron, & Heward, 2007, p. 694).

Example: In the above example, the telephone's ring is the discriminative stimulus.

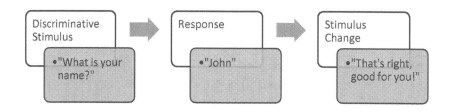

Assessment:

- Label the following: The traffic light turns red, John steps on the break. What is under stimulus control? What is the discriminated operant? What is the discriminative stimulus?
- Ask the supervisee to explain how he can bring a student's behavior of saying "dog" under the stimulus control of the picture of a dog.
- Ask supervisee how they could use stimulus control to reduce the jumping behavior of a man who jumps up

and down so much that he is damaging his feet.

Relevant Literature:

Cooper, J. O., Heron, T. E., & Heward, W. L. (2007). *Applied Behavior Analysis*: 2nd Edition. Pearson Education, Inc.

Related Lessons:

D-19 Use combinations of reinforcement with punishment and extinction

FK-22 Extinction

FK-29 Distinguish between discriminative stimulus and motivating operation

FK-25 Multiple functions of a single stimulus

The same stimulus may serve multiple functions depending on the context. For instance, an aversive stimulus can function as a positive punisher or a negative reinforcer depending on whether it is added or removed contingent on a response. An appetitive stimulus can function as a positive reinforcer or a negative punisher depending on whether it is added or removed contingent on a response.

In a behavior chain, a stimulus can function as a discriminative stimulus and a reinforcer depending on how much of the chain has been completed. Behavior chains are described by Catania as "a sequence of discriminated operants such that responses during one stimulus are followed by other stimuli that reinforce those responses and set the occasion for the next ones" (Catania, 2013, p. 431).

Respondent behavior interacts with operant behavior in ways that can cause a single stimulus to be an eliciting stimulus for respondent behavior as well as a discriminative stimulus for operant behavior. For example, when seeing your best friend arrive to your home for a visit, this may elicit respondent behavior one might describe as "excitement". Seeing your friend may also serve as a discriminative stimulus for waving at him/her.

Assessment:
- Ask your supervisee to give examples of a single stimulus serving multiple functions.
- Look at a task analysis with your supervisee. Have him/her pick a stimulus that serves as a discriminative stimulus and a reinforcer at certain parts of the performance.

Relevant Literature:

Catania, A. C. (2013). *Learning* (5th ed). Cornwall-on-Hudson, NY: Sloan Pub.

Catania, A. C., & Overmier, J. B. (1971). Discriminative stimulus functions of drugs: Interpretations. In *Stimulus properties of drugs* (pp. 149-160). Springer New York.

Bullock, C. E., & Hackenberg, T. D. (2015). The several roles of stimuli in token reinforcement. Journal of the Experimental Analysis of Behavior, 103(2), 269–287. http://doi.org/10.1002/jeab.117

Related Lessons:

E-01 Use interventions based on manipulation of antecedents, such as motivating operations and discriminative stimuli.

D-01 Use positive and negative reinforcement.

D-16 Use positive and negative punishment.

FK-14 respondent conditioning (CS-CR)

FK-15 operant conditioning

FK-16 respondent-operant interactions

FK-26 Unconditioned motivating operations

Definition:

Unconditioned motivating operations - "...events, operations, and stimulus conditions with value-altering motivating effects that are unlearned" (Michael, as cited in Cooper, Heron, & Heward, 2007, p. 377).

Deprivation of basic human needs such as water, food, and sleep all create "evocative effects" that establish these items as reinforcers.

Cooper et al., 2007 identifies nine unconditioned motivating operations (UMOs) including food deprivation, water deprivation, sleep deprivation, activity deprivation, oxygen deprivation, sex deprivation, becoming too warm or cold, and an increase in painful stimulation. The withholding of any of these will lead to an increase in the reinforcing value of obtaining that which has been deprived.

On the other hand, when there is no longer deprivation, this serves as a UMO having an abative effect on behavior, making it less likely to occur.

Example:

Roger has not slept in three days because he has been studying for his chemistry final. Sleep becomes more valuable the more deprived of sleep he gets.

Non-example:

Roger lost his key to his apartment and cannot get in. The locked door serves as motivation for him to find his key to get into his apartment. The key serves as a reinforcer because his learning history identifies this as the only way to unlock his door and get into his apartment.

Assessment:

- Have supervisee identify at least 7 unconditioned motivating operations. Have him/her describe their reinforcer-establishing effect as well as their evocative effect. (see page 379, table 16.1 in Cooper et al., 2007)
- Have supervisee identify UMOs that decrease reinforcer effectiveness and abate relevant behavior. Have him/her describe the reinforcer-abolishing effect and the abative effect of each UMO. (See page 380, table 16.2 in Cooper et al., 2007).
- Have supervisee explain how to weaken the effects of a UMO. (See page 380-381 in Cooper et al., 2007).

- Have supervisee explain the difference between motivating operations and discriminative stimuli. (See page 377 in Cooper et al., 2007).

Relevant Literature:

Cooper, J.O., Heron, T.E. & Heward W.L. (2007). *Applied Behavior Analysis* (2nd Ed.), Upper Saddle River, NJ. Pearson Prentice Hall.

Laraway, S., Snycerski, S., Michael, J., & Poling, A. (2001). The abative effect: A new term to describe the action of antecedents that reduce operant responding. *The Analysis of Verbal Behavior*, 18, 101-104.

Lotfizadeh, A.D., Edwards, T.L., Redner, R., & Poling, A. (2012). Motivating operations affect stimulus control: A largely overlooked phenomenon in discrimination learning. *Behavior Analyst*, 35, 1, 89-100.

Michael, J. (1982). Distinguishing between discriminative and motivational functions of stimuli. *Journal of the Experimental Analysis of Behavior*, 37, 149-155.

Michael, J. (2000). Implications and refinements of the establishing operation concept. *Journal of Applied Behavior Analysis*, 33, 401-410.

Ulrich, R.E., & Azarin, N.H. (1962). Reflexive fighting in response to aversive stimulation. *Journal of the Experimental Analysis of Behavior*, 5, 511-520.

Related Lessons:

D-01: Use positive and negative reinforcement.

E-01: Use interventions based on manipulation of antecedents, such as motivating operations and Discriminative stimuli.

I-02: Define environmental variables in observable and measurable terms.

FK-02: Selectionism (phylogenic, ontogenic, cultural)

FK-13: Reflexive relations (US-UR)

FK-14: Respondent conditioning (CS-CR)

FK-17: Unconditioned reinforcement.

FK-19: Unconditioned punishment

FK-27: Conditioned motivating operations.

FK-28: Transitive, reflexive, and surrogate motivating operations.

FK-29: Distinguish between the discriminative stimulus and the motivating operation.

FK-30: Distinguish between motivating operation and reinforcement effects.

FK-27 Conditioned motivating operations

Definition:

Conditioned motivating operation - "A motivating operation whose value-altering effect depends on a learning history" (Michael, as cited in Cooper, Heron, & Heward, 2007, p. 384).

Three types of conditioned motivating operations (CMOs): surrogate (CMO-S), reflexive (CMO-R), and transitive (CMO-T)

- Surrogate CMOs replace and have the same effect as the motivating operation that it was previously paired with.
- o Example: A rat is placed in a distinctive environment when food deprived. This is repeated a number of times. Over time, the rat is placed in the same environment when they have not been deprived of food. The distinctive environment and it's relation to a state of food deprivation results in an increase in the value of food as a reinforcer and an increase in the frequency of behavior with a history of producing food. In this example, the distinctive environment is paired with a unconditioned motivating operation (food deprivation). Over time, the distinctive environment functions as a motivating operation in the absence of food deprivation.
- Reflexive CMOs create a circumstance in which its own removal serves as the reinforcement.
- o Example: The presence of instructional materials often precedes the presentation of instructional tasks. If an individual engages in behavior maintained by access to escape from instructional tasks, in time they may engage in escape maintained behavior in the presence of instructional materials and the removal of these materials may function as a reinforcer. In this example, the instructional materials serve as a CMO-R.
- Transitive CMOs make other stimuli more effective reinforcers.
- o Example: A locked door functions as a CMO-T to establish a key as a reinforcer.

Assessment:
- Have supervisee describe the three types of CMOs. Have him/her give examples of each.
- Have supervisee explain the definitions for conditioned and unconditioned motivating operations in simple terms that someone who does not have ABA experience can understand.

- Have supervisee explain how to weaken the effects of each of the three types of CMO.

Relevant Literature:

Catania, A. C. (1993). Coming to terms with establishing operations. The Behavior Analyst, 16, 219-224. Catania, A. C. (1994). Learning. Englewood Cliffs, NJ: Prentice-Hall. Clark, F. C. (1958). The effects of deprivation and frequency of reinforcement on variable interval responding. Journal of the Experimental Analysis of Behavior, 1, 221-228.

Cooper, J.O., Heron, T.E. & Heward W.L. (2007). *Applied Behavior Analysis* (2nd Ed.), Upper Saddle River, NJ. Pearson Prentice Hall. 384-389.

Endicott, K., & Higbee, T.S. (2007). Contriving motivating operations to evoke mands for information in preschoolers with autism. *Research in Autism Spectrum Disorders*, 1, 3, 210-217.

Hesse, B. (1993). The establishing operation revisited. The Behavior Analyst, 16, 215- 217.

Iwata, B. A., Smith, R. G., & Michael, J. (2000). Current research on the influence of establishing operations on behavior in applied settings. Journal of Applied Behavior Analysis, 33, 411-418.

Lotfizadeh, A.D., Edwards, T.L., Redner, R., & Poling, A. (2012). Motivating operations affect stimulus control: A largely overlooked phenomenon in discrimination learning. *Behavior Analyst*, 35, 1, 89-100.

Michael, J. (1993). Establishing operations. *The Behavior Analyst, 16*(2), 191.

Related Lessons:

D-01: Use positive and negative reinforcement.
E-01: Use interventions based on manipulation of antecedents, such as motivating operations and Discriminative stimuli.
I-02: Define environmental variables in observable and measurable terms.
FK-02: Selectionism
FK-13: Reflexive relations (US-UR)
FK-14: Respondent conditioning (CS-CR)
FK-17: Unconditioned reinforcement.
FK-19: Unconditioned punishment
FK-26: Unconditioned motivating operations.
FK-28: Transitive, reflexive, and surrogate motivating operations.
FK-29: Distinguish between the discriminative stimulus and the motivating operation.
FK-30: Distinguish between motivating operation and reinforcement effects.

FK-28 Transitive, reflexive, surrogate motivating operations

Conditioned motivating operations consist of "...motivating variables that alter the reinforcing effectiveness of other stimuli, objects, or events, but only as a result of an organism's learning history..." (Cooper, Heron, & Heward, 2007, p. 384).

The 3 types of conditioned motivating operations are surrogate (CMO-S), reflexive (CMO-R), and transitive (CMO-T).

"Any stimulus that systematically precedes the onset of painful stimulation becomes a CMO-R (reflexive- CMO), in that its occurrence will evoke any behavior that has been followed by such reinforcement" (Cooper et al., 2007, p. 385).

"When an environmental variable is related to the relation between another stimulus and some form of improvement, the presence of that variable functions as a transitive CMO, or CMO-T, to establish the second condition's reinforcing effectiveness and to evoke the behavior that has been followed by that reinforcer" (Cooper et al., 2007, p. 387).

Surrogate CMO's are stimuli that have been paired with another motivating operation and "acquired a form of behavioral effectiveness by being paired with a behaviorally effective stimulus" (Cooper et al., 2007, p. 384). There is not strong evidence for this type of CMO.

Example:

- (CMO-R) A child engages in escape-maintained problem behavior during matching to sample instruction. In time, the child engages in escape-maintained problem behavior when the materials for matching to sample are brought out, before instruction has begun.
- (CMO-T) You walk up to your front door and turn the knob, but the door is locked. You reach into your pocket and grab your keys and unlock the door.
- (CMO-S) In the presence of a stimulus that has been paired with a cold environment, the value of stimuli that produce warmth increases.

Assessment:
- Have supervisee list and define the 3 types of conditioned motivating operations.
- Have him/her give examples of each type of conditioned motivating operation.

- Have supervisee explain the difference between conditioned and unconditioned motivating operations.

Relevant Literature:

Carbone, V.J., Morgenstern, B., Zecchin-Tirri, G., & Kolberg, L. (2007). The role of the reflexive conditioned motivating operation (CMO-R) during discrete trial instruction of children with autism. *Journal of Early and Intensive Behavior Intervention*, 4, 4, 658-680.

Cooper, J.O., Heron, T.E. & Heward W.L. (2007). *Applied Behavior Analysis* (2nd Ed.), Upper Saddle River, NJ. Pearson Prentice Hall. 384-388, 390-391.

Laraway, S., Snycerski, S., Michael, J., & Poling, A. (2003). Motivating operations and terms to describe them: Some further refinements. *Journal of Applied Behavior Analysis*, 36, 3, 407-414.

McGill, P. (1999). Establishing Operations: Implications for assessment, treatment, and prevention of problem behavior. *Journal of Applied Behavior Analysis*, 32, 393-418.

Michael, J. (1993). *Concepts and Principles of Behavior Analysis*. Kalamazoo, MI. Society for the Advancement of Behavior Analysis.

Michael, J. (1993). Establishing Operations. *The Behavior Analyst*, 16, 191-206.

Mineka, S. (1975) Some new perspectives on conditioned hunger. *Journal of Experimental Psychology: Animal Behavior Processes*, 104, 143-148.

Rosales, R., & Rehfeldt, R.A. (2007). Contriving transitive conditioned establishing operations to establish derived manding skills in adults with severe developmental disabilities. *Journal of Applied Behavior Analysis*, 40, 1, 105-121.

Related Lessons:
D-01: Use positive and negative reinforcement.
E-01: Use interventions based on manipulation...
FK-13: Reflexive relations (US-UR)
FK-14: Respondent conditioning (CS-CR)
FK-15: Operant conditioning
FK-16: Respondent-operant interactions.
FK-18: Conditioned reinforcement.
FK-20: Conditioned punishment
FK-27: Conditioned motivating operations.
FK-29: Distinguish between the discriminative stimulus and the motivating operation
FK-30: Distinguish between motivating operation and reinforcement effects.

FK-29 Distinguish between the discriminative stimulus and the motivating operation

Definitions:

Discriminative stimulus (SᴰD) - "A stimulus in the presence of which responses of some type have been reinforced and in the absence of which the same type of responses have occurred and not been reinforced; this history of differential reinforcement is the reason an SᴰD increases the momentary frequency of the behavior" (Cooper, Heron, & Heward, 2007, p. 694).

Motivating operation - "An environmental variable that (a) alters (increases or decreases) the reinforcing or punishing effectiveness of some stimulus, object, or event; and (b) alters (increases or decreases) the current frequency of all behavior that has been reinforced or punished by that stimulus, object, or event" (Cooper et al., 2007, p. 699).

Examples:

- A child often asks their parents to play video games after school. The child's father often says "yes" to this request, while the child's mother says "no" and tells the child to get started on their homework. Over time the child continues to ask their father if they can play video games, but has stopped asking their mother. In this example the presence of the father likely functions as an SᴰD due to the history of requests being granted in his presence, but not in the presence of their mother.
- After playing outside for an hour, a child walks into the house and gets a drink of water. In this example, playing outside likely functions as a motivating operation, more specifically as establishing operation, in that it increases the value of water as a reinforce and increases the frequency of behavior with a history of producing water.
- A student earns tokens throughout the school day and can trade them in for a preferred item or activity. Usually the student chooses to trade in their tokens for a small snack, accept after lunch. Usually after lunch the student chooses computer over snacks. In this example, consuming food during lunch likely functions as a motivating operation, more specifically an abolishing operation, in that it decreases the value of food as a reinforcer and

decreases the frequency of behavior with a history of producing food.

Assessment:

- Have supervisee explain the difference between SᴰD s and MOs.
- Have the supervisee to create additional examples of SᴰD s and MOs.
- Provide the supervisee with examples of responses and the reinforcers for those responses. Have the supervisee describe potential ways to increase and decrease the value of the reinforcer.

Relevant Literature:

Cooper, J.O., Heron, T. E., & Heward, W. L. (2007). *Applied behavior analysis*. Upper Saddle River, NJ: Pearson Education.

Michael, J. (1982). Distinguishing between discriminative and motivating functions of stimuli. Journal of the Experimental Analysis of Behavior, 37, 149–155.

Related Lessons:

E-01 Use interventions based on manipulation of antecedents, such as motivating operations and discriminative stimuli.

G-08 Identify and make environmental changes that reduce the need for behavior analysis services.

I-02 Define environmental variables in observable and measurable terms.

J-04 Select intervention strategies based on client preferences.

J-06 Select intervention strategies based on supporting environments.

J-07 Select intervention strategies based on environmental and resource constraints.

K-09 Secure the support of others to maintain the client's behavioral repertoires in their natural environments.

FK-07 Environmental (as opposed to mentalistic) explanations of behavior

FK-24 Stimulus control

FK-26 unconditioned motivating operation

FK-31 behavioral contingencies

FK-33 functional relations

FK-30 Distinguish between motivating operation and reinforcement effects.

Understanding motivating operations (MO) and reinforcement effects are critical components in the analysis of behavior. To briefly explain the difference, MOs are antecedent variables that have behavior-altering effects in that they alter the current frequency of relevant behaviors whereas the process of reinforcement is a consequence-based process (as is extinction and punishment) said to have repertoire-altering effects in that the future frequency of the behavior that preceded the consequence is altered (Cooper, Heron, & Heward, 2007). While this explanation can help clarify the difference between MO effects and reinforcement effects, it is also important to understand the basic features of MOs. Specifically, MOs have a value-altering effect or a behavior-altering effect. As defined by Cooper et al., (2007),

The value-altering effect is either (a) an increase in the reinforcing effectiveness of some stimulus, object, or event, in which case the MO is an establishing operation (EO); or (b) a decrease in reinforcing effectiveness, in which case the MO is an abolishing operation (AO). The behavior-altering effect is either (a) an increase in the current frequency of behavior that has been reinforced by some stimulus, object, or event, called an evocative effect; or (b) a decrease in the current frequency of behavior that has been reinforced by some stimulus, object, or event, called an abative effect (p. 375).

Examples:
- Being deprived of food or water increases the reinforcing value of food and water (i.e., a value altering effect in which the MO functions as an EO), and there will likely be an increase in the current frequency of all behavior that has previously been reinforced with food and water (i.e., an evocative behavior-altering effect). Conversely, if a large meal was just consumed then it is unlikely that food will be reinforcing (i.e., a value-altering effect in which the MO functions as an AO) and there will be a reduction in the current frequency of all behavior previously reinforced with food (i.e., an abative behavior-altering effect).

- This next example can illustrate the difference between MO effects and reinforcement/punishment effects (i.e., repertoire-altering effects). Before leaving for work you realize that it is going to be a cold day. The heater in your car does not work well so you plan ahead by putting a blanket and extra jacket in your car to use if it becomes too cold. During your drive to work, it becomes increasingly cold so you turn on your car heater, put your extra jacket on, and lay the blanket over you so you become much warmer. In this example, there was an increase in the current frequency of all behavior that has been reinforced by becoming warmer (i.e., an evocative behavior-altering effect). For the rest of the winter, to avoid becoming too cold on your drive to work, you leave every morning already wearing an extra jacket and put a blanket on you as soon as you get in the car (i.e., repertoire-altering effect on future behavior).

Assessment:
- Ask supervisee to define MOs and explain the basic characteristics.
- Ask supervisee to discriminate between behavior-altering effects and repertoire-altering effects.
- Ask supervisee to identify potential MOs for client's behavior.
- Ask supervisee to provide examples of behavior-altering effects and repertoire-altering effects that are operating in a client's environment.

Relevant Literature:
Cooper, J. O., Heron, T. E., & Heward, W. L. (2007). Motivating operations. *Applied Behavior Analysis* (pp. 374-391). Upper Saddle River, NJ: Pearson Prentice Hall.

Iwata, B. A., Smith, R. G., & Michael, J. (2000). Current research on the influence of establishing operating on behavior in applied settings. *Journal of Applied Behavior Analysis, 33,* 411-418.

Laraway, S., Snycerski, S., Michael, J., & Poling, A. (2001). The abative effect: A new term to describe the action of antecedents that reduce operant responding. *The Analysis of Verbal Behavior, 18,* 101-104.

Schlinger, H., & Blakely, E. (1987). Function-altering effects of contingency-specifying stimuli. *The Behavior Analyst, 10,* 41-45.

Related Lessons:

E-01 Use interventions based on manipulation of antecedents, such as motivating operations and discriminative stimuli.

FK-25 multiple functions of a single stimulus

FK-26 unconditioned motivating operations

FK-27 conditioned motivating operations

FK-28 transitive, reflexive, surrogate motivating operations

FK-29 distinguish between the discriminative stimulus and the motivating operation

FK-31 Behavioral contingencies

"The AB because of C formulation is a general statement that the relation between an event (B) and its context (A) is because of consequences (C)....Applied to Skinner's three-term contingency, the relation between (A) the setting and (B) behavior exists because of (C) consequences that occurred for previous AB (setting-behavior) relations. The idea [is] that reinforcement strengthens the setting-behavior relation rather than simply strengthening behavior" (Moxley, 2004, p. 111).

"The three term contingency- antecedent, behavior, and consequence- is sometimes called the ABC's of behavior analysis...The term contingency has several meanings signifying various types of temporal and functional relations between behavior and antecedent and consequent variables...When a reinforcer (or punisher) is said to be contingent on a particular behavior, the behavior must be emitted for the consequence to occur" (Cooper, Heron, & Heward, 2007, pp. 41-42).

Example:
When John has not eaten in a while he asks his caregiver for a snack. When John asks he's given a snack. In this case the antecedents are food deprivation and the presence of someone who can provide food. The behavior would be the request for a snack and the consequence is being provided with a snack.

Assessment:
- Have supervisee identify and describe the ABC three term contingency.
- Have supervisee give specific examples of the ABC three term contingency.
- Have supervisee identify and describe other principles and terms related to the three term contingency (i.e., motivating operations, setting events, establishing operations, discriminative stimulus, stimulus control, etc...)
- Have supervisee state how the ABC three term contingency related to both punishment and reinforcement.

Relevant Literature:
Azrin, N.H. & Holz, W.C. (1966). Punishment. In W.K. Honig (Ed.), *Operant Behavior: Areas of research and application* (pp. 380-447). New York: Appleton-Century-Crofts.

Cooper, J.O., Heron, T.E. & Heward W.L. (2007). *Applied Behavior Analysis* (2nd Ed.), Upper Saddle River, NJ. Pearson Prentice Hall. 35, 41-42, 258-259, 261, 263-265, 292-294, 331 (Figure 14.2).

Glenn, S.S., Ellis, J., & Greenspoon, J. (1992). On the revolutionary nature of the operant as a unit of behavioral selection. *American Psychologist*, 47, 1329-1336.

Michael, J. (2004). *Concepts and Principles of Behavior Analysis* (rev. ed.) Kalamazoo, MI: Society for the Advancement of Behavior Analysis.

Skinner, B.F. (1969). *Contingencies of reinforcement: A theoretical analysis*. (pp. 7, 114) New York: Appleton-Century-Crofts.

Moxley, R.A. (2004). Pragmatic selectionism: The philosophy of behavior analysis. *The Behavior Analyst Today*, 5, 108-125.

Sulzer-Azaroff, B., & Mayer, G.R. (1977). *Applying behavior analysis procedures with children and youth*. New York: Holt, Rinehart, & Winston.

Vollmer, T.R. (2002). Punishment happens: Some comments on Lerman and Vorndran's review. *Journal of Applied Behavior Analysis*, 35, 469-473.

Vollmer, T.R. & Iwata, B.A. (1991). Establishing Operations and reinforcement effects. *Journal of Applied Behavior Analysis*, 24, 279-291.

Related Lessons:
B-01: Use the dimensions of applied behavior analysis (Baer, Wolf, & Risley, 1968) to evaluate whether interventions are behavior analytic in nature.

E-01: Use interventions based on manipulation of antecedents, such as motivating operations and discriminative stimuli.

G-04: Explain behavioral concepts using nontechnical language.

I-01: Define behavior in observable and measurable terms.

I-02: Define environmental variables in observable and measurable terms.

FK-10: Behavior, response, response class

FK-11: Environment, stimulus, stimulus class.

FK-15: Operant Conditioning

FK-21: Schedules of reinforcement and punishment

FK-27: Conditioned motivating operations.

FK-30: Distinguish between motivating operation and reinforcement effects.

FK-33: Functional relations

FK-34: Conditional discriminations

FK-35: Stimulus discrimination

FK-41: Contingency-shaped behavior

FK-32 Contiguity

Definition:

Contiguity - "The juxtaposition of two or more events when they occur simultaneously or very closely together (e.g. the succession of a response and a reinforcer in a superstition procedure or of a CS and a US in a respondent procedure)" (Catania, 1998, p. 383).

Example:

- Perseus wears his favorite lucky socks to the Patriots game for the first time. On the same day he wears his socks the team wins the game.
- Dr. Zeus is working in an experimental lab with rats. He trips on a banana peel immediately after a rat pulled a level in the operant chamber.
- Perseus also loves to play Monopoly. He needs a 4 to land on free parking. He blows on the dice and says "come on 4!" He rolls a 4.

Assessment:

- Ask your Supervisee to define contiguity.
  - Ask your supervisee to give an example and a non-example of contiguity
  - Ask your supervisee to explain how contiguity could result in superstitious behavior.

Relevant Literature:

Buehner, MJ. (2005). Contiguity and Covariation in Human Causal Inference. *Learning and Behavior*, 33, 230–238.

Catania, A. C. (1998). Learning (4th ed.). Upper Saddle River, NJ: Prentice Hall.

Shanks, D.R., Pearson, S.M., & Dickinson A. (1989). Temporal Contiguity and the Judgment of Causality by Human Subjects. *Quarterly Journal of Experimental Psychology*, 41B, 139–159

Related Lessons:

FK-14 Respondent conditioning (CS-CR)
FK-24 Stimulus control
FK-32 Contiguity
FK-36 Response generalization

FK-33 Functional relations

Definition:

Functional relation - "An experimentally determined relation that shows that the dependent variable depends on or is a function of the independent variable and nothing else" (Johnston & Pennypacker, 2009, p. 358).

"A 'cause' becomes a 'change in an independent variable' and an 'effect' a 'change in a dependent variable.' The old 'cause-and-effect connection' becomes a 'functional relation.' The new terms do not suggest how a cause causes its effect; they merely assert that different events tend to occur together in a certain order" (Skinner, 1953, p.23).

For every response are a number of factors that influence the likelihood that it occurs. Each one of these factors can be used as an independent measure in an experiment. If an experiment shows that there is a different between a context in which this variable is present vs when this variable is absent, we consider it to be a functional relation (Cooper, Heron, & Heward, 2007).

For behavior analysts, functional relations are important to discover. When we understand how a behavior is related to the environment, we can then decide what treatment to use.

Example:

- Sonny has been engaging in some eloping behavior within a school building. He has been known to leave his classroom area and to run to other rooms within the building. His teachers have started delivering small pieces of candy for on-task behavior, as he works on his schoolwork. The teachers have started seeing an increase in on-task behavior and a decrease in elopement. A substitute teacher came into the classroom for a week but did not know about the on-task candy delivery the first couple of days. Sonny started eloping

again. When the aides told the substitute teacher about the contingency for on-task behavior, the substitute started delivering the candy on the same schedule as the other teacher. Sonny again started sitting down, remaining on task, and elopement decreased. It can be said that there is likely a functional relation between the schedule of candy delivery and the elopement and/or on-task behavior.

- Three semi-busy 3-way intersections in the small town of Passamaquoddy has had a series of accidents over the past few years. These intersections have had yield signs up but there have been several accidents at each location. The town decides to replace the yield signs with 3 stop signs instead. They use a multiple baseline design across locations. After seeing that when, and only when, the new stop signs are implemented, accidents have decreased in that location. It can be said that there is a functional relation between the placement of the stop signs and the change in accidents reported there.

- Non-example:

A child with autism has been engaging in some eloping behavior within a school building. He has been known to leave his classroom area and to run to other rooms within the building. His teachers have explained to him that the other rooms are off limits but this has not had an impact on his behavior nor has simply ensuring that the doors are closed. His teacher decides to put up a green light on rooms that it is o.k. to enter. There has been no change in behavior from the previously recorded levels of entering the off-limits classrooms. It can be said that there is no functional relation between the presence of green light signs and the off-limits classroom entering behavior.

Assessment:

- Ask your Supervisee to give a definition for functional relation.
- Ask your supervisee to create other examples and a non-example of his/her own.
- Ask the Supervisee why it is important to only manipulate one variable at a time
- Ask the Supervisee to state how you would know if a functional relation exists between the independent variable and the dependent variable.

Relevant Literature:

Cooper J.O, Heron T.E, Heward W.L. (2007). *Applied behavior analysis* (2nd ed.) Upper Saddle River, NJ: Pearson.

Johnston, J. M., & Pennypacker, H. S. (2009). *Strategies and tactics of behavioral research*. Routledge.

Skinner, B. F. (1953). *Science and human behavior*. Simon and Schuster.

Related Lessons:

B-03 Systematically arrange independent variables to demonstrate their effects on dependent variables.

FK-33 Functional relations

H-03 Select a data display that effectively communicates relevant quantitative relations.

H-05 Evaluate temporal relations between observed variables (within &between sessions, time series).

I-05 Organize, analyze, and interpret observed data

FK-34 Conditional discriminations

Definition:

Conditional discrimination – "refer to a concept related to stimulus equivalence and can be created using matching-to-sample procedures. Conditional discriminations operate within a four-term contingency that accounts for the environmental context, such that the contingency appears as the following: contextual stimulus → S^D→ response → reinforcement" (Cooper, Heron, & Heward, 2007, p. 400).

The contextual events operating within this four-term contingency become conditional discriminations (Sidman, 1994). Moreover, a specific conditional discrimination implies that there is a specific conditional relation, referring to the direct outcome of the reinforcement contingency (Carrigan & Sidman, 1992). Different conditional relations are reflected in the properties of stimulus equivalence (e.g., reflexivity, symmetry, and transitivity). In order for new conditional discriminations to emerge, at least one conditional discrimination must be directly trained. This initial discrimination is often arbitrary (e.g., training A > B implies that B < A).

Example:
- In a matching-to-sample trial, "A" is given as the conditional sample and is then presented in a series of five letters "z", "k", "a", "t", and "b." By correctly matching "A" to "a" the learner is discriminating stimuli and selecting the correct comparison that will be reinforced. The learner's response will not be reinforced if a stimulus other than "a" is selected. In this example, the conditional sample "A" reflects the contextual stimulus as it creates a context for which stimulus to discriminate.

Assessment:
- Conditional discriminations can be a difficult concept to understand without having adequate knowledge of stimulus control, stimulus equivalence, and matching-to-sample procedures. Therefore, in order to assess for learning, the supervisee should be asked to define and provide examples of conditional discriminations within the context of explaining stimulus control, stimulus equivalence, and matching-to-sample procedures.
- Once the supervisee can explain conditional discriminations, applied knowledge can be assessed by asking supervisee to demonstrate direct training of conditional discriminations by using matching-to-sample and stimulus equivalence procedures. The supervisor will model these procedures, have supervisee demonstrate the skill and provide feedback based on their performance.

Relevant Literature:
Bush, K. M., Sidman, M., & De Rose, T. (1989). Contextual control of emergent equivalence relations. Journal of the Experimental Analysis of Behavior, 51, 29-45.
Carrigan, P. F., & Sidman, M. (1992). Conditional discrimination and equivalence relations: A theoretical analysis of control by negative stimuli. Journal of the Experimental Analysis of Behavior, 58, 183 204.
Cooper, J. O., Heron, T. E., & Heward, W. L. (2007). Stimulus control. *Applied Behavior Analysis* (pp. 392-409). Upper Saddle River, NJ: Pearson Prentice Hall.
Johnson. C. & Sidman, M. (1993). Conditional discrimination and equivalence relations: Control by negative stimuli. *Journal of the Experimental Analysis of Behavior, 59,* 333-347.
Sidman, M. (1994). *Equivalence relations and behavior: A research story.* Boston, MA: Author's Cooperative.

Related Lessons:
E-06 Use stimulus equivalence procedures.
FK-11 Environment, stimulus, stimulus class
FK-24 Stimulus control
FK-35 Stimulus discrimination
FK-37 Stimulus generalization
J-14 Arrange instructional procedures to promote generative learning (i.e., derived relations).

FK-35 Stimulus discrimination

Definition:

Stimulus discrimination – "is when a response consistently occurs in the presence of a specific $^{s^D}$ or controlling antecedent stimulus and not in the presence of new or related stimuli. This is in direct contrast to stimulus generalization in which related antecedent stimuli may evoke the same response" (Cooper, Heron, & Heward, 2007, pp. 395-396).

Example:

- During a tooth brushing routine, a child selects their tooth brush from the cup that holds a number of toothbrushes.
- You own a small white car and can walk directly to your car after leaving the mall even though there are several small white cars parked around your car.
- You are taking three graduate level ABA classes. Two of the professors keep track of attendance and incorporate that into your final grade and one professor does not track attendance or incorporate that into your final grade. As a result, you periodically miss this class since that your grade will not be lowered due to attendance and you regularly attend the other two classes.

Assessment:

- Ask supervisee to identify natural examples of stimulus discrimination.
- Ask supervisee to compare and contrast stimulus discrimination and stimulus generalization.
- Observe supervisee use stimulus discrimination procedures with clients.

Relevant Literature:

Cooper, J. O., Heron, T. E., & Heward, W. L. (2007). Stimulus control. *Applied Behavior Analysis* (pp. 392-409). Upper Saddle River, NJ: Pearson Prentice Hall.

Green, G. (2001). Behavior analytic instruction for learners with autism: Advances in stimulus control technology. *Focus on Autism & Other Developmental Disabilities, 16,* 72-85.

Related Lessons:

E-06 Use stimulus equivalence procedures.
FK-11 Environment, stimulus, stimulus class
FK-24 Stimulus control
FK-34 Conditional discriminations
FK-37 Stimulus generalization

FK-36 Response Generalization

Definition:

Response generalization - "The extent to which a learner emits untrained responses that are functionally equivalent to the trained target behavior" (Cooper, Heron, & Heward, 2007, p. 620).

"Improvements in behavior are most beneficial when they are long lasting, appear in other appropriate environments, and spill over to other related behaviors...When evaluating applied behavior analysis research, consumers should consider the maintenance and generalization of behavior change in their evaluation of a study" (Cooper et al., 2007, p. 250).

Example:

- A young child learns to open a door at their house by turning a door knob. One day, while at a friend's house, they encounter a door that has a handle rather than a knob. The child is able to turn the handle and open the unfamiliar door. This is an example of response generalization because functional both responses are equal (they open result in the door being opened) but the response topographies are different.

Assessment:

- Have supervisee provide examples of response generalization.
- Provide examples of both response generalization and stimulus generalization and have supervisee indicate which type of generalization the example is referring to and describe why.
- Have supervisee describe why response generalization is important when assessing behavior change and skill acquisition.

Relevant Literature:

Baer, D.M., Wolf, M.M., & Risley, T.R. (1968). Some current dimensions of applied behavior analysis. *Journal of Applied Behavior Analysis*, 1, 91-97.

Cooper, J.O., Heron, T.E. & Heward W.L. (2007). *Applied Behavior Analysis* (2nd Ed.), Upper Saddle River, NJ. Pearson Prentice Hall. 250-251, 620-622.

Fantuzzo, J.W., & Clement, P.W. (1981). Generalization of the effects of teacher and self-administered token reinforcers to non-treated students. *Journal of Applied Behavior Analysis*, 14, 435-447.

Goetz, E.M., & Baer, D.M. (1973). Social control of form diversity and the emergence of new forms in children's block building. *Journal of Applied Behavior Analysis*, 6, 209-217.

Sidman, M. (1994). *Equivalence relations and behavior: A research story*. Boston: Author's Cooperative.

Related Lessons:

B-01: Use the dimensions of applied behavior analysis (Baer, Wolf, & Risley, 1968) to evaluate whether interventions are behavior analytic in nature.

E-06: Use stimulus equivalence procedures.

E-11: Use pairing procedures to establish new conditioned reinforcers.

I-01: Define behavior in observable and measurable terms.

I-02: Define environmental variables in observable and measurable terms.

J-11: Program for stimulus and response generalization.

J-12: Program for maintenance.

J-14: Arrange instructional procedures to promote generative learning (i.e., derived relations).

K-09: Secure the support of others to maintain the client's behavioral repertoires in their natural environments.

FK-10: Behavior, response, response class.

FK-11: Environment, stimulus, stimulus class

FK-12: Stimulus equivalence

FK-37: Stimulus generalization.

FK-37 Stimulus generalization

Definitions:

Stimulus generalization - "When an antecedent stimulus has a history of evoking a response that has been reinforced in its presence, the same type of behavior tends to be evoked by stimuli that share similar physical properties with the controlling antecedent stimulus" (Cooper, Heron, & Heward, 2007, p. 705).

Example:

A child says, "mommy" in the presence of her mother, but also says "mommy" when she sees her grandmother or daycare provider.

- Have supervisee identify the difference between response generalization and stimulus generalization.
- Have supervisee identify the difference between stimulus generalization and stimulus discrimination. Have him/her identify the qualities of each and give examples.
- Have supervisee give examples from their workplace of stimulus generalization.

Relevant Literature:

Baer, D.M., Wolf, M.M., & Risley, T.R. (1968). Some current dimensions of applied behavior analysis. *Journal of Applied Behavior Analysis*, 1, 91-97.

Cooper, J.O., Heron, T.E. & Heward W.L. (2007). *Applied Behavior Analysis* (2nd Ed.), Upper Saddle River, NJ. Pearson Prentice Hall.   394-396, Figure 17.1, 616, 632.

Cuvo, A.J. (2003).On stimulus generalization and stimulus classes. *Journal of Behavioral Education*, 12, 77-83.

Guttman, N., & Kalish, H. (1956). Discriminability and generalization. *Journal of Experimental Psychology*, 51, 79-88.

Johnston, J.M. (1979). On the relation between generalization and generality. *The Behavior Analyst*, 2, 1-6.

Stokes, T.F., & Baer, D.M. (1977). An implicit technology of generalization. *Journal of Applied Behavior Analysis*, 10, 349-367.

Related Lessons:

B-01: Use the dimensions of applied behavior analysis (Baer, Wolf, & Risley, 1968) to evaluate whether interventions are behavior analytic in nature.

E-06: Use stimulus equivalence procedures.

J-11: Program for stimulus and response generalization.

J-14: Arrange instructional procedures to promote generative learning (i.e., derived relations).

FK-10: Behavior, response, response class.

FK-11: Environment, stimulus, stimulus class

FK-12: Stimulus equivalence

FK-36: Response generalization.

FK-38 Behavioral contrast

Definition:

Behavioral contrast - "The phenomenon in which a change in one component of a multiple schedule that increases or decreases the rate of responding on that component is accompanied by a change in the response rate in the opposite direction on the other, unaltered component of the schedule; behavior punished in one situation may increase in other situations where it's not punished.....Contrast effects of punishment can be minimized, or prevented altogether, by consistently punishing occurrences of the target behavior in all relevant settings and stimulus conditions, withholding or at least minimizing the person's access to reinforcement for the target behavior, and providing alternative desirable behaviors" (Cooper, Heron, & Heward, 2007, p. 337)

Example:

Rich sneaks candy from home and eats it in class. His teacher catches him one day and he stops eating candy in the classroom. However, he now asks to go to the bathroom every morning and eats candy in the bathroom where the teacher cannot see him.

Assessment:

- Have supervisee describe the principles of punishment and reinforcement and how behavioral contrast relates to each.
- Have supervisee explain why rates may fluctuate based on punishment and reinforcement contingencies in multiple schedules.
- Have supervisee give examples of behavioral contrast from their experiences and what they have done in those circumstances.

Relevant Literature:

Cooper, J.O., Heron, T.E. & Heward W.L. (2007). *Applied Behavior Analysis* (2nd Ed.), Upper Saddle River, NJ. Pearson Prentice Hall. 337-338, 349.

Gross, A.M. & Drabman, R.S. (1981) Behavioral contrast and behavior therapy. *Behavior Therapy*, 12, 2, 231-246.

Koegel, R.L. & Williams, J.A. (1980). Behavioral contrast and generalization across settings in the treatment of autistic children. *Journal of Experimental Child Psychology*, 30, 3, 422-437.

Nevin, J.A. (1992). Behavioral contrast and behavioral momentum. *Journal of Experimental Psychology: Animal Behavior Processes*, 18, 2, 126-133.

Reynolds, G.S. (1961) Behavioral Contrast. *Journal of the Experimental Analysis of Behavior*, 4, 1, 57-71.

Related Lessons:

C-01: State and plan for the possible unwanted effects of reinforcement.

C-02: State and plan for the possible unwanted effects of punishment.

D-01: Use positive and negative reinforcement.

D-02: Use appropriate parameters and schedules of reinforcement.

D-15: Use positive and negative punishment.

D-16: Identify and use punishers.

D-17: Use appropriate parameters and schedules of punishment.

D-19: Use combinations of reinforcement with punishment and extinction.

E-07: Plan for behavioral contrast effects.

FK-18: Conditioned reinforcement

FK-20: Conditioned punishment

FK-21: Schedules of reinforcement and punishment

FK-39 Behavioral momentum

Definition:

Behavioral momentum - "A metaphor to describe a rate of responding and its resistance to change following an alteration in reinforcement conditions" (Cooper, Heron, & Heward, 2007, p. 691).

"In classical physics, momentum is defined as the product of velocity and mass. Translating metaphorically, behavioral momentum is the product of response rate and resistance to change" (Nevin, 1992, p. 302).

Response rate had been used as the measure of response rate for many years. With the introduction of behavioral momentum, Nevin challenges this and describes resistance to change as a better way to measure response strength (Nevin, 1974).

Behavioral momentum is <u>not</u> synonymous with the high-p request sequence. Use caution when describing behavioral momentum this way (Nevin, 1996).

Examples:

- "If you are working at the computer, and you keep working even though you are called to dinner, that is an example of behavioral momentum" (Pierce & Cheney, 2013, p. 134).

- A student is coloring at his desk. The teacher asks him to come down to the rug to listen to a story. He continues to color for a few more seconds.

- James is watching TV. His remote stops working. He continues to push the button despite the battery being dead.

Assessment:

- Ask your supervisee to describe behavioral momentum

- Ask your supervisee to give an example of behavioral momentum.

Relevant Literature:

Brandon, P. K., & Houlihan, D. (1997). Applying behavioral theory to practice: An examination of the behavioral momentum metaphor. *Behavioral Interventions, 12*(3), 113-131.

Cooper, J. O., Heron, T. E., & Heward, W. L. (2007). *Applied behavior analysis.* Upper Saddle River, NJ: Pearson Education.

Nevin, J. A. (1974). Response strength in multiple schedules. *Journal of the Experimental Analysis of Behavior, 21*(3), 389–408. doi:10.1901/jeab.1974.21-389

Nevin, J. A. (1992). An integrative model for the study of behavioral momentum. *Journal of the Experimental Analysis of Behavior, 57*(3), 301.

Nevin, J. A. (1996). The Momentum of Compliance. *Journal of Applied Behavior Analysis,* 29(4), 535–547.

Nevin, J. A., Mandell, C., & Atak, J. R. (1983). The analysis of behavioral momentum. *Journal of the Experimental analysis of behavior, 39*(1), 49.

Related Lessons:

E-09 Arrange high-probability request sequences.

FK-10 behavior, response, response class

FK-40 Matching law

Definition:

Matching law - "a quantitative formulation stating that the relative rates of different responses tend to equal the relative reinforcement rates they produce" (Catania, 2007, p. 449).

Herrnstein (1961) described pigeon's distribution of responding on concurrent schedules of reinforcement. He found the relation between absolute rate of reinforcement and the absolute rate of responding is a linear function that passes through the origin. In other words, if rate of reinforcement and rate of responding are plotted on the x and y axis the result of the data is very close to a line that passes through the origin with the slope of 1. The matching equation can be denoted as follows:

$$\frac{B_a}{(B_a + B_b)} = \frac{R_a}{(R_a + R_b)}$$

The term B_a is behavior measured as rate of response for behavior *a, and* B_b is behavior measured as rate of response for behavior *b*. The term R_a is the scheduled rate or reinforcement for response *a,* and R_b is the scheduled rate of reinforcement for response *b*.

The matching law has been demonstrated across a variety of species including pigeons, cows (Mathews & Temple, 1979), rats (Poling, 1978), free ranging flocks of birds (Baum, 1974), and humans (Conger & Killeen, 1974).

There are also multiple applied examples. For example, Mace, Neef, Shade, and Mauro (1994) found special education high school students spent time on math problems, arranged in different stacks, that was equal to the relative rate of reinforcement for completing math problems from the different stacks. Also, Borrero and Vollmer (2002), after conducting functional analyses to find maintaining variables for problem behavior, found that proportional rates of problem behavior relative to problem behavior matched the proportional rate of reinforcement for 4 individuals with disabilities.

Assessment:

- Ask your supervisee to describe matching law and how it relates to choice (response allocation).
- Have supervisee explain a situation where the matching law could be applied and describe the concurrent rates of reinforcement in place for two different behaviors.
- Relate matching law to the selection of alternative behavior in a DRA.

Relevant Literature:

Baum, W. M. (1974). Choice in free-ranging wild pigeons. *Science, 185*(4145), 78-79.

Borrero, J. C., & Vollmer, T. R. (2002). An application of the matching law to severe problem behavior. *Journal of Applied Behavior Analysis, 35*(1), 13-27.

Conger, R., & Killeen, P. (1974). Use of concurrent operants in small group research: A demonstration. *Pacific Sociological Review*, 399-416.

Herrnstein, R. J. (1961). Relative and absolute strength of response as a function of frequency of reinforcement. *Journal of the experimental analysis of behavior, 4*(3), 267.

Mace, F. C., Neef, N. A., Shade, D., & Mauro, B. C. (1994). Limited matching on concurrent-schedule reinforcement of academic behavior. *Journal of Applied Behavior Analysis, 27*(4), 585.

Matthews, L. R., & Temple, W. (1979). Concurrent schedule assessment of food preference in cows. *Journal of the Experimental Analysis of Behavior, 32*(2), 245-254.

Poling, A. (1978). Performance of rats under concurrent variable-interval schedules of negative reinforcement. *Journal of the Experimental Analysis of Behavior, 30*(1), 31-36.

Related Lessons:

A-14 Design and implement choice measures.

B-03 Systematically arrange independent variables to demonstrate their effects on dependent variables.

E-08 Use the matching law and recognize factors influencing choice.

G-04 Explain behavioral concepts using nontechnical language.

FK-41 Contingency-shaped behavior

Definition:

Contingency shaped behavior – Behavior that is "selected and maintained by controlled, temporally close consequences" (Cooper, Heron, & Heward, 2007, p. 42). These consequences may either be reinforcing or punishing.

Example:

Soda sippers

- Melvin puts a dollar into the soda machine and pushes the cola button. Seconds later a can of soda comes out. He opens the soda and drinks it. He buys 3 more drinks from the same machine that week.

- Simon's friend Ernest is a prankster. Ernest shakes up a can of soda and offers Simon a drink. The can sprays him in the face and soaks his clothing. The next time Ernest offers a soda, Simon is hesitant to accept. Although he'd like to open the soda and drink it, he hands it back expecting another explosive surprise.

- Thirsty Floyd finds a 12 pack of old sodas in the storeroom. He cracks a can and starts to drink. Unfortunately, the soda has gone bad. Floyd gets sick from drinking the soda. In the future Floyd avoids drinking old sodas.

Non-example: Horace's mom tells him that drinking soda is bad for him. Horace avoids drinking soda in the future.

Assessment:

- Ask your supervisee to explain contingency shaped behavior
- Ask your supervisee how contingency shaped is different from rule-governed behavior
- Ask your supervisee to create another example and non-example of his/her own.
- Ask your supervisee to state why it might be better to use contingency shaped consequences as opposed consequences, which are more delayed or rule governed

Relevant Literature:

Cooper J.O, Heron T.E, Heward W.L. (2007). *Applied behavior analysis* (2nd ed.) Upper Saddle River, NJ: Pearson

Malott, R. & Trojan-Suarez, E. (2004) *Principles of Behaviour.* New Jersey: Pearson Prentice Hall.

Michael, J. (2004). *Concepts and Principles of Behavior Analysis* (rev. ed.). Kalamazoo, MI: Society for the Advancement of Behavior Analysis.

Related Lessons:

E-04 Use contingency contracting (i.e., behavioral contracts).

FK-42 Rule-governed behavior

FK-42 Rule Governed Behavior

Definition:

Rule governed behavior - "Behavior governed by a rule (i.e., a verbal statement of an antecedent-behavior-consequence contingency), enables human behavior (e.g., fastening a seatbelt) to come under the indirect control of temporarily remote or improbable but potentially significant consequences (e.g., avoiding injury in auto accident). Often used in contrast to *contingency-shaped behavior*, a term used to indicate behavior selected and maintained by controlled, temporally close consequences" (Cooper, Heron, & Heward, 2007, p. 703).

Examples:

- Matilda's mother told her that if she gets all of her homework done this week that she will take her out for ice cream on Saturday. It is only Wednesday and Matilda still hasn't finished all of the work. This is a new contingency for Matilda, but when Saturday arrived, all of her homework was done.

- Felicia has never put a metal fork in the toaster before but her dad told her that she could be electrocuted if she tried to get her bagel out that way. She always gets a wooden spoon to get the bagel out.

- Non-example: Matilda's mother told her that if she gets all of her homework done this week that she will take her out for ice cream on Saturday. It is only Wednesday and Matilda still hasn't finished all of the work. Her mother brings her to get ice cream every week that she gets her homework done. When Saturday arrived, all of her homework was done.

Assessment:

- Ask your supervisee to explain rule-governed behavior
- Ask your supervisee how rule-governed behavior is different from contingency-shaped behavior
- Ask your supervisee to create another example and non-example of his/her own.

Relevant Literature:

Cooper J.O, Heron T.E, Heward W.L. (2007). *Applied behavior analysis* (2nd ed.) Upper Saddle River, NJ: Pearson

Malott, R. W. (1988). Rule-governed behavior and behavioral anthropology. *The Behavior Analyst, 11*(2), 181–203.

Malott, R.W. & Garcia, M.E. (1991). The role of private events in rule-governed behavior. In L.J. Hayes & P. Chase (Eds.), *Dialogues on verbal behavior* (pp. 237-254). Reno, NV: Context Press.

Schlinger Jr, H. D. (1990). A reply to behavior analysts writing about rules and rule-governed behavior. *The Analysis of Verbal Behavior, 8,* 77.

Skinner, B.F. (1969). *Contingencies of reinforcement: A Theoretical Analysis.* New York: Appleton-Century-Crofts.

Related Lessons:

E-04 Use contingency contracting (i.e., behavioral contracts).

FK-41 Contingency-shaped behavior

FK-43 Echoics

Definition:

Echoic - "An elementary verbal operant involving a response that is evoked by a verbal discriminative stimulus that has point-to-point correspondence and formal similarity with the response" (Cooper, Heron, & Heward, 2007, p. 694).

Examples:

Teaching the class

- Mrs. Platypus is instructing her 3ʳᵈ grade class on their math facts. She holds up a card stating that, "three times nine is eighteen". She then restates the fact asking the class to repeat. The class says, "three times nine is eighteen" in unison. Mrs. Platypus praises the students for their repetition.

- Mr. Penguin is a kindergarten teacher. He is working with one student on his reading skills. He shows little Timmy the letter R. He tells him that the letter R makes the "rrr" sound and asks him to repeat. Little Timmy says, "rrr," and Mr. Penguin comments, "Nice job Timmy."

- Mrs. Dodo the art teacher needs one of her students to run to the office and get some supplies. One of the children volunteers. She tells him that she needs him to get, "Crayons, markers, and paint." He repeats, "Crayons, markers, and paint." "Exactly," Mrs. Dodo says sending him on his way.

Non-example:

Mrs. Platypus is still working on math facts with her class. She holds up the math fact $4x9=$ and asks the students to give the answer. Susie Q raises her hand and answers "thirty-six."

Assessment:

- Ask the supervisee to give the definition of an echoic
- Ask the supervisee to give several examples of echoics
- Ask the supervisee to give a non-example of an echoic

Relevant Literature:

Cooper, J.O., Heron T.E, Heward W.L. (2014). *Applied behavior analysis.* Upper Saddle River, NJ: Pearson.

Sundberg, M. L. (2008). *Verbal Behavior Milestones Assessment and Placement Program.* Concorde, CA: AVB Press

Skinner, B.F. (1957). *Verbal Behavior.* New York: Appleton-Century

Related Lessons:

D-04 Use modeling and imitation training.
D-10 Use echoic training.

FK 44 Mands

Definition

Mand - "An elementary verbal operant that is evoked by an MO and followed by specific reinforcement" (Cooper, Heron, & Heward, 2007, p. 699).

Examples:

- "I want a cookie" (mand for an item; can also include verbs, use of adjectives, prepositions, pronouns etc.)
- A child says "watch me" after learning how to ride a bike independently (mand for attention)
- Asking questions like "what's your name? or "where's the phone?" (mand for information)
- Child says, "No!" when parent is about to use blender (mand for avoidance of an aversive)

Things to remember about mands:

- The form of the response is specific and under control of motivating operations.
- Response topography can vary: vocal, sign language, augmentative communication, pushing, reaching, hitting etc.

Assessment:

- Ask your Supervisee to recall how they asked for supervision
- Ask your Supervisee to list the types of mands they would emit if they were lost in a foreign county and needed directions to a local gas station

- Ask you supervisee to list 5 ways they use mands in an inappropriate way (eg. complain about work to get attention)

Relevant Literature:

Cooper, J. O., Heron, T. E., & Heward, W. L. (2007). *Applied Behavior Analysis* (2nd ed.). Upper Saddle River, NJ. Pearson: Prentice Hall.

Laraway, S., Snycerski, S., Michael, J., & Poling, A. (2003). Motivating operations and terms to describe them: Some further refinements. *Journal of Applied Behavior Analysis, 36*(3), 407-414.

Michael, J. (1988). Establishing operations and the mand. *The Analysis of Verbal Behavior, 6*, 3.

Sundberg, M. L., & Michael, J. (2001). The benefits of Skinner's analysis of verbal behavior for children with autism. *Behavior Modification, 25*(5), 698-724.

Sweeney-Kerwin, E. J., Carbone, V. J., O'Brien, L., Zecchin, G., & Janecky, M. N. (2007). Transferring control of the mand to the motivating operation in children with autism. *The Analysis of verbal behavior, 23*(1), 89.

Related Lessons:

D-09 verbal operant as a basis for language assessment
D-11 Use mand training
FK 27 Conditioned motivating operations
FK 28 Transitive, reflexive, surrogate motivating operations

FK-45 Tacts

Definition:

Tact – "An elementary verbal operant evoked by a nonverbal discriminative stimulus and followed by generalized conditioned reinforcement (Cooper, Heron, & Heward, 2007, p. 705)."

Examples:

- Dexter walks outside with his mother and sees birds in a tree. "Robins," he says. "You're right. Those are robins," Dexter's mom says. "Robins" is a tact.
- Hector is in the store shopping for Valentines Day. He sees a variety of flowers before noticing the ones he wants to buy. "Red roses," Hector says quietly to himself. "Red roses" in this context is likely a tact.
- Chester goes to his friends Super-bowl party. Upon scanning the array of delicious apps and snacks on the counter, he hones in on one that is his favorite. "Ooh, buffalo chicken dip," he comments. "Buffalo chicken dip" would be likely a tact in this context.
- Non-example: Dexter is thinking about buying some cookies the next time he goes to the supermarket. He writes the word "cookies" down on his shopping list.

Assessment:

- Ask the supervisee to define "tact."
- Ask the supervisee to give several examples of tacts.
- Ask the supervisee to give a non-example of a tact. Discuss why.

Relevant Literature:

Cooper, J.O, Heron T.E, Heward W.L. (2007). *Applied behavior analysis* (2nd ed.) Upper Saddle River, NJ: Pearson.

Skinner, B.F. (1957). *Verbal Behavior*. New York: Appleton-Century.

Related Lessons:

D-12 Use tact training.

FK-46 Intraverbals

Definition:

Intraverbal – "An elementary verbal operant that is evoked by a verbal discriminative stimulus and that does *not* have point-to-point correspondence with that verbal stimulus" (Cooper, Heron & Heward, 2007, p. 698).

Examples:
- A new employee shows up for his first day on the job. The man in the cubical next to him asks, "What is your name?" "Harvey," the man replies." Saying "Harvey" is an intraverbal in that context.
- Hanks boss stops his office to let him know that his sales were "outstanding this week." "Thanks. I really put in some long hours," Hank notes. "Thanks," is an intraverbal in that context.

Non-example:

The office phone rings. Harvey picks up the phone and answers "Hello." There is no one on the line so he hangs up and keeps working.

Assessment:
- Ask the supervisee to define "intraverbal"
- Ask the supervisee to give several examples of intraverbals.
- Ask the supervisee to give a non-example of an intraverbal.

Relevant Literature:

Cooper, J.O, Heron T.E, Heward W.L. (2007). *Applied behavior analysis* (2nd ed.) Upper Saddle River, NJ: Pearson.

Partington, J. W., & Bailey, J. S. (1993). Teaching intraverbal behavior to preschool children. *The Analysis of Verbal Behavior, 11*, 9.

Skinner, B.F. (1957). *Verbal Behavior*. New York: Appleton-Century.

Related Lessons:

D-13 Use intraverbal training

FK-47 Identify measurable dimensions of behavior

According to Johnston and Pennypacker (1993), behavior has 3 fundamental dimensional quantities (properties) that can be measured:

Repeatability – Refers to the fact that a behavior can occur repeatedly through time (i.e., behavior can be counted) (e.g., count, frequency, rate)

Temporal extent – Refers to the fact that every instance of behavior occurs during some amount of time (i.e., when behavior occurs it can be measured in time.) (e.g., duration)

Temporal locus – Refers to the fact that every instance of behavior occurs at a certain point in time with respect to other events. (i.e., occurrences of behavior can be measured at points in time.) (e.g., latency, interresponse time) (As cited in Cooper, Heron, & Heward, 2007, p. 26)

Assessment:
- Ask Supervisee to measure their own duration related to a task (eg. give them a timer and crossword puzzle to complete)
- Ask Supervisee to measure and calculate the rate of someone tapping their pen (or another discrete behavior) during a 10 minute meeting
- Ask Supervisee to observe a conversation between colleagues and measure latency regarding question asking-answering. Have Supervisee use a timer/stop watch to record latency

- Ask Supervisee to record their own latency during a supervision meeting when asked to define a task list item, vs. a concept
- Ask Supervisee to measure interresponse time (IRT) by observing someone eating a meal for 5 minutes; have Supervisee record time between swallowing one bit of food and next bite and report the average IRT.

Relevant Literature:
Cooper, J. O., Heron, T. E., & Heward, W. L. (2007). Applied behavior analysis.
Johnston, J. M., & Pennypacker, H. S. (2011). Strategies and tactics of behavioral research. Routledge. Chicago
Thomason-Sassi, J. L., Iwata, B. A., Neidert, P. L., & Roscoe, E. M. (2011). Response latency as an index of response strength during functional analyses of problem behavior. *Journal of applied behavior analysis*, *44*(1), 51-67.
Worsdell, A. S., Iwata, B. A., & Wallace, M. D. (2002). Duration-based measures of preference for vocational tasks. *Journal of applied behavior analysis*, *35*(3), 287-290.

Related Lessons:
A-01: Measure frequency
A-02: Measure duration
A-03: Measure duration
A-04: Measure latency
A-05: Measure interresponse time
A-09: Evaluate accuracy and reliability of measurement procedures
D-21: Differential reinforcement

FK-48 State the advantages and disadvantages of using continuous measurement procedures (e.g., partial. and whole-interval recording, momentary time sampling)

Whole-interval recording
- Advantages
  - o Useful for measuring continuous behaviors or behaviors that occur at such a high rate
  - o These data yield information about the duration of each occurrence of the target behavior, because an occurrence is only scored if the behavior occurs for the *entire* observation interval (Cooper, Heron, & Heward, 2007).
- Disadvantages
  - o Tends to underestimate the overall percentage of the observation period that the behavior occurred for. The longer the observation intervals, the greater the underestimation effect will be (Cooper, Heron, & Heward, 2007).

Partial-interval recording
- Advantages
  - o This type of data collection is similarly useful for measuring continuous behaviors or behaviors that occur at high rates.
  - o Multiple behaviors can be measured concurrently because the observer is only required to record a behavior as having occurred if it occurs for any part of the interval. This makes it easier to record more than one behavior at the same time
  - o If partial-interval recording is utilized with short observation intervals to measure discrete responses, which occur for short periods of time, it can give an approximate estimate of the minimum amount of responses during the observation period (Cooper, Heron, & Heward, 2007).
- Disadvantages
  - o These data cannot yield information about the duration of each occurrence of a target behavior. This is because an occurrence is recorded even if the behavior only occurred for part of the observation interval
  - o Partial-interval recording tends to overestimate the total duration that a target behavior occurred; if the behavior has only occurred for a portion of the interval it still gets recorded as an occurrence, leading to overestimation. It may also tend to underestimate the rate of a target behavior, if the response occurs several times in the interval (Cooper, Heron, & Heward, 2007).

Momentary time sampling
- Advantages
  - o The observer does not have to attend continuously to the measurement, given recording of behavior only takes place at the end of the interval (Cooper, Heron, & Heward, 2007).
  - o May yield less error than interval recording, particularly as interval length increases (Gardenier, MacDonald, & Green, 2004).
- Disadvantages
  - o Is not useful for measuring low-frequency behaviors that occur for short periods (Cooper, Heron, & Heward, 2007).

Assessment:

- Ask your Supervisee to state the advantages and disadvantages of each type of measurement procedure.
- Ask your Supervisee to use one of the continuous measurement procedures and evaluate its effectiveness at representing the behavior being studied.

Relevant Literature:

Cooper, J. O., Heron, T. E., & Heward, W. L. (2007). Applied Behavior Analysis, 2nd ed. Upper Saddle River, New Jersey: Pearson Prentice Hall.

Daboul-Meany, M. G., Roscoe, E. M., Bourret, J. C., Ahearn, W. H. (2007). A comparison of momentary time sampling and partial-interval recording for evaluating functional relations. *Journal of Applied Behavior Analysis, 40* (3), 501-514.

Gardenier, N. C., MacDonald, R., & Green, G. (2004). Comparison of direct observational methods for measuring stereotypic behavior in children with autism spectrum disorders. *Research in Developmental Disabilities, 25*(2), 99-118.

Gunter, P. L., Venn, M. L., Patrick, J., Miller, K. A. & Kelly, L. (2003). Efficacy of using momentary time samples to determine on-task behavior of students with emotional/behavioral disorders. *Education and Treatment of Children, 26*, 400-412.

Powell, J., Martindale, A., & Kulp, S. (1975). An evaluation of time-sample measures of behavior. *Journal of Applied Behavior Analysis, 8*, 463-469.

Suen, H. K., Ary, D., & Covalt, W. (1991). Reappraisal of momentary time sampling and partial-interval recording. *Journal of Applied Behavior Analysis, 24*, 803-804.

Related Lessons:

A-09: Evaluate the accuracy and reliability of measurement procedures

A-12: Design and implement continuous measurement procedures (e.g., event recording)

H-01: Select a measurement system to obtain representative data given the dimensions of the behavior and the logistics of observing and recording

H-02: Select a schedule of observation and recording periods

I-01: Define the behavior in observable and measurable terms

FK-47: Identify the measurable dimensions of behavior (e.g., rate, duration, latency, interresponse time)

FK-48: State the advantages and disadvantages of using continuous measurement procedures and discontinuous measurement procedures (e.g., partial- and whole-interval recording, momentary time sampling)

SECTION THREE
Submitting the Application and Beyond

Chapter 5
Upon Completion of Supervision Hours

The technical guide is now complete. If the guide was effective, you should now have enough knowledge and system tools to do the following:

- Identify and reference the rules for providing supervised experience hours
- Identify and calculate the proper hours for supervising independent fieldwork in applied settings
- Assess supervisees as practitioners
- Assess supervisee's Foundational Knowledge of ABA
- Structure Group Meetings using the Agenda for Group Meetings
- Use the Fourth Edition Task List™ with your group
- Apply the Fourth Edition Task List™ to improve, expand, and maintain each supervisee's repertoire
- Balance individual and group supervision to improve and maintain the supervisee's behavior analytic repertoire
- Identify homework assignments
- Choose from a variety of possible presentation delivery modes for supervisees (i.e., calendar, assigned vs. requested topics)
- Connect with Trainaba.com for videos that can be played at group supervision for Weekly Behavior Analytic Lessons
- Incorporate Behavioral Skills Training into group supervision

We invite you to take an experimental approach to supervising experience hours. Please share your experience with this protocol with ben@trainaba.com. The data received from professionals will shape future versions of this document.

Thank you for using this book. If you like it, please tell a colleague or carry the discussion forward on LinkedIn. If you see a blind spot or something is unclear, please email ben@trainaba.com so we can fix the problem for everybody using the system.

Train ABA's goal is to develop a solid program for supervision through hard work and many trials with feedback. Eventually, we hope to deliver a practical supervision approach that serves the behavior analyst community. We hope you join us in making that dream a reality.

References

Agran, M. (Ed.). (1997). *Student-directed learning: teaching self-determination skills.* Pacific Grove, CA: Brooks/Cole Pub. Co.

Alberto, P., & Troutman, A. C. (2013). *Applied behavior analysis for teachers* (9th ed). Boston: Pearson.

Alessi, G. (1992). Models of proximate and ultimate causation in psychology. *American Psychologist, 47*(11), 1359.

Alexander, D. F. (1985). The Effect of Study Skill Training on Learning Disabled Students' Retelling of Expository Material. *Journal of Applied Behavior Analysis, 18*(3), 263–267. http://doi.org/10.1901/jaba.1985.18-263

Allen, K. D., & Evans, J. H. (2001). Exposure-based treatment to control excessive blood glucose monitoring. *Journal of Applied Behavior Analysis, 34*(4), 497–500. *Analogs to Reinforcement and Avoidance Part 1.* (n.d.).

Anderson, C. M., & Long, E. S. (2002). Use of a structured descriptive assessment methodology to identify variables affecting problem behavior. *Journal of Applied Behavior Analysis, 35*(2), 137.

Anderson, S. R., & Romanczyk, R. G. (1999). Early intervention for young children with autism: Continuum-based behavioral models. *Research and Practice for Persons with Severe Disabilities, 24*(3), 162–173.

Arco, L. (2008). Feedback for improving staff training and performance in behavioral treatment programs. *Behavioral Interventions, 23*(1), 39–64.

Athens, E. S., & Vollmer, T. R. (2010). An investigation of differential reinforcement of alternative behavior without extinction. *Journal of Applied Behavior Analysis, 43*(4), 569–589.

Austin, J., & Carr, J. (2000). *Handbook of applied behavior analysis.* New Harbinger Publications.

Axelrod, S. (1992). Disseminating an effective educational technology. *Journal of Applied Behavior Analysis, 25*(1), 31–35.

Ayllon, T., & Azrin, N. (1968). The token economy: A motivational system for therapy and rehabilitation. Retrieved from http://psycnet.apa.org/psycinfo/1969-15955-000

Azrin, N. H., & Holz, W. C. (1966). Punishment. *Operant Behavior: Areas of Research and Application,* 380–447.

Azrin, N. H., Vinas, V., & Ehle, C. T. (2007). Physical activity as reinforcement for classroom calmness of ADHD children: A preliminary study. *Child & Family Behavior Therapy, 29*(2), 1–8.

Baer, D. M. (1999). *How to plan for generalization.* Pro Ed.

Baer, D. M., Peterson, R. F., & Sherman, J. A. (1967). The development of imitation by reinforcing behavioral similarity to a model. *Journal of the Experimental Analysis of Behavior, 10*(5), 405.

Baer, D. M., & Schwartz, I. S. (1991). If reliance on epidemiology were to become epidemic, we would need to assess its social validity. *Journal of Applied Behavior Analysis, 24*(2), 231.

Baer, D. M., & Wolf, M. M. (1970). Recent examples of behavior modification in preschool settings. *Behavior Modification in Clinical Psychology,* 5–12.

Baer, D. M., Wolf, M. M., & Risley, T. R. (1968). Some current dimensions of applied behavior analysis1. *Journal of Applied Behavior Analysis, 1*(1), 91–97.

Baer, D. M., Wolf, M. M., & Risley, T. R. (1987). Some still-current dimensions of applied behavior analysis. *Journal of Applied Behavior Analysis, 20*(4), 313.

Bailey, J., Bailey, J. S., & Burch, M. R. (2010). *25 essential skills & strategies for the profes-*

sional behavior analyst: expert tips for maximizing consulting effectiveness. Taylor & Francis.

Bailey, J., Burch, M. (2011). *Ethics for Behavior Analysts* (2nd Expanded Edition). Taylor & Francis.

Bailey, J., & Burch, M. (2013). *Ethics for Behavior Analysts: 2nd Expanded Edition.* Taylor & Francis.

Bailey, J. S. (1991). Marketing behavior analysis requires different talk. *Journal of Applied Behavior Analysis, 24*(3), 445–448.

Balsam, P. D., & Bondy, A. S. (1983). The negative side effects of reward. *Journal of Applied Behavior Analysis, 16*(3), 283.

Bancroft, S. L., Weiss, J. S., Libby, M. E., & Ahearn, W. H. (2011). A comparison of procedural variations in teaching behavior chains: manual guidance, trainer completion, and no completion of untrained steps. *Journal of Applied Behavior Analysis, 44*(3), 559–569.

Bannerman, D. J., Sheldon, J. B., Sherman, J. A., & Harchik, A. E. (1990). Balancing the right to habilitation with the right to personal liberties: The rights of people with developmental disabilities to eat too many doughnuts and take a nap. *Journal of Applied Behavior Analysis, 23*(1), 79–89.

Barbetta, P. M., Heron, T. E., & Heward, W. L. (1993). Effects of active student response during error correction on the acquisition, maintenance, and generalization of sight words by students with developmental disabilities. *Journal of Applied Behavior Analysis, 26*(1), 111.

Barger-Anderson, R., Domaracki, J. W., Kearney-Vakulick, N., & Kubina Jr, R. M. (2004). Multiple baseline designs: The use of a single-case experimental design in literacy research. *Reading Improvement, 41*(4), 217.

Barlow, D. H., & Hayes, S. C. (1979). Alternating treatments design: One strategy for comparing the effects of two treatments in a single subject. *Journal of Applied Behavior Analysis, 12*(2), 199–210.

Baum, W. M. (1974a). Choice in free-ranging wild pigeons. *Science, 185*(4145), 78–79.

Baum, W. M. (1974b). On two types of deviation from the matching law: Bias and undermatching. *Journal of the Experimental Analysis of Behavior, 22*(1), 231.

Baum, W. M. (1979). Matching, undermatching, and overmatching in studies of choice. *Journal of the Experimental Analysis of Behavior, 32*(2), 269.

Baum, W. M. (1994). *Understanding behaviorism: science, behavior, and culture.* New York, NY: HarperCollins College Publishers.

Baum, W. M. (1995). Radical behaviorism and the concept of agency. *Behaviorology, 3,* 93–106.

Baum, W. M. (2011). What is radical behaviorism? A review of Jay Moore's Conceptual Foundations of Radical Behaviorism. *Journal of the Experimental Analysis of Behavior, 95*(1), 119–126.

Behavior Analyst Certification Board professional and ethical compliance code for behavior analysts. (2014). Behavior Analyst Certification Board (BACB). Retrieved from http://www.bacb.com/Download-files/BACB_Compliance_Code.pdf

Berk, R. A. (1976). Effects of choice of instructional methods on verbal learning tasks. *Psychological Reports, 38*(3), 867–870.

Bijou, S. W., & Baer, D. M. (1961). Child development, Vol 1: A systematic and empirical theory.

Birnbrauer, J. S. (1999, August). How to Evaluate Intervention Programs. Cambridge Center for Behavioral Studies, Inc. Retrieved from www.behavior.org/resources/552.pdf

Blough, D. S. (1963). Interresponse time as a function of continuous variabes: a new method and some data. *Journal of the Experimental Analysis of Behavior*, *6*(2), 237–246.

Borrero, J. C., & Vollmer, T. R. (2002). An application of the matching law to severe problem behavior. *Journal of Applied Behavior Analysis*, *35*(1), 13–27.

Bosch, S., & Fuqua, R. W. (2001). Behavioral cusps: a model for selecting target behaviors. *Journal of Applied Behavior Analysis*, *34*(1), 123.

Boyce, T. E., Carter, N., & Neboschick, H. (2000). An Evaluation of Intraobserver Reliability versus Interobserver Agreement. *European Journal of Behavior Analysis*, *1*(2), 107–114.

Brandon, P. K., & Houlihan, D. (1997). Applying behavioral theory to practice: An examination of the behavioral momentum metaphor. *Behavioral Interventions*, *12*(3), 113–131.

Buehner, M. J. (2005). Contiguity and covariation in human causal inference. *Learning & Behavior*, *33*(2), 230–238.

Bullock, C. E., & Hackenberg, T. D. (2015). The several roles of stimuli in token reinforcement. *Journal of the Experimental Analysis of Behavior*, *103*(2), 269–287. http://doi.org/10.1002/jeab.117

Bush, K. M., Sidman, M., & De Rose, T. (1989). Contextual control of emergent equivalence relations. *Journal of the Experimental Analysis of Behavior*, *51*(1), 29.

Buskist, W., Cush, D., & DeGrandpre, R. J. (1991). The life and times of PSI. *Journal of Behavioral Education*, *1*(2), 215–234.

Callahan, K., Shukla-Mehta, S., Magee, S., & Wie, M. (2010). ABA versus TEACCH: the case for defining and validating comprehensive treatment models in autism. *Journal of Autism and Developmental Disorders*, *40*(1), 74–88.

Call, N. A., & Lomas Mevers, J. E. (2014). The relative influence of motivating operations for positive and negative reinforcement on problem behavior during

demands. *Behavioral Interventions*, *29*(1), 4–20.

Carbone, V. J., Morgenstern, B., Zecchin-Tirri, G., & Kolberg, L. (2007). The role of the reflexive conditioned motivating operation (CMO-R) during discrete trial instruction of children with autism. *Journal of Early and Intensive Behavior Intervention*, *4*(4), 658.

Carr, E. G. (1993). Behavior analysis is not ultimately about behavior. *The Behavior Analyst*, *16*(1), 47.

Carr, E. G., & Durand, V. M. (1985). Reducing behavior problems through functional communication training. *Journal of Applied Behavior Analysis*, *18*(2), 111–126.

Carr, E. G., & Smith, C. E. (1995). Biological setting events for self-injury. *Mental Retardation and Developmental Disabilities Research Reviews*, *1*(2), 94–98.

Carr, E. G., Smith, C. E., Giacin, T. A., Whelan, B. M., & Pancari, J. (2003). Menstrual discomfort as a biological setting event for severe problem behavior: Assessment and intervention. *Journal Information*, *108*(2).

Carrigan, P. F., & Sidman, M. (1992). Conditional discrimination and equivalence relations: A theoretical analysis of control by negative stimuli. *Journal of the Experimental Analysis of Behavior*, *58*(1), 183–204.

Carr, J. E. (2005). Recommendations for reporting multiple-baseline designs across participants. *Behavioral Interventions*, *20*(3), 219–224.

Catania, A. C. (1993). Coming to terms with establishing operations. *The Behavior Analyst*, *16*(2), 219.

Catania, A. C. (2012). Discussion: The flight from experimental analysis. *European Journal of Behavior Analysis*, *13*, 165–176.

Catania, A. C. (2013). *Learning* (5th ed.). Cornwall-on-Hudson, NY: Sloan Pub.

Catania, A. C., & Overmier, J. B. (1971). Discriminative stimulus functions of drugs:

Interpretations. In *Stimulus properties of drugs* (pp. 149–160). Springer.

Cautela, J. R. (1984). General level of reinforcement. *Journal of Behavior Therapy and Experimental Psychiatry, 15*(2), 109–114.

Charlop-Christy, M. H., Carpenter, M., Le, L., LeBlanc, L. A., & Kellet, K. (2002). Using the picture exchange communication system (PECS) with children with autism: Assessment of PECS acquisition, speech, social-communicative behavior, and problem behavior. *Journal of Applied Behavior Analysis, 35*(3), 213–231.

Cheney, C. D., & Pierce, W. D. (Eds.). (2013). *Behavior analysis and learning* (5th ed). New York, NY: Psychology Press.

Codding, R. S., Feinberg, A. B., Dunn, E. K., & Pace, G. M. (2005). Effects of immediate performance feedback on implementation of behavior support plans. *Journal of Applied Behavior Analysis, 38*(2), 205–219.

Colón, C. L., Ahearn, W. H., Clark, K. M., & Masalsky, J. (2012). The effects of verbal operant training and response interruption and redirection on appropriate and inappropriate vocalizations. *Journal of Applied Behavior Analysis, 45*(1), 107–120.

Conger, R., & Killeen, P. (1974). Use of concurrent operants in small group research: A demonstration. *Pacific Sociological Review*, 399–416.

Cooper, J. O. (2000). Tutoring Joe: winning with the Precision Teaching team. *Exceptional Children: An Introduction to Exceptional Children*, 268–270.

Cooper, J. O., Heron, T. E., & Heward, W. L. (2007). *Applied behavior analysis* (2nd ed). Upper Saddle River, N.J: Pearson/Merrill-Prentice Hall.

Cowdery, G. E., Iwata, B. A., & Pace, G. M. (1990). Effects and side effects of DRO as treatment for self-injurious behavior. *Journal of Applied Behavior Analysis, 23*(4), 497.

Cumming, W., & Berryman, R. (1965). The complex discriminated operant: Studies of matching-to-sample and related problems. *Stimulus Generalization*, 284–330.

Cuvo, A. J. (2003). On stimulus generalization and stimulus classes. *Journal of Behavioral Education, 12*(1), 77–83.

Dattilo, J., & Camarata, S. (1991). Facilitating conversation through self-initiated augmentative communication treatment. *Journal of Applied Behavior Analysis, 24*(2), 369–378.

Davis, H., & Hurwitz, H. M. B. (Eds.). (1977). *Operant-Pavlovian interactions*. Hillsdale, N.J. : New York: L. Erlbaum Associates ; distributed by the Halsted Press Division of J. Wiley.

Deitz, D. E., & Repp, A. C. (1983). Reducing Behavior through Reinforcement. *Exceptional Education Quarterly, 3*(4), 34–46.

Deitz, S. M. (1977). An analysis of programming DRL schedules in educational settings. *Behaviour Research and Therapy, 15*(1), 103–111.

DeLeon, I. G., & Iwata, B. A. (1996). Evaluation of a multiple-stimulus presentation format for assessing reinforcer preferences. *Journal of Applied Behavior Analysis, 29*(4), 519–533.

DeLeon, I. G., Iwata, B. A., Conners, J., & Wallace, M. D. (1999). Examination of ambiguous stimulus preferences with duration-based measures. *Journal of Applied Behavior Analysis, 32*(1), 111–114.

Delprato, D. J., & Midgley, B. D. (1992). Some fundamentals of BF Skinner's behaviorism. *American Psychologist, 47*(11), 1507.

Drash, P. W., High, R. L., & Tudor, R. M. (1999). Using mand training to establish an echoic repertoire in young children with autism. *The Analysis of Verbal Behavior, 16*, 29.

Durand, V. M. (1999). Functional communication training using assistive devices:

recruiting natural communities of reinforcement. *Journal of Applied Behavior Analysis*, *32*(3), 247.

Durand, V. M., & Carr, E. G. (1992). An analysis of maintenance following functional communication training. *Journal of Applied Behavior Analysis*, *25*(4), 777–794.

Endicott, K., & Higbee, T. S. (2007). Contriving motivating operations to evoke mands for information in preschoolers with autism. *Research in Autism Spectrum Disorders*, *1*(3), 210–217.

Engelmann, S. (1975). *Your child can succeed: how to get the most out of school for your child.* Simon and Schuster.

Epling, W. F., & Pierce, W. D. (1983). Applied behavior analysis: New directions from the laboratory. *The Behavior Analyst*, *6*(1), 27.

Epstein, R. (1997). Skinner as self-manager. *Journal of Applied Behavior Analysis*, *30*(3), 545–568.

Etzel, B. C., & LeBlanc, J. M. (1979). The simplest treatment alternative: The law of parsimony applied to choosing appropriate instructional control and errorless-learning procedures for the difficult-to-teach child. *Journal of Autism and Developmental Disorders*, *9*(4), 361–382.

Fabrizio, M.S. (2001). *A Brief Overview of Fluency-Based Instruction for Learners with Autism.* Seattle, Washington: Fabrizio/Moors Consulting.

Fagen, J. W. (1978). Behavioral contrast in infants.

Fahmie, T. A., & Hanley, G. P. (2008). Progressing toward data intimacy: A review of within-session data analysis. *Journal of Applied Behavior Analysis*, *41*(3), 319.

Falcomata, T. S., Roane, H. S., Hovanetz, A. N., Kettering, T. L., & Keeney, K. M. (2004). An evaluation of response cost in the treatment of inappropriate vocalizations maintained by automatic reinforcement. *Journal of Applied Behavior Analysis*, *37*(1), 83.

Fantuzzo, J. W., & Clement, P. W. (1981). Generalization of the effects of teacher- and self-administered token reinforcers to nontreated students. *Journal of Applied Behavior Analysis*, *14*(4), 435.

Favell, J. E., McGimsey, J. F., & Jones, M. L. (1980). Rapid Eating in the Retarded Reduction by Nonaversive Procedures. *Behavior Modification*, *4*(4), 481–492.

Fawcett, S. B. (1991). Social validity: a note on methodology. *Journal of Applied Behavior Analysis*, *24*(2), 235.

Ferster, C.B., Skinner, B.F. (1957). *Schedules of Reinforcement.* New York, Appleton-Century-Crofts, Inc.

Fields, L., Garruto, M., & Watanabe, M. (2011). Varieties of Stimulus Control in Matching-to-Sample: A Kernal Analysis. *The Psychological Record*, *60*(1), 1.

Fillingham, J. K., Hodgson, C., Sage, K., & Lambon Ralph, M. A. (2003). The application of errorless learning to aphasic disorders: A review of theory and practice. *Neuropsychological Rehabilitation*, *13*(3), 337–363.

Fisher, W., Piazza, C., Cataldo, M., Harrell, R., Jefferson, G., & Conner, R. (1993). Functional communication training with and without extinction and punishment. *Journal of Applied Behavior Analysis*, *26*(1), 23–36.

Fisher, W., Piazza, C. C., Bowman, L. G., Hagopian, L. P., Owens, J. C., & Slevin, I. (1992). A comparison of two approaches for identifying reinforcers for persons with severe and profound disabilities. *Journal of Applied Behavior Analysis*, *25*(2), 491.

Fisher, W. W., Kuhn, D. E., & Thompson, R. H. (1998). Establishing discriminative control of responding using functional and alternative reinforcers during functional communication training. *Journal of Applied Behavior Analysis*, *31*(4), 543–560.

Fisher, W. W., Piazza, C. C., BowMAN, L. G., Kurtz, P. F., Sherer, M. R., & Lachman, S. R. (1994). A preliminary evaluation of empirically derived consequences for the treatment of pica. *Journal of Applied Behavior Analysis, 27*(3), 447–457.

Fisher, W. W., Piazza, C. C., & Roane, H. S. (2014). *Handbook of applied behavior analysis.* New York: Guilford Press.

Flora, S. R. (2004). *The power of reinforcement.* SUNY Press.

Foxx, R. M. (1982). *Decreasing behaviors of severely retarded and autistic persons.* Research Press.

Foxx, R. M. (1998). A comprehensive treatment program for inpatient adolescents. *Behavioral Interventions, 13*(1), 67–77.

Fryling, M. J., Wallace, M. D., & Yassine, J. N. (2012). Impact of treatment integrity on intervention effectiveness. *Journal of Applied Behavior Analysis, 45*(2), 449–453.

Gardenier, N. C., MacDonald, R., & Green, G. (2004). Comparison of direct observational methods for measuring stereotypic behavior in children with autism spectrum disorders. *Research in Developmental Disabilities, 25*(2), 99–118.

Gast, D. L., & Ledford, J. R. (2009). *Single subject research methodology in behavioral sciences.* Routledge.

Gersten, R., & Keating, T. (1987). Long-term benefits from direct instruction. *Educational Leadership, 44*(6), 28–31.

Gersten, R., Keating, T., & Becker, W. (1988). The continued impact of the Direct Instruction model: Longitudinal studies of Follow Through students. *Education and Treatment of Children,* 318–327.

Gersten, R., Woodward, J., & Darch, C. (1986). Direct instruction: A research-based approach to curriculum design and teaching. *Exceptional Children, 53*(1), 17–31.

Gewirtz, J. L., & Pelaez-Nogueras, M. (2000). Infant emotions under the positivereinforcer control of caregiver attention and touch. *Issues in Experimental and Applied Analyses of Human Behavior,* 271–291.

Glenn, S. S., Ellis, J., & Greenspoon, J. (1992). On the revolutionary nature of the operant as a unit of behavioral selection. *American Psychologist, 47*(11), 1329.

Goetz, E. M., & Baer, D. M. (1973). Social control of form diversity and the emergence of new forms in children's blockbuilding. *Journal of Applied Behavior Analysis, 6*(2), 209–217.

Graves, A. W. (1986). Effects of direct instruction and metacomprehension training on finding main ideas. *Learning Disabilities Research.*

Green, C. W., Reid, D. H., White, L. K., Halford, R. C., Brittain, D. P., & Gardner, S. M. (1988). Identifying reinforcers for persons with profound handicaps: Staff opinion versus systematic assessment of preferences. *Journal of Applied Behavior Analysis, 21*(1), 31–43.

Green, G. (2001). Behavior analytic instruction for learners with autism advances in stimulus control technology. *Focus on Autism and Other Developmental Disabilities, 16*(2), 72–85.

Gresham, F. M., Watson, T. S., & Skinner, C. H. (2001). Functional Behavioral Assessment: Principles, Procedures, and Future Directions. *School Psychology Review, 30*(2), 156–172.

Gross, A. M., & Drabman, R. S. (1981). Behavioral contrast and behavior therapy. *Behavior Therapy, 12*(2), 231–246.

Gunter, P. L., Venn, M. L., Patrick, J., Miller, K. A., & Kelly, L. (2003). Efficacy of using momentary time samples to determine on-task behavior of students with emotional/behavioral disorders. *Education and Treatment of Children,* 400–412.

Guttman, N., & Kalish, H. I. (1956). Discriminability and stimulus generalization. *Journal of Experimental Psychology, 51*(1), 79.

Hackenberg, T. D. (2009). Token reinforcement: A review and analysis. *Journal of the Experimental Analysis of Behavior, 91*(2), 257.

Hagopian, L. P., & Fisher, W. W. (1994). Schedule effects of noncontingent reinforcementon attention-maintained destructive behavior in identical quadruplets. *Journal of Applied Behavior Analysis, 27*(2), 317–325.

Hagopian, L. P., Fisher, W. W., Sullivan, M. T., Acquisto, J., & LeBlanc, L. A. (1998). Effectiveness of functional communication training with and without extinction and punishment: A summary of 21 inpatient cases. *Journal of Applied Behavior Analysis, 31*(2), 211–235.

Hagopian, L. P., Long, E. S., & Rush, K. S. (2004). Preference assessment procedures for individuals with developmental disabilities. *Behavior Modification, 28*(5), 668–677.

Hagopian, L. P., Rush, K. S., Lewin, A. B., & Long, E. S. (2001). Evaluating the predictive validity of a single stimulus engagement preference assessment. *Journal of Applied Behavior Analysis, 34*(4), 475–485.

Hains, A. H. (1991). Multi-Element Designs for Early Intervention Research Some Considerations. *Journal of Early Intervention, 15*(2), 185–192.

Hake, D. F., & Azrin, N. H. (1965). Conditioned punishment. *Journal of the Experimental Analysis of Behavior, 8*(5), 279.

Hall, R. V., & Fox, R. G. (1977). Changing criterion designs: An alternative applied behavior analysis procedure. *New Developments in Behavioral Research: Theory, Method, and Application,* 151–66.

Hall, R. V., Lund, D., & Jackson, D. (1968). Effects of teacher attention on study behavior. *Journal of Applied Behavior Analysis, 1*(1), 1.

Hanley, G. P., Iwata, B. A., & Lindberg, J. S. (1999). Analysis of activity preferences as a function of differential consequences. *Journal of Applied Behavior Analysis, 32*(4), 419–435.

Hanley, G. P., Iwata, B. A., Lindberg, J. S., & Conners, J. (2003). Response-restriction analysis: I. Assessment of activity preferences. *Journal of Applied Behavior Analysis, 36*(1), 47–58.

Hanley, G. P., Iwata, B. A., & McCord, B. E. (2003). Functional analysis of problem behavior: A review. *Journal of Applied Behavior Analysis, 36*(2), 147–185.

Hanley, G. P., Iwata, B. A., & Thompson, R. H. (2001). Reinforcement schedule thinning following treatment with functional communication training. *Journal of Applied Behavior Analysis, 34*(1), 17–38.

Hanley, G. P., Piazza, C. C., Fisher, W. W., Contrucci, S. A., & Maglieri, K. A. (1997). Evaluation of client preference for function-based treatment packages. *Journal of Applied Behavior Analysis, 30*(3), 459.

Hanley, G. P., Piazza, C. C., Fisher, W. W., & Maglieri, K. A. (2005). On the effectiveness of and preference for punishment and extinction components of function-based interventions. *Journal of Applied Behavior Analysis, 38*(1), 51–65.

Hantula, D. A., & Crowell, C. R. (1994). Behavioral contrast in a two-option analogue task of financial decision making. *Journal of Applied Behavior Analysis, 27*(4), 607–617.

Hardesty, S. L., Hagopian, L. P., McIvor, M. M., Wagner, L. L., Sigurdsson, S. O., & Bowman, L. G. (2014). Effects of Specified Performance Criterion and Performance Feedback on Staff Behavior A Component Analysis. *Behavior Modification,* 0145445514538280.

Harris, F. N., & Jenson, W. R. (1985). Comparisons of multiple-baseline across persons designs and AB designs with replication: Issues and confusions.

Hart, B. M., Reynolds, N. J., Baer, D. M., Brawley, E. R., & Harris, F. R. (1968). Effect of contingent and non-contingent social reinforcement on the cooperative play of a pre-school. *Journal of Applied Behavior Analysis, 1*(1), 73–76.

Hart, B., & Risley, T. R. (1975). Incidental teaching of language in the preschool. *Journal of Applied Behavior Analysis, 8*(4), 411.

Hartmann, D. P., Gottman, J. M., Jones, R. R., Gardner, W., Kazdin, A. E., & Vaught, R. S. (1980). Interrupted time-series analysis and its application to behavioral data. *Journal of Applied Behavior Analysis, 13*(4), 543–559.

Hartmann, D. P., & Hall, R. V. (1976). The changing criterion design. *Journal of Applied Behavior Analysis, 9*(4), 527–532.

Harvey, M. T., May, M. E., & Kennedy, C. H. (2004). Nonconcurrent multiple baseline designs and the evaluation of educational systems. *Journal of Behavioral Education, 13*(4), 267–276.

Hawkins, R. P. (1979). The functions of assessment: Implications for selection and development of devices for assessing repertoires in clinical, educational, and other settings. *Journal of Applied Behavior Analysis, 12*(4), 501–516.

Hawkins, R. P. (1984). What is" meaningful" behavior change in a severely/profoundly retarded learner: The view of a behavior analytic parent. *Focus on Behavior Analysis in Education*, 282–286.

Hawkins, R. P. (1986). Selection of target behaviors. *Conceptual Foundations of Behavioral Assessment*, 331–385.

Hawkins, R. P., & Dobes, R. W. (1977). Behavioral definitions in applied behavior analysis: Explicit or implicit. *New Developments in Behavioral Research: Theory, Method, and Application*, 167–188.

Hayes, S. C., Barnes-Holmes, D., & Roche, B. (2001). *Relational frame theory: A post-Skinnerian account of human language and cognition*. Springer Science & Business Media.

Hayes, S. C., Brownstein, A. J., Zettle, R. D., Rosenfarb, I., & Korn, Z. (1986). Rule-governed behavior and sensitivity to changing consequences of responding. *Journal of the Experimental Analysis of Behavior, 45*(3), 237–256.

Herman, R. L., & Azrin, N. H. (1964). Punishment by noise in an alternative response situation. *Journal of the Experimental Analysis of Behavior, 7*(2), 185–188.

Herrnstein, R. J. (1961). Relative and absolute strength of response as a function of frequency of reinforcement. *Journal of the Experimental Analysis of Behavior, 4*(3), 267.

Hesse, B. E. (1993). The establishing operation revisited. *The Behavior Analyst, 16*(2), 215.

Heward, W. L. (2005). Reasons applied behavior analysis is good for education and why those reasons have been insufficient. *Focus on Behavior Analysis in Education: Achievements, Challenges, and Opportunities*, 316–348.

Heward, W. L., Heron, T. E., Neef, N. A., Peterson, S. M., Sainato, D. M., Cartledge, G., ... Dardig, J. C. (2005). *Focus on behavior analysis in education: Achievements, challenges, and opportunities*. Pearson/Merrill/Prentice Hall.

Higgins, J. W., Williams, R. L., & McLaughlin, T. F. (2001). The effects of a token economy employing instructional consequences for a third-grade student with learning disabilities: A data-based case study. *Education and Treatment of Children*, 99–106.

Holz, W. C., Azrin, N. H., & Ayllon, T. (1963). Elimination of behavior of mental patients by response-produced extinction. *Journal of the Experimental Analysis of Behavior, 6*(3), 407.

Honig, W. K. (1966). Operant behavior: areas of research and application. Retrieved from http://psycnet.apa.org/psycinfo/1966-35017-000

Horner, R. D., & Baer, D. M. (1978). Multiple-probe technique: A variation of the multiple baseline. *Journal of Applied Behavior Analysis, 11*(1), 189–196.

Horner, R. H., Carr, E. G., Halle, J., McGee, G., Odom, S., & Wolery, M. (2005). The use of single-subject research to identify evidence-based practice in special education. *Exceptional Children, 71*(2), 165–179.

Houten, R., Axelrod, S., Bailey, J. S., Favell, J. E., Foxx, R. M., Iwata, B. A., & Lovaas, O. I. (1988). The right to effective behavioral treatment. *Journal of Applied Behavior Analysis, 21*(4), 381–384.

Houten, R. V. (1979). Social validation: The evolution of standards of competency for target behaviors. *Journal of Applied Behavior Analysis, 12*(4), 581–591.

Hughes, J. C., Beverley, M., & Whitehead, J. (2007). Using precision teaching to increase the fluency of word reading with problem readers. *European Journal of Behavior Analysis, 8*(2), 221.

Ingvarsson, E. T., Kahng, S., & Hausman, N. L. (2008). Some effects of noncontingent positive reinforcement on multiply controlled problem behavior and compliance in a demand context. *Journal of Applied Behavior Analysis, 41*(3), 435.

Iwata, B. A. (1988). The development and adoption of controversial default technologies. *The Behavior Analyst, 11*(2), 149.

Iwata, B. A., Bailey, J. S., Brown, K. M., Foshee, T. J., & Alpern, M. (1976). A performance-based lottery to improve residential care and training by institutional staff. *Journal of Applied Behavior Analysis, 9*(4), 417.

Iwata, B. A., Dorsey, M. F., Slifer, K. J., Bauman, K. E., & Richman, G. S. (1994). Toward a functional analysis of self-injury. *Journal of Applied Behavior Analysis, 27*(2), 197.

Iwata, B. A., Pace, G. M., Dorsey, M. F., Zarcone, J. R., Vollmer, T. R., Smith, R. G., … others. (1994). The functions of self-injurious behavior: An experimental-epidemiological analysis. *Journal of Applied Behavior Analysis, 27*(2), 215.

Iwata, B. A., Smith, R. G., & Michael, J. (2000). Current research on the influence of establishing operations on behavior in applied settings. *Journal of Applied Behavior Analysis, 33*(4), 411–418.

Iwata, B. A., Wallace, M. D., Kahng, S., Lindberg, J. S., Roscoe, E. M., Conners, J., … Worsdell, A. S. (2000). Skill acquisition in the implementation of functional analysis methodology. *Journal of Applied Behavior Analysis, 33*(2), 181–194.

Jacobson, J. W., Mulick, J. A., & Schwartz, A. A. (1995). A history of facilitated communication: Science, pseudoscience, and antiscience science working group on facilitated communication. *American Psychologist, 50*(9), 750.

Jarmolowicz, D. P., Kahng, S., Ingvarsson, E. T., Goysovich, R., Heggemeyer, R., & Gregory, M. K. (2008). Effects of conversational versus technical language on treatment preference and integrity. *Journal Information, 46*(3).

Jerome, J., Frantino, E. P., & Sturmey, P. (2007). The effects of errorless learning and backward chaining on the acquisition of internet skills in adults with developmental disabilities. *Journal of Applied Behavior Analysis, 40*(1), 185.

Johnson, C., & Sidman, M. (1993). Conditional discrimination and equivalence relations: Control by negative stimuli. *Journal of the Experimental Analysis of Behavior, 59*(2), 333–347.

Johnston, J. M. (1979). On the relation between generalization and generality. *The Behavior Analyst, 2*(2), 1.

Johnston, J. M. (2013). *Radical behaviorism for ABA practitioners* (1 Edition). Cornwall on Hudson, NY: Sloan Publishing.

Johnston, J.M., Pennypacker, H.S. (1993). *Strategies and Tactics for Human Behavioral Research* (2nd ed.). Hillside, New Jersey: Erlbaum.

Johnston, J. M., & Pennypacker, H. S. (2009). *Strategies and Tactics of Behavioral Research* (3rd ed). New York: Routledge.

Kahng, S., Abt, K. A., & Schonbachler, H. E. (2001). Assessment and treatment of low-rate high-intensity problem behavior. *Journal of Applied Behavior Analysis, 34*(2), 225–228.

Kamps, D., Wills, H. P., Heitzman-Powell, L., Laylin, J., Szoke, C., Petrillo, T., & Culey, A. (2011). Class-wide function-related intervention teams: Effects of group contingency programs in urban classrooms. *Journal of Positive Behavior Interventions*, 1098300711398935.

Kayser, J. E., Billingsley, F. F., & Neel, R. S. (1986). A comparison of in-context and traditional instructional approaches: Total task, single trial versus backward chaining, multiple trials. *Journal of the Association for Persons with Severe Handicaps.*

Kazdin, A. E. (1982). The token economy: A decade later. *Journal of Applied Behavior Analysis, 15*(3), 431–445.

Kazdin, A. E. (2012). *Behavior modification in applied settings.* Waveland Press.

Kazdin, A. E., & Bootzin, R. R. (1972). The token economy: An evaluative review. *Journal of Applied Behavior Analysis, 5*(3), 343.

Keller, F. S. (1968). Good-bye, teacher... *Journal of Applied Behavior Analysis, 1*(1), 79.

Keller, F. S. (1994). The Fred S. Keller School: CABAS at work. *The Current Repertoire, 10*, 3–4.

Keller, F. S., & Sherman, J. G. (1982). *The PSI handbook: Essays on personalized instruction.* TRI Publications.

Kelly, A., & Tincani, M. (2013). Collaborative training and practice among applied behavior analysts who support individuals with autism spectrum disorder. *Education and Training in Autism and Developmental Disabilities, 48*(1), 120–131.

Kelly, M. B. (1977). A review of the observational data-collection and reliability procedures reported in the Journal of Applied Behavior Analysis. *Journal of Applied Behavior Analysis, 10*(1), 97.

Kennedy, C. H., & Meyer, K. A. (1996). Sleep deprivation, allergy symptoms, and negatively reinforced problem behavior. *Journal of Applied Behavior Analysis, 29*(1), 133–135.

Keohane, D.-D., & Greer, R. D. (2005). Teachers' use of a verbally governed algorithm and student learning. *International Journal of Behavioral Consultation and Therapy, 1*(3), 252.

Kerr, K., Smyth, P., & Mcdowell, C. (2003). Precision teaching children with autism: Helping design effective programmes. *Early Child Development and Care, 173*(4), 399–410.

Killeen, P. R. (2015). The logistics of choice. *Journal of the Experimental Analysis of Behavior.*

Kodak, T., Clements, A., & Ninness, C. (2009). Acquisition of mands and tacts with concurrent echoic training. *Journal of Applied Behavior Analysis, 42*(4), 839–843.

Kodak, T., Lerman, D. C., Volkert, V. M., & Trosclair, N. (2007). Further examination of factors that influence preference for positive versus negative reinforcement. *Journal of Applied Behavior Analysis, 40*(1), 25–44.

Koegel, R. L., Egel, A. L., & Williams, J. A. (1980). Behavioral contrast and generalization across settings in the treatment of autistic children. *Journal of Experimental Child Psychology, 30*(3), 422–437.

Kratochwill, T. R. (1979). New Developments in Behavioral Research/Etzel, LeBlanc, Baer (Eds.). *Journal of Learning Disabilities, 12*(3), 209–210. http://doi.org/10.1177/002221947901200321

Krause, T. R., Seymour, K. J., & Sloat, K. C. M. (1999). Long-term evaluation of a behavior-based method for improving safety performance: a meta-analysis of 73 interrupted time-series replications. *Safety Science, 32*(1), 1–18.

Kubina, R. M. (2012). *Precision teaching book.* [S.l.]: Greatness Achieved Pub Co.

Kubina, R. M., Morrison, R., & Lee, D. L. (2002). Benefits of adding precision teaching to behavioral interventions for students with autism. *Behavioral Interventions, 17*(4), 233–246.

Lahey, B. B., & Drabman, R. S. (1974). Facilitation of the acquisition of sight-word vocabulary through token reinforcement. *Journal of Applied Behavior Analysis, 7*(2), 307–312.

Lalli, J. S., Casey, S., & Kates, K. (1995). Reducing escape behavior and increasing task completion with functional communication training, extinction, and response chaining. *Journal of Applied Behavior Analysis, 28*(3), 261.

Lambert, J. M., Bloom, S. E., Clay, C. J., Kunnavatana, S. S., & Collins, S. D. (2014). Training residential staff and supervisors to conduct traditional functional analyses. *Research in Developmental Disabilities, 35*(7), 1757–1765.

Laraway, S., Snycerski, S., Michael, J., & Poling, A. (2002). The abative effect: A new term to describe the action of antecedents that reduce operant responding. *The Analysis of Verbal Behavior, 18*, 101.

Laraway, S., Snycerski, S., Michael, J., & Poling, A. (2003). Motivating operations and terms to describe them: Some further refinements. *Journal of Applied Behavior Analysis, 36*(3), 407–414.

LaRue, R. H., Lenard, K., Weiss, M. J., Bamond, M., Palmieri, M., & Kelley, M. E. (2010). Comparison of traditional and trial-based methodologies for conducting functional analyses. *Research in Developmental Disabilities, 31*(2), 480–487.

Leaf, R., & McEachin, J. (1999). *A work in progress: Behavior management strategies and a curriculum for intensive behavioral treatment of autism.* Drl Books.

Ledford, J. R., Lane, J. D., Elam, K. L., & Wolery, M. (2012). Using response-prompting procedures during small-group direct instruction: Outcomes and procedural variations. *American Journal on Intellectual and Developmental Disabilities, 117*(5), 413–434.

Lerman, D. C., & Iwata, B. A. (1995). Prevalence of the extinction burst and its attenuation during treatment. *Journal of Applied Behavior Analysis, 28*(1), 93–94.

Lerman, D. C., & Iwata, B. A. (1996). A methodology for distinguishing between extinction and punishment effects associated with response blocking. *Journal of Applied Behavior Analysis, 29*(2), 231–233.

Lerman, D. C., Iwata, B. A., Smith, R. G., Zarcone, J. R., & Vollmer, T. R. (1994). Transfer of behavioral function as a contributing factor in treatment relapse. *Journal of Applied Behavior Analysis, 27*(2), 357.

Lerman, D. C., Iwata, B. A., & Wallace, M. D. (1999). Side effects of extinction: Prevalence of bursting and aggression during the treatment of self-injurious behavior. *Journal of Applied Behavior Analysis, 32*(1), 1–8.

Lerman, D. C., Kelley, M. E., Vorndran, C. M., Kuhn, S. A., & LaRue Jr, R. H. (2002). Reinforcement magnitude and responding during treatment with differential reinforcement. *Journal of Applied Behavior Analysis, 35*(1), 29.

Lerman, D. C., & Vorndran, C. M. (2002). On the status of knowledge for using punishment: Implications for treating behavior disorders. *Journal of Applied Behavior Analysis, 35*(4), 431–464.

Libby, M. E., Weiss, J. S., Bancroft, S., & Ahearn, W. H. (2008). A comparison of most-to-least and least-to-most prompting on the acquisition of solitary play skills. *Behavior Analysis in Practice, 1*(1), 37.

Lindberg, J. S., Iwata, B. A., Kahng, S., & DeLeon, I. G. (1999). DRO contingencies: An analysis of variable-momentary schedules. *Journal of Applied Behavior Analysis, 32*(2), 123–136.

Lindsley, O. R. (1985). *Quantified trends in the results of behavior analysis.* Presented at the Presidential address at the Eleventh Annual Convention of the Association for Behavior Analysis, Colombus, OH.

Lindsley, O. R. (1991). From technical jargon to plain English for application. *Journal of Applied Behavior Analysis, 24*(3), 449–458.

Linehan, M. M. (1977). Issues in behavioral interviewing. *Behavioral Assessment: New Directions in Clinical Psychology,* 30–51.

Litow, L., & Pumroy, D. K. (1975). A brief review of classroom group-oriented contingencies. *Journal of Applied Behavior Analysis, 8*(3), 341–347.

Lotfizadeh, A. D., Edwards, T. L., Redner, R., & Poling, A. (2012). Motivating operations affect stimulus control: A largely overlooked phenomenon in discrimination learning. *The Behavior Analyst, 35*(1), 89.

Lovaas, O. I. (2003). *Teaching Individuals with Developmental Delays: Basic Intervention Techniques.* ERIC. Retrieved from http://eric.ed.gov/?id=ED473063

Lovass, O.I. (1977). *The Autistic Child: Language Development through Behavior Modification.* New York: Irvington Press.

Luiselli, J. K. (2008). *Effective practices for children with autism: Educational and behavior support interventions that work.* Oxford University Press.

Mace, F. C. (1996). In pursuit of general behavioral relations. *Journal of Applied Behavior Analysis, 29*(4), 557–563.

Mace, F. C., & Belfiore, P. (1990). Behavioral momentum in the treatment of escape-motivated stereotypy. *Journal of Applied Behavior Analysis, 23*(4), 507.

Mace, F. C., Neef, N. A., Shade, D., & Mauro, B. C. (1994). Limited matching on concurrent-schedule reinforcement of academic behavior. *Journal of Applied Behavior Analysis, 27*(4), 585.

Magee, S. K., & Ellis, J. (2000). Extinction effects during the assessment of multiple problem behaviors. *Journal of Applied Behavior Analysis, 33*(3), 313–316.

Malott, R. (2012). *Issues in the Analysis of Behavior.* Behaviordelia.

Malott, R., & Garcia, M. (1991). The role of private events in rule-governed behavior. In P. Chase & L. P. Hayes (Eds.), *Dialogues on verbal behavior* (pp. 237–254). Reno, NV: Context Press.

Malott, R. W. (1988). Rule-governed behavior and behavioral anthropology. *The Behavior Analyst, 11*(2), 181.

Malott, R. W. (1992). Should we train applied behavior analysts to be researchers? *Journal of Applied Behavior Analysis, 25*(1), 83–88.

Malott, R.W., Tojan, E.A. (2003). *Principles of Behavior* (5th ed.). Upper Saddle River, New Jersey: Pearson Prentice Hall.

Malott, R. W., & Trojan, E. A. (2008). *Principles of behavior.* Pearson Prentice Hall Upper Saddle River.

Martens, B. K., Lochner, D. G., & Kelly, S. Q. (1992). The effects of variable-interval reinforcement on academic engagement: A demonstration of matching theory. *Journal of Applied Behavior Analysis, 25*(1), 143–151.

Matson, J. L. (Ed.). (2009). *Applied behavior analysis for children with autism spectrum disorders.* New York: Springer.

Matson, J. L. (Ed.). (2010). *Applied Behavior Analysis for Children with Autism Spectrum Disorders* (2009 edition). New York: Springer.

Matson, J. L., & Boisjoli, J. A. (2009). The token economy for children with intellectual disability and/or autism: A review. *Research in Developmental Disabilities, 30*(2), 240–248.

Matthews, L. R., & Temple, W. (1979). Concurrent schedule assessment of food preference in cows. *Journal of the Experimental Analysis of Behavior, 32*(2), 245–254.

Maurice, C. E., Green, G. E., & Luce, S. C. (1996). *Behavioral intervention for young children with autism: A manual for parents and professionals.* Pro-ed.

May Jr, J. G., & Risley, T.R., Twardosz, S., Friedman, P., Bijous, S., Wexler, D. (1975). Guidelines for the Use of Behavioral Procedures in State Programs for Retarded Persons. Retrieved from http://eric.ed.gov/?id=ED181619

Mazaleski, J. L., Iwata, B. A., Vollmer, T. R., Zarcone, J. R., & Smith, R. G. (1993). Analysis of the reinforcement and extinction components in DRO contingencies with self-injury. *Journal of Applied Behavior Analysis, 26*(2), 143–156.

Mazur, J. E. (1975). The matching law and quantifications related to Premack's principle. *Journal of Experimental Psychology: Animal Behavior Processes, 1*(4), 374.

Mazur, J.E. (2002). *Learning and Behavior.* Upper Saddle River, New Jersey: Pearson Prentice Hall.

McAllister, L. W., Stachowiak, J. G., Baer, D. M., & Conderman, L. (1969). The application of operant conditioning techniques in a secondary school classroom. *Journal of Applied Behavior Analysis, 2*(4), 277–285.

McCain, L. J., & McCleary, R. (1979). The statistical analysis of the simple interrupted time-series quasi-experiment.

Quasi-Experimentation: Design & Analysis Issues for Field Settings. Chicago: Rand McNally.

McDougall, D. (2005). The range-bound changing criterion design. *Behavioral Interventions, 20*(2), 129–137.

McGee, G. G., & Daly, T. (2007). Incidental teaching of age-appropriate social phrases to children with autism. *Research and Practice for Persons with Severe Disabilities, 32*(2), 112–123.

McGee, G. G., Morrier, M. J., & Daly, T. (1999). An incidental teaching approach to early intervention for toddlers with autism. *Research and Practice for Persons with Severe Disabilities, 24*(3), 133–146.

McGee, G. G., Krantz, P. J., Mason, D., & McClannahan, L. E. (1983). A modified incidental-teaching procedure for autistic youth: acquisition and generalization of receptive object labels. *Journal of Applied Behavior Analysis, 16*(3), 329–338.

McGill, P. (1999). Establishing operations: Implications for the assessment, treatment, and prevention of problem behavior. *Journal of Applied Behavior Analysis, 32*(3), 393–418.

McIntyre, L. L., Gresham, F. M., DiGennaro, F. D., & Reed, D. D. (2007). Treatment integrity of school-based interventions with children in the journal of applied behavior analysis 1991–2005. *Journal of Applied Behavior Analysis, 40*(4), 659–672.

McLaughlin, T. F. (1983). An Examination and Evaluation of Single Subject Designs Used in Behavior Analysis Research in School Settings. *Educational Research Quarterly, 7*(4), 35–42.

McSweeney, F., & Weatherly, J. (1998). Habituation to the reinforcer may contribute to multiple-schedule behavioral contrast. *Journal of the Experimental Analysis of Behavior, 69*(2), 199.

McWilliams, R., Nietupski, J., & Hamre-Nietupski, S. (1990). Teaching complex activities to students with moderate handicaps through the forward chaining of shorter total cycle response sequences. *Education and Training in Mental Retardation,* 292–298.

Meany-Daboul, M. G., Roscoe, E. M., Bourret, J. C., & Ahearn, W. H. (2007). A comparison of momentary time sampling and partial-interval recording for evaluating functional relations. *Journal of Applied Behavior Analysis, 40*(3), 501–514.

Mendonca, P. J., & Brehm, S. S. (1983). Effects of choice on behavioral treatment of overweight children. *Journal of Social and Clinical Psychology, 1*(4), 343–358.

Michael, J. (1975). Positive and negative reinforcement, a distinction that is no longer necessary; or a better way to talk about bad things. *Behaviorism,* 33–44.

Michael, J. (1982). Distinguishing between discriminative and motivational functions of stimuli. *Journal of the Experimental Analysis of Behavior, 37*(1), 149–155.

Michael, J. (1988). Establishing operations and the mand. *The Analysis of Verbal Behavior, 6,* 3.

Michael, J. (1993). Establishing operations. *The Behavior Analyst, 16*(2), 191.

Michael, J. (2000). Implications and refinements of the establishing operation concept. *Journal of Applied Behavior Analysis, 33*(4), 401–410.

Michael, J. L. (2004). *Concepts and principles of behavior analysis.* Western Michigan University, Association for Behavior Analysis International.

Miles, N. I., & Wilder, D. A. (2009). The effects of behavioral skills training on caregiver implementation of guided compliance. *Journal of Applied Behavior Analysis, 42*(2), 405–410.

Millenson, J. R., & Leslie, J. C. (1967). *Principles of behavioral analysis.* Macmillan New York.

Miller, D. L., & Kelley, M. L. (1994). The use of goal setting and contingency contracting for improving children's homework

performance. *Journal of Applied Behavior Analysis, 27*(1), 73–84.

Miltenberger, R. G. (2008). *Behavior modification: principles and procedures* (4th ed). Belmont, CA: Thomson Wadsworth.

Miltenberger, R. G., Suda, K. T., Lennox, D. B., & Lindeman, D. P. (1991). Assessing the acceptability of behavioral treatments to persons with mental retardation. *American Journal on Mental Retardation.* Retrieved from http://psycnet.apa.org/psycinfo/1992-13762-001

Mineka, S. (1975). Some new perspectives on conditioned hunger. *Journal of Experimental Psychology: Animal Behavior Processes, 1*(2), 134.

Moore, J. (2008). Conceptual foundations of radical behaviorism. Retrieved from http://philpapers.org/rec/MOOCFO

Moore, J. (2009). Why the radical behaviorist conception of private events is interesting, relevant, and important. *Behavior and Philosophy,* 21–37.

Moore, J. (2011). A review of Baum's review of Conceptual Foundations of Radical Behaviorism. *Journal of the Experimental Analysis of Behavior, 95*(1), 127–140.

Moore, J., & Cooper, J. O. (2003). Some proposed relations among the domains of behavior analysis. *The Behavior Analyst, 26*(1), 69.

Moran, D. J., & Malott, R. W. (2004). *Evidence-based educational methods.* Academic Press.

Morse, W. H., & Kelleher, R. T. (1977). Determinants of reinforcement and punishment. *Handbook of Operant Behavior,* 174–200.

Moxley, R.A. (2004). Pragmatic selectionism: The philosophy of behavior analysis. *The Behavior Analyst Today,* 5, 108-125.

Mueller, M. M., Palkovic, C. M., & Maynard, C. S. (2007). Errorless learning: Review and practical application for teaching children with pervasive developmental disorders. *Psychology in the Schools, 44*(7), 691–700.

Nevin, A., Johnson, D. W., & Johnson, R. (1982). Effects of group and individual contingencies on academic performance and social relations of special needs students. *The Journal of Social Psychology, 116*(1), 41–59.

Nevin, J. A. (1974). Response strength in multiple schedules. *Journal of the Experimental Analysis of Behavior, 21*(3), 389.

Nevin, J. A. (1992a). An integrative model for the study of behavioral momentum. *Journal of the Experimental Analysis of Behavior, 57*(3), 301.

Nevin, J. A. (1992b). Behavioral contrast and behavioral momentum. *Journal of Experimental Psychology: Animal Behavior Processes, 18*(2), 126.

Nevin, J. A. (1996). The Momentum of Compliance. *Journal of Applied Behavior Analysis, 29*(4), 535–547. http://doi.org/10.1901/jaba.1996.29-535

Nevin, J. A., Mandell, C., & Atak, J. R. (1983). The analysis of behavioral momentum. *Journal of the Experimental Analysis of Behavior, 39*(1), 49.

Newcomer, P. L., & Hammill, D. D. (2008). Test of Language Development: Primary (TOLD-P: 4). *Austin, TX.* Retrieved from http://www.asha.org/SLP/assessment/Test-of-Language-Development-Primary,-Fourth-Edition-(TOLD-P-4).htm

Newman, B., Reinecke, D., & Ramos, M. (2009). Is a reasonable attempt reasonable? Shaping versus reinforcing verbal attempts of preschoolers with autism. *The Analysis of Verbal Behavior, 25*(1), 67.

Noell, G. H., Call, N. A., & Ardoin, S. P. (2011). Building complex repertoires from discrete behaviors by establishing stimulus control, behavioral chains, and strategic behavior. *Handbook of Applied Behavior Analysis*, 250.

O'Neill, R. E., Horner, R. H., Albin, R. W., Sprague, J. R., Storey, K., & Newton, J. S. (1997). *Functional assessment and program development for problem behavior. Pacific Grove, CA: Brooks.* Cole Publishing Company.

O'Reilly, M. F. (1997). Functional analysis of episodic self-injury correlated with recurrent otitis media. *Journal of Applied Behavior Analysis, 30*(1), 165–167.

Otto, J. (n.d.). *Discrete trial procedures vs. free-operant procedures.* Retrieved from http://old.dickmalott.com/students/undergradprogram/psy3600/discrete_vs_free.html

Pace, G. M., Ivancic, M. T., Edwards, G. L., Iwata, B. A., & Page, T. J. (1985). Assessment of stimulus preference and reinforcer value with profoundly retarded individuals. *Journal of Applied Behavior Analysis, 18*(3), 249–255.

Parsons, M. B., & Reid, D. H. (1995). Training residential supervisors to provide feedback for maintaining staff teaching skills with people who have severe disabilities. *Journal of Applied Behavior Analysis, 28*(3), 317–322.

Parsonson, B. S., & Baer, D. M. (1978). The analysis and presentation of graphic data. *Single-Subject Research: Strategies for Evaluating Change*, 105–165.

Partington, J. W., & Bailey, J. S. (1993). Teaching intraverbal behavior to preschool children. *The Analysis of Verbal Behavior, 11*, 9.

Partington, J. W., & Sundberg, M. L. (1998). *The Assessment of Basic Language and Learning Skills (the ABLLS): Scoring Instructions and IEP Development Guide: the ABLLS Guide.* Behavior Analysts.

Pavlov, I. P., & Gantt, W. (1928). Lectures on conditioned reflexes: Twenty-five years of objective study of the higher nervous activity (behaviour) of animals.

Pavlov, P. I. (2010). Conditioned reflexes: An investigation of the physiological activity of the cerebral cortex. *Annals of Neurosciences, 17*(3), 136.

Payne, S. W., Dozier, C. L., Neidert, P. L., Jowet, E. S., & Newquist, M. H. (2014). Using Additional Analyses to Clarify the Functions of Problem Behavior: An Analysis of Two Cases. *Education and Treatment of Children, 37*(2), 249–275.

Pelios, L. V., & Sucharzewski, A. (2004). Teaching receptive language to children with autism: A selective overview. *The Behavior Analyst Today, 4*(4), 378.

Pence, S. T., Roscoe, E. M., Bourret, J. C., & Ahearn, W. H. (2009). Relative contributions of three descriptive methods: Implications for behavioral assessment. *Journal of Applied Behavior Analysis, 42*(2), 425.

Pennypacker, H. S. (1992). Is behavior analysis undergoing selection by consequences? *American Psychologist, 47*(11), 1491.

Perlmuter, L. C., & Monty, R. A. (1973). Effect of choice of stimulus on paired-associate learning. *Journal of Experimental Psychology, 99*(1), 120.

Peterson, L., Homer, A. L., & Wonderlich, S. A. (1982). The integrity of independent variables in behavior analysis. *Journal of Applied Behavior Analysis, 15*(4), 477–492.

Petscher, E. S., Rey, C., & Bailey, J. S. (2009). A review of empirical support for differential reinforcement of alternative behavior. *Research in Developmental Disabilities, 30*(3), 409–425.

Piazza, C. C., Patel, M. R., Gulotta, C. S., Sevin, B. M., & Layer, S. A. (2003). On the relative contributions of positive reinforcement and escape extinction in the treatment of food refusal. *Journal of Applied Behavior Analysis, 36*(3), 309.

Pipkin, C. S. P., Vollmer, T. R., & Sloman, K. N. (2010). Effects of treatment integrity failures during differential reinforcement of alternative behavior: A translational model. *Journal of Applied Behavior Analysis, 43*(1), 47–70.

Poling, A. (1978). Performance of rats under concurrent variable-interval schedules of negative reinforcement. *Journal of the Experimental Analysis of Behavior, 30*(1), 31–36.

Poling, A., Braatz, D., Johnson, C. M., Redmon, W. K., & Mawhinney, T. C. (2001). Principles of learning: Respondent and operant conditioning and human behavior. *Handbook of Organizational Performance: Behavior Analysis and Management,* 23–49.

Potts, L., Eshleman, J. W., & Cooper, J. O. (1993). Ogden R. Lindsley and the historical development of precision teaching. *The Behavior Analyst, 16*(2), 177.

Powell, J., Martindale, A., & Kulp, S. (1975). An evaluation of time-sample measures of behavior. *Journal of Applied Behavior Analysis, 8*(4), 463–469.

Pryor, K., & others. (1999). *Dont shoot the dog.* Bantam.

Rachlin, H. (1971). On the tautology of the matching law. *Journal of the Experimental Analysis of Behavior, 15*(2), 249–251.

Reed, F. D. D., Reed, D. D., Baez, C. N., & Maguire, H. (2011). A parametric analysis of errors of commission during discrete-trial training. *Journal of Applied Behavior Analysis, 44*(3), 611–615.

Rehfeldt, R. A., & Chambers, M. R. (2003). Functional analysis and treatment of verbal perseverations displayed by an adult with autism. *Journal of Applied Behavior Analysis, 36*(2), 259–261.

Reimers, T. M., & Wacker, D. P. (1988). Parents' ratings of the acceptability of behavioral treatment recommendations made in an outpatient clinic: A preliminary analysis of the influence of treatment effectiveness. *Behavioral Disorders,* 7–15.

Resnick, L. B., Wang, M. C., & Kaplan, J. (1973). Task analysis in curriculum design: A hierarchically sequenced introductory mathematics curriculum. *Journal of Applied Behavior Analysis, 6*(4), 679–709.

Reynolds, G. S. (1961). Behavioral contrast. *Journal of the Experimental Analysis of Behavior, 4*(1), 57.

Reynolds, G. S. (1963). Some limitations on behavioral contrast and induction during successive discrimination. *Journal of the Experimental Analysis of Behavior, 6*(1), 131–139.

Reynolds, G. S. (1975). A primer of operant conditioning.(Rev ed). Retrieved from http://psycnet.apa.org/psycinfo/1975-20047-000

Ricciardi, J. N., Luiselli, J. K., & Camare, M. (2006). Shaping approach responses as intervention for specific phobia in a child with autism. *Journal of Applied Behavior Analysis, 39*(4), 445–448.

Richman, G. S., Riordan, M. R., Reiss, M. L., Pyles, D. A., & Bailey, J. S. (1988). The effects of self-monitoring and supervisor feedback on staff performance in a residential setting. *Journal of Applied Behavior Analysis, 21*(4), 401.

Riordan, M. M., Iwata, B. A., Wohl, M. K., & Finney, J. W. (1980). Behavioral treatment of food refusal and selectivity in developmentally disabled children. *Applied Research in Mental Retardation, 1*(1), 95–112.

Roane, H. S., Lerman, D. C., Kelley, M. E., & Van Camp, C. M. (1999). Within-session patterns of responding during functional analyses: The role of establishing operations in clarifying behavioral function. *Research in Developmental Disabilities, 20*(1), 73–89.

Roane, H. S., Vollmer, T. R., Ringdahl, J. E., & Marcus, B. A. (1998). Evaluation of a brief stimulus preference assessment. *Journal of Applied Behavior Analysis, 31*(4), 605.

Rosales, R., & Rehfeldt, R. A. (2007). Contriving transitive conditioned establishing operations to establish derived manding skills in adults with severe developmental disabilities. *Journal of Applied Behavior Analysis, 40*(1), 105.

Rosales-Ruiz, J., & Baer, D. M. (1997). Behavioral cusps: A developmental and pragmatic concept for behavior analysis. *Journal of Applied Behavior Analysis, 30*(3), 533–544.

Rusch, F. R., & Kazdin, A. E. (1981). Toward a methodology of withdrawal designs for the assessment of response maintenance. *Journal of Applied Behavior Analysis, 14*(2), 131–140.

Sailor, W., Guess, D., Rutherford, G., & Baer, D. M. (1968). Control of tantrum behavior by operant techniques during experimental verbal training. *Journal of Applied Behavior Analysis, 1*(3), 237–243.

Sarokoff, R. A., & Sturmey, P. (2004). The effects of behavioral skills training on staff implementation of discrete-trial teaching. *Journal of Applied Behavior Analysis, 37*(4), 535–538.

Sasso, G. M., Reimers, T. M., Cooper, L. J., Wacker, D., Berg, W., Steege, M., … Allaire, A. (1992). Use of descriptive and experimental analyses to identify the functional properties of aberrant behavior in school settings. *Journal of Applied Behavior Analysis, 25*(4), 809–821.

Schlinger, H., & Blakely, E. (1987). Function-altering effects of contingency-specifying stimuli. *The Behavior Analyst, 10*(1), 41.

Schlinger, H. D. (2008). Listening is behaving verbally. *The Behavior Analyst, 31*(2), 145.

Schlinger Jr, H. D. (1990). A reply to behavior analysts writing about rules and rule-governed behavior. *The Analysis of Verbal Behavior, 8*, 77.

Schmidt, F. L. (1992). What do data really mean? Research findings, meta-analysis, and cumulative knowledge in psychology. *American Psychologist, 47*(10), 1173.

Semel, E. Wiig, E.H., Secord, W.A. (2003). *Clinical Evaluation of Language Fundamentals* (4th ed.). Toronto, Canada: The Psychological Corporation/A Harcourt Assessment Company.

Seys, D. M., & Duker, P. C. (1978). Improving residential care for the retarded by differential reinforcement of high rates of ward-staff behaviour. *Behavioural Analysis and Modification, 2,* 203–210.

Shanks, D. R., Pearson, S. M., & Dickinson, A. (1989). Temporal contiguity and the judgement of causality by human subjects. *The Quarterly Journal of Experimental Psychology, 41*(2), 139–159.

Shapiro, E. S. (2011). *Academic skills problems: Direct assessment and intervention.* Guilford Press.

Shore, B. A., Iwata, B. A., Vollmer, T. R., Lerman, D. C., & Zarcone, J. R. (1995). Pyramidal staff training in the extension of treatment for severe behavior disorders. *Journal of Applied Behavior Analysis, 28*(3), 323.

Sidman, M. (1971). Reading and auditory-visual equivalences. *Journal of Speech, Language, and Hearing Research, 14*(1), 5–13.

Sidman, M. (1994). *Equivalence relations and behavior: A research story.* Authors Cooperative. Retrieved from http://psycnet.apa.org/psycinfo/1994-98777-000

Sidman, M. (1997). Equivalence relations. *Journal of the Experimental Analysis of Behavior, 68*(2), 258.

Sidman, M. (2009). Equivalence relations and behavior: An introductory tutorial. *The Analysis of Verbal Behavior, 25*(1), 5.

Sidman, M., & Tailby, W. (1982). Conditional discrimination vs. matching to sample: An expansion of the testing paradigm. *Journal of the Experimental Analysis of Behavior, 37*(1), 5–22.

Sidman, M., Willson-Morris, M., & Kirk, B. (1986). Matching-to-sample procedures and the development of equivalence relations: The role of naming. *Analysis and Intervention in Developmental Disabilities, 6*(1), 1–19.

Sigafoos, J. (2005). From Premack to PECS: 25 years of progress in communication intervention for individuals with developmental disabilities. *Educational Psychology, 25*(6), 601–607.

Singh, J., & Singh, N. N. (1985). Comparison of word-supply and word-analysis error-correction procedures on oral reading by mentally retarded children. *American Journal of Mental Deficiency.* Retrieved from http://psycnet.apa.org/psycinfo/1985-31100-001

Skinner, B.F. (1938). *The Behavior Of Organisms.* New York: Appleton-Century.

Skinner, B. F. (1938). The behavior of organisms: An experimental analysis. Retrieved from http://psycnet.apa.org/psycinfo/1939-00056-000

Skinner, B. F. (1953). *Science and human behavior.* Simon and Schuster.

Skinner, B.F. (1957). *Verbal Behavior.* New York: Appleton-Century.

Skinner, B.F. (1979). *The Shaping of a Behaviorist: Part two of an autobiography.* New York, NY: University Press.

Skinner, B. F. (1981). Selection by consequences. *Science, 213*(4507), 501–504.

Skinner, B. F. (1984). The evolution of behavior. *Journal of the Experimental Analysis of Behavior, 41*(2), 217–221.

Skinner, B. F. (1989). *Recent issues in the analysis of behavior.* Prentice Hall.

Skinner, B. F. (2014). *Contingencies of reinforcement: A theoretical analysis* (Vol. 3). BF Skinner Foundation.

Slocum, S. K., & Tiger, J. H. (2011). An assessment of the efficiency of and child preference for forward and backward chaining. *Journal of Applied Behavior Analysis*, *44*(4), 793–805.

Smith, R. G., & Iwata, B. A. (1997). Antecedent influences on behavior disorders. *Journal of Applied Behavior Analysis*, *30*(2), 343–375.

Smith, R. G., Iwata, B. A., & Shore, B. A. (1995). Effects of subject versus experimenter-selected reinforcers on the behavior of individuals with profound developmental disabilities. *Journal of Applied Behavior Analysis*, *28*(1), 61–71.

Smith, T., Parker, T., Taubman, M., & Lovaas, O. I. (1992). Transfer of staff training from workshops to group homes: A failure to generalize across settings. *Research in Developmental Disabilities*, *13*(1), 57–71.

Snell, M.E., Brown, F. (2006). *Instruction of Students with Severe Disabilities* (6th ed.). Upper Saddle River, New Jersey: Merrill/Prentice Hall.

Spooner, F. (1984). Comparisons of backward chaining and total task presentation in training severely handicapped persons. *Education and Training of the Mentally Retarded*, 15–22.

Sprague, J., Sugai, G., & Walker, H. (1998). Antisocial behavior in schools. In *Handbook of child behavior therapy* (pp. 451–474). Springer.

Spriggs, A.D., Gast, D.L. (2010). *Visual Representation of Data* (D. L. Gast (Ed.)). New York, NY: Routlege.

Stewart, I., McElwee, J., & Ming, S. (2013). Language generativity, response generalization, and derived relational responding. *The Analysis of Verbal Behavior*, *29*(1), 137.

Stock, R. A., Schulze, K. A., & Mirenda, P. (2008). A comparison of stimulus-stimulus pairing, standard echoic training, and control procedures on the vocal behavior of children with autism. *The Analysis of Verbal Behavior*, *24*(1), 123.

Stokes, T. F., & Baer, D. M. (1977). An implicit technology of generalization. *Journal of Applied Behavior Analysis*, *10*(2), 349.

Stokes, T. F., Baer, D. M., & Jackson, R. L. (1974). Programming the generalization of a greeting response in four retarded children. *Journal of Applied Behavior Analysis*, *7*(4), 599–610.

Stokes, T. F., & Osnes, P. G. (1989). An operant pursuit of generalization. *Behavior Therapy*, *20*(3), 337–355.

Striefel, S., Bryan, K. S., & Aikins, D. A. (1974). Transfer of stimulus control from motor to verbal stimuli. *Journal of Applied Behavior Analysis*, *7*(1), 123–135.

Suen, H. K., Ary, D., & Covalt, W. (1991). Reappraisal of momentary time sampling and partial-interval recording. *Journal of Applied Behavior Analysis*, *24*(4), 803.

Sundberg, M. L. (2008a). *VB-MAPP Verbal Behavior Milestones Assessment and Placement Program: a language and social skills assessment program for children with autism or other developmental disabilities: guide.* Concord, CA: AVB Press.

Sundberg, M. L. (2008b). Verbal behavior milestones assessment and placement program: The VB-MAPP. *Concord, CA: AVBPress.*

Sundberg, M. L., Loeb, M., Hale, L., & Eigenheer, P. (2002). Contriving establishing operations to teach mands for information. *The Analysis of Verbal Behavior*, *18*, 15.

Sundberg, M. L., & Michael, J. (2001). The benefits of Skinner's analysis of verbal behavior for children with autism. *Behavior Modification*, *25*(5), 698–724.

Sundberg, M. L., & Partington, J. W. (1998). Teaching language to children with autism and other developmental disabilities. *Pleasant Hill, CA: Behavior Analysts Inc.*

Sweeney-Kerwin, E. J., Carbone, V. J., O'Brien, L., Zecchin, G., & Janecky, M. N. (2007). Transferring control of the mand to the motivating operation in children with autism. *The Analysis of Verbal Behavior, 23*(1), 89.

Sweeney, M. M., & Shahan, T. A. (2013). Effects of high, low, and thinning rates of alternative reinforcement on response elimination and resurgence. *Journal of the Experimental Analysis of Behavior, 100*(1), 102–116.

Tarbox, J., & Hayes, L. P. (2005). Verbal behavior and behavioral contrast in human subjects. *The Psychological Record, 55*(3), 419.

Tarbox, R. S., Ghezzi, P. M., & Wilson, G. (2006). The effects of token reinforcement on attending in a young child with autism. *Behavioral Interventions, 21*(3), 155–164.

Taylor-Santa, C., Sidener, T. M., Carr, J. E., & Reeve, K. F. (2014). A discrimination training procedure to establish conditioned reinforcers for children with autism. *Behavioral Interventions, 29*(2), 157–176.

Terrace, H. S. (1963). Discrimination learning with and without "errors". *Journal of the Experimental Analysis of Behavior, 6*(1), 1–27.

Test, D. W., Spooner, F., Keul, P. K., & Grossi, T. (1990). Teaching adolescents with severe disabilities to use the public telephone. *Behavior Modification, 14*(2), 157–171.

Theodore, L. A., Bray, M. A., Kehle, T. J., & Jenson, W. R. (2001). Randomization of group contingencies and reinforcers to reduce classroom disruptive behavior. *Journal of School Psychology, 39*(3), 267–277.

Thomas, D. R., Becker, W. C., & Armstrong, M. (1968). Production and elimination of disruptive classroom behavior by systematically varying teacher's behavior. *Journal of Applied Behavior Analysis, 1*(1), 35–45.

Thomason-Sassi, J. L., Iwata, B. A., Neidert, P. L., & Roscoe, E. M. (2011). Response

latency as an index of response strength during functional analyses of problem behavior. *Journal of Applied Behavior Analysis, 44*(1), 51–67.

Thompson, R. H., Iwata, B. A., Conners, J., & Roscoe, E. M. (1999). Effects of reinforcement for alternative behavior during punishment of self-injury. *Journal of Applied Behavior Analysis, 32*(3), 317–328.

Thompson, T. J., Braam, S. J., & Fugua, R. W. (1982). Training and generalization of laundry skills: a multiple probe evaluation with handicapped persons. *Journal of Applied Behavior Analysis, 15*(1), 177.

Thoresen, C. E., & Mahoney, M. J. (1974). *Behavioral self-control.* Holt McDougal.

Torneke, N. (2010). *Learning RFT: An introduction to relational frame theory and its clinical application.* New Harbinger Publications

Tryon, W. W. (1982). A simplified time-series analysis for evaluating treatment interventions. *Journal of Applied Behavior Analysis, 15*(3), 423–429.

Twyman, J. S. (1998). The Fred S. Keller School. *Journal of Applied Behavior Analysis, 31*(4), 695–701.

Ulman, J. D., & Sulzer-Azaroff, B. (1975). Multielement baseline design in educational research. *Behavior Analysis: Areas of Research and Application,* 377–391.

Ulrich, R. E., & Azrin, N. H. (1962). Reflexive fighting in response to aversive stimulation. *Journal of the Experimental Analysis of Behavior, 5*(4), 511.

Vanselow, N. R., & Bourret, J. C. (2012). Online interactive tutorials for creating graphs with Excel 2007 or 2010. *Behavior Analysis in Practice, 5*(1), 40.

Vedora, J., Meunier, L., & Mackay, H. (2009). Teaching intraverbal behavior to children with autism: A comparison of textual and echoic prompts. *The Analysis of Verbal Behavior, 25*(1), 79.

Vollmer, T. R. (1994). The concept of automatic reinforcement: Implications for behavioral research in developmental disabilities. *Research in Developmental Disabilities, 15*(3), 187–207.

Vollmer, T. R., Borrero, J. C., Wright, C. S., Van Camp, C., & Lalli, J. S. (2001). Identifying possible contingencies during descriptive analyses of severe behavior disorders. *Journal of Applied Behavior Analysis, 34*(3), 269.

Vollmer, T. R., & Iwata, B. A. (1992). Differential reinforcement as treatment for behavior disorders: Procedural and functional variations. *Research in Developmental Disabilities, 13*(4), 393–417.

Vollmer, T. R., Iwata, B. A., Zarcone, J. R., Smith, R. G., & Mazaleski, J. L. (1993). Within-session patterns of self-injury as indicators of behavioral function. *Research in Developmental Disabilities, 14*(6), 479–492.

Vollmer, T. R., Marcus, B. A., Ringdahl, J. E., & Roane, H. S. (1995). Progressing from brief assessments to extended experimental analyses in the evaluation of aberrant behavior. *Journal of Applied Behavior Analysis, 28*(4), 561.

Vollmer, T., Roane, H., Ringdahl, J., & Marcus, B. (1999). Evaluating treatment challenges with differential reinforcement of alternative behavior. *Journal of Applied Behavior Analysis, 32*(1), 9.

Vorndran, C. M., & Lerman, D. C. (2006). Establishing and maintaining treatment effects with less intrusive consequences via a pairing procedure. *Journal of Applied Behavior Analysis, 39*(1), 35–48.

Walker, G. (2008). Constant and progressive time delay procedures for teaching children with autism: A literature review. *Journal of Autism and Developmental Disorders, 38*(2), 261–275.

Ward-Horner, J., & Sturmey, P. (2010). Component analyses using single-subject experimental designs: A review. *Journal of Applied Behavior Analysis, 43*(4), 685–704.

Ward-Horner, J., & Sturmey, P. (2012). Component analysis of behavior skills training in functional analysis. *Behavioral Interventions, 27*(2), 75–92.

Watkins, M. W., & Pacheco, M. (2000). Interobserver agreement in behavioral research: Importance and calculation. *Journal of Behavioral Education, 10*(4), 205–212.

Watson, D., & Tharp, R. (2013). *Self-directed behavior: Self-modification for personal adjustment.* Cengage Learning.

Watson, P. J., & Workman, E. A. (1981). The non-concurrent multiple baseline across-individuals design: An extension of the traditional multiple baseline design. *Journal of Behavior Therapy and Experimental Psychiatry, 12*(3), 257–259.

Weatherly, J. N., King, B. M., & Arthur, E. I. (2002). Rats' lever pressing for 1% sucrose and food-pellet reinforcement: In search of negative behavioral contrast. *The Psychological Record, 52*(4), 507.

Weatherly, J. N., Melville, C. L., & McSweeney, F. K. (1996). Picking, pecking, and pressing: A cross-species demonstration of behavioral contrast. *The Psychological Record, 46*(2), 351.

Welsh, D. H., Bernstein, D. J., & Luthans, F. (1993). Application of the Premack principle of reinforcement to the quality performance of service employees. *Journal of Organizational Behavior Management, 13*(1), 9–32.

Wheeler, J. J., Baggett, B. A., Fox, J., & Blevins, L. (2006). Treatment Integrity A Review of Intervention Studies Conducted With Children With Autism. *Focus on Autism and Other Developmental Disabilities, 21*(1), 45–54. http://doi.org/10.1177/10883576060210010601

White, O.R., Haring, N.G. (1980). *Exceptional Teaching* (2nd edition). Columbus, OH: Charles E. Merrill.

White, O. R., Sugai, G., & Horner, R. (2005). Trend lines. *Encyclopedia of Behavior Modification and Cognitive Behavior Therapy, 3,* 1589–1593.

Wilder, D. A., Atwell, J., & Wine, B. (2006). The effects of varying levels of treatment integrity on child compliance during treatment with a three-step prompting procedures. *Journal of Applied Behavior Analysis, 39*(3), 369–373.

Wilder, D. A., Normand, M., & Atwell, J. (2005). Noncontingent reinforcement as treatment for food refusal and associated self-injury. *Journal of Applied Behavior Analysis, 38*(4), 549–553.

Williams, B. A., & Fantino, E. (1978). Effects on choice of reinforcement delay and conditioned reinforcement. *Journal of the Experimental Analysis of Behavior, 29*(1), 77–86.

Windsor, J., Piché, L. M., & Locke, P. A. (1994). Preference testing: A comparison of two presentation methods. *Research in Developmental Disabilities, 15*(6), 439–455.

Witt, J. C., Daly, E. M., & Noell, G. (2000). *Functional assessments: A step-by-step guide to solving academic and behavior problems.* Sopris West.

Wolery, M. (1994). Procedural fidelity: A reminder of its functions. *Journal of Behavioral Education, 4*(4), 381–386.

Wolf, M. M. (1978). Social validity: The case for subjective measurement or how applied behavior analysis is finding its heart. *Journal of Applied Behavior Analysis, 11*(2), 203.

Worsdell, A. S., Iwata, B. A., & Wallace, M. D. (2002). Duration-based measures of preference for vocational tasks. *Journal of Applied Behavior Analysis, 35*(3), 287.

Wulfert, E., & Hayes, S. C. (1988). Transfer of a conditional ordering response through conditional equivalence classes. *Journal of the Experimental Analysis of Behavior, 50*(2), 125.

Zhan, S., & Ottenbacher, K. J. (2001). Single subject research designs for disability research. *Disability and Rehabilitation, 23*(1), 1–8.

Made in the USA
Columbia, SC
05 October 2020